GHANA IN TRANSITION

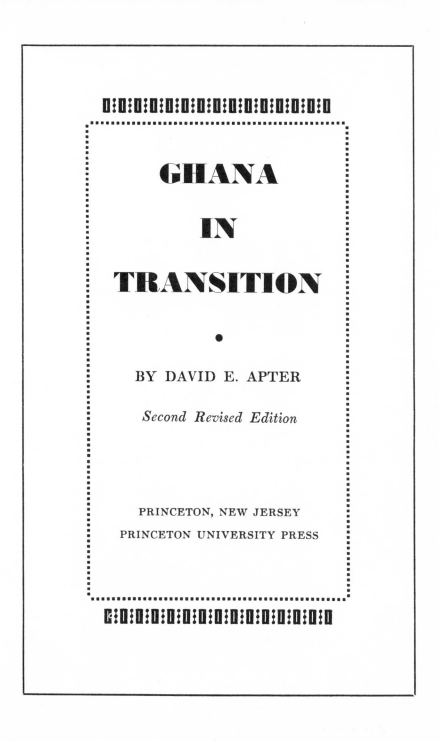

GHANA

IN

TRANSITION

·

BY DAVID E. APTER

Second Revised Edition

PRINCETON, NEW JERSEY
PRINCETON UNIVERSITY PRESS

To

E. S. A.

THIS book, a case study of political institutional transfer, has been planned as the first of two field studies in British Colonial Africa on the development of conciliar organs of rule and self-government. In this task we deal first with the Gold Coast, an area marked by singular success in the transformation from a tribal dependency to a parliamentary democracy, a success which has aroused major interest throughout the world. A second field study, planned for the near future, will try to test some of the hypotheses and propositions which emerge in this volume in a different African environment, one in which the degree of social integration required in nationhood is entirely lacking, and where the effort to create a national state prior to independence is under the leadership of the British Colonial Service rather than an indigenous national movement.

The present volume on the Gold Coast has set the form and the pattern of analysis which we shall follow. If at times it seems unorthodox, I hope that such unorthodoxy has been used with care. The task has been as much to devise a suitable framework for analysis of complex problems of the sort dealt with here as to portray political processes in the Gold Coast—indeed the two are impossible to separate. Nevertheless, the present analytical framework remains tentative. The one argument presented in its favor —that in terms of the problems posed for analysis it has proved an economical and useful research focus—is still not conclusive enough to warrant unusual claims for this method of approach.

Two important omissions from this work must be noted. For several reasons, religious factors have not been handled as a separate category. The use of the word "traditional" is used to subsume religious aspects of traditional social structure. However, neither Christianity nor Islam has been given the treatment it deserves. For this omission there are strong regrets, although the functions of both Christianity and Islam in political institutional transfer are partially treated, albeit in general terms. In the second case study planned, in which Uganda will be contrasted with the Gold Coast, religious factors will be accorded fuller treatment.

vii

Secondly, the formal legal systems of adjudication stemming from British concepts of justice and equity, particularly as they conflicted with traditional legal concepts, have not been specifically treated. What could have been a most revealing study in itself, an analysis of native authority courts and the changing criteria and categories of offenses, forms of punishments, and their consequences for political change, was omitted largely through lack of time and resources. Rather it was felt that from a conceptual point of view, the social and constitutional expressions of differing patterns of legitimized authority, and sources of sanctions, were more susceptible to immediate empirical study in the range of conflicting behavior manifested in group activity. Some of the fundamental factors "behind" law were given greater priority than the body of formal law. The normative and orientational features of law have been treated at their most general conceptual level, e.g., as sanction and legitimacy.

Much of the material regarding central government was gathered in the Gold Coast during the period immediately preceding the 1954 "Nkrumah Constitution." The participation of the chiefs and special interests were apparent, and the last effective remnant of the structure of indirect rule was therefore visible as it played out its role between 1950 and 1954. Today the system has undergone most of those changes which underscore the secular organization of government. Many fundamental political questions have been removed from the arena of central government and placed in more subtle cast, in local issues, and in religious nonconformity. During the period of research a range of loyalties and conflicting reference associations were observed which today operate on a more subsidiary but no less profound level.

Nevertheless, the 1954 Constitution is the logical extension of that promulgated in 1950. Real change came from the latter when Nkrumah left jail to head the first true cabinet in Gold Coast history, and when the country moved from colonial rule to representative and responsible government. The present constitution almost completes the process of the formal secularization of government. That much remains to be done beyond the formal confines of structural change will be evident from these succeeding pages. How much has been accomplished already is a tribute to all who have participated in this dramatic experiment in social change.

This study on political institutional transfer proceeded from a conviction that the development of parliamentary government in underdeveloped areas of the world can be useful for refining our knowledge and our conceptual premises in regard to the political aspects of social change. In the Gold Coast we have an example of such a process inside a continent which looms large in the strategy and interests of America and the Western world. My hope is that from such studies as this both our empirical knowledge and the depth of our understanding of politics will be increased. Most important of all, however, is a deep-seated belief on the part of the author that the efforts of the men and women of the Gold Coast to achieve a democratic system of political rule while simultaneously creating a viable national society is one of the prouder achievements of mankind.

Readers of this book will soon recognize several intellectual debts. An obvious one is to Max Weber, a seminal writer in social affairs too often neglected by political scientists. Perhaps of more immediate importance is my debt to Professor Marion J. Levy, Jr., a scholar with whom it is valuable both to agree and disagree, and from whose book *The Structure of Society* much of the methodology used in the field was taken.

Many acknowledgments are due the people who helped make this study possible. To Professor Harold Sprout and Professor Richard C. Snyder, both of Princeton, gratitude runs deep for the encouragement and support they have given me as well as for some of the tools and concepts of inter-disciplinary work in the social sciences.

To the officers and members of the Social Science Research Council go many thanks for making the study financially possible through an Area Research Training Fellowship which took me to England and to Africa.

To the faculty and staff of Nuffield College and the Institute of Colonial Studies in Oxford my appreciation is particularly great for the kindness and hospitality which they so freely gave. Full working privileges and facilities were provided by them for my use, and they gave of their knowledge and wisdom, their time and their graciousness, to add to my knowledge. Professor S. Herbert Frankel, in particular, gave invaluable help, as did Miss Marjory Perham, Mr. Kenneth Robinson, Sir Reader Bullard,

Mrs. Mary Holdsworth, and many others who made my stay in Oxford both an enriching experience and a cherished memory. Professor Frankel and Mr. Robinson, as well as Mr. Michael de Ensor of the Gold Coast Civil Service, and Professor M. J. Herskovits of Northwestern University, read all or part of the manuscript, and my debt to them is particularly great.

To the many people in the Colonial Office and the Colonial Service in the Gold Coast who had the patience and vision to see value in such a study as I proposed, gratitude is hereby acknowledged. They took time out from the important business of the day to see that I was given access to documents and data, people and places which would have otherwise proved inaccessible. More than anyone, Mr. William Dickinson, formerly senior administrative secretary in the Ministry of Local Government in the Gold Coast, gave unstintingly of his time and knowledge.

To the principal, staff, and members of the University College of the Gold Coast, particularly Professor John Williams and Mr. Walter B. Birmingham, my thanks for working facilities, housing, and the constant help and encouragement which made research in the Gold Coast possible.

Gratitude is acknowledged to the Center of International Studies, Princeton University, for interest and support in this work.

Finally, to the many men and women of the Gold Coast gratitude must be expressed. Their zeal and optimism are matched only by their hospitality. They are challenging the prejudices of people everywhere, and with them the future of Africa is bound up.

In spite of all the help I received from many sources, the work here is, of course, my own responsibility, and the errors contained herein are mine.

D.A.

Northwestern University
July 1955

PREFACE TO SECOND PRINTING

SINCE this volume was written, events of great significance have transpired in Ghana. On March 6, 1957 the Gold Coast became Ghana, an independent country within the British Commonwealth, and the long battle for self-government had reached its end. Independence has already had profound consequences in Africa. Ghana has become, at least for the time being, a center of what might be termed African zionism. It is a country whose self-appointed purpose is not only to be a successful and prosperous Ghana nation, but to serve as inspiration for Africans remaining under colonial rule and, as well, for colored peoples everywhere. Hence Ghana's importance. She has become a symbol of national achievement and African enterprise.

However, the circumstances attendant upon Ghana's independence were not auspicious. The question at independence day was: can a "house divided" still stand? In the last chapter of this book we indicated a range of problems which Ghana would face. One was associated with the removal of chiefs from the legislature without providing them with an upper house. This, we said, would have the effect of removing them from responsible expression. Events have sadly confirmed this analysis. Chieftaincy joined forces with the opposition in a National Liberation Movement which threatened civil war and secession of the North and the Ashanti area and produced a pattern of violence which marred the previous peaceful patterns of transition. One effect was to confirm a hitherto more tentative C.P.P. (Convention People's Party) argument that the opposition was essentially irresponsible and would even slow up the achievement of self-government in order to achieve its ends.

A second and related problem has been the decline in Nkrumah's charisma. Although the C.P.P. has perhaps never been more powerful than today, the earlier pattern of youthful idealism attached to the nationalist movement has, of course, given way to a more reluctant public wariness of the C.P.P. politicians and leadership. Complaints have been voiced against corruption, and against the toughness and arbitrariness of some of the C.P.P. top leaders. As charisma has declined, and as self-government was achieved, the preservation of the party became all important. Considerable respect is shown to parliamentary forms. Parliament is run well by the C.P.P. But it is the party which is important in Ghana and it is the party which chose for quite instrumental reasons to retain the parliamentary pattern. The costs of disengaging from it would be too high in terms of the effective running of the country. Parliament has been used as a forum for the ventilation of grievance, for providing information to the C.P.P. leadership, and as a consultative body. But when, in the summer of 1957, twenty-seven members of the parliamentary backbench threatened to bolt to the other side, the C.P.P. realized that stringent measures would be necessary if they were to retain power. Deportations occurred. A "tough" Minister of the Interior, Mr. Krobo Edusei made it clear that the government would deal harshly with those who in the government's view would be politically irresponsible. Indeed, complaints were heard in some quarters which raised the nice eighteenth-century distinction between liberty and freedom. As one Ghanaian put it, "When the British were here we had no freedom but we had liberty. Now that the British are gone we have freedom, but our liberty is under attack." The first year of independence was thus marred by an emphasis upon restrictiveness. The Ghana Nationality and Citizenship Bill passed just before independence eliminated from automatic citizenship a great many people born in Ghana of Nigerian or French West African parentage. The Emergency Powers Bill gave the government extensive arbitrary powers in case of emergency. The Avoidance of Discrimination Bill attacked chieftaincy and tribalism.

These are acts taken by a government which feels threatened in the midst of its security. Nkrumah can no longer rely only on his popular appeals for support; he has found it necessary to use threats, deportations, and punitive legislation to bolster the party position. The party reigns supreme, but it is a subtly different party from what it used to be.

Yet on the positive side there were other compelling reasons for some of these actions. The opposition position was awkwardly untenable, given its relative impotence—hence its irresponsibility. Threats of civil war were the last-ditch stand of a completely frustrated political opposition. But to Nkrumah, with his devotion to Ghana and African nationalism, the prospect of civil war and its consequences, which he could observe elsewhere in almost every other newly independent state, called for stern measures. As a result, in spite of deep-rooted feelings and the passionate responses of men divided over the issues of chieftaincy, leadership, and constitutionality, the transition to independence has been only superficially a peaceful one.

The parliamentary pattern has been followed, and used with at least partial effectiveness. Ghana is, for all intents and purposes, a one-party democracy. There are genuine elections. Indeed the

C.P.P. went to the polls in 1956 at the height of the troubles with the N.L.M. and won handily. By independence day the party strengths were as follows: Convention People's Party, 72 seats; Northern People's Party, 15 seats; National Liberation Movement, 12 seats; Togoland Congress, 2 seats; Federation of Youth Organizations, 1 seat; Moslem Association Party, 1 seat; and one independent. The party remains characteristically open and fraternal. But it tends to identify itself with its own creation, Ghana, and to remain outside the embrace of the party is to be suspect.

Hence there is great cause both for concern and for satisfaction with the pattern of Ghanaian development. The concern comes from the flaunting of authority in the face of opposition groups by the Convention People's Party. Some of the party leaders have reveled in their power and made it clear that they have no intention of relinquishing it. Personal abuse and some violence have thus marred the performance of the party. But much of this must be taken in the context of Ghana's new "zionism." What the doctrine of socialism in one country was to the U.S.S.R., the doctrine of independence in one country is to Ghana. Only the first phase, independence, is now accomplished. Nkrumah never gave up his dream of a powerful bloc of West African states. Indeed it is in the successful development of some larger federation of African territories that the future of Ghana lies. She must cultivate associations with other independent states. Just as pan-Arabism is the program of President Nasser and the United Arab Republic is the first fruit of his efforts, so pan-Africanism remains the ideology of Dr. Nkrumah and he will join with Mr. Sékou Touré in a republic. A new pattern has been set. Ghana in international affairs is equally important as Ghana as a small democracy. The country is more and more "organized" for Nkrumah's political leadership in pan-African affairs. Whether her democracy will be able to survive remains a moot question.

D.A.

The University of Chicago
November 1958

PREFACE TO FIRST REVISED EDITION

RESEARCH for the original edition of this book was undertaken in 1952-53 in the Gold Coast. The book was written the following year, incorporating certain of the events which occurred subsequent to my visit. It is now ten years since I first went to Africa, and the decade has been most eventful. When I first became interested in the Gold Coast, I was assured that it would be a long time before African territories would become independent. I was, if I may be forgiven a personal reminiscence, warned that a political scientist would find it impossible to obtain an academic post if his specialty was African studies. I felt at the time that such views were wrong in the first instance, and irrelevant in the second, and time has shown that I was right in my judgment.

Today there are twenty-five independent African states in sub-Saharan Africa under African rule. Ten years ago there were two. Ghana's independence was a focal point for this transition on the continent. The structure of her party, the form and practice of government, the blending of traditional and novel forms of association, have much in common with most other African countries.

Moreover, Accra has become a center of pan-Africanism. It is no longer the lively but parochial capital of a small colonial territory, but a cosmopolitan area. South Africans seeking freedom, Southern Rhodesians, Negro Americans, Portuguese Africans can be found earnestly discussing politics. One of the first acts of the new Ghana Government was to organize a Conference of Independent States in Accra in 1958. A much wider grouping of African nationalist and trade-union leaders was gathered together in Accra in the same year. This was the first All-African Peoples Conference. From the very start, then, such conferences have been held. Other countries have come to share with Ghana in pan-Africanist leadership. Nevertheless, the role of Ghana in pan-African affairs and her commitment to it cannot be under-estimated.

Ghana's independence has meant more than the liberation of Africa from colonial rule. It brought together four quite different traditions and political forces. The first of these was the pan-African tradition. The pan-African tradition had its roots in the

West Indies in the Garvey movement, and in separatist churches of the Zionist Episcopal variety (both in the United States and in Africa itself). This strand represented the "in-gathering of the exiles." It emphasized the symbolic unity of all peoples of color, wherever they might be, in the spiritual and racial body of Africa.

The second tradition was socialist and Marxian. It is perhaps most often associated with the name of George Padmore. This tradition accepted the Marxian explanation of colonialism and imperialism, including an explanation of why it was that Africa was in dependent status. The blame for colonialism was not simply one of metropolitan power, but of an inevitable outgrowth of capitalist crisis. Africans were the black equivalent of the European proletarians, a notion that went far beyond the usual connotation of the term working-class. If Europeans thought of colonies in terms of trusteeship and partnership, Marxians thought in terms of superordinate and subordinate relationships. Hence, nationalism was revolutionary, not simply because it sought to remove the political control inherent in colonialism but because, in order to eliminate exploitation, capitalism and socialism had to be changed as well, i.e., the relationship between man and man; producers and consumers. These traditions, one eminently racial and mystical (although not racist except in the case of the Garvey movement); the other eminently Marxist, and therefore political and economic, represented two main currents of nationalist thought. The third and fourth factors are more directly associated with Africa itself. One of these is the force of tradition modified through the chiefs' councils and expressed in religious values and beliefs. This form of nationalism was a recoil against Europeans, who, coming to Africa at the end of the 19th century, were imbued with a sense of moral and technological superiority.[1] Nor were missionaries immune to this. Much of the indigenous nationalism of West Africa was expressed in efforts to

[1] It is of interest that in early contact between Ghana and Great Britain, other attitudes prevailed. Prior to the main thrust of the Industrial Revolution in Europe and before doctrines of racial and cultural superiority became elevated to the proportion of national myths, Africans and Europeans were struck by the similarity of lives of ordinary men in their respective countries. The change in this relationship between ruler and ruled is due to many factors but is perhaps punctuated in colonial history by the Indian Mutiny of 1857. After that event a note of caution and coldness crept into the relationships between Europeans and Africans. It was in this context that traditional nationalism emerged.

make traditional life intelligible to foreigners and particularly to gain recognition for the values and spiritual qualities inherent in relationships between kin groups, political society and land. In the re-writing of African history many of their efforts have been realized.

The fourth tradition in the situation arose directly from the educational and political relationship between metropolitan and colonial powers. England was democratic at home. It was inevitable that the democratic ideas, i.e., liberty of the subject, representative government, universal franchise, free elections, and the other associated factors of law, appeal, and individual rights and liberties were employed as arguments against the restrictiveness of colonial political conditions. Brought to Africa by those who had studied in Europe and England (and those who had worked with local administrators and governors), this element can be called the liberal-democratic one. This tradition was articulated too by nationalists espousing the values of Western democracy. They were demanding independence through constitutional reforms leading to African majorities in legislatures and the transfers of executive authority. Liberal democracy provided a mechanism for the peaceful evolution of authority to local population through the organization of cabinet government. In the original edition of my book it was these latter aspects of transition which were analyzed. This led me to focus upon the internal developments of nationalism in Ghana, the nature of charismatic leadership which brought together, through the procedures of representative government, the new and old elements of nationalism. The real question remained to be answered. What would be the future of the secular liberal values associated with liberal democracy?

Even today no clear answer is forthcoming. Many aspects of constitutional democracy have been fundamentally altered in Ghana since Independence. Nkrumaism as a "political religion" or what perhaps might better be termed a theocratic synthesis, is making a tentative appearance. In this, both the first two political factors which I have mentioned: the element of racial revolution and African socialism are beginning to blend. They are symbolized perhaps by the Black Star, the "Garvey star" in the flag, in the symbolism of the Black Star Line, Ghana's shipping company.

Nkrumaism is one of the new theories of African socialism with an ideological training school in the Kwame Nkrumah Ideological Institute at Winneba. George Padmore is dead, but many of his ideas, some of which were described in a pamphlet not published in Ghana, *A Guide to pan-African Socialism, a socialist program for Africa* (written just before his death), have helped form some of the key ideas of African socialists in Ghana and elsewhere.[2] Both the racial factor and the ideological find expression in pan-Africanism, the African freedom fighters, and African trade-union and farmers' associations.

Nor have traditionalism and liberal democracy, hard hit although both have been, disappeared from the scene. The latter is perhaps still strongest in the court system and, particularly with respect to civil jurisdictions, despite a large and growing body of punitive legislation directed against political acts. Moreover, there is considerable commitment to liberal-democratic principles expressed in the Republican constitution. Nevertheless the entire conception of liberal democracy is increasingly regarded as either premature, to be reconsidered when Ghana has achieved internal political stability around socialist principles and economic development including industrialization, or dangerous and divisive as a current political doctrine. Depending upon whom one talks to in Ghana, liberal-democracy is (a) a cause for nostalgia for what might have been; (b) a counter-revolutionary force in which separatism and division would appear under the guise of individualism; or (c) a revolutionary doctrine wholly inappropriate for the present, but to be reconsidered when the "revolution" has completed its course.

Ghana is not alone in these views. They are shared by many other African states where the questions of one-party rule, and the arrangements between rulers and ruled, have tended to take on a monolithic quality in which society is perceived as an organic whole, rather than a series of contractual relationships between parts. In a curious way the emphasis on unity, community, the party, the state, as well as the "democratic autocrat" who represents the whole people, reflects a real problem. How to create a more genuine corporate social life to minimize differences between

---

[2] See Friedland, William H. and Carl G. Rosberg (eds.), *African Socialism* (Stanford: Stanford Univ. Press, 1964), pp. 223-237.

language and ethnic groups, urban and rural communities, diverse
religious bodies, differing elites; how to fit them into a more integrated pattern is also the business of creating new central values.

It may turn out that it is neither the racial nor socialist nor
liberal views that eventually come to prevail, but rather the enlarged and modified traditional ones. Charisma has declined and
become ritualized. As it becomes ritualized it also becomes tradi-
tionalized and, indeed, often expressed in the actual symbols of
chieftaincy. What Ghana may be passing through is not socialism
and authoritarianism in the form of a parliamentary government,
although that element is clearly and loudly there, but on another
level, modernization and neo-traditionalism in the name of socialism. Whatever the case, the transition is no longer without violence
and difficulty.

The Republican Constitution, while providing parliamentary
government, gives sweeping powers to the first President. The
opposition have gone underground. There have been bombings
and intimidation. There is terrorism and violence. Of course, these
are matters which, in the Western press, have been cast in very
large proportions. The truth is that Ghana, like most new states,
still has not drawn together the various qualities of its political
and social life to form a coherent pattern in accord with its own
traditions, customs, and objectives. It will take time to sort out the
four crucial elements: racial pan-Africanism, or Zionism, African
socialism, traditionalism and constitutional democracy.

It would be impossible for me to describe what has happened in
Ghana since 1953 when I completed my first research there. I have
been back to Ghana for short visits during the summer of 1957,
and subsequently in 1959, 1960 and 1961.[3] To analyze in detail
the great changes that have taken place would require at least
another volume. However, it might be of interest to those concerned both with Ghana and with contemporary problems to see
whether conclusions largely based on work done ten years earlier
have been verified or not, as the case may be.

Originally, I attempted to spell out the conditions of what I
called political institutional transfer. How effective was the estab-

[3] I must record my thanks to the West African Comparative Analysis Project,
under whose auspices, and with support of the Carnegie Corporation, this later
research was undertaken.

lishment of certain norms and roles associated with Western secular democracy, and as well, the structures of government through which those norms and roles could be expressed? The question was whether or not these norms and roles would become so fundamentally institutionalized in Ghana that the structures of government through which they were expressed would take on a meaningful life of their own. I arrived at no clear-cut conclusion, but rather several possible alternatives. One alternative was the possibility of a "premature" decline of charisma.

For various reasons, charismatic leadership was described as one way of shifting and changing the mutual identifications of groups and individuals of many diverse sorts within Ghana and focusing them around a single political leader within a mass national movement and with differential appeals to all, but having as its object an independent Ghana. Historically this alternative has proved to be the case. What has happened with charismatic decline when new tasks of government are imposed upon the society? To examine this question I will take specific propositions and hypotheses from the original analysis and use them as the basis for a few of the developments which have occurred since Independence. But one thing should remain clear. Ghana has taken no irrevocable steps. She has not destroyed either the procedures of democracy embodied in the parliamentary *form*, although she has not followed the spirit of democratic institution. Political institutional transfer, then, has not either failed or succeeded. It remains in a kind of political limbo which I believe will be its fate for some years to come. On the other hand, Ghana is not clearly a dictatorship. There is exorbitant power in the hands of Nkrumah—this is true. There has also been an alienation of good men from the government, so that there is no one clearly to rely on. There are political exiles and some of those most closely associated with Nkrumah, particularly in the early days of "The Revolution," have been punished. On the other hand, the Constitution is referred to constantly, and the potentiality for utilization of that constitution remains. There is, as well, a crystallizing of attitudes among intellectuals and others confronted with the loss of values and norms associated with liberal democracy. The intellectuals have been notoriously antipathetic to the regime. This is, in part, because the regime has been notoriously hostile to them.

However, they possess the talents needed to perform the task of government and economy in a useful way, particularly in a planned society. The intellectuals in the civil service, the military, the professions, and the schools, all those who when liberties are attacked may appear to give way easily, also have a sticking power because they are so needed. "Change" is a long time. This is so obvious we forget it. Rather, we may overstress the day-to-day events which occur in a country as the crucial indicators in change. This is, of course, inevitable. But how we interpret those indicators is the crucial test of theory. Those who are willing to write off Ghana as a new form of dictatorship, and to describe Ghana merely as that, are, in my judgment, wrong. There are clearly very ambivalent tendencies between the various forces that I have sketched out. The burdens imposed by internal discontinuities and culture, the burdens imposed by the pan-Africanist role assumed by Ghana, the difficulties involved in experimenting in economic and social life, all these imposed very severe disabilities on a new state. When one adds to this, lack of experience in government and the changing cadres of leadership (and one must remember that a political generation is perhaps much shorter in new nations than elsewhere), one can readily see how much potentiality for drastic change still remains. I believe that democratic institutions as we understand them will become more and more relevant and more and more revolutionary in the developing areas of the world once the tasks of consolidating independence and the development of new economic and social forms begin to emerge. Hopefully some future edition of this book will be able to describe that phase of Ghana's transition.

DAVID E. APTER

University of California,
Berkeley, 1963

PREFACE TO SECOND REVISED EDITION

ONE OF THE advantages of a case study is that it makes possible the application of general principles of theory to the empirical instance. When, as happened in my lifetime, it has been possible to return repeatedly and under very differing circumstances to review and reexamine the case, then the relationship or fit between actual events and the evolution of one's theory takes on a very special character. In the twenty years which have passed since the primary research for this book was completed, Ghana and the developing world have become substantially different, and so inextricably tied to these changes are my own efforts at theory construction that it would be hard to separate the one from the other.

Indeed, if I were to recast my thinking about Ghana in the terms of some of the analytical constructs I have used recently, I would say that in political terms modern Ghanaian history illustrates certain fundamental contradictions which form an underlying logic to the events that occurred. Basically, what is represented in this book is a sequence of political change in six major stages. The first stage was the formation of elite nationalism, employing highly instrumental objectives—better education, tax reform, commercial development for Africans—to generate structural change, i.e., greater political participation. This period, roughly from 1925 to 1946, transformed the British colonial system from a predominantly bureaucratic political structure to a more representative one, although such representation was for a relatively narrow sector of the population.

Stage two began with the conflict between elite and popular nationalism in which the effort to broaden the base of representation required a mass nationalist movement demanding self-government—a normative and structural change leading to responsible government. This, in our terms a change to a reconciliation system of the parliamentary democratic variety, was the great accomplishment of Nkrumah.

The mass nationalist movement, however, transformed highly instrumental norms into unifying consummatory values, a condition at odds with the essentially "bargaining" character of a parliamentary reconciliation system. This contradiction of norms took three structural forms, residual ethnic or tribal versus the all-embracing C.P.P., elite versus mass, and revolutionary versus reformist. In the effort to consolidate the "revolution" and give primacy to the consummatory values of nationalism and pan-Africanism, a struggle between these groups during stage three resulted in the formation of a single party state, which in our terms constitutes a "mobilization" phase.

The fourth stage, lasting from 1961 until the coup, constitutes the failure of the mobilization system. Characterized by increasing coercion, the attempt to generate a new revolutionary state around consummatory values by and large failed. The mobilization system simply turned into a bureaucratic one, with the party bureaucracy at odds with the new functional groupings, civil servants, and others created with a view to forming a new society at home and a universalizing or transforming influence in Africa more generally. Consummatory values declined, although a radical rhetoric remained. This bureaucratic system produced intense structural competition between government and the party. In a climate of growing corruption and increasing coercion, the ethnic, reformist, and elitist opposition, now underground, gained increasing public support, so that when in 1966 the first Ghana coup occurred and Nkrumah was overthrown, few tears were shed for his demise. The coup in our terms transformed what I have called the "neo-mercantilist" sub-type of the bureaucratic system into a military sub-type of the same system. Strong control plus instrumental values are its chief characteristics. But whereas the bureaucratic system under Nkrumah was *sub rosa*, within the apparent frame of a more mobilization system, the military example was a method of providing power to the opposition coalition composed of ethnics, reformists, and elites. This, the fifth stage according to our analysis, led to the return of a reconciliation system under the leadership of Dr. Busia, and took a parliamentary democratic form.

Here again contradictions arose. Ethnic support was translated into rural benefits and urban austerity. Reformism led to excessive bargaining and inaction. Elitism led to corruption attacks on workers' organizations and urban populists, and fears of a revival of Nkrumaism. These factors, combined with an inability to resolve economic conditions, led to a return to a bureaucratic system in the military coup against the Second Republic of Ghana. The reconciliation system was again overthrown in favor of a bureaucratic type.

The tragedy of countries which like Ghana remain in the early stages of modernization is that they are likely to continue to exhibit a similar political instability. This is because they lack the resources for a genuine transformation of their social and economic infrastructure. Each regime reaches a political ceiling, and each change in political type opens up the opportunity only for a limited reallocation of resources and minor structural change. Then the regime becomes a prisoner of its own decisions.

Ghana exhibits this condition. But she does so with certain special characteristics. Despite all her difficulties, Ghana is the one African country with a genuine parliamentary experience (one hesitates to call it a tradition). How such institutions fare over time, where there are real commitments to democratic methods of rule, ought to serve as a challenge to political scientists and politicians to think about what might be called "development constitutions," urgently needed to avoid the predicaments that countries such as Ghana have experienced. New institutional mechanisms are needed, designed to lift the political ceiling and make the politics of development more possible and humane.

Perhaps I will be forgiven if I end this already lengthy preface on a personal note. This book was, I believe, the first study of African politics which employed modern behavioral categories in the study of nationalism. For this edition I have restored the original methodological appendix (which was dropped from intervening ones) to enable a contemporary reader to see the original methodological perspective with which I came to what was then the Gold Coast. But I would also like to emphasize what will not be visible in the text, the tremendous sense of excitement that accompanied the original research. I had in my own way a feeling of pioneering, of striking out on new lines in a new nation. In short, a moral aspect coincided with my theoretical interest and the research combination was absolutely compelling. This moral aspect was twofold, the creation of the first African nation to emancipate itself from colonialism, and the racial issue. In regard to the first, when I was there so were the British, and the actualities of constructing African freedom formed the substance of my work. Secondly, I knew that, if well begun, Ghana would be the first milestone in a racial revolution which could not end without bringing about the independence of other African states and helping to stimulate black liberation in America. These concerns, together with the scholarly ones, gave to me and to others of my research generation a commitment and intensity of interest which we shared with the builders and shapers of political life themselves. It is perhaps impossible today to recapture the excitement of that period because the moral flavor is gone, shattered on the ambiguities of complex demands and mixed motives. The methodological interests remain, but have become so professionalized that sometimes the substance of the research serves as the means rather than the goal. Gone forever is a certain innocence, moral as well as methodological, which in those days forged a link between research worker and activist, between the observer and the people. What they shared they savored in the form of personal friendships and professional associations.

What is also obsolete is the research year in which a foreign student, coming to observe things African, can really hope to add much to what is known. In my day it was much easier. None of the obvious things had been said. Today they have all been said, and many times. Certain forms of knowledge will require political scientists to do what I have never done, employ the most advanced analytical techniques in a small space over a long period of time, mixing detailed observation of the kind employed by some British or French anthropologists with the most efficient techniques of analysis, both quantitative and analytical. It is perhaps ironic that at the moment when just such scholarly needs are at their height, financial support is declining.

My own emphasis has been the opposite of what I have just described. It has, over the years since the first research for this book was completed, taken a more comparative form. Some of my interests stemmed from the inadequacies of the methods employed here. I did a much more intensive study in Buganda, and found that to use the categories of this book would have caused me to omit much of what seemed crucial there. The effort to put the lessons learned from African research into a more systematic form has been a main preoccupation over the past ten years. The first step in this direction was taken with the publication of my book,

The Politics of Modernization (Chicago: University of Chicago Press, 1965). The inadequacies of the approach employed there were many. For one thing, I still lacked a good theory. For another, the analytical system was too complex. Efforts to simplify and reinterpret these categories in Latin America in a broadly comparative way has led to my most recent effort, *Choice and the Politics of Allocation* (New Haven: Yale University Press, 1971). This, mainly a structural concern, also identified two central behavioral issues which I see as a permanent "dialectic." I call this the relationship between radicalization and *embourgeoisement*.

These themes can also be seen in the context of Ghana. The beginning of the Nkrumah period was an attempt at radicalization, e.g., at the radical redefinition of appropriate roles. In this respect, the regime failed. What occurred was *embourgeoisement*, increased accessibility to the given ensemble of roles. Indeed, if one were to sum up the Nkrumah period, it could be described as radicalization for *embourgeoisement*. That may have been its tragedy.

In the years since this book was written, I had the opportunity to return to Ghana many times, mainly under the auspices of the West African Comparative Analysis Project, supported by a grant from the Carnegie Corporation. I have studied and worked in many places since. It is often said that the country where one does his first field research and defines his original intellectual interests will remain a place of special affection and regard. This has certainly been true in my case.

D.A.

Yale University
New Haven, 1972

◨◨◨◨ **CONTENTS** ◨◨◨◨

PART IV

GHANA IN TRANSITION

CHAPTER 1

THE AFRICAN CHALLENGE
TO DEMOCRACY

HOST to a variety of social, economic, and intellectual stimuli, Africa finds its destiny directed into new and uneasy patterns. In the vast subcontinent today we witness a clash of cultures and ideas as the tribal peoples of many colonial territories move toward Western forms of social organization.

Such a process is a challenge to Western political practice and belief. Can the content and structures of democratic popular government serve as a medium of reintegration for the many peoples of Africa as they seek to modify their activities and their aspirations in the light of modern practice? Is the centuries-old development of parliamentary government in England suitable to the conditions of African life in British colonial territories? If answers to such questions are in the affirmative, then we can say that parliamentary practice is still revolutionary. Reducing the risk of authoritarianism, it gives voice to newly articulate millions, allowing them, increasingly, to make their own decisions and participate in political life. It provides opportunities for expressions of social organization which, possibly, can incorporate older and more traditional systems of politics into a larger scheme of national and democratic society.

It remains an open question whether or not the structures of parliamentary government are suitable for the development of African social organization from tribal to national systems of social interaction. The present task will be to examine the process where it seems to be occurring successfully—in the Gold Coast. We shall treat this process as a case study in political institutional transfer. The policy, problems, and activities of both Gold Coast Africans and British expatriate officials will be examined in detail. We shall attempt to find some of the crucial factors in the process of developing a modern British-type parliamentary democracy in the Gold Coast, where only a half-century ago the rule of the British was limited to the coastal area and the chiefs reigned supreme in the hinterlands. In such a study one set of variables is provided by the indigenous social and political pattern which pre-dated the coming of the European. A second is provided by the impact of European rule upon Africans.

Parliamentary Government in Africa

It is in British Africa that nationalist movements of considerable proportions have developed. British colonial policy, for a considerable time, has involved a program of devolution of powers to a local variety of parliamentary system. Conciliar organs have been adapted and modified to fit the conditions of the African environment and the special requirements of each colony. In parts of East and Central Africa this policy has given European interests a much freer hand in dictating to the African. It has been argued, for example, that the British abdication of imperial responsibility in Kenya would be a way of ducking a formidable multi-racial problem represented in more open and official form in the Malan government of South Africa.[1] Yet the same policy, in areas where Europeans are non-resident, has meant a genuine devolution of authority and responsibility to Africans themselves. In the Gold Coast, Africans are in very real control of the internal decision-making processes of the territory.

Authority patterns which the West has established in Africa have succeeded in bringing forth new images as well as new gods. These new images increasingly reflect concern by African groups for greater freedom of action. Political autonomy has become an insistent theme. As the desire for autonomy sharpens, two great cultural traditions clash with one another. One points to the past, when tribal freedom represented a period of dignity and independence within the traditional pattern of life. The other points to a national future: instead of the tribe, the state; instead of the colonial administrator, the African politician; instead of the mission school, public secular education; instead of colonial status, parliamentary democracy.

Between these two cultural tendencies, Africans today represent all varieties of adaptation and accommodation towards the varied groups with which they have been in contact. In some areas in the Gold Coast they have been dealing with Europeans for over four hundred years. Christianity has made heavy and

[1] See United Kingdom White Paper, Command 1922, London, 1923, p. 10.

4

often strange inroads. Islam has crossed the desert and been incorporated with varieties of religious belief indigenous to the area.

There is the Africa of the European who is born in the White Highlands of Kenya or in the urban centers of Johannesburg. There is the Africa of the bush and the tribe, still the dominant social pattern. There is the Africa of the industrial worker in Nigeria or the Congo, or South Africa, where the family may live in a tribal preserve and the husbands and sons may be away most of the time, seeking their fortunes in more lucrative employment than agriculture. There is the Africa of the politician who may take on the frustrations of others as his own, directing the destiny of his people, or perhaps seeking an easy road towards money and power.

In spite of all these "Africas" which coexist side by side with one another, a gradual redefinition of social life is occurring throughout the continent. What happens in one area has its repercussions in others. People are less bewildered and less passive to European rule. In West Africa self-government has become more than a remote possibility.

Obstacles to Self-Government in British West Africa

British West Africa (including the Gambia, Sierra Leone, the Gold Coast, and Nigeria) is an area having no permanent European settler population. The Gold Coast is the most advanced towards self-government. Nigeria, having gross difficulties with her diverse ethnic and religious groups, has not yet been able to operate successfully even a modified federal system. Yet self-government by 1956 has been a motto of Nigerian political leaders in the southern regions. The Gambia and Sierra Leone trail behind Nigeria in the development of self-government but the pattern has already been demarcated, particularly in Sierra Leone. The main difficulties facing these West African territories in their program of ultimate self-government can be roughly stated as follows:

1. In all cases there is a lack of historical unity. The concept of a nation in any wide territorial sense is largely non-indigenous. Relations between differing areas within a colonial territory were, in the past, conducted mostly on a tribal basis.

2. There are differences in religion, education, and degree of

Westernization between the people of one part of a colonial territory and another. In most cases the coastal regions have had the longest history of relations with the West. The coastal peoples have been engaged in commerce and trade, ruled by British codes of law and justice, and have had longer Western educational traditions and opportunities than have areas farther inland. In the hinterlands of the colonies the traditional systems tend to be more intact, nationalism less pressing and less effective. In some cases traditional disputes between major tribal groups have been enlarged to include religious and political conflicts, such as those in Nigeria between the Moslems in the north and the more Westernized southerners. These conflicts point up sharply the political consequences when differences in indigenous social structure coexist within a larger administrative environment. Ancient rivalries, intensified by the divergent conversions to Islam in the north and Christianity in the south, have crystallized into fear, hatred, and resentment of southern political domination, particularly for the people of the Northern Territories of the Gold Coast and the Northern Emirates of Nigeria.

3. There is a lack of trained and educated personnel to do the jobs of administration both on central and local levels of government.

4. Customs survive which are suitable for tribal government and traditional social systems but which tend to make for corruption and malfunction in parliamentary and secular administrative structures. The traditional African family pattern is an excellent example of some of the conflicts to which Africans are subject. Nepotism, for example, is considered a grave offense in Western bureaucratic practice, yet in African practice providing jobs for the members of one's own family is socially compulsory. It is one of the normal forms of social security and job recruitment in traditional society and one of the crucial elements in the satisfactory maintenance of tribal social structure. When such practices are carried over into the administrative service, they break down into favoritism, corruption, and graft, in a Western-type bureaucratic setup.

5. Differing conceptions of the meaning of participation and representation in government are held by members of the society and the representatives of the public, whether appointed or elected. In most cases, except for those political figures educated

abroad or in the few excellent secondary schools (such as Achimota), there is little notion of representation as known in the Western parliamentary sense.

6. Lack of effective nationalist leadership is coupled with apathy in many parts of a colonial territory and with political aggressiveness in other parts. Particularly where political leadership is lacking, certain areas are at a political disadvantage; this is a real difficulty in the Northern Territories of the Gold Coast, for example, or in the Protectorate of Sierra Leone, where most strong leadership and effective political awareness come from the Colony-proper.

7. An educated elite tends to adopt Western culture and social graces and elects to identify either with the old chieftainship aristocracy or to stand alone, remaining apart from the social body at large in manners, occupation, and politics. Some of these people become nationalist prima donnas without effective popular support.

8. Problems of poverty and disease make it difficult for individual members of the society to adapt and adjust to new behavioral requirements, so concerned are they with their immediate needs for survival. Sometimes the family survives as a socializing structure while becoming less and less adequate as an economic unit.

9. In some cases, as in the Gambia and Sierra Leone, there is no major cash crop sufficient to maintain development, education, occupational mobility, etc., consonant with the solution of immediate problems by parliamentary means.

Where these problems are severe, the task of developing representative self-government is most difficult indeed. It is these problems, as well as others, that make the difficulties and obstacles facing the Colonial Office appear overwhelming to many colonial administrators. Yet the development of self-government in West Africa proceeds without the racial handicaps of other parts of British Africa. In West Africa self-government is with not only the consent but also the demand of the governed. Its development has had official blessing for a long time. It is a policy almost as old as British penetration of Africa, and it has been pursued from time to time with varying degrees of endeavor and exercise. Even with all the handicaps, West Africa remains the only area where the prospects for self-government are real. To the Colonial Office it is an area of experimentation in which a reintegration of society around the processes of parliamentary government is the goal. Such an experiment is subject to all the ills that flesh is heir to, but upon its success African freedom is contingent.

Political Institutional Transfer
in the Gold Coast

In terms of African responsibility the Gold Coast is the most advanced politically of any African colony. It has a British parliamentary structure of government. British-type structures, including patterns of behavior incumbent upon those who would operate them, are of major concern here insofar as we seek to know the kind of adaptation and adjustment which these hitherto tribal peoples in the Gold Coast have made in order to operate parliamentary democracy on a national scale. The processes involved we have phrased *political institutional transfer.* The source is British, and the spirit and form of these British structures have been instituted with due pomp and ceremony in the parliament which meets in Accra, in the local councils springing up in the bush, and in the procedures and machinery of government.

In studying the Gold Coast in an attempt to cast some light on the problems involved when institutional transfer occurs, we need to point out, as most colonial officials are quick to do, that the Gold Coast is not typical of other parts of British Africa, nor even of other parts of British West Africa. Aside from the fact that it has no racial problems on a scale known in East and Central Africa, it is also a prosperous colony in terms of earned receipts from cocoa, bauxite, diamonds, gold, and other products.

The Gold Coast is a small colony having an association with Western nations for over four hundred years. In coastal regions it has the highest literacy rate (approximately thirty per cent) in Africa. For Great Britain, the Gold Coast is the showpiece of successful institutional transfer. It is the model to which people in the Colonial Office point, as do others anxious to see Africans democratically governing themselves. While definitive answers about political institutional transfer will hardly be forthcoming in this study, we hope that an effort to examine the problems consequent on such transfer will cast light on the following:

1. Research theory and methods in political science pointing

8

to some fundamental aspects of politics in terms of political behavior, political perceptions, and political norms.[2]

2. An approach to African political development in terms of the substantive adaptation of tribal to secular culture.

We hope that such a study will have value for those concerned with working out ways and means of studying comparative political institutions and political behavior, both in terms of empirical materials and theory. Our further hope is that this understanding will be useful to those policymakers who are concerned with the trend of developments in Africa.

Political institutional transfer, as it has developed in the Gold Coast, is therefore the central theme of this study. Political institutional transfer will be used here to mean the process of institutionalizing, in the Gold Coast, certain predominantly political structures having concrete memberships, which were modeled after similar political structures in Great Britain.[3] *Institutionalization* as a process deals in this usage with a specific shift of beliefs and perspectives on the part of crucial segments of the Gold Coast public, away from traditional and tribal beliefs and patterns of authority to the acceptance of a set of rules and political objectives which are primarily Western in their inspiration.

The degree of institutionalization will mean the degree of public acceptance of both the form and content of authority which derives from and is manifested through non-traditional sources and governmental structures. The degree of institutionalization ultimately means, in a democratic system, the degree to which the public creates and supports sanctions relating to the norms of political democracy.

The problem of institutional transfer is thus not merely the

---

[2] See Appendix.

[3] A note of caution is offered here. Political institutional transfer is used here as an action phrase. That is to say, the ordinary use of the word "institution," involving a somewhat vague complex of structures, beliefs, and action patterns, is not appropriate. As used here, the word "political" refers to membership structures in the system which are primarily concerned with the source and use of authority in the social system, considered binding upon all the members. The word "institutional" refers to the acceptance by the members of the formal and substantive content of those structures. For the present, it is sufficient to say that "institutionalization" as used here is a process by which predominantly political structures become endowed over a period of time in the eyes of the members of Gold Coast society with normative elements, and as such become a meaningful part of social life.

creation by order in council of a series of political structures such as a parliament, an office of the prime minister, and a cabinet. Rather, the concern here is with the behavioral consequences of setting up these structures in an environment for which there is little meaningful indigenous counterpart. These transplanted structures are not only vehicles for the transporting of government business; they are also orientational foci around which the reintegration of society can develop. The structures themselves become a part of the general range of valued beliefs in the social system. They become operational points for social change.

The structures of parliament, called the legislative assembly, cabinet, prime minister, and civil service, have all been constituted in the Gold Coast.[4] The conciliar system has recently been extended to local government as well. These structural devices, functionally paramount to the maintenance of parliamentary democracy, are a means of facilitating the integration of varied segments of the Gold Coast population into a larger membership unit, the state. The colonial authorities have, in effect, taken the political structures which are a part of their own social environment, saying to the Africans in the Gold Coast that if they can make them work, then they shall be free.

In this process heavy demands and grave disabilities are imposed upon Africans. Asked to give vitality and meaning to a structural pattern not peculiarly designed for their traditional environment, they are further required to change their society at the same time that they solve its problems. Many African leaders are conscious of what is at stake. They know that they are being judged by people who are some of the most adept political sophisticates in the world. Particularly in the Gold Coast, Africans know that if they fail to operate these political structures successfully—institutionalize them to accord with Western criteria of procedure, methods, and stability—they will be quickly criticized and judged.[5] Because the Gold Coast is by far the

4 See *Statutory Instrument*, 1950, No. 2094, The Gold Coast (Constitution) Order in Council, 1950, and *Statutory Instrument*, 1952, No. 1039, The Gold Coast Constitutional Amendment No. 2, Order in Council, 1952.

5 This consciousness of what is at stake is brought home constantly in the press and in public speeches by Gold Coast political leaders. The phrase "the eyes of the world are upon us" prefaces almost every major address. Perhaps of equal importance as the "eyes of the world" to most Gold Coast leaders, are the eyes of other Africans and Europeans, both in West Africa and other parts of Africa. Aware of Malanism and outright hostility on the part of European minorities in

most politically advanced of the British colonies moving towards self-government, Africans know that failure will set back the whole cause of African independence.

The Gold Coast is composed of many tribal groupings. It is divided into three parts; the Colony along the coast; the Ashanti Confederacy in the central area; and the Northern Territories, which begins to approach the Sahara desert.[6] Each of these areas represents considerable cultural and historical differences, and widely differing local institutions. The Gold Coast is a land of many peoples, many religions, isolated groups and groups having a long history of intermingling through trade, migration, and intermarriage.

The varieties of traditional systems in the Gold Coast indicate wide ranges in political structures and expression. Roughly, a bifurcation can be made along the Black Volta River, dividing certain groups which have their orientational affiliations to the north, to Islam, and to desert culture, and those whose affiliations are to the coast and to African tribalism. The Moshi, Dagomba, and Mamprussi groups predominate in the first category. These people wear the long-flowing garments of the Middle East of perhaps four hundred years ago; they are lean-visaged, horsemen, patriarchal. The central and southern groups are predominantly Akan, with a close-knit family-type organization following matrilineal lines in many crucial respects, with similarities to other Bantu groupings of the forest-equatorial belt.

Traditional custom is very difficult to observe. Fortes, for example, in a study of the Tallensi (a Northern Territories group), indicated that it was only after a year in the field, living with these people, that he was able to distinguish between certain types of authentic lineages and other accessory lineages, the latter having less substantial political roles.

One still finds the African woman pounding *fu-fu* in front of her mud hut, but she will probably be dressed in Manchester cloth made expressly for the West African market. In Accra, the

Kenya, Southern Rhodesia, and other parts of colonial Africa under French, Belgian, and Portuguese rule, African leaders in the Gold Coast appear to view their work as the beginning of a historical exercise which can ultimately decide the future of Africans throughout the continent.

[6] See *Atlas of the Gold Coast*, Gold Coast Survey Dept., Government Printer, Accra, 1949.

capital, she might pound *fu-fu*, live in a mud hut, and own a fleet of taxicabs or the house that a European trader lives in. Centuries of culture contact, educational effort, commercial and industrial development, religious intervention—all bear strange fruit, some exotic, some familiar. The calabash is less preferred than the enamel pot. The automobile is a symbol of modernity and success, while books are preferred to the teller of tales and literacy is next to godliness.

The coming of the European has set off countless changes in tribal society. Tribal life, like all other forms of social organization, was a system of integrated efforts by which human beings conquered their environment. Tribal life in the Gold Coast represented sets of ethnically related peoples organized into self-sufficient systems of social action. As in other forms of society it contained a system of beliefs and symbols. It had an elaborate culture and a means of securing the adjustment of its members to its requirements. It created men in its own cultural image, men whose actions would support rather than destroy the systems of social action of which it was made up. It represented, in Africa, a way of life in which certain kinds of relationships—the family, the lineage, or the clan—formed the bedrock of significant social interactions.

Tribal life in the Gold Coast was effective in the rural habitat in which it developed. Tribal cultures, in addition to containing systems of symbols and artifacts which became the social and psychological inheritance of every member, had working explanations of the environment. Symbols were explanatory as well as representational. Magic and religion, labor and crops, land and government, were closely related. The spirits were the spirits of rocks, lakes, the heavens. Labor involved the working of the land, so intimate a part of the natural sequence of the universe. Man was close to his environment, and no great chain of organizations separated the individual from the immediate problems of subsistence and survival.

The overpowering importance of the environment, particularly in the tropics, made all forms of existence precarious. Gifts were often food. Festive rites were occasioned by the harvest or in memory of some great historical obstacle successfully achieved. In some areas the Odwera or Yam Festival not only signified the harvest but was an expression of group solidarity. The entire community participated in cleansing rites, propitiating the ancestors, while newly installed chiefs used the occasion to take their oaths of allegiance to the paramount chief.

Into this intensely personal form of social organization, European institutions were introduced. New forms of activity, new working explanations of the environment, new structures of social and political activity—all helped to change the pattern of Gold Coast life, until today the men and women of the Gold Coast are again managing their own internal affairs, this time with the complex apparatus of a modern political state. It is a young democracy, with all the precariousness which democracy involves. Diverse peoples need to find social and psychological sustenance within its framework.

In dealing with a tribal system of social organization, anyone interested in the predominantly political aspects of social behavior faces severe problems in attempting to step outside the familiar precincts of his discipline and make an intelligent examination of the wider aspects of social action as they seem significant to his study. In examining tribal societies he treads on strange ground in trying to define networks of influence, sanction, coercion, and the forms of political expression outside the façade of formal systems of authority. Some of the tribes in the Gold Coast—the Fra-Fra, for example—have none of the formal trappings of government. In tribal societies the importance of controls on behavior and the expression of those controls is manifest in religious ceremonies, through rites of circumcision, through the expression of solidarity in the election of a chief, through offerings to the gods. The political relevance of these non-political patterns appears again and again as the complexities of political life grudgingly reveal themselves as a network of myth and reality, blood and family, magic and religion.

Authority flows from countless sources, most of which remain unknown to the superficial observer, and, unfortunately, most of us are superficial observers. Traditional societies are no less complex than Western, whether complexity refers to the intricacy of social life or to the difficulty of comprehension. We can make only the briefest of generalizations as they seem pertinent to our focus in the problem of political institutional transfer.

The tribal groups in the Gold Coast are, in the main, personal.

The expression of authority is mostly diffuse, except regarding various specified acts for which offices have been created to dispose of problems arising in connection with those acts. Functions of chieftaincy in war, for example, are specific, regarding a hierarchy much as in Western armies, a chain of command. Crimes draw specific responses in courts. Yet, since in most cases there is an age-grading system, any elder has certain diffuse authority prerogatives over any "youngman."[7] Ritual functions are often precise, but unspecific. The expression of authority is a part of everyday life, as we shall indicate further. The cup of custom is kept with great solemnity.

The traditional systems are the historical as well as the analytical base points of our analysis. It was to these tribal units that the white man came in search of gold or slaves or other forms of commerce. It was these traditional social organizations which became fragmented under Western culture. Showing the differential impact of Western social patterns and economic objectives, tribal affiliations are still dominant as the orientational universe for the non-urbanized Gold Coaster. He still grows up in the bush. He still works the farm. If he goes to a school at all, it is to a mission school. His books deal with affairs remote from his experience. It is still a world in which a close relationship to the ancestors and an uneasy tenure with Christianity or Islam make adjustive demands, some sacred, some secular, upon his pattern of belief, his notion of the spirits, gods, and rites of his natural world.

In the Northern Territories of the Gold Coast organized kingdoms—Dagomba, Mamprussi, Gonja, etc.—have chiefs whose powers are still very much intact. Allegiance to the *ya na* in Yendi is a visible factor in the present efforts to promote secular political structures among the Dagomba, in which the form of secularity has not been followed by its substance.

In Ashanti the functions and activities of the *asantehene*[8] still evoke powerful reactions throughout the Confederacy. The strength of traditional political patterns in their conditional, emotional, and local solidarity aspects is manifested in the be-

---

[7] "Youngmen" are commoner males—of non-royal office, usually members of *asafo* companies (village military groups or militia)—who are not elders. The term does not refer to age.

[8] The *asantehene* is the great paramount chief of Ashanti.

havior of diverse parties, as they reapportion their roles under strikingly different forms of political rules. The very violence of emotional response, characterized by guilt, hatred, and inconsistent behavior, is evident often on the most local levels as the roots of secular authority branch out among the rocks of traditional strength and sentiment.

One important assumption that we make in this examination refers to the generalized functions of culture. Culture we can define as the learned symbols and artifacts held and transmitted by members of a society. In part, culture provides perceptive forms by which members construct their world, their orientational universe. The symbols and concepts held by members of a tribe provide psychological and social security on a relatively homogenous basis. The introduction of secular political forms demands a substitution of new culture forms, new symbols and artifacts either to supplant the old as relevant guides to action, or to replace them.

Which symbols shall replace the old? The word "replace" is a dangerous one since it implies controlled selectivity. In actual fact, changes are partial, and, in terms of the problem of institutionalizing new political patterns of activity, non-selective. What often appear to Western observers as crucial symbols in the appreciation and participation required by secular political structures are often completely missed by the members of the traditional societies in their contact with secularity. To some Africans, perhaps, the adaptation of European behavior standards centers around becoming a nominal Christian, having servants, carrying a briefcase, joining a club, and abusing subordinates. Sometimes the behavior which Africans have observed as characteristic of Europeans has been superficial (seeing the swagger stick, the dress, and the comforts of the European's way of life), missing such basic qualities as devotion to duty, capacity for hard work, standards of honesty.

The standards by which the colonial officer, for example, is governed on his job may be entirely unobserved. Yet the importance of those standards is acute for institutional transfer. How does the Gold Coaster approaching full self-government, operating a host of foreign institutions, perceive the role of the secular administrator, the members of the Legislative Assembly, the role of the prime minister? How he views them will affect the way in which his government will function. Are the things which he does predominantly imitative or based on understanding? Does he act in a parliament according to a mechanical process of following rules, or do the rules have relevance for him as a part of a responsibly functioning group?

To thrust Western democratic political forms into a tribal environment, even by a casual process, entails a drastic set of social consequences. Where the process is dictated by a democratic polity, the creators are hindered by their own values. They cannot manipulate, force, revise, and make demands as if social engineering were the only criterion. Human beings are not steel bridges; one cannot calculate their response to strain. We do not know what is foundation and what is superstructure in social life. But even if we did, those who follow the prescriptions of democratic values must engineer by suggestion, by persuasion, by consent. That the British administrators in the Gold Coast have used these methods is testified by the grudging admiration granted them by latter-day nationalists.

Democracy is based, ultimately, upon consent, and without the active consent of the indigenes, without an awareness of the behavioral considerations imposed by consent, the social engineers, whether academicians, colonial officers, or missionaries, are in difficult waters indeed when they try to plot the democratic course for peoples having political institutions whose form and substance are of another kind. The traditional structures provide a guide to the way in which tribal members view their world, their orientational universe.

The recognized courses of action by which individual behavior is controlled can be called, in the broadest sense, law and order. Whether by statute or custom, constitution or proverb, the larger body of public law is an expression of the governing of means, and the integration of individual efforts into tolerable channels. Law and order, in its expression of political norms, is a fundamental orientational framework, carrying with it public conviction and personal belief. When a new system is posed alongside the old, the old may appear as a powerful, even stifling, framework of blocks against adaptation. The man who lives in tribal society may think of his future as something which was governed by the dictum of his ancestors. He may view an expected role as suddenly unsatisfactory since new alternatives hitherto unthinkable, unperceived, are opened by alien rule. The rules, the law and order of the tribe, may be shattered as a consequence, even though the new law and order of foreign derivation may have little relevance to him.

In such circumstances the individual may forego many of the customs and beliefs most crucial to his traditional way of life. Once this occurs he wanders in a no-man's land for a time, stumbling and halting until he regains his footing on the side of secularity.

The great danger in this process lies in the possibility of prolonged lack of integration. One possible consequence is the withdrawal of segments of the population from effective participation in secular social life—a state of apathy. With wholesale apathy, democracy cannot function. Another possibility lies in the breakdown of order—a state of anarchy. In such an environment the chances for parliamentary development are remote. Time and time again in the Gold Coast, measures which have been attempted to combat disease or to promote efficiency or better living standards have been subverted by local lethargy or have become the center of polite discussion but little action. On the other hand an uncontrolled environment, an environment of lawlessness, is one in which construction is impossible. Without a discipline predominantly self-imposed, in a society which wishes development and rapid social change, the alternative is discipline superimposed. In such situations authoritarianism is incipient.

Sources of Political Institutional Transfer

There are, in the Gold Coast, three main potential sources from which the main outlines of political organization can be drawn.

The first is a return to the traditional system of tribe, lineage, clan, and chief. While the vitality of these traditional systems is difficult to evaluate, it is quite clear that in many places throughout the Gold Coast, they are far from dead. The great value of the traditional systems is the fact that they are indigenous. They are closely tied up with the network of family, lineage, and other kin group systems that are particularly valuable where the older forms of economic and social activity, such as subsistence farming, or age-grading, and other patterns of social life, go on in much their traditional pattern. The traditional systems are local systems. As part of tribal life, they are bound up with the immediate cares of the tribes, which, generally speaking, encompass a small territorial area. They represent patterns of behavior well understood by the members of the tribe. Although the impact of Western culture has resulted in the fragmenting and shattering of many tribal systems, there are a variety of media by which the old societal cohesives are at least partially maintained, and could be resuscitated.

A considerable body of opinion, generally including that of the chiefs, is in favor of recreating the old system insofar as this is possible, with certain modifications. Within this body of opinion is one extreme which seeks a kind of agrarian communism in which the tribe is the corporate owner of land (as was traditional) while modern methods make the land an effective producing unit. Such opinion tends to be sentimental about tribal society, ignoring the close relation between authority and its exercise, and land tenure and land usage in the traditional system, which would be drastically undermined with changes in farming technique and in tenure. At the opposite extreme are those who repudiate Western culture in its entirety and wish to return to the conditions of tribal life in as pure a form as possible.

Interviews with tribal chiefs in the Gold Coast revealed that some return to the traditional patterns of authority was regarded as inevitable, particularly by older chiefs. "We are the rightful rulers," said one, stating a fact of nature as he saw it. To him it was only a matter of time before "the people returned to their senses and stopped playing around with these youngmen and politics." This view, not as naïve as it sounds, depends upon the return to the only political structures which make sense to the people if the honeymoon with secular politics settles down to mass disenchantment.

The range of opinion which in general seeks a revival, in any form, of tribal organization and authority will be described here as "conservative." This term will also include those groups which seek to integrate tribal authority with secular authority; it refers to any affiliation or orientational reference to the indigenous or traditional forms of political and social life.[9]

[9] Such words as "conservative," "liberal," "reactionary," or "progressive" will not be used here except as they are specifically defined with reference to a specific group of people who have a pronounced set of views which can be compared with those of other groups.

The second major source for political institutional transfer can be roughly described as Marxist, or of Marxian derivation. This approach would involve changing the social and economic organization of the society, the setting up of a "bootstrap" economy, and defining goals and objectives toward which the total efforts of the public would be directed. The key elements of the traditional system would be destroyed. The organizational foundations of traditional life would vanish rather quickly. The youth would be reeducated and mass literacy campaigns would enlist the elite to furnish ideas to be communicated while the people were being taught to read and write. At the same time, efforts would be made to keep traditional art forms alive and to capitalize on the pride and historical morale of local social units, the destruction of which might cause apathy.

This form of model has certain advantages. It tackles pressing problems with dispatch. There are few illusions about allowing conflicting views to confuse the public.

The source of this model is the Soviet Union. There is a small group in the Gold Coast which has read of Soviet achievements and which receives Soviet literature. Some find comfort in explaining colonial status as due to the destructive exploitation of capitalist adventurists. There is also the temptation, when organizing political parties, to use the language of Marxism as an ideological weapon against the status quo and a vehicle for rousing public opinion.[10]

How important this second source of political institutional transfer becomes will largely depend upon the success or failure of the third source, the British parliamentary pattern, which is carefully being constructed under the guidance and control of the Colonial Service and the nationalists. Because this third model relates to the form of British rule in all parts of British Colonial Africa, it has wide implications. How the process is taking place in the Gold Coast will form the main body of this study.

The three models—traditional, Marxian, and parliamentarian —are regarded as three of the major sources of inspiration for

---

[10] Insofar as the word "imperialism" will be used here at all, it will be expressed in a very limited sense. In tracing out the perceptions of key individuals who will form part of the study, we find that for many imperialism is a symbol of oppression, denied opportunity, racial antagonism, etc. In this sense it is a symbol through which one group views another group and as such throws some light on political behavior.

political leaders in Africa today. A fourth, stemming from the growth of Islam and other religious influences, will not be discussed.[11] To varying degrees, these three sources are in conflict. Each represents dangers to the other. Each represents efforts to refashion African society either into something which it was or into something which it will become.

So far the British parliamentary model has served as the basis for Gold Coast political development. Therefore a study of its prospects is our major concern. The Gold Coast experiment has important implications for all underdeveloped areas, for it is one test of the processes and prospects of parliamentary government as a means of promoting stability, development, and effective social change. Thus, the Gold Coast is a challenge to political democracy in the West.

[11] So far Islam has not presented major obstacles to the development of secular parliamentary government in the Gold Coast. A new Moslem party founded since this research was done in the field has appeared as an opposition party. This new Moslem Association Party was not very successful at the polls, capturing only one seat in the Legislative Assembly during the 1954 general election.

⧈⧈ | CHAPTER 2 | ⧈⧈

HISTORICAL BACKGROUND

Ethnic Origins

WHILE, in the absence of recorded materials, the early background of the Gold Coast is a compound of mystery and conjecture, there are hints of ancient commerce and contact between the Middle East and the West African coast. It is supposed that the highly prized Aggrey beads found in the Gold Coast are of Carthaginian or Phoenician origin. Hanno, the Carthaginian, is known to have made an expedition along the West African coast, although the narrative of his journey has come down to us in translated and abridged form, the original document having been lost.[1]

Apparently the Stone Age overlapped the Iron Age, and extended until comparatively recent times. Stone neolithic celts, called God's axes in the Gold Coast, have been found which, according to Rattray, have been admitted by some elders to be the implements used by the forebears of the present inhabitants of the Gold Coast. While the celts were commonly supposed by the Akans to be of divine origin, Rattray found some informants who privately admitted their utilitarian past.[2]

The present inhabitants are, for the most part, rather recent settlers in the Gold Coast. Ward even suggests non-African indigenes:

"It is probable, however, that West Africa was inhabited by an earlier race before the Negroes arrived. Apart from the existence of palaeolithic implements and from the Gold Coast belief in the *mmoatia* [spirits], there is stronger evidence that the Negro settlers in West Africa found there in possession a different race. Several nations of the Sudan have a tradition that the original inhabitants were a race of short stature and reddish complexion."[3]

Ward also indicates[4] as does Claridge[5] that the present inhabit-

[1] See Claridge, Walton W., *A History of the Gold Coast and Ashanti*, London, 1915, Vol. i.
[2] Rattray, R. S., *Ashanti*, London, 1924.
[3] Ward, W. E. F., *A History of the Gold Coast*, London, 1948, p. 31.
[4] *Ibid.*, p. 34.
[5] Claridge, *op.cit.*, p. 182.

21

ants of the Gold Coast originally came down from the Southern Sudan.

Meyrowitz and Danquah[6] try to relate the predominating Akan group of the Gold Coast with the ancient Western Sudanese kingdom of Ghana which had a highly developed culture and, for a considerable time, African kings. Attacked in 1076 by the Berbers, its descendants are said to have moved south, the fore-bears of the present Akan peoples.[7] One of the older nationalist leaders in the Gold Coast today, Dr. J. B. Danquah, claims to be the author of the "Ghana myth."[8]

Ward, on the other hand, thinks that the Ghana myth is hardly likely, and he indicates that the Ghana Kingdom was more prob-ably Mandigo than Akan.[9] He feels that by the time the Ghana Kingdom was destroyed, the Akans were already intrenched in the Gold Coast, having moved south to their present locations as a result of local warfare. Regardless of origin, it appears fairly well accepted that the Akans moved southward around the thir-teenth century, not en masse, but in three waves.

The first wave consisted of the Guans and related groups, who came down the Volta valley and probably as early as 1200 were in occupation of a crescent of land stretching from Bole, through Salaga, Karachi, Asum, and Accra, as far west as Winneba.

The second wave, the ancestors of the Fanti who occupy most of the southwestern coastal area, probably came down the Ofin and Pra rivers, arriving on the coast about 1300, thence spreading eastward through Cape Coast until they came in contact with the Guan tribes.

The third wave, the ancestors of the Ashanti peoples, came straight down between the earlier settlers, occupying Ashanti and Akim. The Akwamus, a branch of this group, came into contact with the Accra peoples as late as 1600.

In the Northern Territories, after the Akans had passed through, the Moshi peoples came down from the Sudan, and conquered the

[6] Danquah, J. B., "The Culture of the Akan," in *Africa*, Vol. 22, No. 4, October, 1952.

[7] *Ibid.*

[8] Danquah holds to this notion, based, he claims, on research and documents in the British Museum. But he related in personal interview that his main concern was to find a glorious past for the Gold Coast which would provide a symbol around which nationalists could draw inspiration. After a number of unsuccessful alternatives, the name "Ghana" received popular acceptance and has widespread currency today.

[9] Ward, *op.cit.*, p. 44.

indigenous population. The Moshi split into three groups, establishing the additional kingdoms of Mamprussi and Dagomba under the rule of sons or other relatives of the leaders. These kingdoms were established around the sixteenth century and in the seventeenth the Gonja Kingdom was formed out of Moshi and Akan elements in the southern part of the Northern Territories.[10] These groups originally brought the Moslem influence so widely dispersed in most parts of the Gold Coast today.

The Akans

The Akans are probably the most important of the Gold Coast ethnic groups. Possibly the oldest known center of Akan civilization south of the Black Volta is the Brong city of Bono-Mansu which was founded in 1295. Its ruins lie approximately one hundred miles north of Kumasi.

There is a tradition among the Brong that they were indigenous inhabitants of an area not far from their present establishments. The belief is that the Brong peoples "came out of a hole in the ground." These "holes" are still to be seen today.

The Akans, of whom the Brong peoples are a part, can be divided into two major groupings, Ashanti and Fanti. The Ashanti, occupying the central area of the Gold Coast, once held sway over most of the territory which makes up the modern Gold Coast. They were industrious in pursuing attacks and forays against the Fanti who occupied the western coastal area. The Fanti were quick to ally themselves with European outposts and settlements along the coast, such alliances after European intervention being manifest in collaboration with the British in wars against the Ashanti Confederacy.

The Ashanti Confederacy, a federal grouping of Ashanti states under the control of a paramount chief (*asantehene*), was an elaborate military hierarchy with powerful armies, a bureaucracy, and a taste for imperialism which brought them into immediate conflict with the British, often to the latter's temporary demise. The Confederacy was a remarkable achievement, similar in power to the Dahomey Kingdom to the east.

Needless to say, the Ashanti Confederacy was hated and feared, both by Fanti and other coastal peoples and by northern groups,

[10] An excellent and very brief summary is contained in the *Annual Report*, Gold Coast, 1920-1952, H.M.S.O., London, 1921-1953.

some of which, like the Dagomba, maintained uneasy independence by annual payments of tribute.

Both Fanti and Ashanti stemmed from common ethnic backgrounds. They possessed similar lineages and similar forms of custom and organization. Both Fanti and Ashanti have been in their present areas only a little longer than the Europeans.

The Fanti[11] were in long and continuous contact with the British from the beginning of the seventeenth century, and were the first to participate in a movement which, even in its rudimentary aspects, showed signs of British political influence.[12]

In 1867 the British proposed to cede certain forts and territories to the Dutch, in connection with their policy of temporary occupancy. The Fanti, and the nearby states of Assin, Wassaw, and Denkyera, long subject to Ashanti depredations, formed the Fanti Confederation, one of the first national movements in Gold Coast history.

The Fanti Confederation, formed at Mankesim in 1871, was intended to be more than a military confederation. It expected, in accordance with the proceedings of the Select Committee of Parliament in 1863, that the Gold Coast would receive home rule and therefore self-government within the British sphere of influence. The objects of the Fanti Confederation indicate an early preoccupation with adapting traditional authority patterns to more modern demands. The objects of the Confederation were stated to be as follows:

"1. To promote friendly intercourse between all the kings and

[11] In an interesting paragraph in Claridge we find this comment: "The cowardice of the Fanti has at times been exaggerated, and he has been blamed for it more than he really deserves. His inefficiency as a warrior is due to faults in the system rather than in the individual. Taken man for man, the Fanti is probably nearly as good as the Ashanti. The Ashanti, however, have built up a splendid military organization, to the perfections of which everything else has been sacrificed, and they have learned to rely on themselves and put national interest before their own. The Fantis, on the other hand, have suffered from their long contact with the Europeans. Their surroundings and their mode of life have to some extent become artificial and they have been taught to rely upon the protection of a stronger race, rather than upon their own efforts." Claridge, *op.cit.*, Vol. i. Such a comment is interesting in the light of general traditional cultural dislocation in the Gold Coast.

[12] The Fanti Confederation was partly based on the assumption that the British would leave the Gold Coast shortly after the Select Committee of 1863 indicated that the British government should have no permanent designs on the West African settlements. The element most effective in welding together the "nations" which made up the Fanti Confederation was a conscious effort to formalize through traditional patterns of political authority the objects which Western representatives held as "advanced," "civilized," and desirable.

chiefs of Fanti, and to unite them for offensive and defensive purposes against their common enemy.

"2. To direct the labors of the Confederation towards the improvement of the country at large.

"3. To make good and substantial roads throughout all the interior districts included in the Confederation.

"4. To promote agricultural and industrial pursuits, and to endeavor to introduce such new plants as may hereafter become profitable sources of commerce to the country.

"5. To erect schoolhouses and establish schools for the education of all children within the Confederation, and to obtain the service of efficient schoolmasters.

"6. To develop and facilitate the working of the mineral and other resources of the country."[13]

It had, in addition, provided for a president-king and executive council to which citizens could appear and have recourse, ultimately, to the British courts, in accordance with the Bond of 1844. In addition the Confederation provided for a representative assembly with a right to impose and collect taxes in territories coming within the jurisdiction of the Confederation. The Confederation was never consummated and was, instead, considered a dangerous step, not to be approved by the British government.

A substantially different kind of nationalism was exhibited by the more powerful Ashanti Confederacy, whose expansionist tendencies brought it control over most of the area of the Gold Coast, either by absorption or domination. It was one of the most highly organized military and political systems on the west coast of Africa.

The Ashanti Confederacy was finally defeated by the British only in 1901, after a series of wars extending throughout the nineteenth century which, before protectorate status was established, cost a good many British, Indian, and Hausa troops as well as the head of one British governor, which adorned the *asantehene's* wardrum as a symbol of his prowess.

The Ashanti, like the Fanti, appear to be descendants of the Bona Kingdom. The earliest Twi-speaking Ashanti state was Adansi,[14] roughly corresponding in time to the Elizabethan period in England.

---

[13] Casely Hayford, Joseph, *Gold Coast Native Institutions*, London, 1903, p. 327.
[14] Ward, *op.cit.*, p. 74, says, "The name of the state [Adansi] means 'house-

Only British forces kept the Ashanti from establishing final hegemony along the coast of the Gold Coast. As it was, Ashanti defeats of the Fanti, and alliance with a coastal group, the Elminas, figured for a long time as a sore point of issue between the British and the Ashanti. In January 1824 the governor of Sierra Leone, in charge of the West African settlements, was killed in a battle in Insamankow. An allied force of Akim, Akwamu, Denkyera, and Accra levies was required to defeat the Ashanti two years later at the famous battle of Dodowa.[15]

War between the British and the Ashanti broke out again in 1873 and troops under Sir Garnet Wolseley captured and destroyed the Ashanti capital, Kumasi. After this the Confederacy began to disintegrate. An indemnity imposed by the British could not be met. In 1896 another British expedition was sent to Kumasi and the *asantehene* was deported with his nobles to the Seychelles Islands. In 1900 the governor of the Gold Coast made a visit to the capital of the Confederacy, demanding to sit on the Golden Stool, the "spirit" of the Ashanti Confederacy. War again broke out, the governor narrowly escaping, and in 1901 Ashanti was annexed to the Crown.

Ex-king Prempeh was allowed to return to Kumasi in 1924 and assume, two years later, the position of *kumasihene,* or paramount chief of the Kumasi Division, one of the major divisions of the Confederacy. In 1935 the Confederacy was restored under Nana Sir Agyeman Prempeh II, not without local opposition from some of its members.

As we shall indicate further, the Ashanti Confederacy has provided one of the powerful bases of traditional political authority. Its significance in political institutional transfer will be examined in some detail.

The Ga-Adangme Group

Along the coastal plains and the Volta basin are a series of tribes whose traditions subscribe to those of eastern parts of West Africa, particularly Dahomey and Nigeria.

---

building,' and legend says that the Adansi were the first people in the Gold Coast to build mud or swish houses. If this implies that they were the first to settle down in permanent homes, it confirms the other evidence that makes Adansi the senior Twi-speaking state."

[15] Now the headquarters of the Joint Provincial Council, the organ of the coastal chiefs.

The Ga, who predominate around the capital, Accra, displaced an earlier Guan group (of Akan origin), incorporating Guan gods and shrines with their own. The Ga peoples, consisting of seven disunited groups, were organized into a single unit by an important chief, Okai Koi. Okai Koi was not a popularly supported figure and when the Ga came into conflict with Akwamu, a powerful state near Accra, disaffected elements refused to fight. After defeat, some of the Ga moved to Dahomey, while others remained, occupying seven different areas which exist to this day, as independent divisions having a complicated but tenuous relationship to a single paramount chief, the *ga manche*. Disputes between these divisions recently needed the intercession of the prime minister of the Gold Coast, so disturbing were they to the Accra peoples.

Two areas, Yilo Krobo and Manya Krobo, are important Adangme states. These people represent eastern immigrants who, gradually driven westwards, purchased considerable amounts of land from the Akans. The majority of them refused to accept British authority and a number of campaigns were necessary to remove them from Krobo Hill, a sacrificial hill near the Volta town of Akuse, to two villages, Odumase and Sumanya. As with the Ewe, a Togoland group, one third of whose poulation is now within the Gold Coast, patrilineal succession is one of the distinct differences between their political and social organization and those of the Akan, where matrilineal rule prevails.

Their importance in recent years has centered around the person of the paramount chief of Manya Krobo, the *konor*, who was an important member of the Legislative Council, which preceded the present Legislative Assembly. Problems in this area relating to the larger political atmosphere will be dealt with in a separate section.[16]

The Moshi, Dagomba, and Mamprussi

The Northern Territories and Northern British Togoland present a complexity of ethnic and religious groups. By and large they are opposed to membership in an independent Gold Coast. Their local preferences are strong.

Originally the Northern Territories contained a fairly homogeneous indigenous population whose customs, beliefs, and social

16 See Chapter 12.

organization were closely interrelated.[17] This indigenous population has been considered of remote Akan origin and there is at least one isolated pocket in the northeastern part of the Northern Territories (among the Chakosi) where unmistakable Akan tendencies are indicated. The Northern Territories suffered a series of invasions from the Sudan area by people who, in Rattray's words, were "better armed, better clothed, familiar with the idea of kingship or chieftainship in our modern sense, in some cases conversant with the rudiments of Mohammedanism and accustomed (even if circumstances had not later compelled it) to a patrilineal manner of reckoning descent. These strangers superimposed upon the primitive tribes, among whom they settled, a new and unheard of political conception, namely the idea of territorial and secular leadership in place of the immemorial institution of a ruler, who was the high priest of a totemic clan and dealt only in spiritual sanctions."[18]

Approximately four hundred years ago, then, these Mole-Dagbane strangers migrated southward, superimposing their system of rule upon the indigenous system of priest-kings called *tendana*. In some cases the *tendana* were killed, but usually they were incorporated into the religious and social systems of the invaders in a somewhat ambiguous relationship. Rights, prerogatives, and religious affairs were divided between the *tendana* and the new ruling chief.

At one time the Mole-Dagbane, or Moshi, empire stretched from Salaga in the Northern Territories to Timbuctoo.[19] The three predominating tribal aristocracies in the north—the Dagomba, the Mamprussi, and the Moshi—are all part of this Mole-Dagbane root. They have more or less common traditions, ceremonially ritualized in drum history, the drum beating out the legendary story of the red hunter who founded Dagomba and the other kingdoms.[20]

Adjoining Ashanti, farther to the south, the Gonja nation represents a similar political area, although more sparsely populated. The Dagomba, Mamprussi, Moshi, Gonja, and Wala

[17] See Rattray, R. S., *Tribes of the Ashanti Hinterland*, London, 1932, p. xii.
[18] *Ibid*.
[19] Cardinall, A. W., *The Natives of the Northern Territories of the Gold Coast*, London, 1920.
[20] *Enquiry into the Constitution and Organization of the Dagbon Kingdom*, Accra, 1932.

groups possess a similar form of constitution setting the predominant traditional pattern of rule for three-quarters of the Northern Territories.[21]

These groups were never engaged in large-scale open warfare with British forces. Both British and French were involved in a series of police actions in the Northern Territories against two northern figures, Samori and Babatu, which led them to penetrate deeply into the hinterlands. In the course of pursuing these bandits along the present frontier of the Northern Territories, British officers procured treaties with a number of different tribes in the area. The Anglo-French boundary was secured by three boundary commissions in 1889, 1893, and 1898. The last campaign was fought in the north in 1911 after which Pax Britannica was effectively imposed upon the Gold Coast.[22]

It was worthy of note that Ashanti influence in the north, while less effective than in the south, involved the recognition by the Dagomba of a special subservience to Kumasi. As has been indicated, until 1874 the Dagomba were required to send annual tribute to Ashanti in the form of slaves. A considerable number of Dagomba were kept at the palace of the *asantehene* as hostages, although they had a privileged position at the court.[23]

The people of the north are therefore composed of an indigenous group having little formal social organization insofar as manifest political authority is concerned. Over them are the formal chiefs of the conquering groups. By and large this system is intact, with strong affiliations and emotional ties to chieftaincy still maintained. The pattern has important ramifications in the Gold Coast for the future of political institutional transfer.[24] The people of the Northern Territories are the least affected by the political changes being undertaken. Their orientational affiliations are north to the Sudan, rather than south to the Gold Coast. They have already played a curious role in the secular politics of the Legislative Assembly.

21 *Report on the Northern Territories for the Year 1937-38*, Accra, 1938.

22 See Freeman, R. Austin, *Travels and Life in Ashanti and Jaman*, Constable Co., Westminster, 1898.

23 See Bowditch, T., *Mission to Ashanti*, London, 1819.

24 A new Northern People's Party has emerged as the leading opposition party. The formation of the new party is the first major effort by Northern Territories people to engage directly in secular politics.

As a whole, the history of the Gold Coast peoples is a mosaic of recent migration, strife, and settlements. Most of the present occupants have not been there much longer than the first white man. Gold Coast history is not written; it comes down by word of mouth. The elders in the family, the tribe, and the clan are repositories of information.

Tribal history is a mixture of the factual and the supernatural. "In the beginning there was a man" having supernatural powers, or acted upon by supernatural powers. After a series of tests, or escapades this person sires a people. From the blood affiliations, mythically reckoned, the relationships between other groups and other tribes is defined. The history of battles, famous victories, and exploits are all incorporated in the tribal mythology. Out of the histories, some of which, like the Dagomba drum history, are highly ritualized symbolic expressions, the traditions of the past are related to the peoples of today. Membership in a tribe or ethnic group is participation in a corporate body, the limits of which go beyond the immediate living environment, reaching backwards into the past. In the dance and the beat of the drums this past can be participated in, a process whereby strength is renewed, the ancestors greeted, the gods propitiated, and the devils exorcised.

Out of that past come the hints and overtones of African kingdoms relating to Arab hegemony during the period of Middle East enlightenment. The names of Melle, Songhai, and Ghana are remote to the modern Gold Coast, but their influence can be found in obscure customs of uncertain genre, in dress, in religion, and in the reawakening of the people of the Gold Coast to a historical past, made more golden by its antiquity.

The Introduction of Western Rule

The first Europeans to set foot on Gold Coast soil were the Portuguese.[25] Eleven years after their first landing in 1471, they built their castle at Elmina.[26] Their interests were largely confined to gold (which they found in some quantity, hence the name Gold Coast) and subsidiary products such as spices. The traffic in slaves came somewhat later.

[25] There seems to be some controversy on this point. According to Claridge the French claim to have been the first discoverers of the Gold Coast. The authenticity of the French claims, however, is in doubt.

[26] From Portuguese "San Jarge del Mina." See Claridge, *op.cit.*, p. 100.

By a papal order, the Portuguese were given monopoly rights as well as responsibility for conversion in this part of West Africa. Some British efforts to challenge this monopoly were made, but the Dutch were the first to openly oppose it in 1595.

Subsequently, the development in the American colonies of the plantation system brought a large demand for slaves. The slave trade became the dominant form of commercial enterprise, attracting the British, the Danes, the Brandenburgers, the French, and others. By 1642 the Portuguese were forced to abandon their possessions in the Gold Coast, while other European nations scrambled for a foothold along the coast. The primary objective of these countries was not occupation, but rather the maintenance of "factories" for slaving, and secure trading outlets. The Africans living in the vicinity of these factories, forts, and commercial establishments often found protection under the guns of the Europeans. Trade treaties with Africans were often protective treaties as well. Certain coastal tribes looked to the Dutch for protection; others looked to the English.

In 1750 a serious trading venture was begun in Great Britain with the formation of the African Company of Merchants. The company was subsidized by the Imperial Government to the extent of £ 13,000 yearly. Out of this subsidy, the company was expected to maintain the forts under the British flag, carry on necessary diplomatic negotiations, maintain armed forces, and generally safeguard British interests. Formed for commercial purposes, the company was simultaneously a political administration. This combination of commercial and political rule formed the classic British pattern in the Gold Coast, and is usually referred to by Africans as imperialism. It involved the extension of control and the deprivation of the rights of Africans who often voluntarily entered into agreements with the British, but found that they could not, just as voluntarily, withdraw from these agreements. At the same time, such political encroachment was undertaken by private trading companies by which the Imperial Government incurred no serious responsibilities, meanwhile maintaining the flag in parts of the Gold Coast.

There was little doubt that the African Company of Merchants contained some individuals who were interested in trade in the most ruthless sense of the word, although men of sensibility were certainly among the adventurers. Men were recruited to the

West African trade on the basis of a promise of quick return and margins of profit to be found nowhere else. To go out to the Gold Coast during such times was almost a sentence of death. It took hardy men of the classic entrepreneurial spirit to brave the dangers of disease in the "miasmic marshes and poisonous mists" of the Gold Coast. The troops which went out to garrison the forts were usually made up of a large proportion of convicts. It is not likely that the majority of these men were ambassadors of good will.[27]

The African Company of Merchants was not the first company to be responsible for British trade in West Africa. It succeeded the Royal African Company, which had been formed in 1672 and had held a monopoly over British trade in the Gold Coast until, with the triumph of free-trade doctrines in England, its restrictive practices aroused hostility in Great Britain. The Royal African Company was broken up, after an agreement to turn over ten percent of the profits of the African Company of Merchants to the stockholders of the former. A committee of the African Company of Merchants began the government of the forts and settlements under British control and in 1752 a governor with a council having purely advisory powers was set up. The government had no constitution but nevertheless formalized the relations between the British company and the local tribes in the areas of forts and settlements held by the British.[28]

In 1821 the arrangement with the African company was abrogated, and for the first time the Imperial Government assumed control over the coastal possessions and forts, with a British governor at Sierra Leone. It was during this period that the unfortunate governor, Sir Charles MacCarthy, engaging in a campaign against the Ashanti, was cut off from his troops and beheaded, his skull being used to adorn the drums of the *asantehene*.

In 1828 rule was returned to the Committee of London Merchants.[29] The committee was required to govern the settlements

---

[27] See Martin, E. D., *The British West African Settlements, 1750-1821*, Imperial Studies No. 2, London, 1927, p. 39: "The very heavy mortality among Englishmen in West Africa which constantly raked the forts made promotion rapid, and the promotion was allowed to all ranks from all ranks, the occupation in which a man served his first years having singularly little effect on his subsequent career."

[28] *Ibid.*, p. 33.

[29] In 1828 the government had decided to abandon the coast after the successful promulgation of the Ashanti campaign, but British merchants protested strongly, supported by the Fanti, who did not relish the idea of being left without protection. The government accordingly handed over administration to a committee of three London merchants.

by a governor and a council elected by the committee, with jurisdiction limited to narrowly prescribed areas. The first governor, George Maclean, arrived in 1830. Under Maclean's jurisdiction the first real social and political impact of Western institutions made themselves felt in the Gold Coast.[30]

Maclean, successfully for a time, made peace between the Fanti and the Ashanti. He tripled the country's trade. Through his own personal honesty he gained a considerable local reputation as a judge, a reputation which spread beyond his official court at Cape Coast. Outside his legal authority there speedily grew up an extra-legal jurisdiction over African litigants of every rank and from every district between the Pra and the Volta. Chiefs brought their disputes to Maclean and begged him to decide between them; and unofficial though his position was, his judgment was hardly ever questioned.[31]

It was in the judicial sphere that Maclean's impact was unquestionably greatest, affecting later policies of British rule in the Gold Coast. It carried with it implications for indirect rule in which the consequences of that doctrine were being felt long before indirect rule was formally enunciated as a political policy. When the government again took over the administration of the Gold Coast settlements and forts in 1843, the judicial function was given formal recognition. Maclean was appointed judicial assessor, an office in which he sat upon cases involving Africans under customary law and the principles of British equity.

With the resumption of British government, relations with the local tribes under the general jurisdiction and in the immediate environs of British settlements were undertaken. The position was defined in one of the most important documents in modern Gold Coast history. This document has been subject to considerable misinterpretation and has been the basis of many charges by nationalists that the British government violated its own agreement. Known as the Bond of 1844, it states as follows:

"1. Whereas power and jurisdiction have been exercised for

[30] See Wight, M., *The Gold Coast Legislative Council*, London, 1946, p. 22: "The system had no legal foundation, but arose out of the necessities of a commerce extending into the interior; and it was so efficient that natives of their own accord transferred their judicial allegiance from the native courts to the British courts. This was the beginning, in practice, of the British protectorate on the Gold Coast, which was given a legal basis by the Foreign Jurisdiction Act of 1843."
[31] Ward, *op.cit.*, p. 184.

and on behalf of Her Majesty the Queen of Great Britain and Ireland, within divers countries and places adjacent to Her Majesty's forts and settlements on the Gold Coast; we, chiefs of countries and places so referred to, and adjacent to the said forts and settlements, do hereby acknowledge that power and jurisdiction, and declare that the first objects of law are the protection of individuals and property.

"2. Human sacrifices, and other barbarous customs, such as panyarring, are abominations, and contrary to law.

"3. Murders, robberies, and other crimes and offenses, will be tried and inquired of before the queen's judicial officers and the chiefs of the districts, moulding the customs of the country to the general principles of British law."

The last sentence of paragraph 3 is of particular significance. "Moulding the customs of the country to the general principles of British law" has been, in effect, the object of British political efforts since Maclean's day, setting the dominant tone of political institutional transfer by, in effect, holding such transfer to be possible and desirable.

In 1850 the first legislative and executive councils were set up with members nominated by the governor. Local revenues and the rights of Africans to self-government were bruited about in the very earliest sessions. In 1851 one of the council members stated that "he regards Self Government as the most desirable thing for Africa, and he could not acknowledge the right of the People to this, unless they paid the Expenses of their Government."[32] Self-government for West Africa was a popular doctrine in England and the British in the Bond of 1844 acknowledged only limited jurisdiction, and that in a circumscribed area.

After Sir Garnett Wolseley's successful invasion of Ashanti, following the ceding of Dutch holdings to the British, a new charter was issued, dated July 24, 1874, separating the Gold Coast Colony from Sierra Leone.[33]

In 1901, of the area adjacent to the Colony, Ashanti was annexed and the Northern Territories were made a protectorate. The charge has been made that such annexation was illegal according

[32] Minutes of Meetings of Legislative Council from April 1850 to July 1870, session of March 4, 1851.

[33] At the same time, the Gold Coast was administratively assigned to Lagos, not achieving separate administrative status until 1886.

to the Bond of 1844. A considerable controversy was set off in England itself about the propriety of making the Gold Coast a colony at all, a move regarded as a necessarily unilateral maneuver of dubious legality. The beginnings of a nationalist movement among the educated Africans, as well as among certain chiefs, was given stimulus by this turn of events. The "violation" of the Bond of 1844 is seen by many Africans as an example of British perfidy. It is difficult to see, however, where the Bond of 1844 would apply at all to Ashanti and the north, let alone the areas in the Colony not party to the agreement.

The assumption of territorial responsibility by Great Britain was slow, halting, and to a large extent reluctant. When authority was expressed, it tried to reckon with traditional custom, modified to British concepts of political protection of rights and property, and conciliar processes.

An increasing elite of educated chiefs and commoners began to crystallize opposition to colonial rule in emerging nationalism in the latter part of the nineteenth century. There was no means whereby tribal opinion vis-à-vis British law could be clearly expressed.

In 1888 an African was appointed to the Legislative Council to represent African interests, but this was hardly an effective vehicle for public expression.

The first clearly nationalist and protective body organized in the Gold Coast was the Aborigines' Rights Protection Society. While advocating cooperation with the British authorities, the Society was devoted to the protection of the interests of the Gold Coast Africans which they regarded as under attack. Their objective was "to promote and effect unity of purpose and of action among all aborigines of the Gold Coast." The immediate objective was opposition to the Public Lands Bill, which, according to the Africans, would have destroyed the traditional land tenure system and paved the way for conversion of African holdings to Crown land in all unoccupied lands.[34]

The Society was successful in achieving the withdrawal of the bill in 1897 and continued to lead the opposition to any government policies which it considered contrary to African rights. It was recognized by the governor as a correct channel of local opinion until 1925, when the inauguration of provincial councils

---

[34] There is no such thing as unoccupied land in Gold Coast land tenure.

provided what the government considered a more representative body.[35]

The Aborigines' Rights Protection Society almost achieved the status of a representative body when, after sending its successful delegation to London against the Public Lands Bill, and after its successes against the Forest Lands Bill in 1911, it was hailed by the chiefs and more vociferous public opinion as a body representative of Gold Coast Colony public demands. The Society considered itself the direct successor to the Fanti Confederation. As such it claimed to have inherited the sanctioned allegiance of the coastal Africans.

Frictions between the chiefs and certain educated Africans soon became manifest, however. The chiefs considered the non-royal leaders of the Society as usurpers of legitimate authority.

The Society was finally split apart by the first major constitutional change which occurred in 1925 under Governor Guggisberg. Legislative, executive, and judicial powers were given to the chiefs as agents of British authority, as well as of their own traditional authority. Under the 1925 Constitution, opposed by many members of the Society, chiefs and educated commoners were nominated to seats on the new Legislative Council. After 1926, formal recognition was withdrawn from the Society which became, as an "outgroup" organization, composed of those ardent nationalists who refused to participate in British-ordained political structures. In 1934, when a delegation of chiefs went to London, the Society sent a separate deputation. The chiefs were received by the Secretary of State for Colonies, while the Society representatives were not.

The 1925 Constitution was the first indication of British response to organized nationalist pressure. Compromise and concession made a direct clash between the constituted British authorities and the nationalists difficult. Nationalism never became revolutionary. Rather, it was absorbed into a program, the objective of which was self-government via the construction of parliamentary-type agencies providing, in many instances, a training ground in parliamentary practice. More than that, the program demanded certain types of behavior peculiarly related to British political structures, setting standards by which African partici-

---

[35] Bourret, F. M., *The Gold Coast*, Oxford University Press, London, 1952, second edition.

pation was both judged and rewarded. Those who left the Society were absorbed into the Legislative Council, which now provided for African as well as European members. Far from being denied access to membership in the organs of political authority, Africans were expected to examine problems and give decisions on a wide range of public business to which they had formerly been on-lookers. To many educated Africans it was a satisfying recognition of their status, rewarded through public office.

Certain chiefs as well, having been given an increasing range of public responsibility, found their positions supported by the weight of British authority. They were given representative organs, the provincial councils, and accorded high respect under the new constitutional scheme. We shall return to the complexity of this situation and its implications for the development of nationalism below.[36]

The history of Gold Coast nationalism in modern secular form is a short one. A West African National Congress under the leadership of J. Casely Hayford, which had as its object a pan-African movement that went beyond the limits of colonial boundaries, was influential, but limited in support.

The pattern of political change from 1900 until World War II was marked by the growth of new educated groups aware that their talents were largely unused in the political world, while the position of the chiefs became increasingly unstable in the larger focus of central government. The political reforms emanating from this period attempted to provide political status for a widening range of the elite, while explicitly attempting to make use of their talents within the structural framework of Crown Colony political administration.

Conclusion

This brief excursion into Gold Coast history has been designed to fulfill two purposes. First, it is intended to provide some background for the movements, wars, patterns of colonial penetration, and legal definition of the peoples of the Gold Coast as they moved from independent tribal status into colonial status. Second, it is intended to point out some of the earlier patterns of nationalism and show how such nationalism was met by the British authorities.

We can see the first beginnings of a kind of supratribal identifi-

[36] See Chapters 8, 9, and 10.

cation emerging in the Colony, where the tribal groups had had halting efforts towards confederation, and where others, out of the context of tribal society, took up the cry for greater responsibility. Throughout the Colony at this time there were increasing numbers of people who were suddenly aware of British authority, something which had never been thrust at them in vulgar displays of armed force, but by treaty, by agreement, and by occupation.

In Ashanti, where defeats sustained by the Confederacy were bitter, little overt nationalism emerged; rather, the members of the Confederacy seemed to have largely lapsed into political lethargy, governed separately from the Colony—a defeated people.

In the Northern Territories life went on much as before, with the profound impact visited upon the Colony hardly perceptible in the daily lives of the various groups.

We have, then, a pattern of uneven impact and cultural penetration in differing parts of the Gold Coast. Only the slow growth of coastal nationalism indicated possible political potentials. For the greater part, the mass of the people of the Gold Coast seemed remote from participation in central government political affairs. For many of the British administrators, the quiet reforming process, inhibited very little by overt nationalism, seemed the logical way in which Gold Coast political administration would continue. Such faith was rudely shattered by the sudden growth of the Convention People's Party after 1948, which directed its aim against colonial status and towards independence for the entire Gold Coast. That the C.P.P. should receive widescale support astonished many groups in the Gold Coast, both British and African.

We can now turn our attention to the economic consequences of colonial intervention. Many of the crucial questions of successful institutional transfer will be decided in the economic sphere. Economic considerations are closely tied in with the entire shift of aspirations and activities that indicates social change. As one observer put it, only if the Gold Coast can preserve economic prosperity without the disastrous impact of inflation or deflation will gradual institutionalization of political democracy occur.

CHAPTER 3

THE PHYSICAL AND ECONOMIC
ENVIRONMENT

To SOME, the word "Africa" conjures up visions of dense jungle or arid plateaus, pestilent swamps and miasmic mists, all under a sweltering sun which always shines, even when it is raining. If the visitor to the Gold Coast carries such expectations, he is initially disappointed. He finds forest and savannah, mountains and plains, fertile country, sparse range, but few of the extremes attributed to the tropics.

The visitor will rapidly become aware of the myriads of insects which, because of the lack of temperature extremes, flourish in profusion. He will not see the more lurking dangers, like the parasites which are carried in the water the African drinks, the bugs which systematically demolish the cocoa crop, and the countless tiny creatures which make all life, human, animal, and vegetable, still hazardous if precautionary measures are not used. Even modern drugs, although they have to a remarkable extent reduced the incidence of diseases fatal to human beings, have still to tackle the diseases of the soil, the plant, and water.

It was to such an area that the early commercial travelers came in Africa. Often greedy and rapacious, anxious for a quick and lucrative return, these traders nevertheless brought the Gold Coast into the mainstream of world economic intercourse. Today in the Gold Coast the big commercial companies like the United Africa Company (Lever Brothers) and the petty traders live side by side, the one in large modern buildings, the other in little stalls in the market place or on the streets and highways. Programs for large-scale economic development are changing the contours of the land, harnessing the rivers, and expanding the network of communications and transport, while the small subsistence farmer looks over his hoe to see the strange goings-on.

While the Gold Coast is no longer the white man's graveyard, it is by no means entirely hospitable to man. A high proportion of its inhabitants have malaria. In some areas waterborne diseases, such as guineaworm, river blindness, and bilharzia, are common. The swollen shoot disease threatens the cocoa crop. The tsetse fly carries sleeping sickness to men and cattle. Rinderpest, increasingly under control, threatens those cattle untouched by the fly. There are few means to tackle, on a wide scale, these threats to man and his means of livelihood. The death rate is high, how high no one knows in precise terms. Dispensaries are few and far between. Health facilities are overcrowded. In some areas people are afraid to go to a hospital because so many people die there after having traveled many miles on foot, by canoe, or by lorry, arriving too late for effective treatment.[1]

In the towns venereal disease adds to a host of other diseases born out of slum conditions, poor sanitary facilities, and outdoor drainage ditches. Perhaps the most thorough victory of man over parasite has been the almost total elimination of yellow fever, and a substantial reduction in malarial deaths. In some areas, even in the bush, one sometimes comes across Africans using mosquito netting.

Great as are the hardships imposed by the environment, it also has its advantages. Cocoa grows easily. Laterite soil serves as an effective building material, particularly when mixed with concrete.[2] Fish are abundant along the coast and in the rivers. The Gold Coast is an environment of contrasts under its warm tropical sun.

Population and Area

The total land area of the Gold Coast, excluding Togoland, is 91,843 square miles. The total population, excluding Togoland, is 4,118,450.[3]

The people of the Gold Coast tend to group into towns, and states. Usually a tribal group is made up of several states, each having its central town which is often the headquarters of the traditional authorities. These towns usually became the administrative centers of British district officers, many of them forming the basis for dividing the country into administrative areas.

[1] In a field study in the Tongu Confederacy done by the author in collaboration with Dr. Gustav Jahoda for the Extra-Murals Department of the University College of the Gold Coast, investigation showed that people were afraid to go to a dispensary in Akuse since so many prospective patients died en route.

[2] Called "swish-crete." Swish is laterite soil mixed with water and, sometimes, dung, out of which most local dwellings are constructed. It can be an effective building material and when properly surfaced and painted can last twenty or thirty years. When mixed with concrete it makes a durable building product.

[3] Colonial Reports, *Gold Coast 1951*, London, 1952, p. 75.

The following table will give some picture of the area and density of population in the Gold Coast by major administrative area.

AREA, POPULATION, AND DENSITY, 1948[4]

Administrative Area	Area in square miles	Population, 1948
The Gold Coast	91,843	4,118,450
The Colony	26,401	2,222,810
Accra	918	224,771
Ahanta-Nzima	1,880	179,812
Akwapim-New Juaben	397	113,850
Birim	6,008	370,761
Cape Coast	3,922	495,369
Ho*	2,464	172,575
Keta/Ada	1,954	304,268
Sefwi	2,695	65,208
Volta River	1,458	164,782
Wasaw-Aowin	7,705	131,414
Ashanti	24,379	818,494
Bekwai	2,220	157,894
Kumasi	5,910	376,283
Mampong	6,955	102,758
Wenchi-Sunyani	9,294	182,009
Northern Territories	41,063	1,076,696
Dagomba†	9,611	224,506
Gonja†	14,469	84,415
Karachi†	3,380	31,603
Mamprussi†	6,376	531,130
Wa	7,227	205,042
Togoland	13,041	382,768

* African population.
† Including part of Togoland.

The population, while increasing, has been steadily reducing its nominal rate of growth.[5] From 1921 to 1931 the rate of increase was 3.76 per cent, while from 1931 to 1948 it was only 1.77 per cent. According to the 1948 census figures, the Ashanti area suffered the least proportionate decline, probably in part due to migration from other parts of the Gold Coast, both north and coastal, to its rich cocoa areas.[6]

4 Adapted from the 1948 Census.
5 Government Printer, Census of Population, Accra, 1948.
6 Ibid., Table vii, p. 25.

Geography

There are three main areas in the Gold Coast: the Gold Coast Colony, the Ashanti Confederacy, and the Northern Territories. The Northern Territories are technically a protectorate, although the practical distinction between colonial and protectorate status has been abolished.[7]

Accra is the capital of the Gold Coast, a fact which signifies the predominance of the south. Kumasi is the headquarters of the Ashanti Confederacy and is the historic seat of the *asantehene* or paramount chief of the Ashanti. This city, taken in battle for the last time by the British in 1901, has since become a hub of roads, railheads, and both transit and source points for much of the commerce and trade which ebbs and flows ceaselessly all over the Gold Coast. Tamale, the capital of the Northern Territories, is an administrative center, having little significant traditional background. The 350-mile coastline is bounded on the west by the Ivory Coast, a French territory, and on the east by Togoland, a United Nations mandate area divided between French and British administrative jurisdiction.

Dixcove, Sekondi-Takoradi, Kommenda, Elmina, Cape Coast, Saltpond, Accra, Keta are all coastal towns or villages in which Europeans originally built their factories, established their outposts, and first brought European culture to the Gold Coast in the form of the slave trade.

The major harbor at Sekondi-Takoradi was built during the administration of one of the post-World War I governors, Sir Gordon Guggisberg, against the advice of most advisors. His wisdom has since been proved. Much of the present wealth of the Gold Coast comes from trade which flows through this port, which is thereby partly responsible for the economic position of today's Gold Coast, in which political independence is at least economically feasible. Most sea-borne arrivals to the Gold Coast disembark at Takoradi, seeing the familiar cranes, abutments, warehouses, railroad lines, and wharves of any major port. It is a big harbor and a busy one. Out of a total import and export tonnage of

[7] See Wight, M., *British Colonial Constitutions*, Oxford, 1952.
   See also *Parliamentary Affairs*, "Special Issue on Parliamentary Government in the Colonies," Hansard Society, Vol. vi, No. 1, p. 1; Latham, R. T. E., *The Law and the Commonwealth*, London, 1949.

3,233,000 entering the Gold Coast in 1950, Takoradi handled 1,865,000.[8] The recent completion of harbor extensions should substantially increase this total.

The deep basin of the harbor has joined two large municipalities of the Gold Coast, Takoradi, the original harbor, and Sekondi. As with other major towns in the Gold Coast, many immigrants from the Northern Territories and from French West Africa came down to work in the docks, the roads, and other construction gangs in this rapidly growing urban area. In Kumasi, Accra, Cape Coast, and other towns there are modern houses and slums, shanty-towns and office buildings. The urban areas are a congested mixture of races and religions, a polyglot of tongues and tribes where nationalism breeds many of its more formidable recruits.

Contrary to expectations, the long low coastline is neither jungle nor swamp, desert nor forest. The road from Takoradi to Accra passes the mud villages with their thatched or tin roofs, their market places where women squat alongside a rude table selling plantain, or red peppers, or enamel pots from England. Low scrub trees are punctuated by the stately silk cotton trees which grow to enormous heights yet are hollow inside, occasionally falling across the road to make it temporarily impassable. Oil palms and cassava, plantain, corn, yams, and groundnuts grow in the small cleared places in the bush. Part of what grows is wild, part is food, but the vegetation is neither sparse nor heavy.

The road to Accra stretches some 170 miles: past Elmina, where the Portuguese first came to the Gold Coast almost five hundred years ago to find gold, past Cape Coast, where the first permanent English headquarters was established, and which, for many years, rivaled Accra as the potential capital of a Gold Coast nation.

The road dips through Saltpond, where, near the lagoons and old castles of slavers long departed, the present political party system was born in 1949 in a dramatic break between Kwame Nkrumah, the young nationalist politician now prime minister who was schooled in America, and the intelligentsia of the organization which originally hired him as their chief organizer, the United Gold Coast Convention. Saltpond is a small town,

[8] Ministry of Finance, *A Survey of Some Economic Matters*, Accra, 1950, Table 15, p. 28.

44

and the casual visitor would be wise to view with respect what such small villages have been heir to.

The road moves inland through hills covered with cocoa trees, to Swedru and its Syrian traders, across the Accra-Kumasi railroad and Achimota, seat of the new University College of the Gold Coast, where men and women from the bush and from the town take their London degrees and learn about a world most of them have never seen, and into Accra, the capital.

A few miles outside Accra is the old Danish castle, Christiansborg, where the governor resides, the surf still pounding against its ancient walls. Here the cabinet meets in spacious rooms built over the dank holds once used as dungeons. In the town itself the streets overflow with brightly dressed market women or blue-clad Hausa traders from Nigeria, bargaining in time-honored fashion. Near spacious bungalows of the colonial service officers is the sleek modern secretariat. This is the home of the Gold Coast government and Kwame Nkrumah's third-floor office looks out over a hubbub of activity and building.

Along the coast there are few heavily luxuriant farming areas. Most of the coastal plain is sandy red soil. The Accra plains, potentially fertile, suffer from lack of irrigation part of the year and floods during the rainy season.

Annual rainfall along the coast is between thirty-five and forty-five inches yearly. The temperature is moderate, never rising above ninety-six degrees, although the coast is only about five degrees above the equator.[9]

Both Accra and Sekondi-Takoradi have main highway and rail connections with Kumasi, the capital of the central area of the Gold Coast, the Ashanti Confederacy. For the most part, Ashanti is lush green forest country. Not as heavily populated as the coastal areas, it is partly mountainous and mostly fertile. Before the trade of the West found its way inland to Kumasi and thereby out into the surrounding countryside, trade across the Sahara in slaves and kola drew Kumasi into communication with the Moslem world.

[9] All of the crop, precipitation, and land-use information derives from the following: *Information Transmitted to the Secretary-General of the United Nations by her Majesty's Government in the United Kingdom* in Accordance with the Provisions of Article 73 (3) of the United Nations Charter, Concerning the Gold Coast for the Year 1951.

Behind the coastal plains and the Ashanti Confederacy lie rich cocoa-producing areas and the forest reserves. Commercially, cocoa is the most important revenue-producing crop of the Gold Coast. The forest zone occupies some 25 per cent of the land area of the Gold Coast. It has a double-peaked rainfall of from fifty to eighty inches yearly. Within this rich area, in addition to a large proportion of the cocoa which provides most of the Gold Coast revenue, are gold mines, timber resources, and other forest products.[10]

This wealthy area, with its center in Kumasi, is traversed by the Gold Coast railway, which runs northward from Takoradi to Kumasi with a spur to the Tarkwa gold mining areas, thence southeast towards Accra. A considerable amount of food crops, particularly maize, cassava, cocoa, yams, plantains, groundnuts, and rice, is grown in the forest area (and in recently felled forest which comprises an additional 15 per cent of the Gold Coast).[11]

As one travels northwards on the Kumasi-Tamale road one sees an abrupt vegetational line which demarcates savannah from forest country. The luxuriant greens and tall trees suddenly give way to dry, parched soil, scrub trees, and pastels that hint of the desert. Behind the forest belt, this savannah country cuts diagonally across the northern edges of the Ashanti Confederacy to cover most of the Northern Territories. Here the dry heat of the Sahara can be felt. The people live in round mud huts formed in compounds with mud or thatch walls. In some areas a family will occupy one village-compound with another exactly a bow's shot away. The people are poor, scratching a bare existence out of the unyielding soil. Many of the indigenous inhabitants, as distinct from the Dagomba conquerors, such as the Fra-Fra, the Konkomba, and others provide the manual work force of the Gold Coast. To the southerners, manual labor is work for slaves.

Occupying a total land proportion of 40 per cent, the Northern Territories are, in spite of their hostility to cultivation, intensively farmed. Here most of the cattle population of the Gold Coast is to be found. The area has a single-peak rainfall of about forty to forty-five inches each year.[12]

Rivers form the main boundaries between the historic tribal areas of the Gold Coast. They have been barriers rather than commercial highways. For example, the Pra provided a tentative

[10] *Ibid.*   [11] *Ibid.*   [12] *Ibid.*

barrier for the coastal Fanti against the frequent forays and invasions of the Ashanti. The principal river, the Black Volta, soon, it is proposed, will be harnessed in order to irrigate the Accra plains and to produce aluminum from the large bauxite reserves of the Gold Coast and hydroelectric power essential to that production and sadly needed for the development of subsidiary light industry. This proposed development should substantially increase Gold Coast revenues, provide jobs, and further change the social organization of Gold Coast peoples.[13]

The Gold Coast economy today can be described as an individualized system of small holdings within the larger compass of a tribal-communal system of land ownership. Cocoa is, of course, the main cash crop and most important product. Subsistence farming has become subsidiary to the production of cocoa wherever this is feasible. Cocoa is grown almost entirely by small farmers. The swollen shoot disease, however, has made severe inroads on production. From 1946 to March 1951, 12,000,000 trees were cut out because of the disease. Since it takes four or five years before a newly planted cocoa tree begins to yield, this is a sizable proportion of the cocoa reserves. One index of the importance of cocoa to Gold Coast revenue is its proportion of the domestic exports. In 1935 cocoa represented 56 per cent of the value of domestic exports; in 1945, 47 per cent; in 1950, 71 per cent.[14]

Other than cocoa, there are small yields of palm kernels, palm oil, copra, coffee, kola, lime juice, and bananas. A considerable timber export trade has developed since the war. Other export resources are negligible, although coffee, rubber, bananas, and other products could be developed if it became economically feasible. Certainly citrus fruit production could be expanded, with processing plants built in the Gold Coast for exporting tinned grapefruit, oranges, and other fruits.

With the exception of gold, industrial diamonds, bauxite, and manganese, however, the Gold Coast is not richly endowed for industrial purposes. Its main energy potential lies in the Volta Development Scheme.[15] There is no coal or oil, and very little

---

[13] See Davison, R. B., "The Volta River Aluminum Scheme," in *The Political Quarterly*, Vol. xxv, No. 1.

[14] Ministry of Finance, *An Economic Survey of the Colonial Territories*, London, 1952, Vol. iii, p. 26.

[15] Davison, *op.cit.*

iron ore. Even the soil does not appear to be particularly well-endowed for ordinary farming, being especially deficient in organic matter and short of calcium and phosphates.[16]

From a nutritional point of view, the population does not appear to suffer unduly as compared with other tropical countries. "In general deficiencies in the local diet appear to be protein, B vitamins, and possibly calcium and iron. Diet analyses show iron levels to be rather low, while so far as can be estimated, the number of calories is from 20 to 25 per cent below the desired level."[17] In the light of economic demands, ability to adapt and to learn, required alertness, as well as general capabilities, a properly nourished population would seem a minimal requirement for the working of a democracy.

The Economic Picture Today

The usual concomitants of capital investment—an immediate growth in secondary and tertiary industries for processing and distribution—have proceeded slowly in most African territories. This is partly due to the flow of income or profits to the respective mother countries rather than to local reinvestment. It is also because the uncertainties and risks of economic development derive from high cost schedules, including high labor and overhead costs, inadequate transport facilities, a largely reluctant labor force with low motivation, a high degree of apathy, disease, which lowers efficiency, and notions of labor time that are contrary to those of the West. Efficient production is most difficult to achieve, but at the same time efforts to produce more diversified commodity schedules in Africa have rarely seen a simultaneous attack on labor problems.

Investment in Africa has, of course, almost invariably been made in enterprises which showed some prospect of immediate gain. The risks were, of course, inordinately great, due to the large turnover and the vicissitudes of climate, disease, marauders, and other obstacles to quick profit. No one really knows how much money was lost in Africa in one scheme or another.

The Gold Coast area is still largely a single-crop or single-commodity producer. It has been used as a base for raw material export to the factories of England and the United States. After

[16] Ministry of Finance, op.cit.   [17] Ibid.

materials have been processed and finished in the plants of the United Kingdom, they have found their way back to the Gold Coast as finished products. Chocolate is the most obvious example. At the same time, the rate of reinvestment within the Gold Coast has been low, with a correspondingly low capital gain in the territory itself.

From the point of view of human, material, and technological resources, the modern Gold Coast of today has a problem of wealth assessment for program priorities and developmental scheduling from within her own resources, and the best use of Colonial Development and Welfare Act funds made available to the Gold Coast.

Since the economic limitations and assets of the Gold Coast provide important ramifications for political development, we shall use the concept of wealth as *resources for development.*

As resources for development, wealth will be discussed here as an amalgam of land, labor, and capital resources. However, specialized problems arise in regard to the traditional categories of land, labor, and capital. Our primary purpose in examining these aspects of the Gold Coast economy will be whether or not they hinder or help institutional transfer. As a prefatory warning, it must be emphasized that what is of significance here are the social consequences of economic factors.[18]

Land

As previously indicated, most land is used either for subsistence farming or cocoa production. Disease and water shortages reduce its use for large-scale cattle grazing and herding. A considerable amount of land, particularly in the Northern Territories and the coastal plains, is unusable much of the year because of alternative periods of drought and flood. A high proportion of arable land necessarily lies fallow during the year, due to the indigenous practice of shifting agricultural methods of cultivation.

Few modern means of land exploitation are widely used. The most common implement is the short hoe, involving hours of backbreaking toil for, on the whole, meager crops. Cocoa, the excep-

18 This discussion is designed as background to the Gold Coast. It is not intended to raise questions of the place of economics in politics or social change. It does not conceive of the economic variable as the independent variable.

tion, flourishes with little labor. Particularly in the forest belt, climatic, social, and economic factors have made this an extremely popular crop.

Customary practice demands soil clearance by burning. This practice, on the one hand, inhibits insect and small animal growth. On the other hand, it destroys valuable soil properties. Difficult to change, the traditional methods of cultivation are reinforced by religious, family, and related social factors above and beyond mere technical efficiency. Under such circumstances, it is hard for agricultural experts to get the farmers to accept modern agricultural methods.

Closely related to problems of land usage are those of land tenure. The traditional concepts of land tenure have been complicated by Western commercial notions of ownership upon which both trade and distribution are often based. It would hardly be an exaggeration to say that the customary laws regarding the ownership and disposition of land are one of the roots upon which the complicated lineage systems of tribal society, and many of the subsidiary forms of customary law and political authority, rest. An almost Ricardian pattern of recent land valuation, due to the increase in export crops and rent, has been a crucial difficulty in the adjustment of tribal political patterns to those of Western origin.

Large-scale alienation of native land (exhibited in other parts of Africa, particularly South Africa, Kenya, and other areas of permanent European settlement) has not taken place in the Gold Coast. The plantation system has been resisted. No European can own land. After the abolition of the slave trade, palm oil, a more virtuous if less profitable product, became the object of commercial operations. To expand palm oil production, numerous efforts were made by Europeans to develop a plantation system. This would have resulted in wholesale land alienation to Europeans and a rapid disintegration of tribal society. Strong efforts along these lines culminated in failure in the 1920's after particularly strenuous attempts by Lever Brothers. All subsequent efforts by large corporations were frustrated by the government of the Gold Coast, although some of the arguments used by the interested corporations were compelling. The plantation system involved the advantages of large-scale organization, combining scientific methods of agriculture with a rationalized system of marketing and distribution, if properly controlled by the government. The African system was based on small holdings, the extensive use of middlemen, low productivity, and costly methods of agricultural production. At the height of such efforts to foster the plantation system, the Empire Resources Committee argued, during the First World War, for the thorough and open exploitation of the colonial empire. This argument was persuasively in favor of the plantation system.[19]

In resisting efforts of this nature, the governor of the Gold Coast, Sir Hugh Clifford, stated what is probably a classic of sophisticated awareness of the problems of economic and social change. It is indicative of the best in British colonial policy in the Gold Coast. He stated that "a plantation system is not a society; it is an economic agglomeration created for the pursuit of profit. It substitutes itself for those primitive societies which in sickness and in health sustain their members."

Under such terms it became quite clear that no sudden shattering of traditional social patterns was being undertaken. By the preservation of the traditional pattern of land tenure and land usage, one of the crucial factors in the maintenance of tribal systems and tribal authority—the power deriving from traditional prerogatives and social patterns deriving from land usage and ownership—has been sustained. Permanent alienation of tribal land has in the main not been allowed to take place. For the most part, in rural areas, the traditional land tenure system is legally and operationally intact.

Except for tribal lands in mining areas, where considerable alienation has occurred, problems of land tenure are most severe where a balance must be struck between the demands for disposal and usage rights over land which has had its value increased through trade and commerce. The customary concepts of ownership and land holding, which are not precisely formalized, have caused social and economic disruption. That this balance often appears to defy logical reasoning is demonstrated in the custodial functions of chieftaincy, and the notion that final ownership resides with the ancestors. Decisions taken in regard to land disputes are rarely regarded as final by the disputants.[20] The major

[19] This organization pointed out that intensive cultivation of the Empire would pay off war debts and give Englishmen a six-hour working day.
[20] See *Land Disputes in the Adansi Division* (mimeographed document, n.p., n.d.).

product has been litigation rather than marketable surpluses. In one study of a fairly typical Ashanti village in the cocoa area, it was clearly indicated that while increases in trade with the outside world nominally increased village income, they also increased local indebtedness due to extensive litigation with other towns and stools as the value of land increased along with the value of cash crops. The chief beneficiaries in such cases are the lawyers, a factor not unremote from their increasing unpopularity in the nationalist movement.[21]

Gold Coast concepts of land tenure and ownership have few genuine counterparts in Western society. Analogies which have frequently been drawn between feudal property relations and African land tenure systems in the Gold Coast are somewhat misleading. In the Gold Coast all land is occupied insofar as it is claimed by tribal authorities or lineages; there is no such thing as open or free land, although there is much uncultivated and fallow land. Because stool land is ancestral land, it could never be sold in any final Western sense.[22]

This is not to say, however, that wide-scale land alienation has never taken place. At one time, chiefs and elders had, in fact, alienated more land than the total amount of land in the Gold Coast.[23] This was only one index of the breakdown of key features of political authority which originated with European intervention, insofar as chiefs and elders violated the prescriptions of office by allowing such alienation.

In attempts to control alienation and maintain land control in the hands of the traditional authorities, a series of ordinances governing concessions was passed. Other protective ordinances which aimed at vesting forest and mineral lands in the Crown— such as the Ordinance of 1894 and the Public Lands Bill of 1911 —all met with bitter local opposition.[24] The opposition to the Public Lands Bill of 1897 was the occasion for the foundation of the Gold Coast Aborigines' Rights Protection Society,[25] one of the most important early nationalist organizations.

In discussion of land tenure problems from the standpoint of

[21] For an excellent monograph on Gold Coast village life, see Beckett, W. H., *Akokoaso*, A Survey of a Gold Coast Village, London, 1947.
[22] See Meek, C. K., *Land Law and Custom in the Colonies*, London, 1946.
[23] See Hailey, Baron, *African Survey*, London, 1938, pp. 775-780.
[24] See above, p. 35.
[25] See Buell, R., *The Native Problem in Africa*, New York, 1928, p. 822.

native customary law, Casely Hayford, one of the leading figures in the Aborigines' Rights Protection Society, wrote in 1913:

"There is no conception which is clearer to the mind of a student of Gold Coast customary law than the broad distinction between paramountcy and ownership. . . . From time immemorial, lands in this country have been held by family groups, the members of each family being such persons as can trace a clear descent from one maternal ancestress. Succession runs through the female line, and a brother by the same mother, or a nephew being the son of one's maternal sister, would succeed to a man's property and not his son. Failing succession in the female line, a 'domestic' would succeed for the reason that the customary law regards him as a member of the family.

"But such succession does not imply that the successor, as the head of the family for the time being, has vested in him the right of ownership to the exclusion of the other members of the family. He is, indeed, a co-owner with the rest; and so zealously do the members of the family restrict him to a legitimate use of his position that the slightest trespass on their rights entails deposition. Theirs is the right to nominate to the headship of the family. Theirs is the right to depose from such headship; and no act of the head for the time being is valid without the consent and concurrence of the members of the family, nor is his permission necessary in the enjoyment of family land."[26]

The importance of these notions of land tenure, rooted in the basic economic problems of rural and tribal life, lies in their consequences for chieftaincy and authority in the traditional pattern of social life. Chieftaincy and land trusteeship are two sides of the same coin; one cannot be understood without the other.

Because of this close relationship between land tenure and patterns of tribal authority, concessions and land alienations to Europeans strike at the heart of the customary social patterns and authority systems. The decision on the part of the Colonial Office against allowing ownership of land by Europeans prevented the breakdown of traditional authority. At the same time, no white settler population having permanent residency in the Gold Coast has developed. From an economic point of view there is little question but that this has somewhat retarded the development of

[26] Casely Hayford, Joseph, *The Truth about the West African Land Question*, London, 1913, pp. 52-53.

agricultural and other resources. However, the advantages to be derived from a non-plural society, at least from the African standpoint in social and political terms, would appear to make any loss of potentialities a small price to pay indeed. This factor alone has made African self-government possible in West Africa, as compared with areas where Europeans, though in a minority, are in control.

In the Northern Territories of the Gold Coast, land tenure differs somewhat from that of the Colony and Ashanti. The religious aspect of land ownership is less closely related to the religious functions of chieftaincy, as in the south and central areas. This is partly due to the fact that the suzerain chiefs of the north are recent arrivals, having conquered the indigenous inhabitants. In most of the areas, the new chiefs respected the traditional pattern of land tenure by coming into alliance with the predominantly religious figures (*tendana*) caring for the land. A separation of tribal authority and land trusteeship has therefore occurred, which differs from the south and central areas where the functions of authority and land trusteeship are both part of the role of the chief.

The religious aspects of land tenure in the Northern Territories are of major importance. Land tenure was the basis of local indigenous administration. In the Northern Territories, as Hailey puts it:

". . . all religion centered on the worship of the Earth God and of the ancestral spirits. The land itself was mapped out into a network of well-defined areas (*tengani*) each of which had its own particular designation, as a domain of the Earth God. The principal mediator between the people and the Earth God was the *tendana*, a priest holding an hereditary office, who lived the life of a recluse in communion with the god and the ancestral spirits, and had considerable control over the lives of the people in his particular *tengani* area. Since the *tendana* of one area could not propitiate the Earth God or ancestral spirits of another, the area for which a *tendana* was responsible came to be recognized as a land unit, with its own established boundaries. The land itself was regarded not as the property of a family or other unit, but of the Earth God; the *tendana* was its trustee, and was the final authority in any issue such as the allocation of the bush for cultivation."[27]

[27] Hailey, Lord, *Native Administration in the British African Territories*, London, 1951, Vol. ii, pp. 259-260.

The jurisdiction of the chiefs, particularly in those areas where the chief had by treaty or by war subdued the local population, derived from other than land tenure sources. As a result, little of the instability and litigation over tribal holdings and tribal borders has affected the Northern Territories, as has been true in the Colony and Ashanti. No land could become private property, since any abandoned holdings reverted to the care of the *tendana*. Few major questions of chieftaincy, ownership, and authority developed. As a result, chieftaincy is, in the north, far more intact than in other parts of the Gold Coast to the south. There is comparatively little rebellion against the traditional authorities, and very little feeling for self-government and nationalism.

There is little doubt that the imposition of Western commerce, trade, and cash crops upset the balance between land tenure concepts and the role and limitations of chieftaincy. In their haste to benefit from the payment of a small fee, chiefs allowed concessionaires proprietary rights, thereby diminishing their own status in the eyes of the public and of the British administrators as well. Many chiefs were thrown out of office—destooled. Chieftaincy suffered a blow from which it could never recover. It was necessary for the British administration to step in and by ordinance control concessions.

In Ashanti and the Colony, concessions for mineral or mining rights can be directly negotiated between Africans and the concessionaires. However, validation of any such proceedings is subject to the Concessions Ordinance of 1939. Broadly speaking, this ordinance, read in conjunction with the Order of the Governor in Council Number 9, 1926, requires that any grant of rights over land (except land situated in a town) or grant over minerals, timber, or other products of the land, shall be subject to judicial review and inquiry if the area of the land exceeds five acres in the case of a grant to a native (and involves a period of some twenty-five years). It is the duty of the court to ensure that a just bargain has been made and that the essential rights of the inhabitants of the area are protected. The ordinance limits a grant to a term of ninety-nine years.[28]

In the Northern Territories land is regulated by the Land and Native Rights Ordinance, which empowers the governor to grant

[28] Colonial Reports, *Gold Coast, 1951*, London, 1952, p. 66. See also, *Gold Coast Handbook of Trade and Commerce*, G.P.D., Accra, 1951.

certification of occupancy to Africans and non-Africans for terms not exceeding ninety-nine years.[29]

In effect, Northern Territories land is legally a form of Crown land over which the government has final control. Colony and Ashanti land is subject to grants which must be validated by a divisional court, and the control over such grants is by a judicial rather than an executive authority. "Thus, in the south, the Crown has assumed no general rights over land. If it requires land for public purposes it may have to purchase it, on full consideration. All unoccupied land is at the disposal of the local or paramount native authority (stool)."[30]

In view of the fact that the Gold Coast is primarily a tribal-agrarian society, it is clear that the question of control over land, the relations of power and decision arising from land holding and land use affect the foundations of the legal and customary norms of the traditional authorities.

That such concepts of land right and usufruct are not easily commensurable with Western legal notions is evidenced not only by the consequences of the wide-scale alienations which had occurred in grants to concessionaires in the past, but also by the extensive legal disputes which are still rampant. In 1901, when the Concessions Ordinance was first passed, alienation reached 25,508 square miles in the Colony, an area larger than the Colony itself.

In many cases this situation was due either to unscrupulousness on the part of chiefs or to ignorance of Western notions of land tenure. The chief never had the right to grant permanent alienation of land since it, properly, was not his to grant. The ultimate title lay with the stool ancestors, and all dispositions were ultimately accountable to them.

Around the turn of the century, concessionaires brought deforestation, non-tribal forms of labor such as mining, and the related social consequences of commercialization marked in increased de-tribalization and the growth of urban centers. Even when the government tried to control the worst effects of concessions, and the wholesale deprivation of Africans of their land the political consequences were profound.

In order to control irresponsible behavior by the chiefs in regard to land, the government had to restrict their activities and their

29 *Ibid.*   30 Meek, *op.cit.*, p. 169.

disposition of land. This control violated the chief's prerogatives and sources of sanction. The responsibility of the chief, in his actions, tended to be removed from the tribal members and the exercise of their traditional powers, to the British government.

Yet even the effort to control land, in some of its most consequential aspects, was successfully fought off by the Africans. Efforts to prevent wide-scale deforestation by vesting forest areas as Crown land—which would have made tribal land the property of the Crown—were bitterly opposed. Meek sums up the situation as follows:

"Until recent times, the position of the chiefs or 'stools' in regard to land was generally the same as other African communities. The people looked to the chief and elders to administer the land on their behalf. The chief allotted such areas as were sufficient for each subdivision, and held the remainder in reserve against the further needs of the future. But the demand for gold-mining concessions, which began about 1880, led to wholesale alienations by chiefs at the expense of native occupiers. With the development of the cocoa industry at the beginning of the present century, the demand for land became greater, and this, coupled with the spread of English principles of conveyancing, led to a rapid growth of private or individual forms of ownership. At the present time it is said that the Gold Coast farmer of the south is so land conscious that it is becoming the rule rather than the exception that he could obtain his farm by way of absolute grant, evidenced by a written instrument."[31]

No real statistics exist to indicate the distribution of types of land holdings and the standards by which a clear title, or even the validity of various titles, can be indicated.[32] In effect, ownership is residual. Contrary to Western common law, there is no single property right involving private ownership; there is only provisional proprietorship. "The rights of the chief in respect of land is [sic] not separable from those of his people who have conjoint right in the property as well as a joint control. . . . The king, qua king, does not own all the lands of the states. The limits of his proprietary rights are strictly defined."[33]

Land has become a political issue, wrapped up with the per-

[31] Ibid., p. 171.
[32] Meek, Macmillan, and Hussey, Europe and West Africa, Oxford, 1940, p. 82.
[33] Casely Hayford, Joseph, West African Land Question, op.cit., pp. 54-55.

quisites and obligations of traditional chieftaincy and society. For the present Gold Coast government, embarking upon developmental projects infringes upon customary patterns of land tenure. Any changes involving land and land usage infringe upon the prerogatives of chieftaincy. The government must provide new forms of social and community life to replace the tribe, insofar as the old system is increasingly less satisfactory in the light of modern Gold Coast national objectives. In addition, the customary tradition of land tenure is one of the strongest inhibiting factors militating against the rapid development of individualized and Western patterns of competitive practice so closely bound up with private ownership and an atomistic social structure. Whether or not such competitive practice would tend to undermine social discipline and make the task of the present government even harder is difficult to decide. In any case, land and land tenure remain a real dilemma for the nationalist government.

Labor

In a primarily subsistence economy, where capital investment as compared with that of more industrialized countries is proportionately low and where limitations upon the efficient utilization of resources abound, labor assumes great significance. This does not mean that there is a well-organized and numerically strong trade union movement at present, nor anything remotely approaching a proletariat in any meaningful terms. Rather, labor power and efficiency are the most available form of wealth. It is upon labor, and its use in conjunction with other resources, that the economic future of the Gold Coast depends, particularly since the nationalists have been brought to power through demands by increasing segments of the population for Western standards of subsistence.

Increasingly, skilled labor is required for the development projects and the highly technical operations in a modern state. Where is such labor to come from? Laborers will have to be trained from a rural working force whose desire for Western standards of life does not include Western standards of work.

A general occupational classification is provided in the 1948 census returns. Figures for the male population are as follows:

MALE OCCUPATIONAL GROUPS*

	Number	*Per cent*
Cultivators of cocoa	150,020	11.5
Artisans, craftsmen, and skilled workers	127,251	9.7
Shopkeepers, traders, and sellers	56,144	4.7
Unskilled workers	177,560	13.6
Remainder (mostly farmers)	797,025	60.5

* Adapted from the 1948 Census.

However, as aggregates the figures are somewhat misleading. The high proportion of cocoa farmers in Ashanti and the small proportion in the Northern Territories indicate a substantial difference in occupational distribution in these two areas. Farming in the north is back-breaking, while cocoa farming involves less labor, often of the absentee landlord type. In the north only 0.4 per cent of the male population is engaged in cocoa cultivation, while 90 per cent is engaged in other forms of farming.

Women, as well, form a large part of the working force. For the female working population, 67 per cent are engaged in commerce, petty trading in fish, cloths, and manufactured objects. Petty trading is a woman's occupation by and large. Everywhere in the Gold Coast market women carry their wares on their heads, to the market place or along the roads, bargaining furiously with the passers-by. Much of the small trading in the hinterlands done by women is a social function which a more rational system of distribution would upset. To change the system of petty trading would, in a democratic system just beginning to take root, be a dangerous political step, yet it is expensive.

In addition to trading, women often own farms. Half as many women are engaged in cocoa cultivation as men. In many cases women own their own cocoa farms.

The general occupational division of labor therefore breaks down along predominantly agricultural lines, indicating a population primarily engaged in subsistence farming and cocoa cultivation. The proportion of part-time laborers and traders is most difficult to estimate, but it can be assumed that in almost every family, some trading, particularly by women, occurs. Women still predominate in petty trading, although men are gradually moving into general commercial life. Most of the large-scale non-European commerce is in the hands of Syrians and Lebanese, who occupy a kind of middle position in the occupational structure of the Gold Coast and are disliked by both Europeans and Africans. There remain cultural barriers against African males engaging in petty commerce and, for southerners and Ashanti groups, against manual labor. Educated Africans tend towards the professions, with law extremely popular in view of the extent of land litigation. A considerable number of non-university but successful politicians go into contracting, an occupation which promises good returns for the successful entrepreneur and places a heavy burden on virtue. Bribery and corruption, particularly in the awarding of contracts, is not uncommon.

Rather than an extensive and highly differentiated division of labor, there are significant regional and tribal occupational clusters. Particular tribes from different areas tend to follow occupational patterns deemed most in keeping with their traditions or their sense of prestige. Ewes tend to go into service occupations, for example, which no proper Ashanti would engage in.

Instead of a rigid class stratification system, based upon income and occupation, there are status group clusters devolving around membership in a tribal group and around lineage status. Particularly in rural areas, tribal membership and lineage fix the status patterns on a traditionalistic basis. "Class" based on occupation has only just begun to appear in the urban areas, particularly among the Western-oriented and educated groups. Except for these groups, the predominant pattern of trade and agriculture admits of a real variation in incomes which may add to the prestige of the tribe or village rather than of the individual. In most parts of the Gold Coast, occupational status does not involve a highly articulated built-in system of statuses, and monetary income and traditional prejudices tend to reinforce one another on an inter-tribal and inter-regional basis. The poverty of the north is taken by many southerners and Ashanti as a reinforcement of the traditional prejudice against the northerners, who have always been considered inferior and were mostly used as slaves. New reasons reinforce old prejudices. It is no accident that the northerners, many of them, are bitterly opposed to self-government, finding the protection of the British more salutary than the dubious advantage of independence in a nation dominated by southerners.

The division of labor is not extensive. It reflects the lack of skilled and even semi-skilled workers available for present developmental tasks. Many of those groups considered skilled or artisan are goldsmiths or ivory-carvers, whose immediate value in the general productive process would be limited.

Labor Efficiency

It can be stated rather categorically that labor efficiency is, for the most part, low. Problems generally seem to derive from several sources. In most enterprises the labor turnover is extremely high. Traditional attitudes toward manual labor reduce potential recruitment as well as morale. A high premium value placed upon leisure reduces the motivating aspects of monetary reward as compared with the rewards of leisure time. Differing concepts of labor time involve working as inclination dictates, and no idea of "time as money." A lack of technical understanding and skill reduces the effectiveness of capital equipment and job performance. Traditional responsibilities to the tribe and the family often demand leaving the job, and reduce labor mobility as a sustained force. Traditional responsibilities to land call the worker home for harvest, for festival occasions, and for customary rites. High rates of disease make systematic and sustained effort impossible for many. The climate tends to make rapid work over long periods of time difficult.

In the mines, in particular, labor turnover is exceptionally high. Figures gathered in 1949 indicate that the turnover in mines amounted to nearly 80 per cent of the labor force, while the turnover of underground labor amounted to over 90 per cent. In the following year labor turnover percentages increased to 85 per cent in the first instance and almost 100 per cent in the latter. Nearly 40 per cent of those leaving employment had been employed for less than six months. Almost half of the mining force is migrant.[34] "Labor in the Gold Coast is cheap per day, but expensive per unit of output" indicates the Seers and Ross Report.[35] Its efficiency, by comparison with Western standards of productivity, is low.

One of the major factors in low productivity is the unstable labor force which shifts from job to job, and frequently from urban to rural life and back again. Particularly in the semi-skilled

[34] Heigham, J. B., *Some Notes on Labor in the Gold Coast*, Accra, 1952.
[35] Seers, Dudley, and Ross, C. R., *Report on Financial and Physical Problems of Development in the Gold Coast*, Accra, 1952, pp. 102-103.

occupations, the scarcity of labor gives a premium value to those with some training and background in the industrial process. Recruitment of skilled workers is extremely limited. "The skilled craftsmen must, therefore, be largely recruited from those already in the industry. This means training not merely the unskilled, but also those that are allegedly skilled."[36] Even then there is no guarantee that a newly trained man will remain in his employment. According to Seers and Ross, "A further cause of low productivity is the continuous change of jobs, turnover rates as high as 50 per cent a month were reported to us for projects in areas short of labor. This is to some extent inescapable: the Gold Coast laborer likes to change his job often, and many regularly return home, particularly men from the Northern Territories (or French territory) who form a high proportion of the unskilled labor force, even in the Colony."[37]

An aggravating factor in labor turnover is involved in payoffs to find or retain employment. A report done several years ago on labor conditions in West Africa states:

"An evil element which is a burden to all the poorer paid sections of the population is the 'rake-off' which must be paid to secure, or sometimes even to retain, employment; this is an old established practice, almost openly regarded as the prerequisite accompanying a position of authority. Not only is this an imposition in itself; it also tends to the ready discharge of an employee to make room for another victim, and where the extortioner is not in a position to do this himself, he will invent causes of complaint on which the employer may unwittingly act."[38]

As more and more jobs with the government become available to Africans at all levels, these same pressures apply. Recent investigations, following the confessions of a Minister of Communications to taking bribes, indicates that such practices are not unknown on the highest levels of government. We shall return to this problem in another context.

In the Colony and Ashanti, where present and potential manpower requirements are large, local personnel are not anxious to do manual labor of any kind. In Ashanti, in particular, manual work is considered appropriate only for slaves. The larger pro-

[36] *Ibid.*, p. 205. [37] *Ibid.*, p. 98.
[38] Orde-Browne, Major G. St. J., *Labor Conditions in West Africa*, Command 6277, London, 1941, p. 24.

portion of manual labor is performed by the Northern Territories people, and at best it is subject to social, regional, and historical biases which associate it primarily with captives and slaves. Even recruitment for the new Kumasi College of Technology, a British-operated technical college, carries less prestige than the University College of the Gold Coast at Achimota. In the value hierarchy of present-day Ashanti, the modern specialist's engineering degree counts for less than the classical British tradition of scholarship. The former indicates labor; the latter, leisure.

There are, in fact, few of the prejudices against leisure which exist in the Western world. Few people are judged by how hard they work, unless such work is communal and within the tribe, village, or family as part of joint enterprise. While commerce in slaves and gold has traditionally been acceptable, it does not require sustained effort or regular hours. Similarly, the cultivation of cocoa, one of the most popular forms of production—popular not only because of its high pecuniary return—requires little attention. The tree does not have to be carefully nurtured. Many cocoa farmers build houses in Kumasi or some other large town, using women or boys to harvest the crop when necessary. Another popular means of income with little effort is participation in the Convention People's Party, the nationalist political organization now in office, where the sale of favors can provide an effective source of income and serve as a vehicle for social mobility.

These conditions are of course related, as well, to differing concepts of labor time. Particularly for those whose tribal and rural affiliations are strong, for recent migrants from the bush and from French territory, time is related to the cycle of the seasons, to births and deaths, to rituals and ceremonies. Time is, in a way, history, in which there is a tendency to regard the present as embodying all time.[39] The time of the clock, the day, the hour, has little immediate impact. Consequently, it is extremely hard, without careful supervision, to maintain a disciplined working force. Some managers begin the work-day extremely early in the morning, with a nine o'clock stop for breakfast, and a diminished rate of working throughout the remainder of the day.

Traditional labor in the Gold Coast has been, in the main, a

[39] See Fortes, M., *Dynamics of Clanship Amongst the Tallensi*, London, 1945, in which this factor is discussed in some detail.

social affair. Except for farming, the requirements of the family and the tribe have mostly been met by joint efforts. The occasions for successful joint work in manual labor outside tribal and personal village associations have been rare, since the social and familial aspects of joint participation are often more important than the cooperative aspect, at least from the conscious point of view of the members.

Even where the incentives and motives for a particular form of labor are high, the individual often must bear the burden of the extended family coming to share in the fruits of his toil. The traditional family security system involved the sharing of the return as social obligation. One observer writes that the:

". . . successful wage-earner often finds himself bearing the major costs of the family. 'I met with one case where a clerk on £ 27 a month was maintaining a household of nineteen persons and two domestic servants; even more remarkable examples are said to exist. . . .

"Another curious factor in family expenses is the high value set on social status; anyone above the humblest class has numerous obligations, most of which entail additional expense. Thus a clerk on a salary of £ 6 10 s. monthly maintained the necessity of a black dinner jacket, while an elderly widow, dependent upon an allowance from her daughter in domestic service, found it necessary to employ a woman on a meagre wage to save her from the social stigma of having to make her own purchases in the market."[40]

These are obviously extreme cases, at least for the Gold Coast, but their general implications are valid enough. The new government must take steps to reduce this kind of practice if it is to have savings held by the population, less corruption and graft in its own circles, and differing behavioral standards appreciated by the members, in the long pull to a viable secular political system.

Finally, disease and climate understandably reduce the efficiency of labor. The problem of maintaining a highly active work force under such conditions is great. Much depends upon the physical capacities and endurance of the workers. In a village rural survey done in connection with this research, it was found that in one village sampled, having a population of some two hundred people,

[40] Orde-Browne, *op.cit.*, pp. 23-24.

only five males roughly over fifty survived. In a survey quoted in the Seers and Ross Report in 1950, it was found in a typical cocoa village that 32 per cent of the inhabitants had malarial infection, 52 per cent showed hookworm, 76 had ascana, and 75 per cent had active or quiescent yaws. The report goes on to say: "Altogether, it would seem that a very high proportion of Gold Coast citizens are ill from parasitic diseases, and that almost all of them have had such diseases at some time."[41]

From the point of view of labor efficiency and the potential labor force, it is important to consider that the participation by an African in non-traditional forms of work is a departure from a host of related social and economic activities. In many respects, it means the removal of the African from his way of life. As stated by Greaves:

"When we consider the labor situation which confronts foreign capitalism in backward territories, therefore, it is important to remember that these places have already an integrated economy in which all the factors of production are represented. It is misleading to think that because they so patently lack capital, they compose only one factor, labor, awaiting more advantageous employment. The population is not comparable to a proletariat which has no alternative to wage labor, for when they are left free, backward people have a choice between the conditions of their customary system of production and the terms offered by the foreign employer.

"Hence when foreign interests attempt to alter the methods of production in the direction of greater efficiency, they meet obstruction. What they consider to be only a simple economic adjustment, native opinion regards as a menace to its whole social fabric. It is easy to see that while the native may be willing to work at his economy, changes introduced from the outside which require the alteration of that framework will appear to be of quite a different order. Economic matters cannot be isolated from the rest of the social system of ideology and sanctions, and when a change in the system of production is of a kind which requires a change in social laws and ceremonies which are regarded as of the utmost importance to the preservation of tribal integrity, it

[41] Seers and Ross, *op.cit.,* pp. 101-102.

will be accepted if the tribe realizes that it is impossible or undesirable to continue under the old system."[42]

In its implications for development, for achieving the larger political objectives of the Gold Coast, and for preparing the public for a new set of social institutions by shaking them out of the old, the role of labor is significant. In its immediate consequence it tends to break down the tribe and, because of this breakdown, contribute to general social disorder, urban overcrowding, and the social tensions which characterize periods of rapid social change.

It is through the effective use of labor skills, labor time, and labor efficiency that the prospects for institutional transfer will be greatly enhanced. In the long run, the decisions of secular democratic government will be developmental rather than constitutional decisions. These developmental decisions are bound up with the program of the present Gold Coast government. Development is the tangible aspect of the new world to come. If labor costs are too high to attract foreign investment, or if inadequately trained personnel play havoc with rationalized operations and productive units, then the chances for achieving some of the very goals which make democratic self-government attractive to at least some Africans will be minimized.

Income and Distribution

"Before 1874, when dealing in domestic slaves was abolished and existing slaves were declared emancipated, wage earning existed in the Gold Coast only in the very restricted sphere of government and European commercial and missionary employment. . . .

"Although industrialization has developed in the Gold Coast to an extent which was probably inconceivable in 1874, wage earning . . . is still the exception rather than the rule, since only approximately one in five of the adult population is engaged in it."[43]

A wage economy, almost entirely new in the Gold Coast, has had dramatic effects upon the entire social and political environment. With the acceptance of European valuations upon con-

[42] Greaves, I. C., *Modern Production among Backward Peoples*, London, 1935, pp. 59-60.
[43] Heigham, *op.cit.*, p. 2.

sumer goods, the desire for monetary return has grown. Almost nowhere are cowrie shells still an acceptable medium of exchange.

In traditional Ashanti, gold dust had been used as a payment of honorifics among chiefs in the form of tribal dues, customary obeisance, and tribal fees or payments. It was not a normal medium of exchange. Indeed, among the Ashanti, the rule was that any gold dropped in the market place belonged to the *asantehene*, or paramount chief of Ashanti, and failures to adhere to this rule were punishable by death.

Closely paralleling the development of a wage economy was the steady growth of migratory labor, which after 1911 had grown to an estimated 300,000 people of non-indigenous Gold Coast origin in 1950.

Wage payments by commercial firms and government are generally monthly, with the result that a host of related occupations (landlords, cateresses, moneylenders, and traders) all base their practices on monthly payments. A high proportion of workers pay their bills and rent at the end of each month and live on credit for the rest of the next month. Very little saving is recognized, and there are traditional barriers to saving. The government has tried with some success to encourage thrift by the use of postal savings.

Wide gaps between the rising cost of living from 1938 onward and the small rewards to labor and cocoa farmers helped to increase general dissatisfaction with British colonial rule. At least part of the support received by the nationalist movement derived from public outrage against rising living costs. Only after a series of major disturbances did post-war incomes begin to rise as follows:

INCOME AND DISTRIBUTION[44]*

	1948-1949	1949-1950	1950-1951
Wages and salaries	8	11	13
Cocoa incomes	35	24	36
Other mixed incomes	34	47	56

* £ million.

One of the most important consequences of a change to a wage economy was the development of a host of secondary distributive

[44] Adapted from Table 2, Seers and Ross, *op.cit.*, p. 33.

and middlemen agencies. Very often these middlemen add a considerable amount to the final purchase price of the article. In farm products a large gap exists between farm prices and the ultimate market price of the produce. The price received by the farmer is rarely high.

In 1937 dissatisfaction over prices received by cocoa farmers led to a voluntary boycott which seemed to be spontaneous and unorganized but exceedingly effective. A commission sent to examine the causes of the cocoa holdup proved extremely influential in determining future government policy. Stating that the major evils derived from two sources—competition among the export merchants and questionable practices of the middlemen who, in effect, cheated both the producer and the merchant—the report concluded that the producer was not getting a reasonable price for cocoa in the light of market conditions.[45] As a consequence, a more rationalized system of buying and marketing cocoa was set up. Today this market system is under the control of the Gold Coast government through the agency of the Cocoa Marketing Board, one of the most crucial statutory boards in the Gold Coast today.

The reserves of the Cocoa Marketing Board are derived from the difference between the price paid to the cocoa farmer and the price of cocoa on the world market. When the world price is high, the reserves of the board accrue from the margin between the world price and the price which the board pays the farmers. If the world price drops, then the reserves cushion the impact, acting as an insurance fund. The policy of the Cocoa Marketing Board is calculated to maintain a steady return of income to cocoa farmers, in spite of possible drastic fluctuations in the world price of cocoa.[46]

[45] See *Report of the Commission on the Marketing of West African Cocoa*, Cmd. 5845, London, H.M.S.O., 1938.

[46] One indication of how significant is the policy of the Cocoa Marketing Board and the responsibility of the government in such matters is the political impact of price policy. The first act of the 1954 Nkrumah government after it took office was to fix the price of cocoa at 72 s per load (60 lbs.) and in Ashanti bitter disagreement with the price helped sponsor a national liberation movement. This movement has the backing of members of the Asanteman Council and has stated as its object the establishing of a federal system in the Gold Coast and the abolition of the present governmental structure. A good deal of latent Ashanti separatism has come to the fore, with the price of cocoa serving as the main grievance unifying individuals against the regime. See the Gold Coast *Daily Graphic*, September 13, 1954, and *West Africa*, October 2, 1954, p. 924; October 9, 1954, p. 937.

The Cocoa Marketing Board policy has been, at different times, dictated by three major considerations. After the disastrous effects of the world economic depression in the 1930's, it was decided that a large reserve fund was needed as insurance, operated through the mechanism of price stabilization in order to reduce the impact of a severe drop in the world price of cocoa on the Gold Coast economy. During the war, when prices rose, such a reserve became feasible with an added consideration—inflation control. By the control of the amount of money in the hands of farmers (all having a high propensity to consume) the inflationary pressures during the war and post-war periods were held down. The Gold Coast has been one of the few primary producers to avoid major inflation. Finally, reserves were looked upon as a possible source for general development. In other words they are part of the capital reserves of the Gold Coast available for investment. The creation of reserves has been, in effect, forced savings.[47]

Problems of employment, income, and prices will provide issues increasingly central to the stability and balance of the nation. Immediate problems have been posed for the nationalist government. If food prices continue to rise, for example, there will be demands that the government take steps to make price controls more effective. The steps taken might be unpopular and, in any case, would have to be taken on many fronts.

The shift away from subsistence and other forms of farming to wage employment has put large urban populations at the mercy of local price rises. From 1949 to 1952, when prices rose considerably, the urban populations suffered the most. It is in the urban areas, as well, that the most aggressive feeling for independence resides.

[47] This view of the beneficial effects of the Cocoa Marketing Board is sharply contradicted by P. T. Bauer, who regards the Statutory Marketing Boards as having "socialized" peasant saving in British Africa, yet done so to the advantage of the exporters. Bauer states his criticism regarding stabilization (one object of such an export monopoly under government control) as follows: "In neither of the two White Papers, nor in any other official statement, was there any attempt to define stabilization, or to distinguish between stabilization of incomes and prices, or to refer to any of the various fundamental conceptual and practical problems and difficulties of stabilization. Yet without a consideration of these ambiguities and problems, stabilization becomes a meaningless omnibus term of no value as a guide to policy." See Bauer, P. T., "Origins of the Statutory Export Monopolies of British West Africa," in *The Business History Review*, Col. xxviii, September 1954, No. 3, p. 211.

Some indication of local price conditions can be found in the following table on food prices.

LOCAL FOOD PRICES: INDEX NUMBER[48]
(1948 equals 100)

	1st quarter	*2nd quarter*	*3rd quarter*	*4th quarter*	*Annual average*
1949	130	161	151	140	145
1950	144	143	143	149	145
1951	172	194	189	189	186

It is, of course, obvious that people most dependent upon wages were hardest hit by prices on food. Insofar as the urban population represents the more "detribalized" elements of the population, the nationalist movement found more recruits who had felt the inflationary pinch, had few roots in traditional society, and made more willing party zealots and functionaries.

Effective demand and purchasing power is much higher in the Colony and Ashanti than in the Northern Territories. In many rural areas the farmers are victims of the middlemen, who, particularly for perishable crops, will pay the farmer or in some cases the fisherman extremely low prices for a year's work on the farm or along the river. Knowing that the farmer or fisherman cannot keep his produce indefinitely, the middleman can afford to wait until the price is low enough for his satisfaction.

Since national income figures are not available and income breakdowns are unreliable, perhaps the most adequate picture of Gold Coast income and expenditure can be found by examining an ordinary rural household budget. The table on the following page has been taken from the *Agricultural Statistics Survey* produced by the office of the government statistician.[49]

Demand for imported foodstuffs, household goods, clothing, and farm equipment tends to place the cost of imported goods in a crucial position when family income increases. Small increases in cocoa income, for example, result in a multiplier effect which stimulates substantial inflationary pressures. Even in the villages it is rare that an entirely subsistence economy is maintained.

The larger implications of the shift from subsistence farming to a wage economy of light industrial products, consumer demand,

---

[48] Ministry of Commerce, *Survey of Some Economic Matters*, Accra, 1952.
[49] Report No. 4, Accra, 1953.

THE HOUSEHOLD BUDGET

Average Monthly Income and Expenditure per Household
(items recorded daily)

	£	s.	d.
Income			
Sale of farm produce (excluding cocoa)	2	10	6
Casual labor, etc.		5	8
Crafts, etc.		3	1
Resale of purchased goods	1	5	7
Other	1	3	3
	—	—	—
TOTAL	5	8	1
	£	s.	d.
Expenditures			
Food for home consumption			
Local	2	1	1
Imported		5	1
Goods for processing and resale	1	4	9
Clothing		6	10
Fuel and light		4	9
Household goods		2	10
Farm equipment		1	1
Casual labor		2	10
Transport		4	1
Other		14	10
	—	—	—
TOTAL	5	8	2

and cash crop agriculture can be summed up as follows:

1. It supports a system of distribution and exchange of non-subsistence commodities, including imported goods and the agents and institutions thereof.

2. It serves as an object to which action in the form of urban migration, de-tribalization, etc., is oriented and which serves as a stimulus for power and prestige in new occupational roles.

3. It results in an evergrowing labor force.

4. It attracts immigrants from areas other than the Gold Coast.

5. It directly ties the welfare of increasing proportions of the population to world trade and world prices of raw materials and finished products.

6. It creates a public interest in developmental projects using large quantities of labor.

7. It creates a public interest in government wage and price policies since government is the largest employer of labor and the accustomed agency of price-fixing.

In general, the introduction and spread of a wage economy produce problems to which solutions can be found only in the operations of government. Rarely does one find the purely subsistence farmer paying no heed to the vicissitudes of the market. Everyone buys imported goods. People's lives are tied directly to the economic and welfare decisions which the government takes.

Capital Investment

As has been indicated, the Gold Coast today is a commercial economy. It is a hive of building and development. Goods come carried on the head, by canoe, lorry, and even air freight. At times it seems as if the entire Gold Coast is engaged in commerce and construction.

Yet, as in most underdeveloped areas, the Gold Coast is an economy of shortages. Limited port facilities, uneven peak periods of effective demand, an uncertain political pattern, in addition to the high cost of labor, make investment risky. The Gold Coast, which has been the scene of so much commercial activity for over four hundred years, has seen little in the way of permanent capital investment in productive enterprise.

In the past, a governmental economic policy has been almost entirely lacking until around the turn of the century. While the West African settlements were the first to receive funds from parliamentary enactment, these funds were given in pursuit of minimal administration for safeguarding trade and commerce.[50] In 1750 the African Company of Merchants was founded with a subsidization by the Imperial Government amounting to £13,000 per annum.[51] Control by a merchant company indicated the nature of imperial policy in regard to West Africa.

When serious efforts to develop the Gold Coast began, the coastal areas, where the impact of commercialism had resulted in larger urban areas, received immediate attention. In 1901 a railway was built from Sekondi to Tarkwa, the center of the gold mining area, and in 1904 it was extended to Kumasi. In 1911 work was begun on extension of the line from Kumasi to Accra.

[50] See *Annual Reports, 1937-1938*, No. 1882, London, 1939.
[51] *Ibid.*

By 1919 lorry roads reached over a thousand miles, building upon the military communications links which had been established by British forces in their forays into the interior.

Up until the First World War, however, only the barest essentials in schooling, hospital and medical resources, housing and migrant labor camps were developed. Gold mining corporations, cocoa firms, and general commercial establishments for retail trade were just getting organized on a large scale.

According to Bourret[52] Gold Coast economic history can be divided into three main periods. The first, from the sixteenth to the eighteenth centuries, consisted primarily of slave trading until it was abolished by the British government in 1807. The second period, the trader's heyday, lasted until the middle of the nineteenth century. The third dates from the establishment of Crown Colony government in the Gold Coast and the serious exploitation of the resources of the Colony and the creation of a market for British exports.

After 1919, under Sir Gordon Guggisberg as governor, investment was oriented by the government towards the future needs of the Gold Coast. The large harbor at Takoradi was built. Achimota College, one of the finest secondary schools in all Africa, was established, and promptly began to turn out graduates destined to be some of the most important political figures of today's Gold Coast. Hospitals were built, roads and permanent public buildings were constructed. Under a ten-year plan of development the concept of a viable social and economic Gold Coast was for the first time injected into official governmental policy. Provision was increasingly made for the needs of Africans. During this period a constitution was drafted which gave Africans their first opportunity to participate in the top levels of conciliar government.

As a primary producer, however, the Gold Coast was particularly vulnerable to the effects of the economic depression of the 1930's. While a company such as the Ashanti Goldfields Corporation was returning dividends in 1930-1931 of 90 per cent and a 33 1/3 bonus in fully paid shares,[53] the new harbor at Takoradi remained empty of ships and Gold Coast revenue dropped from £4,000,000 in 1927 to £2,000,000 in 1931.[54]

[52] Bourret, F. M., *The Gold Coast*, London, 1952, p. 120
[53] Hinden, Rita, *Plan for Africa*, London, 1941.
[54] Bourret, *op.cit.*, p. 121.

Bourret indicates as follows: "As a result of this experience the government made some attempts to foster more varied types of agriculture, but with only moderate success. The cattle and timber industries were also stimulated, but though far-seeing African leaders asked for the introduction of local industries, the administration did not, at that time, adopt a policy of official encouragement of manufacturing. It was to take the changed conditions and the challenge to Britain's colonial policy of the 1939-1945 war years finally to procure strong governmental support of a more balanced economy."[55]

For African local investment there are few resources. Except for Cocoa Marketing Board reserves now approaching a hundred million pounds, there are practically no internal savings by Africans. On the contrary, theirs is more usually a condition of indebtedness.[56] Government financing has proceeded partly out of Colonial Development and Welfare funds, payments out of the Cocoa Marketing Board reserves (for such items as the building program of the University College of the Gold Coast, at Legon Hill),[57] and customs and revenues, excises, etc., which provide a bulk of the funds for governmental operations. It is estimated that ninety per cent of the income tax paid in the Gold Coast is paid by the large European commercial firms.

The biggest developmental project, calling for large sums of investment capital, is the proposed Volta River aluminum scheme. Under the present proposals, ninety per cent of the scheme will be financed in equity capital held by British and Canadian investors, the Gold Coast buying the remaining ten per cent with an

[55] *Ibid.*

[56] The traditional system involved peasant cultivation in which land was tribally owned, and to increase income or holding it was necessary only to plant on uncultivated land, which was plentiful. No cash holdings were necessary and the farmer could remain in undisturbed possession of all land worked. The present system is based more on absentee ownership with hired migrant workers. The owner frequently owns more than one farm. Land has received a commercial valuation with consequent legal disputes. Under the present marketing and purchasing arrangements, cash is a necessity. With cocoa as collateral, the moneylenders have prospered. In lending, the entire future crop might be mortgaged with interest payments up to 50 per cent. In the absence of further collateral, "pawning" of daughters and nieces—indenturing them to the creditor—is common. It is estimated that 30 per cent of the farmers have pledged their farms in exchange for long-term loans. Most loans are used for non-economic purposes such as weddings. The last thing the moneylenders want is to see the complete repayment of debts. For further discussion, see Hinden, *op.cit.*, pp. 119-122.

[57] See The Gold Coast Cocoa Marketing Board, *First Annual Report and Accounts*, Accra, 1949.

option to buy an additional ten per cent in twenty years. A proposed hydroelectric station would be financed by British bonds, while a new harbor and railroad would be the responsibility of the Gold Coast government.[58]

Since the stabilization of internal incomes by using the Cocoa Marketing Board, which was organized on its present basis in 1947,[59] a considerable number of developmental projects calling for diverse government investments have been initiated. Agricultural stations are being established in major rural areas doing both advisory and experimental work. Subsidiary to these stations are veterinary posts, where efforts to inoculate cattle against rinderpest and other diseases and to advise on husbandry practices have increased cattle herds.

Recently, an Agricultural Loans Board was set up to be financed by Cocoa Marketing Board funds. This board, whose purpose is to grant loans to farmers, would allow them to avoid the loan sharks who are ever-present in the Gold Coast; it encourages thrift and enterprise on the level of farm investment. At present, this system has not yet come into operation, a situation which has been severely criticized in the Legislative Assembly.

The Gold Coast Agricultural Development Corporation was established in order to undertake specialized experimental schemes. One of its major operations has been a large-scale resettlement and cooperative farming venture, the Damongo Scheme in the Gonja area of the Northern Territories. The Gonja Development Company, formed as a subsidiary of the corporation, plans to finance and construct a farming area of 30,000 acres, complete with modern hospital, school, low-cost housing, recreation facilities, piped water, electricity, and most of the features of a modern community. There is evidence, however, that the scheme has run into considerable difficulties with labor, problems of efficiency, and other factors which qualify schemes of this sort in Africa.[60]

The Agricultural Produce Marketing Board has been set up as a statutory body, for the marketing of agricultural produce other than cocoa. At present it is authorized to export palm

[58] See Davison, R. B., *op.cit.* See also *Legislative Assembly Debates*, 1953, Issue No. 1, Volume II, for a detailed discussion of the pros and cons of the Volta Scheme, and, in addition, below in Chapter 11.

[59] Which was changed from the West African Produce Control Board.

[60] See Damongo, Supplement to the Gold Coast *Weekly Review*, Vol. II, No. 13, March 26, 1952.

kernels, copra, and coffee. If the plans are fulfilled, its activities should expand to include other export crops such as rubber, tobacco, and shea butter.

The Gold Coast Industrial Development Corporation was established in 1947 and, in addition to setting up its own workshops for furniture and crafts industries, it has given financial assistance to three timber mills, six printing presses, two weaving concerns, and other new industries. Mostly it has sponsored handicrafts workshops and trade outlets within the Gold Coast.

The mining industry is the largest private investment and capital development factor in the country. It is in private hands and has a relatively steady output. The companies supply a large proportion of government revenue through taxes. Next to cocoa gold mining is the ranking export commodity in the Gold Coast. Under the Volta Scheme, processed aluminum should eventually provide an additional major source of revenue.

For the immediate future, cement and tobacco industries are planned. In 1950 the Gold Coast had to import cement valued at £1,120,000, and it is expected that the government will invest £2,000,000 in a cement industry for local production.

Under the auspices of the Department of Cooperation, a Gold Coast Cooperative Federation was formed in 1944. Although some local opposition to the cooperative movement has developed, partly because of financial malpractices, a Gold Coast Cooperative Bank was formed in 1946, and is the central banking organ of all the cooperative societies. In addition, the Cooperative Wholesale Establishment was founded in 1949 as a central importing agency for consumer societies. In 1953 the C.W.E. was subject to special investigation for financial irregularities, several of its employees were placed upon trial in the courts, and it was closed down in 1954.

The general proposed expansion of the Gold Coast economy has been delineated in the *Development Plan, 1951*.[61] Its planned operations and expenditures, excluding the Volta River Project, are listed on the following page.

Problems of development are perhaps indicated by the financial priorities listed in the plan. Communications is the largest single

[61] For a complete survey of development projects excluding the Volta Scheme see *The Development Plan, 1951*, Accra, 1952.

DEVELOPMENT PLAN[62]

	Planned expenditures	Per cent of total
Economic and productive services	£12,444,000	16.85
Communications	26,110,000	35.3
Social services	24,542,000	33.1
Common services and general administration	10,896,000	14.75

item, for example, while only 16.85 per cent is available for economic and productive services.

While it should seem that a variety of local crops and manufactures would thrive in the Gold Coast, large-scale problems still await solution. In his report on industrialization in the Gold Coast, Professor Lewis indicates favorable prospects for the following industries: oil expressing, canned fruit and vegetables, salt, beer, bricks and tiles, cement, glass, lime, industrial alcohol, miscellaneous chemicals, and wood products. Almost all other possible industrial products are either considered to have unfavorable or at best marginal prospects in the Gold Coast.[63]

In his conclusions Professor Lewis states: "Measures to increase the manufacture of commodities for the home deserve support, but are not of number one priority. A small program is justified, but a major program in this sphere should wait until the country is better prepared to carry it. The main obstacle is the fact that agricultural productivity per man is stagnant. This has three effects. First, the market for manufactures is small, and is not expanding year by year, except to the extent of population growth; consequently it would take large subsidies to make possible the employment of a large number of people in manufacturing. Secondly it is not possible to get ever larger savings out of the farmers, year by year, to finance industrialization, without at the same time reducing their standard of living; hence industrialization has to depend on foreign capital, and large amounts of capital for this purpose could be attracted only on unfavorable terms. And thirdly, agriculture, because it is stagnant, does not release labor year by year; there is a shortage of labor in the Gold Coast which rapid industrialization would aggravate."[64]

[62] *Ibid.*
[63] See Lewis, W. A., *Report on Industrialization and the Gold Coast*, Gold Coast Government, Government Printer, Accra, 1953, p. 7.
[64] *Ibid.*, p. 22.

Conclusion

As this brief discussion of the Gold Coast economy indicates, profound problems await solution in the Gold Coast. Political institutional transfer, in substance, means the operation of a host of financial schemes, statutory boards, agencies, welfare and housing projects, cooperatives, banks, within the context of parliamentary government. How these complex operations and functions fit into the entire range of political operations must be learned by the Africans themselves. For this, well-trained personnel is needed, with high standards of honesty, efficiency, and adaptability. Yet these operations must be handled within the give-and-take of secular democratic politics. A series of technical tasks must be learned at the same time as a philosophy of government is absorbed.

The present nationalist government of the Gold Coast looks forward to independence in the near future. For the most part the complex administrative jobs of the nation are still being performed by expatriates. Yet rapid Africanization is the goal.

While these processes of institutional transfer occur, the Gold Coast is in a precarious economic position. In their report on the Gold Coast economy, Seers and Ross state in their very first paragraph, "If we were forced to sum up the Gold Coast economy in one word, the word we would choose would be 'Fragile.' "[65]

There are few efficient inflationary checks within the system. Developmental programs mean more income distributed within the economy as laborers, technicians, and others receive sustained income payments. Limited port facilities mean that imported goods cannot enter the Gold Coast in quantities large enough to keep pace with the rising income levels. Prices are already very high for imported items, and an African often must pay considerably higher than a European for a manufactured product. Domestic foodstuffs have risen even higher in prices, proportionately, than imported items.[66]

Inflation is one horn of the dilemma facing the government of the Gold Coast as it seeks to promote institutional transfer and increase living standards in accordance with its objectives. Scarcity is the other horn of the dilemma. Scarcity pertains not only

[65] Seers and Ross, *op.cit.*
[66] *Ibid.*, Appendix D.

to finance, but to skills, expertise, natural resources, and, above all, to lack of a reservoir of social stability. Coupled with scarcity are high costs of production and development. In the building industry, for example, the cost of labor is in fact higher in the Gold Coast than in the United Kingdom, in spite of the lower wage rates prevailing.[67]

If the economy of the Gold Coast is precarious, so is the basic social framework. Any government taking office in such an environment faces acute problems of instability and change. Within an economic milieu of instability and change, as well as of great expectations, stresses and strains upon a new democratic government will be severe.

From an economic point of view the problems of the Gold Coast are similar to those of other underdeveloped countries of the world. As Professor S. H. Frankel puts it: "The real problem confronting the 'underdeveloped' countries of the world is therefore not only how to economize in the use of foreign capital, but how to utilize all capital—the very social indigenous heritage itself—to achieve new goals of social action with the *least* unnecessary social disintegration and disharmony. . . ."[68]

The task in the Gold Coast is to develop new standards of social and economic life within the framework of political democracy. It needs to mobilize all its resources—human, technological, and material. In this respect, political institutional transfer has become part of the apparatus of mobilization.

[67] *A Survey of Some Economic Matters, op.cit.,* p. 12.

[68] Frankel, S. H., *Some Conceptual Aspects of International Economic Development of Underdeveloped Territories,* Essays in International Finance No. 14, May 1953.

CHAPTER 4

THE TRADITIONALLY ORIENTED
SYSTEM

IT WOULD be impossible to comprehend the substance of political institutional transfer without some understanding of the indigenous systems upon which the secular structures impinge. The traditionally oriented system forms the base point from which our analysis will proceed. The materials in Parts I and II have been predominantly descriptive, placing the Gold Coast in both historical and modern settings. Yet so far we have ignored the more complex processes by which institutional transfer is manifest in political behavior, nor have we attempted to account for certain patterns of behavior which appear significant in Gold Coast political development. The attempt is made here, therefore, to indicate some of the crucial aspects of the traditional patterns of political life. By discussion of some of the traditionally oriented systems we hope that some aspects of political institutional transfer will become clear as its ramifications become more obvious.

The particular form of traditional society which we shall deal with here can be called tribal. As used here, "tribal" is a restricted term referring to a particular form of social organization, the basis of which is the recognition and integration of kinship structures as the "nuclear" units of the social system. Tribal society as it existed in parts of the Gold Coast was an amalgamation of family units into larger and larger kinship groupings in which totemic genealogy provided a major social guide.

Stemming from this definition of tribal or traditionally oriented systems is a major hypothesis which shall underlie the succeeding pages of this presentation. This hypothesis will, at present, neither be proved nor disproved within the confines of this study but will remain tentative. Simply stated it is: *some of the structures crucial to the maintenance of the tribal system substantively conflict with and would, if maintained, contravene crucial Western patterns of social and political organization around which a structural reintegration of society is taking place.* Some of these structures deal with functional aspects of chieftaincy for which the political necessity at the central secular level is entirely lacking, and others refer to the behavioral conflicts which ensue, given contradictory patterns of approved social behavior.

It is intended, in a further volume, to expand upon this hypothesis in a more careful and systematic fashion. Within our present reference, however, we shall attempt to support it on an impressionistic basis, often without restating it, and without more careful formulation.

To the extent that the perceptive world of the indigene is intact, alien political structures will operate in a political vacuum. To the extent that this world is modified, a range of possibilities, from apathy to revolution and even to tribal adaptation (such as in Uganda), is possible. What happens depends on the nature of alien contact, on timing in relation to orientational factors, and on the substantive policy elements which have been provided by the colonial officers.

We enter a world in which problems of race, religion, and social structure are intertwined. It is a complex world, and an extremely adult world, which has weathered many storms over many centuries.

Some Aspects of Tribal Systems

We shall not discuss in any detail the various kinds of tribal systems in the Gold Coast. There are many kinds. The Akan system predominates as far as the bulk of the population is concerned, and we will examine the most highly developed of the Akan systems as found in Ashanti. In the Northern Territories one can find the Tallensi having almost no recognizable formal political authority, as we are accustomed to regard it, and in the same general area we find the Dagomba with highly articulated systems of chieftaincy. We find different systems of lineage demarcation, systems of succession, etc., among different tribes. The Krobo along the coast have elective chieftaincy with a patrilineal system. Among the Ewe one finds the least tribal hierarchy among coastal groups and perhaps the strongest sense of Ewe identification. Except, however, in the most backwoods areas, one finds a high level of indigenous sophistication, manners, culture, and belief which is characteristic of the West African ethnic groups. Considered all together, they seem to be a most impressive group of peoples.

The various tribal systems which had currency before and during colonial rule have been here called traditional, to use Weber's term. In examining the traditional systems we shall occupy ourself with three orientational variables. The first we can call *behavioral alternatives*. They are the systems of authority roles, particularly as they are legitimized in various clusters such as the family, the chieftaincy hierarchy, the state council (*oman*), and other membership structures entailing the direct exercise of authority.

The second we can call *goal orientations*. This term refers to the types of expectations which were built into the traditional system by which individuals viewed their future and patterned their activities. We will, of course, be preoccupied with predominantly political goal orientations.

The third we can call *social norms*. This variable refers to the sanctioned aspects of social action. We shall be concerned with the predominantly political aspects of social norms, and particularly with those aspects which refer to the limitations of action placed upon those occupying political roles. As such, the term refers to legitimacy and the nature of extended public support to the activities of those actually occupying authority roles in the system.[1]

Of crucial significance to any appreciation of the political norms encompassed by tribal social structure is their sacred derivation. Political norms, both in the institutionalization of ultimate ends and in control over behavioral limits, are enshrined in tribal religious patterns.

Religion as law or dicta, as well as generalized norms, has certain fairly well-defined maxims. Guides to political and other social behavior are enunciated in proverbs, which we can call "proverb law." These proverbs are usually interpreted by a chief or a priest as part of the living code of behavior.[2] In addition to

[1] Weber, Max, *The Theory of Social and Economic Organization*, translated by Parsons and Henderson, London, 1947, p. 119. Weber says, ". . . a belief in the legitimacy of what has already existed"; and later on, p. 301, he says, "resting on an established belief in the sanctity of immemorial traditions and the legitimacy of the status of those exercising authority under them."

[2] See Moore, Wilburt, *Industrialization and Labor*, Ithaca, 1951, p. 99: "In most primitive and peasant societies the idea and significance of change are strictly limited. In the most general sense, societies are conservative. This means that the notion of progress, or of orderly development, is not commonly encountered. For the group as a whole, the emphasis is upon preservation of the established struc-

the interpretation of such maxims being part of the chief's functions, the public, as well, was quite aware of these maxims. By this means the general behavioral limitations expressed in proverb law conditioned the limits of legitimate authority. The proverbs, in addition, stemmed from the past and often were associated with certain "prophets."

The Structure of Tribal Authority

Most tribal systems have one important element in common, a basic commitment to the past, to time immemorial. The best way to act, in traditional systems, is "the way our fathers have ordained." That which is legitimate is that which has been enshrined in the past.[3]

For those whose orientations are within the traditional focus, the past becomes more and more significant as threats to its continuity and sacredness occur from secular sources. Attacks by other religious forms, particularly Christianity and Islam, have vitiated much of the structure of traditional legitimacy, yet it is still intact in many areas, raising its head even today in the discussions of the modern functions and performances of chiefs, as for example, whether or not they should sit in a parliament as chiefs.[4]

The particular role alternatives which were institutionalized in traditional terms prescribed the limits within which political activity was manifest. Criteria of legitimacy derived from nonsecular sources. An individual could act in a particular fashion, regularized within a role pattern, because it was interpreted as pleasing to the gods or to the ancestors. The actual limits of public sanction and tolerance of role behavior—the limits on *actual* as

---

ture. When shortcomings are recognized, they are likely to be interpreted as departures from received norms, often viewed as having been more honored in past generations. Improvement then consists of going backward. This difference in cultural orientation, stated here as a difference in kind, is actually one of degree. The degree is often so great, however, as to mark a fact of fundamental importance in the spread of industrial patterns." Moore's statement would be applicable to the spread of Western structures of political rule as well.

[3] This is not to say that no changes took place whatever, or that tribal society was structurally static. Changes occurred under varying circumstances, but the ultimate determination of right and wrong insofar as social and interpersonal relations were concerned was very much affected by the historical justification from which legitimacy derived.

[4] See *West Africa*, Nov. 21, 1953, p. 1095, for a brief summary of the Legislative Assembly debate over the place of chiefs in the parliamentary system of the Gold Coast.

compared in their divergence from *ideal* roles—basically had religious boundaries. Religious beliefs often provided the overt limits when role prescriptions were violated, bringing into play tribal control mechanisms. The entire weight of public sanctions, in such cases, would be operative in terms of the maintenance of the prescribed behavioral requirements in order that they be kept orthodox. For a variety of miscellaneous deviations, beheading, both as penalty and as ancestral propitiation, was customary.

The limits to the role of chief, for example, which was a specialized composite of sacred and non-sacred functions, were carefully delineated and watched by the elders and the *asafo* companies. The chief had an elaborate system for sounding out public attitudes about his own activities, and if he was treading on dangerous ground, for finding out the extent of opposition. The chief kept his ear to the ground through the elders and other public officials so that he could be aware of public sentiment. If he went beyond the bounds of his office, he could be, and frequently was, removed or destooled.[5]

RECRUITMENT TO OFFICE

Role alternatives open to tribal members, particularly among the Akan groups, basically depended upon a set of criteria determining availability. That is to say, certain roles were open to individuals who possessed certain qualifications and who met certain requirements. These requirements were particularistic, being based on specialized qualifications due to birth. The basic pattern of recruitment to office, with which we are primarily concerned, is defined largely in terms of three types of criteria listed below. In addition, other factors would come into play in selecting among candidates whose general qualifications were proper. Such other factors varied. For a chief, for example, a good skin was a requirement; blemishes, scars, and other disfigurements were sufficient cause to rule out an otherwise accepta-

---

[5] The "stool" refers to the "soul" or spiritual heart of the group. The stools are carved seats, often of considerable beauty, and regarded as sacred objects. Each family has a stool. The state has a stool. They are the symbols of membership and are ancestral in origin. Particularly among the Ashanti and other Akan groups, the process of removal or destoolment was a fundamental aspect of the political structure. The stool, which contained the soul of the tribe or family or village, as the case may be, was considered violated if the chief went beyond his prescribed limits. Therefore, in order to preserve the public well-being, the chief had to be removed if he violated sanctional limits.

ble candidate. Among Akan and other coastal groups, a chief who suffered such disfigurement subsequent to his election might be removed from office.

The pattern of recruitment to office can be based on the following distinctions: (a) Availability on the basis of lineage. (b) Availability on the basis of membership. (c) Availability on the basis of sex.

Availability on the basis of lineage refers to three major distinctions: (1) slave-non-slave distinction; (2) elder-commoner distinction; (3) royal-non-royal distinction. In terms of these distinctions, the particular lineage descent of an individual determines his qualifications for a position within the tribal role system.

Availability on the basis of membership refers to the clusters of clans which formed territorial units—villages and towns, as well as larger complexes of tribal groupings. Two distinctions here of importance stand out: (1) slave-non-slave distinction; (2) tribe-stranger distinction.

Some slaves will be of other ethnic origin than the group in which they reside if their maternal lineage is of stranger origin. They may be members of a family unit in which they are slaves, without being tribal members.

Almost the same thing may be said for the stranger groups. In many cases, however—and almost every village has its *zongo* or stranger quarter—these strangers are tolerated in an area at the pleasure of the chief. "Stranger populations" refer to non-tribal immigrants residing either temporarily or permanently in a particular tribal area. While these strangers may often intermarry and otherwise become part of the tribal group, there is almost always a clear understanding of the limits on their participation. To the casual observer, the stranger populations may appear indistinguishable from the local population, but regardless of the length of time they or their families have spent in an area it is rare that they lose their separate identity as far as the local population is concerned. Particularly where land is involved, it is always known which elements use land at the pleasure of the chief, i.e., do not have it granted by right of ancestral occupancy in perpetuity, since land belongs ultimately to the tribal rather than stranger ancestors. Where generations of intermarriage have taken place, some stranger elements may become candidates for chieftainship, but almost invariably in such cases a struggle takes place over the legitimacy of the descendant of strangers occupying the stool.

In many cases, however, strangers may play important advisory positions around the stool. They may, for example, become specialized functionaries. Bowditch speaks of the Moors around the *asantehene* who enjoyed special prerogatives and were important in advisory capacities. These Moors, so-called, were mostly Moslems from the Northern Territories, probably Dagomba.

Availability on the basis of sex refers to the types of positions open to either males or females. Formal political roles such as that of chiefs or elders are almost invariably male roles among the Akans, with the one major exception of the role of queen-mother. This job, which has important advisory as well as selection functions, is crucial in the political system of the Akan states. The queen-mother is, for example, the representative of the women. She sits with the chief when he hears cases. She nominates a new chief from among prospective candidates. She is a major power in the community.[6]

These criteria of availability provide the broad guides to offices and roles of many varieties. The most important are those of lineage succession. They reinforce the belief patterns of the unit and are integrated with the structural standards of the society.

Descent among the Akans is reckoned matrilineally.[7] "The theory of procreation held in Ashanti is that a human being is compounded of two principles: the 'blood' (*mogya*) which . . . [is inherited] . . . from the mother, and the other 'spirit' (*ntoro*) which is derived from the father."[8] A man may have a number of wives, but the children take the lineage affiliation of the mother. "Descent is traced through the mother, for the traditional conception is that physical continuity between one generation and another is maintained by the blood which is transmitted through her. A man is therefore legally identified with his maternal kins-

---

[6] Not all Gold Coast tribes had a clearly demarcated political structure in a formal sense. Such groups as the Tallensi had almost no formal political structure at all. See Fortes, M., *Dynamics of Kinship Among the Tallensi, op.cit.*, and "The Political System of the Tallensi of the Northern Territories of the Gold Coast," in Fortes, and Evans-Pritchard, *African Political Systems*, London, 1950.

[7] As is succession to the stool and to land and inheritance. The system is not, however, uniform throughout the Gold Coast.

[8] Busia, K. A., *The Position of the Chief in the Modern Political System of Ashanti*, London, 1951, p. 1.

men: his maternal grandmother and her brothers and sisters, his mother and her brothers and sisters, and his own brothers and sisters. It is his membership within this group that determines his succession to different offices or property, and his jural rights and obligations."[9]

The children of a slave woman and a non-slave man are thus considered slaves, even though part of the family of the father. They are excluded from certain types of roles, and may perform a more restricted area of work. The same holds true for children of strangers: the child belongs to the mother's lineage.

A chief is selected from royal lineages. The successor to the chief can never be his son, among the Akans, but can be his sister's son. The lineage has its mystical totem which cannot be changed and which supports the pattern of matrilineal descent. Blood deriving from the particular totem having mystical powers is ancestral blood. To counter it by behaving outside lineage limits is to commit heresy. The ancestors of the lineage are believed to act instrumentally in favor of the living lineage member if he behaves properly or against him if he does not.

As a sanctional source, therefore, lineage and its religious aspects are an important control feature in traditional society. Where it is obstructed or modified, disturbances usually follow.

An excellent illustration of the integration of procedure, structure, and precedent as embalmed in custom is provided by an area where a slight departure from customary tradition has been tolerated for many years. In one area it is sometimes possible for a royal-stranger—an immigrant who was of royal lineage in his own state—to become a chief. In Wenchi State today, for example, periodic difficulties between rival factions are occasioned by the presence of two royal families which regularly struggle for power. Apparently a member of the royal-stranger family many years ago once saved the Wenchi State from defeat in battle. As a result he was rewarded with chieftainship by the queen-mother, since no Wenchi male royal was available. The precedent became established and the descendants of the royal-stranger family became acceptable candidates for the stool.[10] As a consequence, the state

9 *Ibid.*

10 The example is valid even if the facts are not precise. One of the difficulties involved in research into traditional materials of the Gold Coast is the amount of misinformation carefully given by Africans to the research worker so that the genuine tradition of the tribe will not be known by outsiders. The genuine tradition

is riddled with intrigue, factionalism, and even violence, which in this particular case is significant in the politics of the latter-day Gold Coast. The history of the state is a history of disputes over legitimacy.

The entire social structure is divided by lineage, membership, and sex into available groups of individuals playing significant roles in the authority system. The divisions reinforce the authority structures. They provide the links with authority of the past, the sources of legitimate activity.

THE POLITICAL SIGNIFICANCE OF THE FAMILY

Westermann remarks that: "The tribe is in many parts of Africa the typical political unit. As an agglomeration of groups and individuals, not necessarily related, it forms a cultural and political unity through living in a common territory, having a common leader, one language, and similar customs and usages. In West Africa a tribe will often consist of three elements: the group which migrated to the district; the original inhabitants of that district; and later migrants composed of offshoots from other groups. Though each of the component parts may be conscious of its origin, they have all been welded together into a close union. The tribe is ruled by a chief, and each individual settlement by a sub-chief who is dependent on the chief in a greater or lesser degree."[11]

However, "tribe" in this context does not necessarily involve a political entity, a mistake which many, including Westermann, make. Essentially, the tribe is an ethnic group in the Gold Coast, not necessarily acting as a single social or political unit, although having similarity of custom. Some tribes are composed of a number of states, each independent of the other. For some groups, tribe is a membership unit having no sovereignty implications, but rather ethnic congruity. Within this structure, the family is a basis for ethnic identification. Among the most organized tribes in the Gold Coast, the Ashanti, it is impossible to gain an adequate

---

may have important consequences for tribal policy if known by an outsider, and therefore the responsibility of the informant to his tribe is paramount. The present *wenchihene* states the above story to be true. The royal family not occupying the stool denies the story, as they must, for to admit it would be damaging to their case. See below for a fuller discussion of the Wenchi dispute, Chapter 12.

[11] Westermann, Diedrich, *The African Today and Tomorrow*, London, 1949, p. 72.

picture of tribal social and political organization without an examination of family structure.

The impact of the family, as an extended unit, upon present secular government in the Gold Coast is immense. Its paramountcy in the formation of tribal political role prescriptions is genuine. It was the basis for continuing lineage, and as such a crucial social unit. Most important of all, perhaps, is the fact that in traditional society, particularly in Ashanti, tribal roles were family roles writ large. As the nuclear social unit within a system of ritualized politics, the family was the structural rock on which, ultimately, the state stood or fell. It was the center in which the spirit male and blood female were manifested in the procreation and perpetuation of the social unit. Out of this, the lineage was maintained, the social organization reinforced, and the solidarity of the tribal unit protected.

Of immediate political interest, however, is the fact that the lineage mythology—the history and foundation of the lineage which gave it its special qualities in kinship, such as royal or non-royal qualities—is a directly historical mythology. The genealogy of the lineage, in regard to its ultimate origin, is the history of the foundation of the village, or the clan, or the state, or the tribe itself.

In many respects Aristotle's concepts of the ever-larger units of social organization, merging finally to embrace the city state, is perhaps more appropriate here than anywhere else.[12] According to Rattray, the family unit was the concrete membership basis of political organization, at least among the Akans. As we have indicated, the Akans had migrated to the Gold Coast in the not very distant past. The migrations by family and clan to various new territorial areas gave specific functions of control and decision-making to the head of the family.[13]

Decisions affecting the family were made according to certain fixed procedures. The responsibility and authority of the head of the family was tempered by the significant role played by the mother, and the general interpretations of ancestral obligations

[12] See Aristotle's *Politics*, Book I.

[13] Family refers to extended family, the larger kinship unit in which nuclear relational ties govern the economic, social, and political orientations of the members, who include grandparents, parents, children (regardless of lineage), aunts, maternal uncles, nieces, and nephews.

by which moral restrictions on the father's or headman's authority were sanctified.

In the migrations into the territory presently occupied by the various tribes of the Gold Coast, the head of the family was responsible for major decisions. He led his family to an area and occupied the land. He gave offerings to the gods. He allocated the lands to the several members of the family. He prepared for their defense and their well-being.

When new immigration brought additional families into his area, he was responsible for further allocating land, adjudicating disputes, pouring libation, and acting as a kind of priest. The family head combined the temporal and spiritual "swords" in such fashion that there was no empirical distinction between them.

As more and more families came to settle on the site of the first settlements, the job of the father became that of headman. With further increases in migration his job became more complex. Other family heads in charge of their own clan groups were ranged under his authority, and responsible to him, since his priorities of leadership derived from the original occupancy of land. As larger social units consisting of groups of families, or clans, accrued to the settler family and its descendants, the senior family headman became a sort of chief (*odikro*), whose authority extended to custodianship over land held by clan members not immediately related to him. He dispensed land to newcomers. His dispensation was more or less final, insofar as these acts were in fact the creation of ancestral lands. The descendants of the first recipients observed the original terms of the contract.

The relationships between members of the group, based in part on the grants of land, became permanently defined, with the descendant of the early *odikro* now deriving from a royal-lineage, as the only proper candidate for local chieftainship.

The ancestral relationship was to a large extent religiously static. The day-to-day relations between descendants mirrored the ancestral network of relationships.

What was enshrined in the past became the proper and compulsory source of sanctioned behavior in the descendants. The *odikro* maintained his authority in part as a matrilineal descendant of the *odikro* ancestors, i.e., by the blood ties as distinguished by the members, whose job was publicly sanctioned as one of trusteeship or custodianship over the land and the welfare of the members. The maintenance of this essentially family system was in fact a family matter. The mother or grandmother was revered as the repository of ancestral lore, and had an honored place among the family members. It was often the mother or grand-mother whose knowledge of the proverbs and history of the family or the clan made possible effective adjudication by the *odikro* of disputes. Her function in the family as historian as well as her control over the socialization of the young in accord-ance with tribal precepts formed the nucleus for the later official position of queen-mother, among the Ashanti.

According to Rattray, "The family was a corporation; action and even thought were corporate affairs. . . . The routine, the half-formulated rules binding the individuals in the family, rules relating to property, inheritance, ownership of land, collection of family contributions, became the customary laws governing the larger group."[14]

In regard to the traditional system of the Gold Coast, particu-larly amongst the Akans, the family was a central factor of social and political organization. The traditional family pattern of rights and obligations, which by its defined relations perpetuated on the one hand the defined legitimized use of authority, and on the other hand the rules by which authority could be handed down, played its crucial role in the maintenance of traditional society.

The criteria of availability were thus first formulated and later maintained at this most local level, the family, where the religious and social indoctrination of individuals is closely wrapped up in the affectual and relational processes of daily living. The family was a social and administrative unit, differentiated in functional roles. The father or headman was responsible for the general well-being of the group. His slave wives were responsible for the cook-ing or the farming. His non-slave wives were responsible for taking care of the children.[15] The aged, having a place of honor, were the transmitters of myth and custom and in many ways arbi-ters of proper conduct even for the headman.

The family as a unit was a personalized unity of a high degree of solidarity, with slave members and non-slave members, stran-gers and non-strangers, with as many lineages as the father had

---

[14] See Rattray, *Ashanti Law*, *op.cit.*, p. 62.
[15] Insofar as socialization and education were concerned.

wives, plus those of the sons and their maternal derivations. The family, essentially, was the foundation of political organization. It had its own priorities of obligation and responsibility. It had its own system of social security. Its legal codes were those of the tribe, binding the members by coercion as well as custom at this most local and intimate level of social life.

THE POLITICAL SIGNIFICANCE OF THE VILLAGE

According to Rattray, the extension of authority beyond its most local sources occurred as "various family groups, in course of time, came under the head of one particular family, to whom in all important matters, the appeals were made. This process of amalgamation went on in independent localities, and in this manner numerous territorial divisions grew up under different heads, independent and often rivals of one another."[16]

In these larger units, the network of kinship formed the foundation of formalized political structures. In the village, organization was essentially on the basis of clusters of families or clans. These clans, whose lineages often cut across clan limits, had their own stools. They were political as well as social units. Their representatives, or headmen, performed the functions of advisors to the *odikro*.

The members participated in ritual ceremonies around their own stool, but also around the stool of the *odikro*. The stool of the *odikro* was the symbol of group solidarity and the expression of common membership and affiliation.

The stools embodied the spirits of the ancestors. In fact, they are usually carved wooden affairs with a seat shaped in the form of a slight crescent, and with no back. No one sits on these stools, and at various times of the year on ritual occasions a sheep or rooster is sacrificed, and the blood from its slashed throat allowed to run over the stool.

The stools embody the spirits of the ancestors and are the living symbols of their presence. To be made a chief is to occupy the stool. The stool signifies the closeness between living and dead, between land and law (all land is stool land), and between law and behavior. In traditional Ashanti, acts of sacrifice were acts of propitiation and grace, expressed in their most elaborate form in human decapitation.

---

[16] Rattray, *Ashanti Law, op.cit.*, p. 63.

The clusters of clan stools around the village both expressed an organizational membership and defined both loyalty and functions. The local units in their separateness had specialized obligations, usually semi-military, which jointly made village life a corporate enterprise.

Orientational horizons were narrow and immediate. There was little conception of a larger public and impersonal membership affiliation, although an awareness of tribal identity was derived from totemic and mythological history.

Such affairs as the regulation of demand, the allocation of scarce means, and the control of deviant behavior and other control factors were local matters. The exercise of authority was watched at every turn for violations of norms, violations of ancestral obligations, in other words, violations of customary law.

In the village, groups of commoners formed semi-military companies (*asafo* companies) who would protect the stool against enemies within and without the village. They would safeguard the interests of the village against chiefs or *odikro* who were going beyond the limits of their powers, participating as the members of the corporate unit in the determination of decisions and in the definition of a proper course of activity. They could, through the elders, have a chief removed (destooled).

If the family was the nuclear unit of social life, the village was the indigenous corporate entity, particularly in Ashanti. It remains to this day the primary organizational unit where many issues pertaining to shifts in legitimized authority are worked out, sometimes in a climate of bitterness and anguish.

THE TERRITORIAL DIVISION

As migrations from larger to smaller villages occurred, the affiliations of the newly founded villages and their clans were maintained with the older ones. The lineage affiliations of members formed strong ties, and the *odikro*, gradually elevated to a more formalized status of chieftaincy, could effectually intervene in matters affecting the affairs of more than one village.

As these new centers grew, the new headman became, in turn, an *odikro*. The *odikro* of the greatly enlarged central village, which provided the source of migration to newer settlements and villages, in turn became a chief. Usually the main village was the affiliational center for these smaller and newer villages, gaining in economic stature as a market center and in symbolic significance as a place of origin.

Sometimes the old village declined in size, but remained the custodian of the stool. When this process of expansion by village reached a point where it could no longer go farther and was stabilized by wars with other groups pushing out from other central villages, a defined unit was established; all members had bonds to the central stool, the unit being independent of any other unit. In Ashanti, where this process occurred in an elaborate form, the stabilization unit has been called the territorial division.

In Ashanti, in particular, the process evolved until there were a number of fairly large divisions, each independent of the other and each with a network of authority extending down to the feeder villages.

The warfare which occurred during the latter stages of this process had a profound effect on the social and political structure emerging along with territorial definition. The division changed from a kinship group having historical bonds to a military-administrative formation, with a system of formalized offices carrying more specialized responsibilities and military functions. A separation was recognized between civil, military, and religious functions, although a chief in his turn would be involved in all three.

The various sub-chiefs and *odikro* in the division formed a hierarchical pattern of offices and responsibilities. The sub-chiefs, along with other military personnel such as classificatory brothers of the chief and important advisors, were members of the divisional council.[17] The chief became known as the *omanhene* or head of the council, among the Ashanti.

Membership of the council was therefore composed of representatives from village units having lineage propriety deriving from original occupancy as intermediate or local royals, and having been given specialized but diffuse functions of office in divisional administration, with specific military obligations and places in military formations—"right wing" or "left wing" etc., each with a responsibility to both the subordinate and the superordinate authority. All were liable to removal. All, when sitting

17 In Ashanti these divisions became part of the Confederacy. However, they are in Gold Coast terms separate states. We shall use division when referring to states which are members of a confederacy. Both signify independence, with a division usually part of a federalized system.

on the council, spoke for their units whether village or division in the case of the *omanhene*. At these divisional or state council meetings, the members, sitting as chiefs, had their elders behind them in a group, with other members of the village scattered behind the elders. No statement by any member of the council, therefore, could be taken without public knowledge by his own unit, and the elders were required to give their assent to any statements made by their chief, who, as a divisional sub-chief, was participating in the council. In these respects the divisional structure was a large-scale kind of democracy, if public participation and the responsibility of the authority to the electorate is any guide.

The *omanhene* or paramount chief of the state or division, while rigidly limited in his prerogatives, was, within these limits, an autocrat. Indeed, it was expected that a chief should act as autocrat and as a fierce and terrible fellow. Fear of the chief appeared to be a major element in social control.

Within a certain sphere each individual member, in addition to the chief, had his sphere of absolute inviolability. For, while the process of consultation and democracy was rigidly enforced, the chief's sphere of autocracy could often extend to capriciousness, and frequently was manifested in human sacrifice. "The group over which he is head is a democracy, but a democracy very different from those of modern Europe. In one sense it is a communistic body, yet in another the rights of each unit to individual enjoyment of property are absolute during his actual enjoyment thereof."[18]

The chief as custodian over land was by no means the owner of land. Ownership was communal-ancestral.[19] He had officials to watch over the treasure of the stool. He used the hierarchy to obtain certain revenues which were utilized for stool purposes. He could not sell land, however, as a source of revenue.

Rather, revenues were received in the form of court fines, ritual dues, and gifts, levies, as well as customary payments by sub-chiefs as they expressed their allegiance or sought favor at the court. The treasury belonged to the divisional stool. Its funds were used for express purposes, rigidly defined. Strangers were often expected to pay a certain portion of their income derived from the

---

[18] Rattray, *Ashanti Law, op.cit.*, p. 63.

[19] The chief kept only his own property, that which he possessed prior to his chieftainship.

land which they were allowed to use, and each family reserved portions of their income to the stool.

The division was in more recent times essentially a military unit. The well-being of the villages and the families was tied up with its fortunes. It was the most inclusive integrated authority system in which by blood and by immediate history members were bound together. Ultimately, in Ashanti these divisions were formed into a confederacy, but even in confederation the primary prerogatives of the division were maintained. They were independent except in certain matters affecting two divisions or more, where the *asantehene* could intervene, or in war, when they occupied positions in the confederacy armies. It was to the division that national loyalty was given by members. The division was the most effective expression of commonality. There is little question, however, but that common Ashanti identification contained an idea of racial supremacy.

Family, clan, village, and state or territorial division are the crucial concrete membership structures of Ashanti tribal groupings in the Gold Coast. Each of these units represents a limited range of expressed authority, integrated into a decentralized pattern of checks and balances. Within each of these units, however, chiefs, *odikro*, and headmen had their clear prerogatives in the exercise of their authority.

SOCIAL DIFFERENTIATION

Compared to many non-Western systems, Gold Coast social organization in the south and central areas was, for the most part, open even though rigidly circumscribed. Slaves were part of the family. Denied certain forms of eligibility to full membership in the social unit—such as being disbarred from access to chieftainship—they often achieved positions of importance. Moreover, they were protected by the same norms which governed the behavior of all.

For non-slaves, depending upon their kinship and lineage relationships, a wide range of subsidiary and other posts were available if chosen. There was little rigid class structure, and even lineage carried few invidious connotations, except in regard to certain types of work. For example, the Ashanti non-slave held manual labor in contempt as work for slaves.

In spite of this open quality, manifested particularly in relationships between members, certain cognitive factors affected interpersonal relationships. According to Rattray, in spite of this comparatively free social group, ". . . in Ashanti, a condition of voluntary servitude was the essential basis of the whole social system. In that country there existed no person or thing without a master or owner."[20] What appears to be, superficially, a highly differentiated system of status groups and even classes (except for the bottom class of slaves) was more like the highly developed system of obligations in the family.

It is clear that any notion of class distinction was at best rudimentary and not a recognizable category perceived by members. Very little invidiousness appeared to be involved in the types of relations between people belonging to the same family, clan, village, or divisional unit, although unit parochialism often appeared. Rather, the relations between people were in some respects sacred as enshrined in ancestral history. Not social onus but individual restraint in crucial features of tribal life seemed to be the major supporting factors which made reciprocal relations self-sustaining. This fact perhaps provides some basis for an understanding of the disastrous consequences of even slight contacts with Western culture. Self-restraints seemed to be most amenable to cultural seduction.

Class distinction, then, was rudimentary. The limited division of labor, and consequent social differentiation by economic class, was of only slight relevance. Almost everyone did roughly the same kind of work. There were artisans and farmers, weavers and armorers, etc. An important man might have more slaves than someone else, but his basic livelihood was roughly limited to farming or hunting or weaving or blacksmithing or drumming. More crucial distinctions derived from affiliation to the social unit, particularly on a local level, which formed the basis of divisional or state association. Particularly, as has been indicated, in divisional association or membership, local patriotism was strongly manifested. The ritual history of the division was a repetition of its glories and its achievements. Any ignominies were passed over or attributed to malevolent spirits. A formalized loyalty was created which helped to support social discipline.[21]

---

[20] Rattray, *Ashanti Law, op.cit.*, p. 34.
[21] Again, tied to the glorification and deification of the ancestors.

Divisional solidarity manifested itself at the expense of other divisions.[22] Even the bottom class of slaves participated, as did strangers, in the glory of their association with the local units.

Status groupings on the basis of lineage and more formalized roles carried certain privileges. Yet status did not involve a personal set of qualities involving superiority or inferiority, but rather impersonal relationships having ritual antecedents which all members were obliged to sustain. Emotional feeling ran high if participants attempted to break out of this social pattern.

[22] It is noteworthy that in the public recitation of the history of the division or tribe at ceremonial occasions, the defeat and death of a chief in combat, or major losses suffered, are loosely touched upon, passed over entirely, or divine intervention is invoked to explain an embarrassing historical point. The influence of the ancestors is involved, since to embarrass them is not only to cast a negative reflection upon them but possibly to invoke their wrath as well.

CHAPTER 5

POLITICAL ORGANIZATION
AMONG THE AKANS

IN SPEAKING of tribal political organization, we shall use the Ashanti system for discussion purposes. While this is by no means the only form of political organization, it is perhaps the most highly developed of those found in the Gold Coast. Its component features are useful for the purpose of this study. In addition, more anthropological materials of a high standard are available for Ashanti than for any other highly organized ethnic group in the Gold Coast.

One of the basic differences between the primitive family units[1] and those which subsequently developed was the attribution of more specific functions and consequently the appearance of membership structures devoted to the allocation and use of power and responsibility. As the tribal system became more elaborate, the basic family model as a division of authority was modified in: (1) the separation of individual from office, (2) the formalization of access to power, (3) the formalization of remedial measures against the misuse of power, and (4) the formalization of the consultative and decision-making processes.

Ultimately, with the development of Ashanti suzerainty over a large part of the Gold Coast, this system grew in size into a dominating bureaucracy, more like a legitimized holding company of partially independent divisions than like a formal kingdom. Yet at the center a very real monopoly of power was held by the paramount chief of Ashanti, the *asantehene*, whose central position of monarchy was as absolute as was consonant with custom and the maintenance of public support. A highly differentiated system of councils, a bureaucracy, and a court surrounded the Golden Stool, the symbol of Ashanti nationhood. We shall examine the emergence of the Ashanti system in some detail.

---

[1] We use the word "primitive" here to refer to an undeveloped state or condition of the family as a political unit.

The Ashanti Confederacy

Rattray divides the history of the Ashanti Confederacy into two historical and structural epochs. The first is the pre-Feyiase period.[2]

The pre-Feyiase period refers to the days of emerging political structure based on the family system and the migrations under its aegis. The first migrant families to the Gold Coast became the "first" political families. The subsequent migrants made themselves subordinate to the first family for the purposes of government. Those from different tribes at the source areas—having totally different tribal origins, such as the Dagomba or Moshi or Wala—lived in a *zongo* or stranger area. These, as we have indicated, were not able fully to participate in the affairs of the village or other social unit, particularly those pertaining to ethnic integrity, such as the election of a new chief. Rather, they owed their ultimate allegiance elsewhere, and would often return to their ancestral villages when death approached.

A hierarchy of chiefs and their councils developed, each having certain clear-cut prerogatives over the immediately affiliatory lesser chiefs. Each had certain limits of power. Each had a rank. The lines of authority went through clan and lineage. A small village chief, of a different clan group from that of a subdivisional chief, did not owe allegiance and deference to him. Rank was meaningful in relation to kinship and village association. The village chief would owe obligation to a subdivisional chief. But no other subdivisional chief, in the formal course of affairs, had authority over him. A system of authorities, each having certain independent qualifications, was the rule.

At each level of the administrative hierarchy, from family to division, every governing unit was composed of a headman or chief, and the lineage elders or senior headmen, depending on the rank order of the unit, the latter acting as a council. In both pre- and post-Feyiase periods, all matters of public interest were dealt with by the chief in council, and unilateral action was barred to him. As Busia indicates:

"Often they [chief and elders] discussed matters of a general nature: the prospects of the yam harvest, the meat supply, the

---

[2] Feyiase is the name of a battle in which the Ashanti emerged victorious and out of which the temporary alliance of independent divisions became a permanent association under the *asantehene*.

state of the paths and roads, whether the court should sit that day or not. So important were these informal meetings for the administration of the division that it was obligatory for every elder to call at the chief's house every morning 'to greet the chief.' Failure to do so without explanation was regarded as disaffection towards the chief. The first sign of disaffection on the part of an elder was his failure to go to the chief's house in the morning. A chief whose elders relaxed in this duty, or abstained from going to his house in the morning, surmised that there was something brewing against him, or that the elders were displeased with him. If at a morning meeting it was decided that no court or other business would be done during the day, the elders went and worked on their farms, or visited one of the villages directly under them.

"If other meetings were necessary in addition to the morning meetings to discuss matters of importance, the chief sent a messenger to call the elders, usually in the evenings, after the day's work had been done. The chief had to keep strictly the injunction that he was to act only on the advice of his elders. There were rare occasions, however, when in an emergency, he could act on his own initiative."[3]

The highest set of internal authorities was at the apex of the affiliatory hierarchy. The heads of these hierarchies, together with the paramount chief, formed a major part of the state council. These same kinship structural groups formed various parts of the state armies. The military formations preserved the solidary identifications of each of the sub-units in battle. Their performances reflected upon their ancestors. To lose a battle, or suffer defeat or disgrace, was to fail as an individual leader. Captains of military formations would often blow themselves up on a keg of gunpowder, rather than contribute to the disgrace of the stool.

In the pre-Feyiase period, the Ashanti tribe consisted of a number of independent states, or divisions, each sovereign. These Ashanti divisions—Kumasi, Mampon, Dumawu, Offinsu, Juaben, and Assumegya—were often linked in voluntary informal alliance against other states. The Confederacy was founded when the Kumasi Division achieved paramountcy over the other divisions. The paramount chief of Kumasi, in addition to his functions

3 Busia, *Position of the Chief, op.cit.,* pp. 15-16.

as a divisional chief (*kumasihene*) became paramount chief of Ashanti (*asantehene*).

The particular circumstances surrounding the formation of the Ashanti Confederacy reveal a good bit of the myth and history found in Gold Coast traditional lore. It is perhaps worth while spelling out the formation of the Confederacy in some detail since it does indicate the formation and institutionalization of certain traditional norms which survive to this day in Ashanti custom.

The Confederacy began with a temporary defensive Ashanti alliance against an invading state, Denkyera. The war, which broke out in 1699,[4] saw victory for the Ashanti at the battle of Feyiase. It was a particularly significant victory since a curious series of events had preceded success. An alliance between Osei Tutu, the *kumasihene*, and Anokye, a priest, played an important preliminary part. Since the five most powerful chiefs of the Ashanti Divisions were of the same "family" as Osei Tutu, they already had certain types of social obligations towards one another. This made possible the frequent, albeit temporary, alliances of the past. In order to formalize their unity, Anokye "made some 'medicine' mixed it with palm wine, and all the Ashanti chiefs drank it; under his instructions, Osei Tutu made new swords for his army officers, and each swore to fight to the end."[5]

Shortly thereafter, in Kumasi, Anokye "brought down from the sky, with darkness and thunder, and in a thick cloud of white dust, a wooden stool adorned with gold, which floated to earth and alighted gently on Osei Tutu's knees. This stool, Anokye announced, contained the spirit of the whole Ashanti nation, and all its strength and bravery depended on the safety of the stool."[6]

[4] Ward, *op.cit.*, p. 114.

[5] *Ibid.*, p. 111. Osei Tutu got into trouble with the *denkyerahene* because of intrigues with the latter's sister. When she became pregnant he had to flee to Akwamu country. In Akwamu Osei Tutu became friends with a priest, Kwame Frimpon Anokye, who returned to Ashanti with Osei Tutu after the death of the uncle, Obiri Yeboa. It is commonly supposed that Anokye had magical powers which made it possible for the Ashanti Confederacy to be formed. Since the Ashanti were split at the time Osei Tutu assumed office, the amalgamation of the chiefs of Ashanti was an important prerequisite of Ashanti power. Five of the most powerful chiefs were of the same *abusua* or blood clan. The others were united by Anokye's persuasion, and by the successful use of myth and magic to unite everyone behind a common stool which was the soul of the nation. The Golden Stool, as it was called, was supposed to contain the spirit and strength of the Ashanti Confederacy. See Rattray, *Ashanti Law, op.cit.*, pp. 272-274.

[6] Ward, *op.cit.*, p. 112.

Shortly thereafter the war with Denkyera ended in victory for the Ashanti. The Golden Stool became enshrined as the most sacred object of the Ashanti peoples. All Ashanti chiefs owed their allegiance to it, and therefore to the *asantehene.*[7]

This myth, essentially, is a main "derivation of legitimacy" for the Ashanti Confederation. Having its non-empirical as well as its historical aspects, to deny it is to deny the traditional religion as well. As a result of this series of events the foundations of a national solidarity emerged.

The development of the state was, as we have indicated, at least partially due to military operations as grave conflicts arose in the period of expansion. Some of the sub-chiefs were directly military in function. Such a sub-chief would be militarily supreme within the limits of his office and as far as his subordinates were concerned. The top of the hierarchy was controlled by the paramount chief.

When the Confederacy was established, subsequent to the remarkable events mentioned above, certain classificatory relatives of the new *asantehene* were elevated to important positions on the council and in the administrative system, in addition to the division chiefs of the member divisions of the Confederacy. The family and village units, as extended in migration, now became territorially defined units rather than units defined by kinship.[8]

The divisional chiefs maintained their independent authority in most domestic matters, but in military and certain judicial functions they were responsible to the Ashanti Confederacy council as well. In military matters the divisional chiefs formed a part of the *asantehene's* armies, and in domestic matters formed a part of the Confederacy council.

The resulting system was a confederation. The issues of state's rights were by no means unknown to the Ashanti. Different divisions often had to be rallied against a rebel, and civil war was common. Alliances were often made between subordinate divisions and other states seeking to destroy Ashanti power.

It is important to remember that the Confederacy always contained a large proportion of dissenters. These, particularly members who had been conquered by the Ashanti, were kept in the

---

[7] For a study of the religious and political significance of the Golden Stool, see Smith, Edwin, *The Golden Stool*, London, 1927.

[8] Rattray, *Ashanti Law, op.cit.*, p. 80.

Confederacy by the threat of force. Secessionist movements were generally incipient. Hostility to the Confederacy by some members, aggravated by British restoration of the *asantehene* in 1935, was an important factor in the rise of nationalist leaders who later repudiated both the Confederacy and the colonial government.

The System of Political Roles

A typical Ashanti Division is composed of a hierarchy of positions. In addition to the divisional chief and the queen-mother, there are two senior sub-chiefs.[9] The two are considered *primus inter pares*; the *kontihene*, and the *akwamuhene*. Among the others, the *adontenhene* is the commander of the main body of troops. The *nifahene* commands the right wing of the army. The *benkumhene* leads the left wing. The *kyidomhene* is a leader of the rearguard. The *abusuahene* is head of the chief's lineage. The *ankobiahene* was responsible for the safety and security of the state. There were several *akyeame* or spokesmen for the chief. These were almost all lineage posts, the occupants being the heads of the lineages.[10]

The elders in any Ashanti community, whether village, subdivision, or division, are essentially the same. They comprise the *abusuatiri* of the principal family groups, with the addition of a few other persons whose ancestors, either by their prowess in war or their wisdom as councillors, have gained distinction.[11]

In addition to the elders there is a list of minor functionaries attached to the household. Rattray lists these as spokesmen, stool carriers, drummers, horn blowers, umbrella carriers, caretakers of the royal mausoleum, bath attendants, chief's soul washers, elephant-tail switchers, fan bearers, cooks, hammock carriers, floor polishers, shield bearers, minstrels, and executioners.[12]

The Functions of the Chief

We can define the functions of chieftainship as follows:

1. *Sanctional source.* This refers to the legitimacy stemming

[9] These sub-chiefs are really elders. In time of war they are captains.
[10] See Rattray, *Ashanti Law, op.cit.*, p. 163, and Busia, *Position of the Chief, op.cit.*, pp. 18-19.
[11] Matson, J. N., *A Digest of the Minutes of the Ashanti Confederacy Council from 1935 to 1949 and a Revised Edition of Warrington's Notes on Ashanti Custom*, Cape Coast (n.d.), p. 57.
[12] Rattray, *Ashanti Law, op.cit.*, p. 91.

from the chief, who as a trustee for the ancestors is a semi-deified figure who prescribes norms of behavior.

2. *Symbolic referent.* The chief is the central orientational symbol of tribal unity, continuity, and integration. When, for example, the *asantehene* was exiled, the Ashanti Confederacy not only broke apart but was marked by widespread apathy.

3. *Integrational integer.* The chief serves as the chief decision-maker, not only exerting control but dissolving conflict. His authority is taken as final.

4. *Sub-ethnic or ethnic definition.* The chief serves as the his-torical membership totem representative in which the ties of lineage, blood, clan, as expressed in social organization, have historical genealogical reference from the qualifications of the chief, and membership definition deriving thereto.

These functions are expressed in the following structures as regards Ashanti:

1. *Military*: expressed in formal organizational powers in the relationship of lineage affiliation to military formations, defining subordinate status for functional purposes of members of the unit.

2. *Religious*: expressed in the theocratic functions displayed in almost every aspect of his authority, whether in pouring libation before an offering to the gods, or the death penalty for shoving a chief, or in the expression of his decisions.

3. *Legal*: the chief maintains his court for the adjudication of disputes on formal grounds, but is the advisor and consultant on all aspects of human affairs.

4. *Administrative*: the expression of his authority is part of a far-reaching network of communications, information, orders, and subordinate authority.

5. *Trusteeship*: or custodianship manifested in his responsibility over land use and land disposal, as well as for the general well-being of his people.

These structures are manifested in a variety of social acts, and in a variety of concrete membership structures, which may involve sitting in court, sacrificing a sheep, leading a military campaign, etc. The network is complex between, for example, residual trustee-ship over land from which specific powers of economic allocation derive. Military capacities provide formal organization powers under certain circumstances, manifested in concrete military for-mation. The royal lineage provides non-empirical sources of authority demanding deference, reinforcing the authority of adjudicatory performances, such decisions that are made being considered binding upon the members.

The authority of the chief, expressed in the functions listed above, is a combination of symbolic and instrumental derivatives, closely linked with history.

In addition, the chief has a monopoly of age; that is to say, in a system where age provides certain prerogatives, the chief is called *nana* or grandfather. This is both a token of his family-inspired role and a symbol by which the equation between age and wisdom can be conferred on him, regardless of his actual age. The patriarchal title is thus conferred even though the chief may be a young man.

The chief plays the central role in most of the religious ceremonies of the division or the village. He pours the libation and whispers the incantations over the sacrifice to the gods. He is the living link with the dead.

Since chieftainship developed out of the family system in which the father played both advisory and adjudicative roles, as the number of social units under his jurisdiction increased, his judicial responsibilities became more formalized. A host of "proverb norms" were available from which decisions could be derived. They were, in effect, a publicly recognized standard for behavior.

On various mornings, the chief would sit in court and hear cases along with his elders and the queen-mother. Cases of destoolment often came before him, as well as land disputes, theft, adultery, crimes against oath (perjury), etc.

As the descendant of the *odikro* who had allocated lands, the chief was the responsible custodian of all stool property. In collaboration with his council, he could revoke the tenancy of all unworked land.[13] Much of his constitutional position was maintained through the formation of part of the chief's role as derived from land custodianship.

[13] The procedure essentially was that land could be granted to a family, in perpetuity so long as it was used, but ultimate ownership was ancestral. The long and difficult pattern of land disputes was one of the major judicial concerns of the chief. Land tenure is closely linked with his whole concept of office. To discuss land tenure is to discuss the constitutional position of the chief.

For a thorough discussion of this, see the *Committee on the Tenure of Land in West African Colonies and Protectorates*, Minutes of Evidence, Colonial Office, 1916.

The concrete manifestations of the chief's traditional authority is perhaps best expressed by Ellis:

"The king, or head chief of each tribe, is the suzerain lord over all the other chiefs of the tribe, and receives tribute from, and exercises certain rights over them. His dealings are generally only with the chiefs, who, in turn, exercise authority over the sub-chiefs and head-men of the districts under their jurisdiction. Five, six, or more villages are grouped under the jurisdiction of a town, where a chief resides and the chiefs of all such towns in the territory of the tribe are under the direct authority of the king of the tribe. The chiefs have the ablebodied men of their towns organized for war purposes into what are called town companies, the captains of which are under the direct authority of the chiefs; and in time of war each chief takes the field in person with his own contingent. Each chief has his own local court, but in any matter of importance which concerns the whole tribe, the king sits in court with all his chiefs, in the open air, and in the presence of the people. . . .

"The king of the tribe is not by any means an absolute monarch possessed of unlimited power, and he is always controlled to a certain extent by the chiefs. The king alone cannot make peace or war nor can he enter into negotiations or treaties which concern the interests of the whole tribe, without the consent of the chiefs."[14]

Yet, in spite of the controls upon him, the chief was made to appear an autocrat. This was an expression of functions in the various structural manifestations in the system. Ellis, for example, says that the chief's power was maintained by sheer terror. Rattray perhaps indicates a more subtle appreciation:

"To all outward appearance and to superficial observers, who included the populace, the chief was an autocrat. In reality every move and command which appeared to emanate from his mouth had been discussed in private and had previously been agreed upon by his councillors, to whom everyone in the tribe had access, and to whom popular opinion on any subject was made known. Such at any rate was the ideal; serious departure from the custom would eventually lead to destoolment. Although nominally the Ashanti Constitution was intended to appear to be autocratic, in

---

[14] Ellis, A. B., *The Tshi-Speaking Peoples of the Gold Coast of West Africa*, London, 1887, p. 275.

correct practice it was democratic to a degree. The person of a chief was, moreover, invested with sanctity just so long as he sat upon the stool of his dead ancestors. This is the reason why there was a reaction the moment a chief was destooled; when that happened, insults, abuse, and even personal violence were used."[15]

The chief was thus a sanctified figure who was the nerve center of the tribe. His authority, deriving from the past, coursed through the blood in his veins and was made manifest by election to office. The lineage line gave authenticity to the ancestral heritage. Each new installation of the chief was a reinforcement and expression of solidarity. Each ceremony over a new chief was in effect a social contract.

The chief, in this view, represented the crucial political unit in Akan organization. It is held here that the chieftaincy as a sanctional source, a symbolic referent, an integrational integer, and for sub-ethnic and ethnic definition, represents the orientational base out of which the charismatic authority of Nkrumah, the present prime minister of the Gold Coast, has developed. Without an understanding of the functional requisites of Gold Coast chieftaincy, the present role of Nkrumah in political institutional transfer cannot be fully comprehended. We shall return to this further.

The Queen-Mother

The queen-mother, according to Busia, is described as the "mother" of the chief, although most often she is his sister, or the sister of his maternal uncle. It is the responsibility of the queen-mother to advise the chief. She has the freedom to scold him and to deal with him as no one else can. Busia indicates that two queen-mothers in the state of Juaben were destooled for not advising the chief well.

The queen-mother selects or nominates the candidate to fill a vacant stool. "As the 'mother' of the members of the royal lineage she is regarded as the authority on the kinship relations of the lineage and therefore, questions as to whether or not any candidate possesses a legitimate kin-right to the stool are referred to her."[16]

The queen-mother is in charge of the women of the village or

[15] Rattray, *Ashanti Law, op.cit.,* p. 82.
[16] Busia, *Position of the Chief, op.cit.,* pp. 19-20.

division. She advises them. Her position is such that she is a powerful figure in the community. Rattray speaks highly of these women who exert their influence in many subtle ways little understood by the foreigner.

The Separate Identity of Individual and Office

The tribal groups, expanding and changing through migration and land occupation, often conflicted with other groups engaged in a similar occupation. It is not difficult to see the office of the chief emerge from the nuclear family system. Its authority was expressed in increasingly precise terms, although the manifestations of authority were functionally diffuse. The prerogatives of office became ceremonially endowed with certain types of authority from which the sources of law and right descended.

The separate office of chief consisted of a set of functional prerogatives combined into a recognized set of procedures by which the functions of chieftaincy were satisfactorally discharged. Further, it involved the institutionalization of these procedures within certain concrete structural patterns. We can, in fact, say that the offices in the traditional Ashanti system had *ritual precision and functional diffuseness.*

The office had precise limits insofar as behavior was concerned. The occupant of the office had a well-defined set of roles to play. Of course the limits varied somewhat for an exceptionally popular chief or under situational pressures, but constitutional or ideal roles were rarely remote from actual roles or performance patterns. The Ashanti, as well as other tribes of the Gold Coast, had a clearly demarcated system of constitutionalism, a fundamental law which limited discretionary powers and provided effective means of enforcing these limits.

The separation of office from occupant further involved a set of procedures for selection among available candidates, and the removal of chosen individuals if such need arose. All Akan groups in the Gold Coast had such provision for removal of offensive chiefs or other authorities who violated their terms of office, and for the selection of new replacements.

As has been indicated, particular lineages provided acceptable candidates. At the same time, a plurality of available candidates demanded a selection process which would not tend to create too much factionalism and division, hence disrupting basic consensus in the system. Instead, the selection of the chief became a ceremony of religious and social significance in which a major consequence was an expression of public solidarity around the stool.

The selection of a chief was a formal process in which the candidate was selected by the queen-mother from the royal lineage.

"A new chief is generally chosen from that particular kindred branch of the clan to which the stool belongs. There may be, as we have seen, many separate kindred groups all tracing descent from a common ancestress, but as a general principle the line from which the chiefs are chosen is confined to one branch. There are exceptions, however, and sometimes a clear 'jump' is made and succession transferred from one kindred group to another of the same clan. Again, the chieftainship may pass alternatively from one branch to another, or even in rotation, the heads of three or four different kindred groups holding the office in turn."[17]

The lineage selection is carefully defined:

"The eldest son of the senior woman of the royal family may or may not succeed. Brother may succeed brother; nephew, uncle; grandson, grandfather; and the younger may be chosen before the elder. Who then decides who shall be the next chief, assuming all these possible aspirants to the stool? During the lifetime of a chief there is generally a member of the royal house who has been marked out to succeed the reigning chief on the death of the latter. He is the heir apparent and is called in Ashanti the *badiak-yiri*. His selection is, to all outward appearances, in the hands of the chief and the queen-mother. In one sense, therefore, it would appear that they select the successor. This, however, is not the case. There is in the vernacular one of those sayings or proverbs which have all the force of legal maxims. It states . . . one of the royal blood does not place a chief on a stool. It is true that the *abediakyiri* may and often does succeed to the chief, but if such be the case, *it will only be because he has been selected independently by the votes of the majority of the mpanyimfo*[18] *who must include two officials called the ko'ntire and akwamu.* Nominally, it will be seen that it is the queen-mother who does so, and for a long time I [Rattray] believed that her wishes in this matter

[17] Rattray, *Ashanti Law, op.cit.,* pp. 84-85.

[18] *Mpanyimfo* are elders. These elders are family members in an area to which they have migrated. They receive allegiance of the village or clan in which they have lineage priority, and they owe allegiance to the *omanhene*.

were absolute, but I know now that such commands would not be constitutionally in order, and that although in every enstoolment it is she who publicly nominates the successor to the late chief, she does so only after discussion, consultation, and agreement in private with the *mpanyimfo*, who in turn take good care to find out the wishes of the majority of the populace. Democracy is again triumphant, though ready to allow autocracy to boast the semblance of power. This was always necessary if the central authority was to be upheld in its dealings with a somewhat wild and turbulent populace."[19]

A formal process was involved whereby the queen-mother, the commoners, and the elders, each a lineage-sanctioned group membership, elected a chief to the stool. The elders, themselves, were the heads of the differing lineage groups of the unit.[20] The account offered by Busia of the procedure in Wenchi is revealing:

"When a chief died and a new one had to be appointed, the elders held a meeting at which the *kontihene*[21] presided. At the meeting the elders selected two from among themselves to approach the queen-mother and ask her to nominate a candidate for the stool.

"The queen-mother then held a meeting with all the adult men and the senior women of the branches of the royal lineage. They considered the eligible candidates in turn and chose the one they thought most suitable. The necessary qualities were intelligence, humility, generosity, manliness, and physical fitness.[22] When they had decided on a candidate, the queen-mother sent to inform the *kontihene*. The latter summoned a meeting of the elders and told them of the queen-mother's nominated candidate. The elders sent a message back thanking the queen-mother, and adding that they could not say whether or not the candidate was acceptable, but that a meeting of the whole division (*oman*) would be summoned to consider the candidate. A day was appointed for this meeting and the queen-mother was informed.

"The *kontihene* then sent a message to all the heads of villages through the respective elders, asking them to be present for

[19] Rattray, *Ashanti Law, op.cit.,* p. 85.
[20] According to Busia, the elders were once distinguished from one another by the names of their lineages. This practice gave way to the military titles deriving from the position occupied by elders in military formation.
[21] The *kontihene* was one of the two most senior elders in a division.
[22] The African terms for these qualities have been omitted in quoting.

the election of the chief. This was an important affair in which everyone took a keen interest, and all the headmen, elders, and commoners came to the meeting on the appointed day."[23]

The spokesman of the commoners, the *nkwankwaahene*, would indicate to the elders if there was widespread dissatisfaction with the chief selected by the queen-mother.[24]

At the general meeting the spokesman indicated the name of the candidate. This immediately called forth a response from the assemblage—hoots or applause or hisses, as the case might be. In Wenchi, Busia describes the process as follows:

"The elders would appear to deliberate over the matter, and then ask the commoners what they thought about it. The *okyeame* [spokesman] would say: 'Thus has the queen-mother said. What do the people say?' The commoners would then approve or disapprove of the decision of the elders. If the candidate was not accepted, the queen-mother was informed and the royals proceeded to make another nomination. If after three nominations, the queen-mother's candidate was still unacceptable, the divisional council nominated a candidate from the royal family. It was for the queen-mother to say whether or not the popular candidate had a kin-right to the stool. Both parties usually agreed on one of the eligible candidates. In case of disagreement, the popular candidate, that is, the one who had the backing of the divisional council, won."[25]

After the election of the candidate, any prior controversies between the chief-elect and the members of the royal family were adjusted. All lineage members then swore an oath of allegiance. The importance of this oath, as Busia points out, is great. "The precaution, besides expressing the solidarity of the royal lineage, imposed the moral and religious sanction of the oath on any member of the royal lineage who might feel injured at being passed over, to prevent him from working against the chief."

At the moment of enstoolment, the admonitions of the public are repeated to the chief. Rattray gives the recitation of these admonitions for one Ashanti division:

"Tell him that
We do not wish greediness
We do not wish that he should curse us

[23] Busia, *Position of the Chief, op.cit.,* p. 9.
[24] *Ibid.,* p. 10.   [25] *Ibid.,* p. 11.

We do not wish that his ears should be hard of hearing
We do not wish that he should call people fools
We do not wish that he should act on his own initiative
We do not wish things done as in Kumasi
We do not wish that it should ever be said 'I have no time. I
    have no time.'
We do not wish personal abuse.
We do not wish personal violence."[26]

The chief was enstooled with words of caution ringing in his ears. His election was a signal for rejoicing, and a sharing of group identity and participation.

Remedial Measures against the Misuse of Authority

Particularly among the Akans, chiefs or sub-chiefs who went beyond the prescriptions of their office could be removed. In Ashanti and other Akan groups the general principle holds that those who elect a chief have the power to destool him.

Advice given to the chief at the time of his enstoolment is more than symbolic. It is a warning that for any prolonged and major violations of the advice given at the time, destoolment can follow. If, after his election, a chief "behaves in an unbecoming manner, his elders should warn him privately that his conduct is alienating his subjects and bringing the stool into disrepute. The type of conduct complained of in this manner is usually excessive drinking, going after other men's wives, being overbearing in dealing with his subjects, neglecting the advice of his elders, or getting in a rage and flogging the young men. Individual complaints against the chief are heard privately by the elders and they may ask the chief to pacify the offended person."[27]

As has been indicated, the general rule is that those who enstool a chief can destool him. The sources of pressure for destoolment are varied, however. The nominal authorities who press the enstoolment and destoolment proceedings are the queen-mother, the elders, and the commoners, who must agree. Commoners, however, can initiate destoolment proceedings by bringing pressure on the elders through the *asafo* companies. These military companies

---

[26] Rattray, *Ashanti Law, op.cit.*, p. 82.
[27] Matson, *op.cit.*, p. 68.

protect the village. They are the auxiliaries of the chief, without whom he could not exercise his functions.

One immediate consequence of British rule was to upset this delicate balance of power. *Asafo* companies found simple and effective means to destool chiefs whom they regarded as against their own best interests. According to Field, since any disgraceful performance involving the chief meant automatic destoolment, the *asafo* companies accomplished their purpose in the following manner:

"In the recent past there was, I am told, an outbreak of destoolments of chiefs brought about by *asafo* companies. A chief had only to make himself in the mildest degree unpopular and the *asafo* would promptly destool him by the simple ceremony of seizing and bumping his buttocks three times on the ground. This practice was stopped by a government ordinance which provided that no destoolment should be recognized by the government unless it had been approved by the elders and ratified by the state council."[28]

In bringing destoolment proceedings, the elders called a meeting of the state council. If their destoolment attempts failed, they were often "made" to eat "dirt," exiled, or in the case of irresponsible charges, put to death. Ridicule, a particularly abhorrent form of abuse, was extensively used against whichever party lost. A destooled chief was most generally exiled. It was by no means impossible for him to be reinstated.

Conclusions

The Ashanti Confederacy was a decentralized bureaucracy. The *asantehene* had a large staff. He was assisted by a queen-mother and the *birempon*. He had his spokesmen and officials. An elaborate pattern of specific relationships existed between the chief and his principal officers in which their various performances were carefully worked out, while their functions were not. The positions were, relative to Western standards, functionally diffuse.

The federalized basis of the Ashanti Confederacy in which, for the most part, divisional chiefs exercised most of their tra-

---

[28] Field, M. J., *Akim Kotoku*, Accra, 1948, p. 34. For an extensive discussion of the role of the *asafo* in Akan society, see Christensen, James, *Double Descent among the Fanti. Asafo* political controls are related to a patrilineal aspect of Akan kinship.

ditional prerogatives while recognizing allegiance to the *asantehene*, permitted the structural maintenance of local units. Formal controls against intrigue and subversion existed all along the line. For example, the stool was protected by *wirempefo*, a group of vigilantes whose job it was to keep the stool from being taken by a usurper.[29]

The systems in the Northern Territories are substantially different. Among the dominant political groups, authority is a three-fold variation in Moshi practice. The Moshi, Dagomba, and Mamprussi, for example, have a patriarchal system of political authority involving the election of chiefs from lineage heads arranged in hierarchical status groups. Acceptable lineage heads are elected over a period of time to higher and higher office, with final selection of the paramount chief made from three liege posts ("gates") directly below the paramount chief in the hierarchy. By the time a chief is eligible for the top posts he is an old man.

Although the chief is obliged to discuss affairs with his council, his authority is far more absolute than in the central and coastal areas of the Gold Coast.

Among the Akans the range of tribal goal orientations, or perceived objectives, was local and intimate. The individual's goals were linked to the maintenance of the family, and through the family to the larger social unit. There was little individual competition to achieve objectives. Social action was usually performed with others, whether family members or village associates. The allocation of duties, prerogatives, and rights within the tribe depended to a large extent upon the cognitive and affective content of the elder-youth relationship, the royal-non-royal lineage

[29] See Rattray, *Ashanti Law, op.cit.*, p. 86. "The persons who select a chief are those who can destool him. We have thus two checks upon despotism. There is yet a third. It is perhaps hardly necessary to say that in Ashanti the stool is greater than the chief who sits upon it. This we know to our cost. . . . In every division there are a group of officials whose title must never be mentioned during the lifetime of the chief. These are the *wirempefo*. The composition of this body varies considerably in various localities, as we shall see when an examination comes to be made of the separate divisional constitutions, but everywhere it has one aspect in common. A member of the kindred group which supplies the ruler may not be one of the *wirempefo*. On the death of the chief, the *wirempefo* constitute themselves into an armed body, sweep down upon the ancestral stoolhouse, and carry off the 'blackened' stools, without which a new chief cannot be legally enstooled . . . [this] shows the effective practical means at the disposal of the hereditary councillors of the reigning house to counter the intrigues of ambitious queen-mothers, or of persons of the royal blood who might get ready to force their individual claims on the stool."

relationship, the slave-non-slave relationship and the elder-commoner relationship. Depending upon the individual's birth within these relational configurations, factors of specific social desirability were inculcated in him. These factors involved the fulfillment of social roles, open by lineage, towards which the individual's hopes were directed.

Choice in the system was, by Western standards, severely restricted. Goal orientations were limited to a restricted and integrated pattern of mutually compatible choices in which factors of kinship, age, and sex provided the efficient bases.

The major normative aspects of goal orientations were those of religion and consequently proverb prescriptions. In the main these were parochial, stemming from the past.

With a rudimentary division of labor, the range of role alternatives was not possible on an extensive basis. Most individuals performed similar predominantly economic roles, depending upon their membership in slave or non-slave lineages and their sex. Most people were occupied with the same over-all types of economic activity. Almost everyone worked on subsistence farms. Some worked on the farms of others. The system of roles was elaborated in the hierarchy of political and military posts which were comparatively formalized. Selection to these posts was based on predominantly particularistic criteria.

The system of roles was institutionalized in the shadow of past performances of the ancestors, real or mythical. It was the maintenance and enhancement of ancestral society which was paramount in the performance of these roles.

For the same reason the limits of tolerance were clearly demarcated. Aside from the socially dis-equilibrating consequences of unsanctioned behavior, the balance of public support and actual performance was manifest in a high degree of conformity between ideal and actual role prescriptions. The hierarchy of roles was, in some respects, a system of mutual checks on behavior. The roles themselves, while authoritarian in many respects, were so only within the limits of public consensus. The system of checks and balances was essentially based on religious sanctions demanding a high degree of social obedience.

Tribal society in the Gold Coast was essentially contractual in the classic sense of the word. The ceremony of contract was repeated at intervals throughout the political life of the tribe, throughout its various administrative levels. The contract could be broken, hence the crucial importance of swearing an oath. The contract, so long as its terms were observed, demanded a set of reciprocal behavioral relationships understood as correct. Variations were regarded as deviation, and controls against deviation were well articulated. Either a chief could be destooled, or a member severely punished.

Yet the contract was hardly a legalistic affair. Rather, it was an expression of the terms of relationship of members out of which law stemmed. Indeed, the contractual form was a normative basis for a system of repressive law in which the violation of public law could lead to drastic consequences. For example, to pick up gold in the market in Kumasi was punishable by death. The law stipulated that all gold dropped in the market place belonged to the *asantehene*.

The contract essentially was an expression of social solidarity. The proverb norms were the formal guides for behavior and adjudication. The degree of behavioral institutionalization was intense. The level of affect was maintained at a high pitch in a context of vengeance, fear, magic (*ju-ju*), and exorcism. The non-empirical sources of behavioral criteria stemming from specifically religious sources granted rationality to the wisdom of the gods, and obedience at the level of social action. To offend the ancestors brought their vengeance. The repressive act against the deviant actor was thus to prevent vengeance from falling on the tribe or the village. Repressive acts in this same sense promoted the social and political solidarity of the tribe or other unit. Durkheim, calling this a "mechanical solidarity," indicates drastic consequences against deviant behavior. Thus religious integrity is social integrity, and the religious supports to social structure are fundamental to the maintenance of the system. Originally, religion "pervades everything: everything social is religious"; Durkheim,[30] as well as Mary Kingsley, regard the two words as synonymous.

In such a society, the individual is not, self-consciously, a free agent having a wide imaginative scope for purposeful change. He reaches, with his classificatory brothers, certain types of roles. He plays these roles within well-defined limits. Such limits are difficult to change since their definition comes from the past.

[30] See Durkheim, E., *Division of Labor in Society.* Glencoe, 1949, p. 169.

It is hoped that this discussion provides some guide to the integrated pattern of Gold Coast tribal life. To change this society without a breakdown of social order is possible only if the society admits some flexibility. But traditional societies cannot tolerate substantive change: they can accomplish modest accommodation but not drastic modification. These distinctions were overlooked by the early British administrators, who changed the content of tribal activity but retained the shell. In such highly coordinated and subtle systems the consequences of intervention are complex. Indeed, the consequences of alien impingement in this traditional social environment were such that certain orientational, particularly symbolic and inspirational, aspects of tribal life shifted from chieftaincy to Nkrumah, and from local to national membership via nationalism.

⊡⊡ CHAPTER 6 ⊡⊡

PATTERNS OF INDIRECT RULE

THE general impact of formal British authority upon the indigenous political systems of the Gold Coast will be the object of concern in the discussion which follows. Adequate statements regarding policy are abundant in British government publications and documents as well as in various recent studies, and we shall not discuss British administrative policy during the period from World War I to World War II in great detail.[1] Nevertheless, most of the events which form the basis of this discussion occurred between the two wars. It is sufficient to mention that earlier consolidation of British power in the Gold Coast proceeded in two steps. First, the coastal area was made a Crown colony in 1874. Then Ashanti was declared a conquered colony and the Northern Territories were made a protectorate in 1901. As in other Crown colonies, the coastal area continued to have a legislative council and an executive council, even though no African members were appointed for a considerable time. The Ashanti Divisions and the Northern Territories were directly the responsibility of the governor and his delegated officers, the chief commissioners. No legislative council or executive council for the protectorates developed. It was not until 1946 that the Ashanti Confederacy was incorporated into the conciliar jurisdiction of the Legislative Council.[2]

For the most part, after the initial declaration of colony and protectorate status for the various parts of the Gold Coast, a network of district commissioners was rapidly provided. The district commissioners were directly responsible to the governor. They ruled through indigenous tribal groupings, however. It is from the juxtaposition of British authority represented by district officers and traditional authority represented by tribal chiefs that an increasingly unstable political situation arose. This situa-

---

[1] See particularly Wight, M., *British Colonial Constitutions*, Oxford, 1952; Wight, M., *The Development of the Legislative Council*, London, 1947; Wight, M., *The Gold Coast Legislative Council*, London, 1946; Latham, R. T. E., *The Law and the Commonwealth*, London, 1949; Bourret, F. M., *The Gold Coast*, London, 1950; Hailey, *Native Administration in the British African Territories*, London, 1952, Part III, Chap. VIII.

[2] See Statutory Rules and Orders No. 353, Gold Coast Colony and Ashanti (Legislative Council) Order in Council, 1946.

tion finally was expressed in intense nationalism after World War II.

A basic hypothesis here is that conflicting sources of authority, so different in nature as to be directly contradictory, were procedurally integrated into one system, indirect rule. The contradictions were made manifestly clear insofar as the codes and rules of behavior in the tribal systems broke down as the chiefs were identified with British authority. At the same time, the codes and rules of behavior which the British stood for were not adopted, partly because they were not understood and partly because few opportunities presented themselves for Africans to act and be received as British officials.

Indirect rule is an omnibus term which covers a considerable number of colonial policies by various British authorities in their different areas. It is not a precise term; in fact, it is considered one of the most confusing expressions in the colonial lexicon. It is associated particularly with Sir Frederick Lugard, who devised the system for ruling the newly conquered Moslem Emirs in Northern Nigeria while having only a small force of officers. The Emirates were preserved as administrative units and the Emirs kept on in their traditional leadership capacities. It was intended that, except for extreme practices contrary to British standards of morality, traditional social life should continue unimpaired.[3]

[3] Lugard lays out three alternative conceptions of indirect rule. The first is the ideal of self-government by evolution, as in the case of Europe and America. This Lugard rules out for Africa because of the diversity of the groups, and the unevenness and primitiveness in stages of evolution represented by Africans. Further, Lugard felt that educated Africans, particularly those clamoring for self-government, tended to seek monopolization of power in their own hands, as against the natural rulers or chiefs. This would tend to destroy the old system, which Lugard holds to be an undesirable eventuality. In fact, he quotes a famous Gold Coast chief, Nana Sir William Ofori Atta, to the effect that the "claim of a handful of educated lawyers and doctors to represent the people, instead of their chiefs, was a base attempt to denationalize the institutions of the country."[4] Evolution to self-government is therefore ruled out.

The second alternative noted by Lugard is the notion that "every advanced community should be given the widest possible powers of self-government under its own rules, and that these powers should be rapidly increased with the object of complete independence at the earliest possible date in the not distant future." Lugard indicates that this position is a deception since underlying it is the assumption that attempts to train "primitive tribes in any form of self-government are futile, and administration must be wholly conducted by British officials."[5] In other words, while this proposal intends self-government, in actual fact it seeks to isolate traditional authority from colonial rule and thus provide a completely unreal form

The system, as Lugard defined it, has as an essential feature the native chiefs constituted as an integral part of the machinery of administration. "There are not two sets of rulers—British and native—working either separately or in cooperation, but a single government in which the native chiefs have well-defined duties and an acknowledged status equally with British officials. Their duties should never conflict, and should overlap as little as possible. They must be complementary to each other and the chief himself must understand that he has no right to place and power unless he renders his proper services to the state."[7]

Indirect rule shifted the source of traditional power to British law. Attacks against duly constituted traditional authorities were a punishable offense. This was an attempt to retain the organizational structure of traditional social life without impairing its efficiency. The general control principles laid down by Lugard are as follows:

"1. Native rulers are not permitted to raise and control armed forces, or to grant permission to carry arms.

"2. The sole right to impose taxation in any form is reserved to the suzerain power.

"3. The right to legislation is reserved.

"4. The right to appropriate land on equitable terms for public purposes and for commercial purposes is vested in the governor.

"5. The right of confirming or otherwise deciding the choice of the people of the successor to a chiefship and of deposing any ruler for misrule or other adequate cause, is reserved to the governor. [Succession is governed] by native law and custom, subject in the case of important chiefs to the approval of the governor, in order that the most capable claimant may be chosen."[8]

The concept of indirect rule in terms of the political prescriptions which it involved was, therefore: a belief in colonial govern-

---

of self-government in which direct and autocratic British government would actually make the important decisions.

The third alternative, which Lugard considers the best, is based upon the presumed inferiority of the black race to the white, at least as regards the arts of government. "The third conception is that of rule by native chiefs, unfettered in their control of their people as regards all those matters which are to them the most important attributes of rule, with scope for initiative and responsibility, but admittedly—so far as the visible horizon is concerned—subordinate to the control of the protecting power in certain well-defined directions."[6]

[4] Lugard, *The Dual Mandate in British Tropical Africa*, Edinburgh and London, 1922, p. 194.

[5] *Ibid.*, p. 196.   [6] *Ibid.*, p. 197.   [7] *Ibid.*, p. 202.   [8] *Ibid.*, p. 213.

ment through the principal chiefs as agents, with residual and plenary powers reserved for the colonial authorities. The objective was a promotion of a system of law and equity in which slavery and the worst effects of tribal insobriety and license were abolished and a Pax Britannica let loose upon the land.

The following admixture of factors of indirect rule can be listed: (a) the use of indigenous structures as agencies of both continuity and decentralization in administration; (b) the co-operation of the chiefs and people with the colonial service; (c) the congruity of colonial policy and traditional social life; (d) the residual authority of the Crown.

Lugard states: "If continuity and decentralization are, as I have said, the first and most important conditions in maintaining an effective administration, cooperation is the key-note of success in its application—continuous cooperation between every link in the chain, from the head of the administration to its most junior member—cooperation between the government and the commercial community, and above all, between the provincial staff and the native rulers. Every individual adds his share not only to the accomplishment of the ideal, but to the ideal itself. Its principles are fashioned by his patient and loyal application of these principles, with as little interference as possible with native customs and modes of thought."[9]

The Effects of Indirect Rule

One of the first effects of this doctrine was to shift the focus of authority and responsibility away from the legitimate properties of chieftaincy to those of British power. An immediate consequence was to identify the chiefs as agents of British rule.

This is not to say that British officials were necessarily unpopular. On the contrary, many of the British officers were revered almost as much as the chiefs. But the popularity of the British authorities was almost inevitably cloaked in the garb of paternalism. Some officers manifested a genuine fondness for and appreciation of the traditional modes of life. Often it was the Colonial Service officer in some lonely bush station who saw the cycle of tribal culture in its diverse aspects. Indirect rule in the field was a personal relationship as chief and district commissioner learned to know, deal with, and often like and respect one another.

[9] *Ibid.*, p. 193.

Yet paternalism carries its own consequences. Tribal societies are by no means societies of children. At times the district commissioner acted the role of father, at times guardian and mentor. He was often admired, and sometimes beloved. He was respected and feared. He was a participant but never a member. However, as Joyce Cary eloquently showed in his novel *Mr. Johnson*, the district commissioner in his various capacities infringed on traditional life in almost every major requirement of his job. If he built a road, commerce would follow. If commerce developed, new elements entered into village life. If new elements entered, traditional restraints on behavior were altered. Tensions and adjustments required new kinds of controls, including legal controls and the definition of classes of offenses which could not be handled under customary law. The essential features of village life might be modified. Migration from the village and the breakup of family life often occurred. If subsistence farming gave way to the production of cash crops, a new premium was placed on money while food had to be imported to the community. What often seemed to the district commissioner as a necessary and progressive measure —the control of disease or the halting of certain customary practices—had hidden consequences. The congruity of colonial policy and traditional life of which Lugard spoke presumed a continuous process of adjustment beyond the capacity of traditional culture.

More than anything else, the residual authority of the Crown was the ultimate destructive factor in indirect rule. Chiefs, whose powers were traditionally kept in balance by a continuous process of consultation and whose source of authority affected the maintenance of lineage, kinship, and clan integrity, suddenly became figures whose ultimate legitimacy derived from British law. No chief could be considered a chief unless gazetted as such by the governor. The most disruptive element of all was introduced by transmuting traditional legitimacy into legitimacy derived from Great Britain.

Actually, the classic application of indirect rule of the type developed by Lugard in Northern Nigeria was never applied in the Gold Coast. In an excellent examination of the position in regard to the Gold Coast, Rita Hinden indicates:

"The system of 'indirect rule'—that local administration should be entrusted to native institutions having their roots in age-old custom, subject to the supervision and overriding authority of the central government—has never been applied wholeheartedly in the Gold Coast (except in the Northern Territories). . . . The Gold Coast system was designed to show the greatest respect to the position of the chief as representative of the stool. But this in itself made it impossible to exert that control which was demanded of native institutions to be effective agencies of local government. In practice the Gold Coast system has been described as a 'mixture of direct and indirect rule with a steady bias towards the latter.'

"Administrative difficulties in the Gold Coast have centered around the position and powers of the chiefs—do the chiefs and native administrations derive their powers from their traditional position in native society, or by delegation from the government? Is the government the sole source of authority without whose recognition and approval they cannot legally function?"[10]

Indirect rule, as the basis of a particular form of administration, provided substantial structural modification of the traditional system of authority occurring within a framework of British law and order. Its intent was not major social change, but modified adjustment. The result, however, was major social change, within an administrative scheme which sufficed until new organs of authority were required, on a basis deemed somewhat less than satisfactory in the light of the problems involved. "The British ideal was the ideal of a good African, pagan or Mahomedan, weaned from savage and cruel practices, humane to his fellow creatures and to animals, but otherwise staunch to his attachment to African traditions and institutions."[11]

The Structures of Indirect Rule

Role Differentiation

As has been indicated, the general criteria of traditional roles derived from availability on the basis of lineage, membership, and sex.[12] By far the most important of these, both as a source of recruitment and as a cognitive element sustaining social structure, was the lineage system. The lineage patterns in social structure we have discussed at some length. The recruitment occurring

---

[10] Hinden, Rita, *Local Government in the Colonies,* London, 1950, pp. 95-97. See also Bourret, *op.cit.,* Chapter iv.

[11] Evans, E. W., *The British Yoke,* London, 1949, p. 218.

[12] See Chapter 4.

under indirect rule, which paid little attention to lineage and great attention to training and ability, immediately set up certain kinds of affective and cognitive conflicts. Suddenly access to roles was provided on grounds other than traditional ones.

For example, when the British first came into some areas they were followed by mission schools. The chief might be told to send his children to school. Often the chief and other important figures would be annoyed at this and send a slave son (a son from a slave mother) to school. The slave son, having achieved a measure of education, would be eligible for junior posts in the civil service or as a clerk with a European firm. The sudden rise in the political and influence status of these slaves immediately created potential friction and along with other factors undermined stability within the traditional framework. Some of these slaves became members of the nationalist organizations, and some rose to positions of eminence otherwise barred to them.[13]

The more the British sought selective recruitment on the basis of skill, the more were valuations on kinship and lineage factors inhibited. Where such inhibitions were present, motivation to leave the tribal scene was more acute. Not only did education promote this tension, but the work of the missionaries as well. Tribal politics was, as has been indicated, closely linked with tribal religious elements. To undermine the religious sanctity of the chief drastically reduced the effectiveness of his sanctional control. With traditional normative restraints vitiated, and his other ultimate weapon, force, battened down firmly by British authorities, the chief no longer served as a central orientational and authority figure. A new range of perceived criteria centering around newly created roles emerged, fostered by the spread of educational opportunities, European recruitment for the junior service, clerical positions in European, Syrian, and Lebanese firms.

The respect for age, which in the Northern Territories reached the proportions of a semi-gerontocratic political hierarchy and in the south required certain types of obedience, was vitiated by the diminished prestige attached to certain positions. Under the traditional pattern of authority when a conflict developed between a youngman and an elder, it was difficult for the youngman to

[13] According to Busia, some of the nationalist members of the legislative assembly are slave descendants. This fact is unverified, however, and was related to the author in personal interview.

protest. Such a protest is almost an admission of guilt, demanding an apology in elaborate and ritualized form particularly degrading to the youngman. At the head of the system is the chief. "Any chief is called *nana*, even if he is a boy, so that he goes to the top of the age-grading hierarchy. Part of the system of government is based on respect due to age, and the formal authorities are men of considerable age, like the elders who are the councillors of the chief."[14]

The impact of differential non-traditional roles affected the younger elements particularly, therefore. As roads, schools, lorries, and other tangible evidences of the material culture of the West filtered into the tribal village, even the nuclear family suffered.

Differentiation on the basis of religion was undermined by Christianity. By making manifest hostility against the past and providing an invidious standard of judgment of traditional religious patterns, not only Christianity but Islam as well often spread more rapidly.

Differentiation on the basis of lineage or kinship was greatly disturbed, particularly where the British set up chiefs or other political leaders having no traditional legitimization.

Differentiation on the basis of age was undermined in the general repudiation of tribal life by the young, a repudiation which varied in its proportions from extremes in the growing urban coastal centers to very little in the Northern Territories.

Differentiation on the basis of solidarity broke down in some important concrete structures of tribal life such as age-grading societies, the family, and other predominantly kinship solidarity units. New agencies of solidarity based on education, having substantively different contexts of role definition, became more common, later including cooperative associations, trade unions, occasional secret societies, burial societies, and political youth movements and parties.

The traditional clusters of roles in the *oman*—the clan, the chiefs, and sub-chiefs with their honorifics and status—gradually gave way to a new pattern of role definition, all the more exciting for being frowned upon by the traditional authorities. Those without money, the illiterate, the representatives of tradition, were

[14] Quoted from an interview with Mr. J. De Graft-Johnson.

barred from these more prestige-bearing occupations. The beginnings of a stratification system based on economic class rather than on ancestral prerogatives rapidly conflicted with the traditional, providing a permanent source of tension which continues until the present.

Solidarity

Indirect rule, particularly as it strengthened the chief and thereby allowed him to go beyond traditional boundaries, broke the effectiveness of the political sub-structures which had been integrated with restrained and restraining aspects of chieftaincy. New types of membership units, such as branches of the nationalist movement, slowly cut across the traditional units. Traditional kinship affiliations often aided in this process. It is remarkable, for example, to find the number of brothers or classificatory brothers, or other relatives, working together in the same party or political sphere. Kinship bases proved a reliable organizational core in the nationalist movement.

The tendency was a new development of religious and political solidarity units. These solidarity units were aided to some extent by the web of kinship which provided reinforcement of traditional supports within these newer units. In other words, the solidarity factors associated with traditional kinship structures tended to be *eufunctional*[15] for the adaptation to new solidarity units, but *dysfunctional*[16] for the maintenance of the old kinship structures themselves. Brothers tended to follow one another to Achimota School, the youth movements, or a political party. Secondary school students at Achimota, who were to form a nucleus of trained and aggressive but responsible political leadership in the Gold Coast, provided a solidarity grouping which cut across traditional kinship and authority lines.

These new solidarity units on the whole adopted, in tentative

[15] "A eufunction is a condition or state of affairs that (1) results in the operation (including in the term operation mere persistence) of a structure of a given unit through time and (2) increases or maintains adaptation or adjustment to the unit's setting, thus making for the persistence of the unit as defined of which the structure concerned is a part or aspect." Levy, Marion, *The Structure of Society*, Princeton, 1952, p. 77.

[16] "A dysfunction is a condition or state of affairs, that (1) results from the operation (including in the term operation mere persistence) of a given unit through time and (2) lessens the adaptation or adjustment to the unit's setting thus making for the lack of persistence of the unit as defined of which the structure concerned is a part or aspect." *Ibid.*

and preliminary fashion, the standards and styles and symbols of Western clubs. Boy Scout organizations fostered by the missionaries played their part. For a time anything African was looked upon, by these educated youth groups, with a measure of embarrassment or even contempt. As Dr. J. B. Danquah wrote in a poem which adequately sums up the tenor of these new groups:

> "Buck up, O youth and kill the bogey!
> The bogey that your race is infant!
> Know ye not that God is very busy,
> And helps only the few who are constant?"[17]

These youth movements proved a basis for a more serious political organization along nationalist lines after World War II. Whereas before the war they bent their political efforts toward moderate reform in collaboration with the "natural rulers," the chiefs, in the postwar period the language and the aspirations were more drastic. An interesting comparison is offered by an article written by the Gold Coast Youth Conference, appearing in pamphlet form under the title *First Steps towards a National Fund*. This pamphlet, which recognizes the Ashanti Confederacy Council, the Aborigines' Society, and the Joint Provincial Council as the proper agents of authority, is preoccupied with basic questions of race. There is none of the lusty self-confidence which characterizes later proclamations from the Convention People's Party. On a somewhat plaintive note the pamphlet states:

"Neither the integrity nor ability nor the spirit for cooperation is wanting in the African. The youth of the country does not believe that these calumnies are true of the African as such, or of the European as such, for that matter. Individuals may prove themselves dishonest, incompetent, self-centered and vain not because they are Africans but because they have so been brought up. Heredity alone is not responsible for what an individual turns out to be in society; environment counts for much, and the social milieux, and it is the duty of the country's leaders to improve the environment and the conditions of the social balance in which the growing child must weigh his future possibilities."[18]

The reforms called for pertain to marriage, inheritance, "The

---

17 From Youth Conference pamphlet, *First Steps towards a National Fund*, Achimota, 1938.
18 *Ibid.*

son vis. the Nephew," and other social structures in the indigenous pattern of social life. Little is said of colonialism, government, independence, or of major political change. This is a striking contrast to the language and spirit of later youth manifestos. For example, in 1948 the *Ghana Youth Manifesto* links the Gold Coast demands for political freedom to the war against fascism. It identifies Gold Coast youth with all youth. The manifesto states:[19]

"To British Youths we send special greetings. You are lovers and exponents of freedom and democracy. Thousands of you fought in this last world war against fascism to maintain your well-earned freedom. . . . We trust that you, Youth of Britain, would co-operate with us in our struggle for freedom and self-government so that we could both freely work together to build the Brave New World which is the dream of us youth."

Speaking to the Gold Coast youth, it continues:

"Youth of the Gold Coast, the new Ghana, the struggle for self-government gains unrelenting momentum, that brings us daily near our goal. However hard the struggle, whatever the stratagems of the imperialists, or whatever the opportunism of traducers, stooges, and quislings to lead us astray, we shall not deviate an inch from our avowed goal."

To make sure that no one confused the "avowed goal," the manifesto states as point one of its ten-point demand: "We demand a constitution that would give this country nothing less than FULL SELF-GOVERNMENT."

The first statement is from 1938, the *Manifesto* from 1948. The ten years not only make a difference in the kinds of demands expressed by those dissatisfied with traditional life; they also deny easy refuge in Western systems adopted on Western terms, i.e., under colonial domination.

The variety of solidarity units which emerged during the period of indirect rule, however, provided the first bases for political institutional transfer. They represented groupings whose sustaining strength was their common adherence to Western political and social standards.

These earlier more secular solidarity groupings represented for the most part intellectuals, siphoned off the main stream of

<hr>

[19] This quotation and the two following are from the *Ghana Youth Manifesto*, Accra, 1948.

rural tribal life. Wooed and accepted by liberal British educators, they discussed Gold Coast problems long and earnestly. An intellectual elite emerged, often divorced, as far as social habits were concerned, from the less well-educated youth and the larger social organization of the tribe.

Two sets of authority patterns were therefore visible in the period of indirect rule. These patterns were manifested in two sets of role clusters, integrated into a formal organizational network which can be called Gold Coast colonial government. One, the British administrative service, was supported by norms of rationality and acceptance based upon criteria indigenous to the British themselves. The other, the native authorities, found themselves deriving *effective legitimacy* at least in part from the British source. To the degree that such effective legitimacy derived from British sources, traditional authority was weakened.

⃝⃝⃝ | **CHAPTER 7** | ⃝⃝⃝

THE POLITICS OF INDIRECT RULE

The British Colonial Service

THE British Colonial Service is the agency of colonial rule. Through its functions and organization it has created a distinctive pattern of authority which is adaptive to conditions of local administration and territorial governance. It is both a fully articulated bureaucracy, and yet a flexible system of role structures. The balance in the bureaucratic system between office and role, between rigidity and flexibility, is perhaps one of the unique features of British colonial rule which can, without changing organizational structure, promote political evolution to self-government while assuming a position of residual control.

As a system of offices the Colonial Service is, in each colonial territory, the arm of the Crown which, under the Secretary of State for Colonies, legislates in colonial areas.[1]

The letters patent and royal instructions of the Crown together form a kind of organic foundation for a colony. The legal flexibility of the system lies in the order in council and letters patent system, which allows ready amendment. By prescribing the limits of immediate Crown discretion, action prerogatives can devolve upon local authorities. The crucial discretionary figure is the governor: "The governor is the central institution of the crown colony system. He is the representative of the king, the head of the executive government, and usually the president of the legislature. He is his own prime minister."[2] As the governor of the Gold Coast put it, before the constitutional changes of 1950 he was an autocrat, a representative of the Crown, who ruled with the advice of the Executive Council. He was under no obligation to accept that advice.[3] Now his position is somewhat like a constitutional monarch.

The governor, as representative of the Crown, had plenary powers under indirect rule. He was the keystone in the arch of central government although constitutional changes have made

---

[1] See Wight, M., *The Development of the Legislative Council 1606-1945,* London, 1946, pp. 41-42.

[2] *Ibid.,* p. 142.

[3] Although he always did.

many of the governor's powers purely formal in the Gold Coast.[4] Responsible to him was the formal political administration which ranged from the colonial secretary in the secretariat to the district commissioners out in the field, the latter having full administrative discretion.

While the governor was head of the government and all acts were done in his name and by his authority,[5] the colonial secretary was his executive officer. The secretariat was a technical departmental establishment, the heads of which coordinated the functions of government. They were not similar to ministerial or cabinet posts, which came about after the abolition of indirect rule in 1950. They were responsible to the chief secretary, not the Legislative Council.

Just as the governor represented the Crown in the Colony, so the district officer represented the government in the field. "He is expected to control or regulate all aspects of labor, commerce, land tenure, and exercise judicial functions. His model is not that of English local government but that of the prefect system on the continent."[6]

Comparatively late as compared with other British colonies, the system of native authorities was integrated into this almost purely Western façade of administration in which the essentials of autocratic rule were present. Legal autocracy was softened perforce, through the toleration of custom, and administration through the traditional authorities. In many respects, indirect rule was little more than direct rule, with some of its decisions

[4] It is important to note, however, that the Crown's prerogative powers to legislate in the colonies were affected by the case of Campbell vs. Hall as far back as the eighteenth century. "It was there decided that when the king had granted a constitution to a ceded Colony and had not reserved to himself the power to legislate, that power was lost. The actual decision related only to ordinary laws and not to constitutions, but the case has been widely regarded as having also established the principle that the Crown could not amend a constitution which had been granted unless power in this respect was reserved in the constitution itself. It appears to me that this interpretation of the decision goes too far, but it may be that the principle should now be regarded as settled law. And though the Colony actually concerned was ceded, the decision is considered to apply to all colonies." Sir Kenneth O. Roberts-Wray, C.O. /6780/52 (Mimeo.), Speech at the Second Devonshire Course, September 1952, Queens College, Cambridge.

[5] "He has the power, by direct legislation from the Crown, of life and death and the sovereign's prerogative of mercy." He is responsible to the Secretary of State and it is in this fashion that the Colonial Office and the Colonial Service are formally linked, through ultimate responsibility to the same operating authority. See Bertram, Sir Anton, *The Colonial Service*, Cambridge, 1930.

[6] *Ibid.*, p. 68.

deriving from customary authorities rather than the district officer or decree law.[7] However, authority under the period of indirect rule stemmed from the British political administration. This was clearly recognized by the members of the traditional system who were supposedly integrated with the secular pattern of rule in coordinate but separate spheres. It was also clearly recognized by British officers in the field. The effect was to allow few illusions as to the nature of sovereignty in the Gold Coast. No traditional power existed beyond the sufferance of British tolerance. The resulting "de-institutionalization" of the traditional we can state here as one important prerequisite to effective institutional transfer.

The indirect rule system as evolved in the Gold Coast was peculiar insofar as the establishment of organs of central government preceded the pattern of native authorities in local government. The native authorities system did not go into effect until 1932 in the Northern Territories and 1935 in the Colony and Ashanti. This system was a belated attempt to resuscitate disintegrating tribal structures, particularly in coastal areas.

The modern construction of the Legislative Council dates, however, from the Gold Coast Colony order in council dated April 8, 1925. The general purpose of this constitution was to amplify participation by chiefs and other African members in advisory organs of the government and in houses of assembly through which the chiefs could advise the country. It was a move to bolster the waning support of the chiefs and to avoid incipient nationalism by building a more representative system based partly on the traditional democracy of the Gold Coast tribal system. The 1925 Constitution was important for the ultimate development of a national society although its terms of reference included only the Colony.

The Provincial Councils

The setting up of provincial councils was a logical product of

[7] As was indicated above, nothing is more confused than the term "indirect rule." Buell, in *Native Problem in Africa* (New York, 1928), states: "Indirect rule means immediate self-government in local affairs through native institutions, constantly being strengthened by the accretion of new political experience derived from contact with the western world, and subject only to European supervision, which becomes less and less with a realism based on experience" but Bertram, on the other hand, indicates that the district officer rules his district directly. (Bertram, *op.cit.*, p. 68.) Both are in a sense correct and therein lies the confusion.

the process of the informal consultation and mutual advice which had been going on between the chiefs and the administrative authorities since the British entered the Gold Coast. We have indicated the close and intimate kind of consultative process traditional to tribal politics:

"Sovereignty in the Gold Coast tribes lives in the people themselves who elect their chiefs and who can, if they so desire, deprive them of office. Each chief is, in fact, but the mouthpiece of his state (*oman*) council without whose approval no chief can perform any executive or judicial act. Accordingly, when the head chiefs of a province are summoned to the provincial council in order, say, to elect representatives of their peoples as members of the Legislative Council, each head chief carries with him the instructions of his state council as to the policy which he is directed to pursue and the manner in which he is to record his vote."[8]

The chiefs and their newly established provincial councils in the Colony were to serve as an intermediary link between the actual local administration which took place via the district commissioner with the cooperation of traditional authorities, and the central government, represented by the governor and assisted by a legislative council on which sat elected chiefs as well as elected members from municipalities. This structural arrangement placed the chiefs at a crucial position between central and local political structures, linking secular organs of political administration and traditional organs of rule. As Governor Guggisberg indicated:

"I have never concealed my conviction that it is on the native institutions of this country—with the exception of the necessity of giving certain populous municipalities a voice—that the gradual development of the constitution must be founded. It was at the preservation of native institutions that I aimed when devising what is the outstanding feature of the new constitution—the provincial councils. These provincial councils are really the breakwaters defending our native constitutions, institutions, and customs against the disintegrating waves of Western civilization. They are the chief means by which the nationality of the Africans of the Gold Coast will be built up out of the many scattered tribes; for it must be remembered that, although each council functions for its own

---

[8] See Guggisberg, F. G., *A Review of Events, 1910-1926*, Accra, 1927, p. 21.

province, yet arrangements have been made by which these councils can meet and discuss common questions, as had already been done in the case of the Native Jurisdiction Bill."[9]

The foundations of territorial solidarity and political integration were thus viewed as created through the procedural mechanism of the provincial councils. On the one hand this would tend to revive and strengthen the prestige and status of chieftaincy. On the other, it was felt that the allegiance and sanctioned support extended to the chiefs could, thereby, be extended to the central organs of government, particularly the Legislative Council.

With the provincial council pattern established, chiefs gained a prominence on a national level quite out of keeping with their traditional limits. In many cases the new position of the chief only served to strengthen the opposition to him, and chiefs were poisoned, destooled, or forced to abdicate in increasing numbers.

Their local position, in addition, was formalized in 1932 and 1935 in the case of the Northern Territories, and Colony and Ashanti respectively, with local native authorities ordinances constituting the chief and his council as the unit of local administration.[10]

The pattern of provincial councils was maintained in Ashanti through the Ashanti Confederacy Council, a body having genuine traditional precedent.

Up until the basic structural change imposed by the Local Council Ordinance of 1951, which abolished the native authorities system, the period of indirect rule was structurally characterized by a system of native authorities having financial, judicial, administrative, and policy powers. It was constituted on traditional lines with administrative changes deemed necessary for effective supervision and operations such as the control of native authorities treasuries, native courts, and regulations pertaining thereto, etc.

The native authority was supervised by the district commissioner and responsible to the state councils presided over by the

9 *Ibid.*, pp. 23-24.

10 See Hailey, *Native Administration, op.cit.*, Part III. The native authorities were set up by ordinance in 1935 in the Colony, with powers increased and modified extensively in 1944 and 1952. In Ashanti the same principle prevailed, although in the Northern Territories local administration was applied according to the principles of indirect rule in 1932, under the Native Authority Ordinance of 1932.

divisional or other chief. Ranging above them were the provincial councils as the highest units of the native authorities structure. They dealt not only with customary problems but any issues which they felt could be profitably discussed. Their formal association as artificial but high-ranking organs was with the chief commissioner who was the agent of the governor at the regional or territorial levels—for the Colony, Ashanti, and the Northern Territories.[11]

Both British and native authorities representatives met on the Legislative Council, so far as the Colony was concerned, the latter being nominated and elected by the provincial and municipal councils, the former usually being nominated or ex officio.

The Executive and Legislative Councils

As far back as 1850, areas in the Gold Coast under British jurisdiction were governed with the advice of executive and legislative councils. These councils, the powers of which were purely advisory, were composed of European members, and it was not until 1889 that the first African[12] member was appointed. In 1916 the Legislative Council consisted of 11 official members and 10 unofficial members.[13] In 1925 it was enlarged to include elected members. The Executive Council was increased to include 8 members: the governor, the colonial secretary, the chief commissioner of Ashanti, the chief commissioner of the Northern Territories, the attorney-general, the financial secretary, the director of medical services, the secretary for native affairs.[14]

The Legislative Council consisted of 30 members with the governor as president, 15 official members, and 14 unofficial. Nine Africans, including 6 provincial and 3 municipal members, sat in the Legislative Council. The former were elected through the Joint Provincial Council. The latter were composed of elected members of the municipalities. Three towns—Accra, Cape Coast, and Sekondi—were enabled to elect one member each to the Legislative Council.[15]

The municipalities, rapidly filling with people of many tribal

11 Hailey, *Native Administration, op.cit.*, Bertram, *op.cit.*, Hinden, *op.cit.*, and others. There are numerous sources for the evaluation of the native authorities system under indirect rule.

12 See Coussey Commission Report, Appendix.

13 Hailey, *Native Administration, op.cit.*

14 See Wight, *Gold Coast Legislative Council, op.cit.*

15 Municipal Corporations Ordinance, 1924.

and regional associations, were the main centers of incipient nationalism. The serious opponents of the British and the chiefs at this time, the nationalist lawyers of the Aborigines' Rights Protection Society and the West African National Congress, were opposed to the use of chiefs by the British in the formation of central agencies of government. Influential barristers like Joseph Casely Hayford clearly saw the contradictory position of the chiefs, Casely Hayford himself stating that anyone who sat on the Legislative Council was in effect a traitor.

The Legislative Council under the 1925 Constitution contained an official majority. As Wight indicates:

"The theory of a Legislative Council with an official majority is that of a morally homogenous advisory body. Its subordination to the executive government is its primary feature, its composition only secondary; and the organization of a party system would be as improper as it is unnecessary."[16]

With this composition the government could ensure a favorable decision if it demanded, by instructions to the official members who had a majority. In addition, in the Gold Coast the officials could always count on unofficial mining and commercial members who were appointed by the governor as representatives of special interests. Finally, it was rare that either elected or appointed representatives of special interests were characterized by extremist attitudes and debate was joined in a climate of mutuality, rather than in the spirit of division and policy determination.

As part of the mechanism of indirect rule, the Legislative Council was conceived not as a representative body, expressing public demands, but rather as an agency to advise, through its composite membership, on important issues. It was a communications center in which the governor found out public attitudes by quizzing African members, and through whom information was transmitted to native authorities through the provincial and municipal councils. As Wight states, "As the form of Legislative Council is not parliamentary, so its psychology is paternalistic and not democratic."[17]

As a consequence, demands issued by political groups were decided in the judgment of central British authorities. For practical purposes, the people of the Gold Coast had little genuine

[16] Wight, *Gold Coast Legislative Council, op.cit.*
[17] *Ibid.*

participation in national government, except on the tolerance of the governor.

Nevertheless, bills were heard and debated in the council and for the most part the governor would abide by the council's decisions. The processes of debate and passage of bills conformed to parliamentary rules. Committee practice was common. In addition, bills of a non-financial character were sent to the provincial councils for their comment, and an elaborate process of multi-level debate served as a sounding board for public feeling.

Members of the Executive Council in their capacities as departmental heads presented matters for the discretion of the Legislative Council, including financial estimates, ordinances affecting their departments, and the general laws of the Gold Coast Colony. It is important to remember that neither Ashanti nor the Northern Territories was represented. Ashanti separation was not overcome until the 1946 Constitution, and even then the Northern Territories remained the stepchild of central Gold Coast politics.

With the new responsibilities placed upon them, certain chiefs responded with a brilliant political showing which no doubt raised the Gold Coast people in the esteem of the British administrators. Not all of the new role performances by the traditional authorities resulted in negative violations of sanctions. Many of these chiefs were decorated by the British government. They were looked upon as the repositories of Gold Coast wisdom, were treated with exquisite respect and courtesy, and their words carried weight.[18]

---

[18] The Secretary of the Joint Provincial Council, Mr. Magnus Sampson writes as follows: "From the beginning of Gold Coast history, the chiefs have always reacted to their oaths of office not to be caught napping in their vigilance over the general affairs of the country. It was in that spirit that they vehemently opposed the Governor Maxwell's Lands Bill of 1897 which sought to vest Gold Coast lands in the British Crown. The successful outcome of that opposition was the founding of the Gold Coast Aborigines' Rights Protection Society, and the passing into law of the Concessions Ordinance of 1900 and 1939. . . . So that but for the chiefs, the development of the country would have been well-nigh impossible. They have, in this particular respect, saved the country from the fate of the Matabeles and the Kenyas.

"During the administration of Sir Hugh Clifford (1912-1919) it became necessary for government to make use of the experience of certain leading chiefs of the country in the central legislature, and accordingly Sir Hugh reconstituted the Legislative Council and admitted for the first time to the council four well-educated and distinguished chiefs, namely, the late Nana Sir Ofori Atta, K.B.E., *omanhene* of Akyem Abuakwa State, the late Nana Sir Mate Kole, Kt., *konor* of Manya Krobo State, the late Nana Amonco V., *omanhene* of Anomabu State, and Togbi Sri II, O.B.E., *awoame fia* of Anlo, all of whom served on the Legislative

A high proportion of the chiefs who were directly involved in provincial council or central government politics regarded themselves as a ruling aristocracy and in this way they were supported by honorifics, orders and knighthoods, as well as membership in the Legislative Council. Rarely was their advice disregarded.

For a limited number of partially educated chiefs, therefore, the road to political authority was through participation in secular organs of authority which pertained to customary matters as well as other issues, such as the Joint Provincial Council and the other provincial councils. From these organs, they bent their weight in the central legislature. British authorities regarded them as the only true spokesmen for African affairs since they were, by custom, allowed to act only in accordance with consultation and discussion with elders and commoners of the tribe. Indirect rule was thus considered close to the general public. Political development seemed to involve increasing the comprehensive responsibility of adequately trained chiefs and intelligentsia in the running of conciliar organs—a notion denied only by a few members of the Aborigines' Rights Protection Society, and the West African National Congress. The chiefs apparently envisioned their position as conservative-nationalist and their increasing responsibility was called "orderly progress." As Sampson puts it:

"It must be clearly understood that the chiefs have never at any time stood in the way of political progress because they quite realize that there is no fundamental difference between them and their people whose interests are interwoven, since they swim or sink together in all national questions or emergencies. What they definitely stood for is *orderly progress* and that political advance should go hand in hand with economic development and Africanization of the public service. Apart from this the chiefs are also conscious of the necessity to adapt native institutions and tradi-

---

Council with characteristic dignity and sagacity.

"Under the 1925 Constitution, Sir Gordon Guggisberg made it possible for more chiefs to take part in the deliberations or activities of the Legislative Council and from that time up to January, 1951, the chiefs played an important and noble part in the central legislature, notably the late Nana Sir Ofori Atta, K.B.E., *omanhene* of Akyem Abuakwa State, Nana Sir Tsibu Darku IX, Kt., O.B.E., *omanhene* of Asebu State, the late Nana Amanfi III, C.B.E., *omanhene* of Asin Atandaso State, the Nana Ayirebi Acquah III, O.B.E., *omanhene* of Effutu State and Nana Ofori Atta II, *omanhene* of Akyem Abuakwa State."

The above information derives from a personal communication with Mr. Sampson.

tions to the needs of a more democratic age but preserving the best in the spirit of the old, remembering the fundamental truth that adaptation to changing conditions is the condition of survival and remembering also that unhappy are the people who cut themselves from their past."[19]

This indeed is the language of indirect rule. In fact, one of its major achievements is the effective recruitment, training, and participation of such men as those who involved themselves in provincial and central politics.

However, for increasing groups in the population, indirect rule was viewed as government by seduction. Orders, knighthoods, and political posts awarded to the chiefs were regarded as a kind of pay-off. It was argued that some chiefs paid little attention to local affairs, so concerned were they with cutting a large political swath through the Colony. Today most of these chiefs are under a cloud. Some, like the *konor* of Manya Krobo, are under fierce pressure to abdicate. Some have been destooled. The language of indirect rule is not the language of nationalism. Today's counterpart of indirect rule, with its stress on moderation and conservatism, is found in the parties of the North (Northern People's Party), the chiefs (Ghana Congress Party), and the Moslems (Moslem Association Party).

Under indirect rule the attempt was made to blend traditional authority by maintaining as much as possible of traditional social organization compatible with conciliar secular structures. Indirect rule provided new and wider functions for chiefs. It initiated in this fashion the process of institutional transfer by demanding Western-type standards of behavior and secular norms in the performance of predominantly Western-type role structures. It sought to endow chieftaincy with a supporting cloak of secular authority, and to endow secular authority with the traditional participation of traditional authorities. Out of such a pattern, most British leaders felt that a new structural synthesis would emerge, close to the public, and in that sense indigenous. Rattray's warning is an effective pointer to what followed:

"In introducing indirect rule into this country, we would therefore appear to be encouraging on the one hand an institution which draws its inspiration and validity from the indigenous religious beliefs, while on the other we are systematically destroying

[19] *Ibid.*

140

the very foundation upon which the structure that we are striving to perpetuate stands. Its shell and outward form might remain, but it would seem too much to expect that its vital energy could survive such a process."[20]

The Constitution of 1946

After the Second World War, in which the Gold Coast regiment distinguished itself, the Colonial Office decided that the fruits of victory should take the form of political reform. The groundwork had been laid by the strengthening of local government units, viz., the reform in 1944 of the native authorities. Each territorial area and administrative division had its councils of chiefs. Each territorial area was subdivided into native authority units in which the state councils (*oman*) were the conciliar foundation of the consultative hierarchy. Each native authority had its own treasury, its native courts and police, and often took commoners on the council.[21]

An amalgamation of petty states into confederacies operating as native authorities took care of more atomistic communities such as in the Tongu area composed of Ewe groups among others. Larger areas were given subdivisional treasuries, courts, and councils. At the peak of this structure was the territorial council. This structure appeared as a substantial organizational pattern having, at the local level, the district commissioner, and at the territorial level, the chief commissioner, British colonial officers providing advice, handling complicated matters beyond the purview of traditional authority, and responsible for keeping the peace and good order of the areas under their jurisdiction.

Under the Constitution of 1946, the Burns Constitution,[22] the Colony and Ashanti were both put directly under a common legislative and executive instrument, the newly reconstituted legislative and executive councils.[23] This instrument integrated the traditional and secular—the chiefs on the one hand and the municipal elected members and nominated and ex officio members on the other— into an advisory organ whose powers to recommend were profound and whose assent to ordinances was considered essential to the

[20] Rattray, *Ashanti Law, op.cit.*, p. ix.
[21] See Hailey, *Native Administration, op.cit.*, pp. 208, 216.
[22] After the governor, Sir Alan Burns.
[23] See Statutory Rules and Orders 1946 No. 353, Gold Coast Colony and Ashanti (Legislative Council) Order in Council, 1946.

enactment of internal law. The provincial members were elected by the Joint Provincial Council,[24] the Ashanti members by the Confederacy Council, the municipal members, as hitherto by ballot, the electorates being the same as for municipal elections. The nominated members were to be appointed at the governor's discretion. "It was intended that they would be Africans rather than Europeans, drawn from interests that were otherwise unrepresented or under-represented minorities (e.g., the Ewes, Togoland, the unconfederated units in Ashanti), commercial interests, missions, education, the cooperative movement, etc."[25]

The effort was therefore made to draw in all of the representative groups in the Gold Coast deemed capable of taking a responsible part in the decision-making processes of the Colony and Ashanti. At the same time the constitution drew in the wealthier political malcontents—those dissident educated Africans tending to the fringe between traditional and secular patterns of political life.[26]

For the first time in West Africa the 1946 Constitution gave to the Gold Coast an African-dominated Legislative Council, and, more important, a representative legislature. As Wight points out:

"The new constitution presents two great contrasts with the old. Legislative Council has become the legislature for Ashanti as well as for the Gold Coast Colony, and at the same time it has been transformed into a representative legislature. The first change marks the political union of the Colony and Ashanti, and it brings five Ashanti members to the council at Accra: four representing the Confederacy Council, the fifth representing Kumasi. It is contemplated, moreover, that though the governor will continue to legislate for the Northern Territories at present, these too will come under the authority of Legislative Council when their unofficial representation becomes possible. The unification which Ashanti failed to accomplish by military force in the eighteenth and nineteenth centuries has been brought about, within a frame-

24 For the Colony.

25 See Wight, *Gold Coast Legislative Council, op.cit.*, pp. 203-204.

26 The new Legislative Council consisted of the governor as president, 6 official members; the colonial secretary, the 3 chief commissioners, the attorney-general and the financial secretary; 9 provincial members for the Colony, 5 from the eastern and 4 from the western provinces; 4 Ashanti members; 5 municipal members, 2 for Accra and 1 each for Cape Coast, Sekondi-Takoradi, and Kumasi; 6 nominated members. See Part II, The Legislative Council, Statutory Rules and Orders.

work of British power, in terms of Western constitutionalism. The year 1946 may well come to have the same significance in Gold Coast history as 1707 has in British.

"But if the new constitution thus makes a landmark in Gold Coast history, it has also a wider significance. For with the replacement of the official majority by an elected majority, the council becomes a representative legislature. The contrast between the old and the new council is striking. Its total number has been increased by no more than one, and this only if the new position of president without a vote be included in the reckoning; but whereas in the old council the fourteen unofficial members faced the impregnable majority of sixteen official members, and only nine of the unofficials were Africans, in the new council there are eighteen elected African members against six officials, and the remaining six are nominated unofficial members who may as likely be Africans as Europeans. The council has thus advanced at a bound from an official majority to an unofficial majority, an elected majority, and an African majority."[27]

The Burns Constitution was considered a logical climax to the system of indirect rule. With effective political representation of the chiefs, the "responsible" educated Africans, and the British, it seemed destined to mark the solution to the political demands of the Gold Coast nationalists. Members came to it from the territorial councils and as elected municipal members, in addition to those appointed from official or other bodies. The two hierarchies —the native authorities territorial councils hierarchy and the British colonial service hierarchy—met, in company with other representatives, to debate the bills and ordinances of the Gold Coast. It seemed that this constitution would last for a good many years; in actual fact, it lasted four.

The Legislative Council often reached high levels of debate. The governor almost never ignored its decisions. While not yet a responsible organ, it at least represented Africans in the majority on the council. The members of the council were exclusive members, an elite, having been given their posts either by franchise in the municipalities, by appointment, or from the territorial councils.

The chiefs were, in the main, pleased with their important func-

[27] Wight, *Gold Coast Legislative Council, op.cit.*, pp. 205-206.

143

tions. They had become figures with extra-traditional authority, having a hierarchy in which they could exercise influence that had important consequences for the public at large. They ruled their local areas with the majesty of British legal sanction and with a district commissioner to advise them and back them up if necessary. Where they went beyond their jurisdiction in traditional matters they could be, and frequently were, destooled. Destoolment of lesser chiefs was a common practice. For the more powerful political chiefs, destoolment was more difficult since their violation of traditional prescriptions of chieftaincy was less telling than their new functions.

One fatal weakness of the constitution perhaps more than any other reduced its effectiveness and eventually provided for its downfall. The constitution failed to accord responsibility in full measure with representativeness, and also to accord representativeness in due proportion to the more basic power blocs in the Gold Coast itself. These basic power blocs were to show their hand later on, but in a very real sense the British authorities were not aware of their existence. The repudiation of the Burns Constitution came as a genuine shock to many British officers who saw in nationalism the subversion not only of British rule but of traditional Gold Coast institutional patterns as well.

The Orientation of Leadership Roles

One of the peculiar features of Gold Coast patterns of indirect rule was the emphasis on the development of central governmental political structures partly in collaboration with a network of increasingly traditional sub-structures as concrete membership units in the territorial and local areas. In this fashion, it was felt, the close and intimate relationship of chiefs and people could be maintained while the larger aspects of more secular government business could be handled with greater public understanding and participation. A second assumption which emerged in practice rather than design resulted from the use of outstanding chiefs in advisory capacities so that they became representatives on parliamentary bodies, more skilled in the ways of secular decision-making. Increasingly, their traditional legitimacy (still a formal requirement of participation) became residual; their functioning roles involved two substantively different patterns. They had to perform, on the one hand, ritual functions and conform to the procedures and norms of tribal society. On the other hand, the legislative structure provided access to more secular political power. The chiefs were not devoid of nationalist utterances, but they saw nationalism in terms of the devolution of responsibility to the natural rulers within a modified structural parliamentary arrangement which emerged out of indirect rule and reached its fullest development in the Burns Constitution. A few chiefs attained remarkable status in the secular political structure achieved in the latter days of indirect rule, but for the mass of lesser chiefs the association with the British was a destructive influence. Only certain important chiefs who had reached remarkable success under indirect rule could envision with equanimity their political roles within the framework of Gold Coast indirect rule. The apparent integrative aspects of this system were misleading. The strengthening of chieftaincy for a few by adding to its functions was not repeated down the line. Instead, the contradictory aspects of secular and traditional legitimacy and its extended sanctions undermined the pattern of rule of chiefs in general. Busia puts it as follows:

"The support which government gives to the chiefs is on the basis of the chief's subordinate status. The chief's powers are limited and defined by ordinances: both he and his subjects are under the control of the government, which the people associate with limitless power, endless wealth, and a high prestige. By comparison, the chief has limited powers, scanty wealth, and a lowered prestige, daily in evidence in his relationships with the district commissioner or chief commissioner or the governor.

"It is in these circumstances that the Ashanti chief today is called upon to perform many new functions of government, and to rule over the subjects, some of whom have acquired a new status in the community, having gained more power, greater wealth, and a higher prestige, because of the opportunities offered by the white man's presence, as government official, trader, or missionary within the framework of British rule."[28]

Some educated Africans were hostile both to British demands for secular standards of behavior if secular roles were to be sought, and traditional demands insofar as they had not cut themselves off from the traditional environment, their family or their clan groups. As Rattray states:

[28] Busia, *Position of the Chief, op.cit.,* p. 117.

"The educated African, however, has been cut off from and is out of sympathy with the life of his own people. He has learned in nine cases out of ten, if he has not actually been taught, to despise his own illiterate brethren and the unlettered part of his race. Concerning that past he really knows little or nothing and generally cares less. . . .

"[The educated Africans] feel, and they have been trained to believe that they are brands plucked from the burning. It is almost impossible that such persons can be sympathetic with their own past, a past which after all few of them have really known, seen, or clearly understand."[29]

For many of those who sought to develop more fully the latent Gold Coast nationalism rather than utilize existing traditional or other organizations, the emphasis was upon educational elites, having a firm organizational base. One of the founders of the youth movement, Dr. J. Danquah, in a pamphlet entitled *Self-Help and Expansion*,[30] discusses the importance of organization, which in practice turned out to be the precursor of present-day political parties insofar as the United Gold Coast Convention was largely the expression of Danquah's political hopes. Danquah asks for the intensified organization of society with people like himself in the crucial position. Hardly a mention is made of independence. Rather, Danquah calls for industrialization, speaking "in the name of science" with the grandiloquent plea, "Please, God, let a column of fire go forth before us, behind us, to bring to us and

---

[29] Rattray, *Ashanti*, London, 1923, pp. 87-88.

[30] Published by the Gold Coast Youth Conference, Accra, 1943. See pages 13-14. Danquah says: "Liberty is power. Freedom is power. Education is power. Not power in a vacuum, but power in an organized community where your capacity, your attainments, your resources can be put to beneficial use.

"When therefore we cry for a better system of education, when we cry for liberty and freedom, what we are crying for is this, that this community should be so highly organized that our capacity to do the thing we like to do can be practicalized. We wish to be powerful. We wish that we could have the power to travel where we like, to learn what we like, to eat what we like, to obtain the music we like, the kind of bedstead we like to sleep in, the room, the house, the locality, or street, the town, the bicycle, the sewing machine, the car, the clothes, the wife—educated and trained—the children, the society, the confraternity, the companions, the friends, the books, the hobbies, and above all, the kind of employment or work or service we most like to have or do. Liberty is the power to command the thing you like to have.

"That power is denied us if our community is not highly organized, and if the community we live in is not highly organized, then we are weaklings, we are like children, like a primitive people, born in chains without any increased increment in our liberty for greater locomotion, the liberty to walk, or talk, or act, or to stand on our own feet. We are slaves."

the country, to the people, to the ignorant, poverty-stricken and subject people of this Gold Coast a light into our darkness."[31] It is clear that Dr. Danquah, "a brand plucked from the burning," saw himself with a few sparks of his own. Traditional economic and social life was viewed as something of the dark past— sordid, squalid, and in no way to be preferred to Western civilization. Western aspirational definition served to recruit adherents such as the Achimota School graduates who demanded that Europeans respect them on European terms by according them positions of responsibility. The symbols of progress, science, freedom, youth, all became cues which the new leadership evoked and reinforced. "When some people want to come to Africa, they say they want their place in the sun; and they go to war for it. We live in Africa, we have plenty of sun, but we want our share of cash, because we want to be happy and do our duty to the world, so as to make human life, in black man, or in white man, a dignified thing, and not the sordid thing in squalor round about us," says Danquah. Indirect rule, in supplanting the range of traditional goals and objects of utility with those of Western style, provided the nationalist leadership with ammunition. It evoked a range of demands which were impossible to fulfill. No colonial government or government of an underdeveloped area can move very rapidly towards fulfilling the goals it has inspired. Particularly for the educated, and for the youth, impatience and hostility were turned against both the traditional leadership and the colonial officers, leaving people embroiled in confusion, while underneath like an ugly current was the self-consciousness of race.

The orientational effects of the structure of indirect rule on role definition were, of course, complex. The decorated and admired chiefs had their affiliations to the members of their tribe, of course, but these links became less close and personal. Instead, the tribe was a base from which chieftainship qualified a few individuals for positions of national honor in British-inspired councils. When the nationalist movement did develop, the chiefs were identified with British imperialism. They donned traditional robes and business suits with equal dispatch, without realizing the inconsistencies in these positions.

With the sacred restrictions on their own activities undermined, the entire traditional structure of tribal politics was threatened.

[31] *Ibid.*

The native courts, usually presided over by a chief or elder, took bribes.[32] The sanctity of a fair decision given in accord with proverb and custom was dissipated since local opposition often would spring out of an unfavorable decision. Increasingly the effectiveness of tribal politics was based upon the district commissioner's support, a local by-product of which was tension and hostility to both the district commissioner and the chief.

The chiefs, then, modified the traditional system, but they were careful to preserve the fiction of ultimate traditional legitimacy. The very language of chieftainship—natural rulers—indicates a condition of cultural orientation which is basically unstable, once the natural order as conceived in traditional society is subverted.

The only other group which effectively challenged the leadership of the chiefs, and who also were encouraged by the British, were educated and responsible elites. Mostly trained in Britain, or else professional men of one sort or another, they formed a group attempting clearly to play roles assigned in terms of Western education, dress, behavior patterns, values, and religion. These were the people whose affiliations were to the municipalities, to the de-tribalized, urbanized, restive, and aggressive Westernized society of the coast. Where the chiefs retained in form, but less in substance, their old associations and reference orientations, the educated group had to create their own support. Partly they received esteem from the high prestige placed upon education. For the most part, as has been indicated, they served as orientational inspiration for younger people whose desire to emulate them turned them into willing, if sometimes unreliable, associates. Some of those who joined the youth movements received support from civil authorities, the schools (particularly Achimota), the churches, and most of the other responsible segments of the population.

A considerable number of these educated Africans had strong lineage and family ties to royal families. If they were lawyers, they received some of their income from land litigation or from professional duties which enabled them to devote part of their time to politics. Some of them, like Justice Korsah or Sir Emmanuel Quist, the latter the speaker of the Legislative Assembly, set the standards for a responsible British-type African who would represent the interests of his fellow-Africans with a dignity made

[32] See Blackall Commission on native courts.

more impelling by his exquisite understanding of the need of proceeding slowly towards political independence.

Into the comparatively open society of the Gold Coast, these new barristers, educators, and churchmen thrust a new prestige group, represented as a cluster of roles, political and social, towards which tribal youth, more and more restive under the rule of the chiefs and rural life, aspired. This new group moved with comparative ease in British social circles. By African standards they had wealth and crucial items of conspicuous consumption.

This group, gradually interpreted to be a class—at least by the British, who dubbed it a middle class—were the business-suited professional men. They were presumed to be conservative (in the sense that they wanted no drastic or revolutionary change), responsible, and fitting products of indirect rule. They were provided places by election to municipal councils and were often nominated or elected members of the provincial and legislative councils. Regardless of how nationalist they sounded, in retrospect they were identified with British custom. Some grew very wealthy and became objects of suspicion; the disparity between their mode of life and that of the ordinary African widened.

Both the chiefs and the educated elite tended to regard themselves as the inheritors of British power. They sought to enhance their responsibility and power in the political picture and were alternately pro- or anti-British in these terms, but mostly cooperative. They considered themselves logical trainees under indirect rule for positions of authority.[33]

The net effect was to fragmentize orientational affiliations into new social subgroupings, marked on the one hand by a bureaucratic chieftainship, affable and able, and on the other by a new middle class which was to act as a responsible lever against the whims and fancies of the mob. Through this middle class it was

[33] Much of the material in this section comes from interviews with educated Africans who had achieved positions of eminence in the period of indirect rule, as well as from chiefs and civil servants. I am particularly indebted to Kenneth Bradley, former acting colonial secretary in the Gold Coast, the Reverend Mr. Baeta, a member of the Coussey Commission and now at the University College of the Gold Coast, Mr. J. de Graft Johnson, Nene Azzu Mate Kole, the *konor* of Manya Krobo, Dr. K. A. Busia, chairman of the Department of Sociology, University College of the Gold Coast, the *assumejehene*, the *ashympemhene*, the secretary of the Ashanti Confederacy Council, and many others. I have not identified particular individuals with the statements made since they are generally corroborative, and in any case might cause personal embarrassment to the individuals themselves.

hoped that a new and stable group would provide a source of recruitment on secular lines.

One effect was the widening of goal orientations toward secular and material positions which on the one hand either promoted achievement by British standards, and which involved self-images of responsibility and authority while aligning roles with significant membership subgroups in the system, and on the other hand provided a source of motivation particularly for political action. Membership in this significant group received support from official, educational, religious, and other groups composed of Europeans.

The limiting factor remained social mobility. The evidence of a small but effective group of professional people, as well as some of the titled chiefs, served to attract larger numbers of people hitherto integrated into traditional patterns of society. Yet opportunities to enter these groups were small, often stimulating deviant and illegal efforts toward goal satiety.

The system of political norms was essentially bimodal, with a procedural harmony which was adequate for the functioning of government, but which promoted fundamental behavioral conflict stemming from contradictory forms of legitimacy, traditional and secular. Procedural harmony was maintained by the use of secular force to preserve traditional roles, in which crucial issues of constitutionalism and legitimacy were postponed, but which helped, in the long run, to undermine the effective authority of the chiefs.

Analytical Aspects of Relationship Structures under Indirect Rule

Indirect rule has been used to signify a particular form of political association in which traditional and non-traditional political structures coexist in complementary association for the good governance of the country. We have tried to indicate that in this process a set of social and orientational consequences were unleashed which made heavy demands for the readjustment of individuals and groups to new social conditions, the adjustment itself being complex and diffuse. Insofar as it was the design of the colonial authorities to maintain the traditional system intact and use it as a basis of political administration, much of the effective maintenance of the traditional system increasingly came from external sources rather than from internal support by the members. This fact, evidenced in the changing roles of chieftaincy and the structures provided for the chiefs to ventilate their political advice, aided in producing a basically unstable situation relating to the shift in goal orientations, behavioral alternatives, and political norms of tribal groups in the Gold Coast. The net effect was that, in terms of subsequent events, the maintenance of the structure of traditional authority was in fact countenanced by law, and by British support to the chiefs, while internal support waned. *The use of external—non-traditional—means to support traditional legitimacy was dysfunctional to the maintenance of traditional authority.*

The changes wrought under indirect rule were therefore profound. They indicate both the astonishing resiliency and fragility of traditional societies. Indirect rule demonstrated that at crucial points of contact between European and traditional patterns of authority, the latter as an expression of social cohesiveness declined. With its decline, a visible source of conflict remained —the question of the terms of social behavior and group membership. Such a source of conflict is one of the prerequisites of nationalism. In this manner, indirect rule, which is often charged with being unwise, illogical, imperialistic, etc., produced the conditions whereby social groupings could emerge, cutting across traditional lines to create a larger political unit: a Gold Coast in more than name only.

We shall try to outline some of this material as shifts in analytical and normative factors governing interpersonal association during this period. Certain aspects of these shifts will be discussed in terms of Levy's analytical aspects of relationship structures.

Levy[34] defines a relationship structure as "any social structure (or set of structures) that defines the actions, ideally and/or actually, that interrelate two or more individual actions." Under these relationships we can subsume the conflicting patterns of interpersonal relations of traditional and secular Gold Coast social life. We shall use some of Levy's relationship structures for this purpose, particularly as regards the Colony and Ashanti.

a. The Cognitive Aspect.[35] Traditional society in the Gold

---

[34] See Levy, Marion J., *The Structure of Society, op.cit.*, particularly Chapter vi, from which much of the succeeding materials derive.

[35] Levy says, "However elementary it may be, every socially defined human

Coast was one in which religion and magic played crucial roles, the former embodying the value and belief systems of the society, and the latter a means of employing certain non-empirical instrumentalities to achieve empirical ends.[36] Christianity and Mohammedanism and other nativistic and messianic cults tended to subvert the traditional relationship between religion and traditional authority and its use. Where people adopted Christianity, they usually attempted to conform to Western patterns of behavior, although occasionally some remarkable interpretations of Western appeared. Those who moved towards Mohammedanism tended to retain some of the intimacy of tribal association, meanwhile adapting more effectively to commercial demands of Gold Coast life. The impact of Islam is a most complex one and properly would be a study in itself. Those who joined the nativistic or messianic cults tended to avoid newly provided patterns of Western social behavior, seeking solace in religious beliefs, yet rarely regarding a particular form of social life, tribal or not, as highly desirable.

In the cities, however, the pattern of Christianity took hold for increasing numbers of mission school gentry whose objectives were the normal type of Western social intercourse, at least in form if not in substance. The middle class of intellectuals or professional men—teachers, doctors, lawyers—tended to be Christian, Western-oriented towards empirical rather than non-empirical ends. Christianity was a fashion to which proper men, responsible and upright, gave service. However, their behavior was consciously determined by criteria of rational rather than religious or magical thought.

For the rural, pagan, and rural messianic or nativistic groups, what has been termed methodologically arational action in the main applies[37] as a category into which magic or *ju-ju* would

---

interrelationship involves some elements of cognition. There is, for example, the cognition involved in the recognition of those eligible for the relationship, and there is always some cognition involved in the action carried out in terms of the relationship." *Ibid.*, p. 240.

[36] Such as protection of one's farm, ridding one's self of an enemy, etc. It is called *ju-ju*, and the Gold Coasters make a clear distinction between religion and magic. The latter is an immediate political weapon in some cases, particularly on a local or rural level.

[37] Methodologically arational action "is that action in which the ends of the actor are empirical but the means are nonempirical, at least in part." Magic or *ju-ju* would fall into this category. See Levy, *op.cit.*, pp. 242-244.

fall, as does ultimately arational action,[38] a category into which religion itself would fall. The urbanized and educated Africans tend to view these positions with contempt. Instead, their standards became more logical in an empirical sense. The distinction has given rise, in some circles, to a mistaken notion of "pre-logicality" on the part of primitive people. Such is not the issue here; the essential logicality of mental processes is not in question, but rather whether or not it deals with non-empirical limits. One even finds educated Africans speaking of the "pre-logicality" of his illiterate compatriot, using this term with full invidiousness. One consequence of this has been the placing of education on a very high prestige level. With several notable exceptions, a gulf emerged between the illiterate public and the educated intellectuals. One of the most important political aspects of such a gulf has been that these intellectuals were never able effectively to reach the public, whereas less well-educated nationalists were.

The political effects of these cognitive differences are profound since they establish orientational boundaries which divide people from one another in terms of criteria of action and norms of rationality. We can not only classify the action criteria of different portions of the population, but point out the divisions within the population itself in patterns of social intercourse and affiliations.

b. The Membership Criteria Aspect. Consonant, to some extent, with the cognitive aspects of relationship structures was the "membership criteria aspect." Levy indicates "In all relationships the question of choice of membership in the relationship is posed."[39] We have indicated that in traditional society, membership and recruitment were on the basis of high specific qualification which we can call particularistic. The actual criteria of selection were not logically germane to actual choice, but rather to other considerations. On the other hand, during indirect rule more non-traditional and secularized sectors of society tended to affiliate to and maintain social relations with others on the basis of more universalistic criteria, in keeping with the standards of impartiality, merit, and technical requirements of the British civil service.

Again and again throughout the literature of this period we

[38] Ultimately arational action "is that action in which both the ends and the means of the actor are at least in part non-empirical." Religion would fall into this category.
[39] Levy, *op.cit.*, p. 248.

find references to the need to democratize chieftaincy and the traditional pattern of authority. It is clear that the term does not have reference to the consultative processes under traditional authority, which even by Western standards are democratic to an extreme. Rather, it refers to the range of offices and positions around the chief which can be entered only on the basis of particularistic membership criteria, a barrier which to a large extent is removed in secular social life.

An earlier mentioned example of disbarment on the basis of lineage serving to stimulate high attainment on more secular levels is the move of educated children of slave lineages (slave mothers) to join the more secular ranks of the intellectuals. According to Busia, some of the most effective nationalists in the Convention People's Party have been products of slave lineage and high education.

Essentially, the contradiction between universalistic and particularistic membership criteria under traditional and secular patterns of authority which developed during the period of indirect rule is one of the crucial problems of political institutional transfer. A definition of the spheres in which traditional particularistic criteria shall apply means a definition of the groups which shall persist having predominantly traditionalistic orientations. Like the place and role of chieftaincy, such a question can never be met head on, but rather will work itself out in the heat of politics.

A number of immediate questions are of course posed. Should an African civil servant remain a full member of his family and act on their behalf in terms of traditional criteria? Action on their behalf might mean the use of very particularistic criteria indeed as an efficient cause of activity.

c. The Substantive Definition Aspect. "In every relationship there are activities or considerations or rights and obligations that are covered by the relationship. These factors comprise the *substantive definition* of the relationship."[40]

The structural system in tribal society was functionally diffuse. For example, the same ceremony or the same ritual might at one and the same time propitiate the ancestors, strengthen the stool, bring forth a more bountiful harvest, and help to select a new chief. The kinds of relationships established and built around these

[40] *Ibid.*, pp. 255-256.

social phenomena were ceremonial and prescribed, but lacking in the functional precision of a highly specialized system where extensive division of labor and a highly differentiated set of social obligations and responsibilities set the pattern of the relationships, as in modern business communities, for example.

In traditional society, just as the family as a network of social relations fulfills many differing kinds of functions through membership participation and activity, so the tribal system was the functional enlargement of the family in many ways and the product of a more extended structural arrangement. As such, the same personnel and the same general pattern of social intercourse characterized many differing kinds of functional expression in the tribal authority pattern.

The impact of indirect rule upon this system was to introduce a more highly specific set of role requirements fitted to performances which had European valuations placed on them. The Colonial Service was made up of a highly differentiated and functionally specific set of administrative relationships. To be drawn, even tentatively, into this network meant a drastic change in role performance in order to integrate with the system established by the British authorities. For example, while the role of the chief had ritual precision and functional diffuseness within the tribal nexus, the role was modified in a functionally specific direction as it involved participation in the provincial, territorial, or legislative councils, or in the local or native authorities structure as laid down by ordinances. Such functional precision played havoc in the relationship among elders, commoners, and chiefs which had been articulated on a delicate balance of power. The chiefs began to have more and more things to do. They were responsible for courts, for building local roads, for financial matters—in other words, for administration. The functional precision created in this manner directly violated the sacred and diffuse role of the chief in traditional authority, where specific obligations referred to diffuse functions.

d. The Stratification Aspect. One of the most significant aspects of traditional authority was, as we have indicated, the modestly hierarchical and only slightly invidious differentiation of status on the basis of lineage. Group participation and group superiority took the form of local patriotism, with contempt expressed for other integral groups outside the tribe, village, or family. Otherwise, in regard to internal structure, hierarchy was not elaborate and there was little or no class awareness. Status groups were probably most articulated for the Ashanti Confederacy, and for the north, among certain groups like the Tallensi or Konkomba, social organization was in many respects egalitarian. The independent unit was the family, with its own stool and its own magical devices for protection.

The cluster of British-type roles, both for professionals or intelligentsia and for educated chiefs, tended to create a new status hierarchy which for some proved to be a barrier to effective communication with the traditional unit.

In addition, status groupings around such symbols of wealth, and others stemming out of the shift from subsistence farming to a variety of means of earning income, tended to shift the status of individuals out of the traditionally conceived pattern.

In the political sense, to be a powerful chief was to violate the traditions of the past. The old status of chieftaincy was rarely found in a secure state. Within the new status hierarchies, new political and social organizations were formed having some of the properties of exclusiveness, such as the Achimota group, from which the partially educated who had repudiated traditional authority were barred. They, in turn, had to find some publicly recognized vehicle to status. Such motives were no doubt important in the founding of the Convention People's Party.

e. The Goal Orientation Aspect. For the most part, the demands made by secularism on traditional social action tended to require the development of more individualistic attitudes coupled with a concept of individual responsibility. Whereas the traditional pattern directly involved a predominantly responsible behavioral network, orientation was towards the collectivity rather than towards the individual himself, except in certain modes of economic activity such as working the farms. It is most difficult to speak with much authority on this subject since little material was gathered which would support a carefully elaborated discussion. It suffices to say that by comparison with the responsibility orientations demanded by tribal social life, a strong development of individualism has occurred in which each person tends to regard his success as an individual matter, and the means legitimate if they further the goal. It might be added that such a process among the educated and partially educated groups clearly had occurred, but where both kinds of aspects, individualistic and responsible, coincided, wide ranges in the behavior of the individual, often appearing erratic and irresponsible, were observed.

Conclusions

The period of indirect rule was the period of maximum flux, Western cultural impact, and adjustive demands made upon Africans in the Gold Coast. We have roughly set the limits of this period from the 1925 Constitution to the 1946 Constitution. The contradictory elements engendered in indirect rule as we enunciated them created basic instabilities in the pattern of social order so that questions of basic legitimacy regarding traditional and secular roles and structures were raised, as were the questions pertaining to behavior. Although legally a pattern of procedural integration was evident in the system of secular political administration which utilized the native authorities and chiefs as a means to provide stability, to maintain traditional authority patterns, and to sustain the network of consultation and communications of intimate tribal social structure, these attempts raised crucial problems of transition without providing adequate bases for substantive reintegration around new units of authority. By the time the Burns Constitution was promulgated, the latent strains in the social structure under indirect rule had already made it an inadequate basis for supporting a central system of authority receiving the dual legitimacy of traditional and secular sanctions. It was impossible to maintain a system whereby effective power was still in the hands of the British officials, and responsibility, in the full sense of the word, was granted and demanded of widely differing groups of Africans who were judged in terms of their performances by Western political standards.

Role performance and achievement, particularly in the performance of functionally specific roles of secular authority, made demands on Africans divided between tribal and secular orientations. Often the poor performances of Africans in government were held up as examples of their unreadiness to participate in greater shares of political authority at central government levels, while satisfactory performances were judged as exceptional.

The system, on the surface, attempted to integrate tribal and secular authority systems in their forms, without an appreciation by colonial officials of how some of the more substantive aspects of traditional society might be functionally integrated with more modern demands. Apparently, little attention was given to modifying traditional land tenure notions into communal cooperative rural enterprise, for example; instead, the legal framework of a secular, British cooperative was proposed. Petty commerce and trading which adjusted easily to the traditional marketing pattern and matrilineal kinship system became the rule, with all the costs of an encroaching competitive system in which concepts of individual gain were rarely coincident with the maintenance of corporate responsibility.

For those who moved to Westernized patterns of life, the pressure of traditional social obligations appeared as a millstone. Detribalized Africans formed a social status group composed of solidarity units having British type orientations. These people provided a reservoir from which Africans were selected, recruited, and rotated in the important offices and duties under the system of indirect rule.

For those still remaining in tribal society, and for the growing numbers of partially educated groups whose chances of entering either the society of decorated chiefs or the society of the intelligentsia were small, and whose opportunity for economic advancement was limited, there were few outlets. They became marginal in their own society. At the very top, the class which had been created under indirect rule was siphoned off into the requirements of the political structure. At the very bottom of the political hierarchy, in the villages and tribal areas, the system of native authorities provided for roles which sometimes strengthened the overt position of the chief. Among the general public, both in the tribe and in the urban centers, the old allegiances tended more and more to be subverted. Young men turned sourly against them. Pressures on the family were greater and the family tended to be less a source of strength than an obstacle. The old tended to view the young with fear. In the process new aspirations toward independence, status, reward, and wealth were being defined for those who composed this marginal group. In some cases the gap between aspiration and achievement was met with apathy; in most parts of the Gold Coast, particularly in the south and central areas, it was met with nationalism.

CHAPTER 8

TOWARDS AUTONOMY WITHIN THE
COMMONWEALTH

UNDER indirect rule, as has been indicated, a conflicting set of political norms, deriving sanctity and legitimacy from fundamentally different sources, was counterpoised within the organizational framework of the political administration. During this period greater access to the formal secular organs of government was granted both to the chiefs, whose authority increasingly came from secular sources, and to the intelligentsia, whose authority was directly secular in derivation, although many were of or related to a royal lineage.

Yet the peculiar feature of Gold Coast indirect rule was its emphasis upon the reintegration of social life around the structures of central government. The few successful chiefs felt that they would inherit the mantle of British power, as did a good many of the politically groomed intellectuals and businessmen like Danquah and Grant, the founders of the United Gold Coast Convention, Grant being its president. Even the British administrators, in the main, considered that the pattern established under the 1946 Constitution, in which certain chiefs and intellectuals achieved majority status on the Legislative Council, would only be carried another step further if the need arose. Few saw the immediate necessity for the Order in Council of 1950 or predicted the effective parliamentary use of the Legislative Assembly set up under that Constitution. Hardly anyone saw the Legislative Assembly as a parliament with an elected membership coming from exactly the people who had rarely enjoyed formal participation in the structures of authority during indirect rule. Only one member of the Convention People's Party, Kwesi Plange, sat in the old "Legco." Under the new constitution, the Convention People's Party formed the government.

The material which will preoccupy us in this section on secular government covers the period from the last war until the present "Nkrumah" constitution.

We shall attempt first to indicate some of the crucial factors which have operated first to create a national society out of an arbitrarily defined territory and second to endow the structures of parliamentary democracy, as taken from Great Britain, with legitimized and effective power.[1]

Changes in the Setting

We have discussed earlier some of the economic problems facing the Gold Coast from the standpoint of future development.[2] It must be clearly borne in mind in any discussion of Gold Coast politics that to many people "Free-dom," the nationalist slogan, is a vague kind of freedom to enjoy the blessings of Western standards of subsistence. The rock of parliament could easily submerge if improvements in material well-being are not soon forthcoming. Since the Convention People's Party came to power, a climate of buoyancy and expectancy has prevailed in many areas, with a pronounced feeling that with freedom all good things will be better tomorrow than today and that the new is better than the old. This new attitude has in many areas replaced the sanctional demands stemming from time immemorial.

Meanwhile, substantial shifts in social structures, including political sub-structures, heightened by increased migration an education, have jeopardized older institutions until today we find disagreement over basic questions relating to the place of chieftaincy in secular political organization. For example, in a leading Gold Coast daily we find the following discussion:

"The establishment of British administration and modern democracy dealt the political sovereignty of paramount chiefs a fatal blow. One constituency may cover the territories of four paramount chiefs. No paramount chief, not even the *asantehene*, can override a decision of the cabinet.

"The intricacies of modern government demand the intelligence and exertions of trained people. Local government cannot succeed unless qualified and well-paid people are employed to do the job. The cry for modern amenities grows stronger and stronger and modern amenities are expensive. Will it be possible to give all our chiefs substantial salaries which will maintain their prestige, while we pay adequately qualified local government staff and provide expensive modern amenities? The answer is obviously in the negative, if we may borrow a parliamentary term.

[1] See *The Government Proposals for Constitutional Reform*, Accra, 1953.
[2] See Chapter 3.

"Are chiefs, as they are at the moment, a dying nobility? We must face facts—the forces that assail chieftaincy are many and inexorable. We may say that in half a century its nature will be very different from what it is in Ashanti now. Wherever literary education is widespread the dignity and prestige of a chief suffers greatly. In fact it is in inverse proportion to the spread of formal education."[3]

The old institutions and structures of rule are being rapidly "de-institutionalized." The traditional standards of legitimacy are giving way. In the latter stages of indirect rule, nationalists, having no traditional sources of sanction, found themselves awarded a measure of responsibility if they could rally a significant following, conform to an image of Western behavior (including professional or intellectual status), and promote themselves as effective symbols of the African transformed. Lineage barriers served only as incentives to destroy lineage distinctions. Traditional offices were undermined by affiliation and support from British secular authorities or from others whose allegiance to traditional authorities was at best nominal. Effective authority stemmed from secular sources and operated through alien offices, filled for the most part by British Colonial Service personnel. *Only one alternative to such effective authority remained—the amalgamation of disassociated groups around a particular leader, or symbol, or set of ideas, or combination thereof.*

If public support centers around a local figure in such fashion as to take on the proportions of an organized movement, and the goals of the movement are basically to restore legitimacy and effective authority to internal (non-colonial) sources, we shall call this "nationalism." If public support and effective authority diverge, then a politically unstable situation exists. If the divergence can be modified by shifts in such fashion that public support and effective authority reach increasing identity, then a manifestly integrative process is occurring. If public support and effective authority continue to diverge, the situation will result in the open breakdown of any kind of consensus—a breakdown of the system of order, with anarchy or apathy as the polar extremes. It is the process of devolving effective authority upon the representatives of effective public support through parliamentary political struc-

[3] Apea, Kwadwo, "The Problem of Chieftaincy," in the *Daily Graphic*, Accra, November 16, 1953.

tures in such fashion that they become institutionalized which is the nub of the problem of political institutional transfer, once the decision has been taken that such devolution shall in fact take place.

These propositions, which we have discussed earlier, should be kept in mind as we proceed with the discussion. It must also be remembered that for the British colonial officials, effective public support was, for the most part, presumed to be with the chiefs and the intelligentsia who had reached high status and prestige. This error was corrected only after the war, when the political repudiation of chieftaincy and the intelligentsia was as complete as voting processes and elective procedures could indicate. The image of responsibility roles devolving in slow and solemn manner to the intelligentsia did not serve as an acceptable definition of public interest or of the interests of the growing nationalist groups in the system. The normal enactment, debate, and questioning of parliamentary business in the old Legislative Council took place in a comparative vacuum. The chief performed a role remote to the intimacy of his normal duties. The intellectual was outside the pale of ordinary social intercourse. A widescale political organization was lacking through which effective communication and participation in political solidarity could be expressed. Where the old chief was the trustee of the ancestors, the new intellectual tried to become the political trustee of the general public. The repudiation, by important elements of the public, of both meant the repudiation of indirect rule.

In traditional social life, the village, the territorial division, and the family were the major structural units of social interaction and political authority. The period of indirect rule saw the domination of the urban areas as orientational foci, particularly for the young. In some respects, the towns maintained certain features of tribal life, such as the local exclusiveness of totem and tribal affiliations, providing an immediate ease of initial adjustment. Most of the personnel emerging as significant—that is having been awarded a public following and esteem—lived in urban areas. If the wealthy cocoa farmer could afford it, he would build a house in the capital, or in a major town such as Kumasi or Korforidua. The markets in these towns and municipalities increasingly showed an assortment of imported manufactured products which served to attract those from the bush.

Youngmen, coming to the towns, for the most part found homes in slum quarters (such as in Usshertown in Accra), often residing with kinsmen who had previously migrated. In the later period of indirect rule many of those who migrated to the towns were partially educated, mostly in mission schools. The varied migration picture can be demonstrated in figures gathered from the 1948 *Census of Population* and privately analyzed by the census commissioner. In Kumasi, for example, only approximately 44 per cent of the population was Ashanti, with members of other tribes or foreigners making up the rest,[4] although about 41 per cent of the Ashanti were not migrant.

In the Tarkwa district, a gold mining region, the local tribe dispersed. Instead of the growth of this area and subsequent benefits to the residential population, the residential population, Wasaw, refused to work in the mines. As a result only 4 per cent of the total population in the district is Wasaw, and "it appears that the Wasaw likes neither the town nor the mine. The result of this is that the population of the group consists mostly of migrants, only 11 per cent having been born in the area compared with 29 per cent in Kumasi and Accra."[5]

Heavy migrations, the growth of effective demand for imported commodities, the expansion of roads, transport, and communications all played their part in creating a climate of change and expectancy. Urban growth from 1931 to 1948 was as follows:

CENSUS FIGURES OF TOWN POPULATIONS[6]

Town	1931 Census	1948 Census
Accra	70,000	135,926
Kumasi (including suburbs)	35,829	78,483
Sekondi-Takoradi	22,431	44,557
Cape Coast	17,685	23,436
Korforidua	10,529	17,806
Tamale	12,941	17,164

[4] The next largest group is Fanti, then Hausa, Nigerian, Ewe, and Ga in that order. The information is derived from an unpublished study by the census commissioner, compiled in 1953. I am indebted to him for similar figures for other urban centers.

[5] Quoted from an unpublished manuscript on the Tarkwa group by the census commissioner.

[6] Adapted from the *Census of Population*, Accra, 1948, report and tables.

By 1950 twenty daily papers were being published, with a circulation limited mostly to the towns. One, the *Daily Graphic*, has taken on the proportions of a national daily; another, the *Evening News*, is the organ of the nationalist movement. Newspapers have become, increasingly, a source of communications, and as education has become more widespread, have helped to channel latent nationalism into an organized political movement.[7] Except in the Northern Territories, where literacy was rare, the public became more aware of affairs in Accra. The *African Morning Post*, owned for a time by Azikiwe, printed articles by well-known anti-colonialists such as George Padmore. The castigation of the imperialists for all the ills of the Gold Coast became commonplace.

Simultaneously, the cinema showed to ever-larger audiences a picture of other places and other things that was largely distorted but nonetheless stimulating. American films are popular, along with American prize fighters, automobiles, and wealth.[8] Jazz can be heard in the towns which sprouted night clubs with titles like Weekend in Havana or Hollywood Bar, where one could dance high-life or Western dances with young ladies of undeniable charm and dubious reputation. For those with more pretensions and money, the Rodger Club, modeled after the British club system, provided formal dances, sherry parties, and receptions.

The wartime promise of tomorrow, aided by sentiments of gratitude for colonial loyalty expressed by Great Britain, heightened disappointment that peace did not suddenly bring prosperity and freedom. The deprivations suffered by Gold Coasters for their participation in the war, even though relatively slight, were considered by many as incommensurate with the benefits received. The Burns Constitution itself was viewed with circumspection, particularly since Governor Burns had not acted with dispatch in order to curb postwar inflation. Ex-servicemen, having returned from other parts of the globe with an appreciation of differing material standards of life, felt that postwar hardship was a malicious colonial plan to inhibit the development of the Gold Coast.

[7] Almost all papers are daily English-language papers. See *Colonial Reports*, Gold Coast, 1950, London, 1952, pp. 85-86.

[8] The influence of the town and particularly American films can be observed. A random selection of films in Accra showing on November 13, 1953 was: Globe—Where No Vultures Fly; Opera—The Lone Rider Texas Justice [sic] with the caption, "He pulled punches to oblige a gal"; Park—California Conquest; Regal—The Toast of New Orleans; Rex—The King of Jungleland; Roxy—Gung Ho; Royal—To Please a Lady. All of these were American films.

In these terms the 1946 Constitution stood little chance of providing satisfactions in full measure to postwar demands and expectations.[9]

The government, as the largest employer of labor in the Gold Coast, received the antagonism directed against the high cost of living which was partly a product of inadequate wage policies, especially for lower salaried and unskilled employees.[10] Those who shouted imperialism and exploitation as charges against colonial government found a ready response among those who worked for government and considered themselves exploited. Meanwhile "Standard VII" boys, those who had completed elementary education, were on the whole loath to take jobs involving menial or degrading labor and were not readily absorbed into the government or private clerical posts, partly because many of them were badly trained, sometimes dishonest, and often unreliable. Such personnel was plentiful, but superior clerks were hard to find. Those who were not absorbed formed a literate and aggressive group, linked to both the rural areas and the towns. They were close to the ordinary public and not divorced from the social and institutional structure of Gold Coast life as the intelligentsia might be. Occasionally among these groups Marxist literature found a ready if only partially understood response. These Standard VII boys were recruited by the nationalist movement. Their partial education helped contribute to the general decay of traditional orientations, while new outlets for prestige positions and orientations were not available in the form of jobs.[11] The significance of education in creating a pool from which nationalists were recruited is well described in a recent Colonial Office report on education in Africa:

"In the first stage, when education is being introduced, it is bound to be regarded as a means of escape from the hard and

---

[9] For a brief but excellent discussion of the Gold Coast in the Second World War see Bourret, *op.cit.*, Chapter IX.

[10] See *Report of the Commission on the Civil Service of the Gold Coast, 1950-1951*, Vol. I, Accra, 1951, particularly Chapters VI and VII. This report indicates as follows, p. 50: "On the basis of figures relating to price levels up to the third quarter of 1948 and of other relevant information, the working party came to the conclusion that civil servants, senior, and junior, and daily-rated were suffering hardships as a result of price increases since 1945-46."

[11] See Final Report, Office of the Government Statistician, *Survey of Standard VII Boys*, Accra, 1951. This is an excellent study of the consequences of elementary education as broken down in occupation, income, and general employment categories. The sample is derived entirely from Standard VII boys.

primitive conditions of the life of subsistence farming; for while the number of the schooled is very small, schooling is a passport to employment outside agriculture—generally clerical employment. The leaders of the community tend to distrust and oppose an influence which turns young men away from the land and so seems to threaten the very existence of the community."[12]

These partially educated young men tended to migrate to the towns in search of work. Some owed traditional responsibilities to the family, or the mother, or the maternal uncle, particularly if helped with their schooling by the family.

Some suffered under cross-behavioral pressures. A man might be married to an illiterate woman whose orientations were predominantly traditional. Particular strains were put on the marriage patterns of such people. For most, the youth movements served as outlets of common expression for those of common experience. These movements, increasingly nationalist, served as a major social outlet. Association with others in a movement towards a remote-appearing goal served to subdue the daily conflicts of social and economic reality.

After the war the identities of problems and interests which increasingly cut across tribal boundaries enabled new groups to form having common psychological and social frontiers. Those who had hitherto been marginal men were now tantamount to effective public opinion. They were organized, and they were many. They had a goal—self-government. They had a devil— British imperialism. They found a God—Kwame Nkrumah. With the permissiveness of the British regime, acts of daring often won accolades in the press and in public praise. Activities such as strikes and aggressively worded demands for self-government were at one moment taken as examples of subversive activity, and treated accordingly, and other times taken as examples of the readiness of Africans to assume larger shares in politics. Confused action boundaries provided a stimulus to further political organization and activity, while the inconsistent responses on the part of officialdom served to aggravate political tension and focus political grievances. Clamor was raised by Africans against things which only a few years previously no African would have dreamed of questioning. Basic rights and freedom were issues posed against

[12] *African Education*, A Study of Educational Policy and Practice in British Tropical Africa, London, 1953, p. 24.

the legality of political domination, providing a more ready basis for hostility and distrust of anything colonial. In its report, the commission which investigated the 1948 riots indicated that "by far the most serious problem which the administration [had] to face in the Gold Coast [was] the suspicion which surrounds government activity of any sort. Its origin, apart from political propaganda, is disperse [sic] and often obscure. It does not attach to persons or individuals in government service. It is an attitude of mind based on no one specific grievance. That it exists we had evidence on all sides. That it must be overcome is the hard core of the problem of healthy relations between government and the governed."[13]

In the increased tempo of postwar Gold Coast life, the more delicate nationalism of the Achimota elites and the intelligentsia which had founded the United Gold Coast Convention in 1946 and advocated self-government in the "shortest possible time," gave way to the more robust and popular mass following of Kwame Nkrumah in the Convention People's Party and its demand for "self-government now." Its membership was primarily the partially educated, the Standard VII boys, those whose roots with rural areas were not dissolved but whose urban affiliations made possible quick and effective organization.[14]

The United Gold Coast Convention, whose most powerful figure was Dr. J. B. Danquah, a lawyer and London Ph.D.,[15] suffered

[13] *Report of the Commission of Enquiry into Disturbances in the Gold Coast,* 1948, Colonial No. 231, p. 7 (Watson Commission).

[14] The nationalist movement before the present Convention People's Party was the United Gold Coast Convention. This organization held its organizational meeting in August 1947, with the object of ensuring by "all legitimate and constitutional means the direction and control of government should pass into the hands of the people and their chiefs in the shortest possible time." It is noteworthy that the emphasis upon the chiefs, and upon legitimate constitutional means, is the trademark of the conservative nationalists in the Gold Coast. They were schooled under the tradition of indirect rule and were those who such people as the acting colonial secretary, Mr. Kenneth Bradley, felt would logically inherit the mantle of British rule. The chairman of the organization was one of the wealthiest African businessmen in the country, Mr. George Grant, and most of the top leadership were lawyer-intellectuals such as J. W. de Graft Johnson, Francis Awoonor Williams, Obetsebi Lamptey, Akufo Addo, and others. Some of these people later on formed the opposition to the Convention People's Party in the first Legislative Assembly, and helped found the Ghana Congress Party, the leading opposition party at that time.

[15] The Watson Report described him as follows: "Dr. Danquah might be described as the doyen of Gold Coast politicians. He has founded or been connected with most political movements since his adolescence. He is a member of the Legislative Council and but for the accident of birth might have been a notable chief. He is a man of very great intelligence but suffers from a disease not unknown to

from its inability to symbolize the public demands of large segments of the population. Its leadership was composed of part-time politicians of dubious constancy. On December 16, 1947, Dr. Kwame Nkrumah, after returning from studies in the United States and Great Britain, was invited to take the post of secretary of the United Gold Coast Convention. A capable organizer and a sophisticated politician, he became a popular idol almost overnight. His objective was immediate self-government, and toward this end he threw his energies. His acquaintance with Marxism and his abilities as an orator gained him a following among the young, the disadvantaged, the disillusioned, and the idealistic. He was untainted by cooperation with the authorities and his aggressiveness and success alarmed the leadership of the United Gold Coast Convention and earned him the enmity of the colonial authorities. With the youth groups firmly on his side, and a network of organizations spreading throughout the country, he proposed a political program which seemed to sum up the aspirations of thousands of people, to point a path of progress, and to lead them out of the confusion wrought by the uneven pace of social change.[16] To many his name became deified. He was the messiah who would lead the country to Free-dom, the slogan he adopted, and to new stature and dignity. Meanwhile Nkrumah was able to use the events and situation of the postwar Gold Coast in aid of his cause.

---

politicians throughout the ages and recognized under the generic name of expediency."

[16] In February 1948 Nkrumah recommended: "The formation of a shadow cabinet should engage the serious attention of the working committee as early as possible. Membership is to be composed of individuals selected *ad hoc* to study the jobs of the various ministries that would be decided upon in advance for the country when we achieve our independence. This cabinet will forestall any unpreparedness on our part in the exigency of self-government being thrust upon us before the expected time."

Nkrumah further recommended that organization work be divided into three periods, the first involving; "a. Co-ordination of all the various organizations under the United Gold Coast Convention: i.e., apart from individual membership the various political, social, educational, farmers and women's organizations as well as native societies, trade unions, co-operative societies, etc., should be asked to affiliate to the convention. b. The consolidation of branches already formed and the establishment of branches in every town and village of the country. . . . c. The setting up of convention branches in each town and village throughout the Colony, Ashanti, the Northern Territories and Togoland. The chief or *odikro* of each town or village should be persuaded to become the patron of the branch. d. Vigorous convention week-end schools should be opened wherever there is a branch of the convention. The political mass education of the country for self-government should begin at these week-end schools." See p. 93, Appendix 12 of the Watson Report.

Inflation following the war was highlighted by a boycott organized in January 1948 by an Accra sub-chief, Nii Kwabena Bonne III, which lasted about a month and was directed against the high cost of living. At its conclusion, although the government made certain concessions, a demonstration was held by ex-servicemen. They claimed, among other grievances, that promises made to them while they were in service had not been fulfilled, that pension rates were insufficient due to inflation, that grants had not been made to men too old to start business on their own account, that Africanization of the Gold Coast Regiment was not effectively maintained and promoted.[17] The demonstration which began as a procession along a route approved by the authorities turned into a march on the governor's castle at Christiansborg. Refusing to halt when advised by the police, the demonstrators were fired upon. Two men were killed and four or five wounded.

News of the disturbance spread rapidly throughout the Gold Coast, and riots were touched off in other towns and villages. Public disgruntlement at the terms agreed to by the Accra Chamber of Commerce in the proposed reduction of prices added to the excitement. Emotional feeling against Syrian and Lebanese shopkeepers ran high. Europeans were stoned, shops raided, and violence spread rapidly.[18] The governor, Sir Gerald Creasy, arrested six of the United Gold Coast Convention leaders, including Nkrumah, and deported them to the Northern Territories for a short time.[19]

After the disturbances died down a commission was set up to inquire into causes. This commission[20] felt that Kwame Nkrumah was "imbued with a Communist ideology which only political expediency had blurred."[21] It went on to say that "he was occupying

17 *Ibid.*, p. 22-23.

18 The Syrians and Lebanese occupy a peculiar position in the Gold Coast. They operate retail stores, transport companies, a brick and tile plant, and residual trading generally which is not taken up by the big commercial houses like United African Company (Unilever), John Holt and Sons, etc. They occupy a marginal position in Gold Coast society, considered with some dislike by both Africans and British. They bore the brunt of much of the rioting, many of their stores and shops being wrecked.

19 The six were J. B. Danquah, Kwame Nkrumah, William Ofori Atta, Akufo Addo, Ako Adjei, and E. Obetsebi Lamptey.

20 Hereinafter referred to as the Watson Commission.

21 Most observers agree that this judgment was scarcely warranted. If it was, however, then Nkrumah's growth and stature as a statesman is all the more impressive. Nkrumah, as prime minister, has shown a respect for his office which few could have anticipated.

the role held by all party secretaries in totalitarian institutions, the real position of power."[22] Finally, the commission concluded that Nkrumah "has never abandoned his aims for a Union of West African Soviet Socialist Republics and has not abandoned his foreign affiliations connected with these aims."

More important, the commission made an evaluation of the larger Gold Coast situation. It examined the social and economic bases of the disturbances, advising constitutional and political reforms. As far as the Burns Constitution was concerned, the commission concluded:

"The new constitution ushered in with such promise in 1946 was no doubt well intentioned. Its weakness in our view lay in its conception. It was obviously conceived in the light of pre-war conditions. Six years of total war had naturally arrested development in British administration. For that no apology need be made. But the same period had been marked by rapid advancement in the experience of Gold Coast Africans. Large numbers had their horizons widened and their political consciousness stimulated by service in the forces abroad and close contacts with other peoples. In that background the 1946 Constitution was outmoded at birth."[23]

The report of the Watson Commission received full consideration. A new governor, Sir Charles Noble Arden-Clarke, replaced his less fortunate predecessor, and younger Colonial Service personnel replaced those near the age of retirement. A new commission on constitutional reform was set up which reported its conclusions to the governor on August 17, 1949.[24] The commission, composed entirely of Africans, on the whole represented the intellectuals of the United Gold Coast Convention. Its chairman, Justice Coussey, was an eminent African jurist. Its members represented older and more educated professional men of the Gold Coast.

While the Coussey Commission was holding hearings and formulating plans for constitutional reform, Nkrumah set about expanding his control over the youth organizations. Particularly in Ashanti, aggressiveness against the chiefs and British administrators ran high. A committee of youth organizations was formed,

[22] Watson Commission, p. 17.   [23] *Ibid.*, p. 19.
[24] See *Report to His Excellency the Governor by the Committee on Constitutional Reform*, 1949, Colonial No. 248 (Coussey Commission).

composed of a variety of youth movements usually dominated by Nkrumah adherents. They formed a powerful bloc, anxious to take political action.

Nkrumah designed a campaign of "Positive Action"[25] in which all tactics other than open insurrection and mass violence were to be utilized against the regime. Opposition immediately developed from the executive board of the United Gold Coast Convention, and conservative opinion branded Positive Action as subversive and dangerous to the nationalist cause.[26] The leadership of the United Gold Coast Convention attempted to force Nkrumah to dissolve the youth organizations. An attempt was made to remove him from the secretaryship. The attempt failed. Rather, after a secret session in Kumasi in December 1948, the new committee of youth organizations issued a manifesto:

"Youth everywhere are in action against the forces of evil, of suppression and repression, and we youth in the Gold Coast have not been found wanting. Together with the struggling youth of other lands we shall not rest until we have built the Brave New World of free and independent nations bounteously enjoying the blessings of life."[27]

In June 1949, at a meeting in Saltpond, the youth organizations forced Nkrumah to resign from the United Gold Coast Convention. Leaving the meeting place, Nkrumah is reported to have shouted that his life was in danger. Mrs. Hannah Cudjoe, one of his most devoted followers and now a propaganda secretary and organizer of the women's branch of the Convention People's Party, is supposed to have climbed onto a platform and led the crowd in singing "Lead Kindly Light." A new party, the Convention People's Party, was proclaimed shortly thereafter in a burst of self-righteous martyrdom.[28] Six months later, on January 8, 1950, Positive Action was launched.[29]

[25] See Nkrumah, Kwame, *What I Mean by Positive Action,* Accra (n.d.).

[26] See Danquah, Moses, *Political Agitation in the Gold Coast,* Accra, 1949, in which the conservative, moderate, and positive action positions are examined, with the latter being opposed. Strongly influenced by Gandhi, the pamphlet urges truth as the most effective weapon.

[27] C.Y.O., *The Ghana Youth Manifesto,* Accra, 1949. The above quotation is signed by Kojo Botsio, then secretary of the C.Y.O., who later became. one of the top leaders of the Convention People's Party, and whose first cabinet post was as Minister of Education and Social Welfare.

[28] See *The Gold Coast Observer,* February 11, 1951.

[29] See Padmore, *Gold Coast Revolution,* London, 1953, p. 72.

By the time the Coussey Commission handed down its report, the Convention People's Party was well established, with a network of branches throughout the coastal and central areas of the Gold Coast. Even though several political parties were on the scene, none received a real grassroots following as did the Convention People's Party. A Gold Coast Liberal Party under Nii Bonne III, the Accra chief who had led the boycott, had a short and ineffective life, as did the Freedom Defence Society. The National Democratic Party, under the leadership of Dr. Nanka Bruce, a highly respected figure, had limited appeal in the towns, having been made up of the predominantly municipal Ratepayers Association and the Mambii Party. A Ghana Freedom Party was given even shorter shrift while the United Gold Coast Convention had its popular strength depleted by the split with Nkrumah. The Convention People's Party emerged as the spearhead of a popular mass movement, opposing the Coussey Commission Report and demanding self-government in 1949.

When the Convention People's Party launched the Positive Action campaign, three party journalists and officials were sent to prison for sedition. Meanwhile in municipal elections the Convention People's Party began to win victories. When three imprisoned party leaders, Gamesu K. Amegbe (now the new Cocoa Marketing Board chairman), Kwame Afryea (until recently acting general secretary of the C.P.P.), and K. A. Gbedemah (now Minister of Finance), were released from jail, Nkrumah and others were sentenced from six months to five years. This was precisely the cap of martyrdom needed by the party. As Amegbe related in interview, "As soon as they put Kwame in jail we toured the country with Gbedemah. We went up and down the land, into almost every village, making seven or eight speeches a day, and covering thousands of miles in a week. We brought C.P.P. into every village. With Kwame in jail, Gbedemah was in command and he really organized the party."[30]

The incarceration of Nkrumah spelled the end of the United Gold Coast Convention as an effective organization. Nkrumah became a household name.

The Coussey recommendations were accepted by the governor and an order in council promulgating the Constitution of 1950

[30] Interviews with Amegbe, now chairman of the Cocoa Marketing Board, and Boi-Doku, assistant propaganda secretary of the C.P.P.

was received. Just at the time the C.P.P. was becoming popular, the Coussey recommendations called for a widened electorate. A legislative assembly was set up with plenary powers, except for those residual to the Crown and reserved to the governor. The Gold Coast was to have an African prime minister[31] and an African cabinet except for three ex-officio ministers. In the elections which followed, the Convention People's Party won a resounding victory. Nkrumah was released from jail and the nationalist movement was in power.

Of the members of the Coussey Commission, most have either joined the ranks of the conservative opposition or retired from political life. Two became non-party cabinet ministers, some are chiefs who were elected by the territorial councils to the first assembly, but most feel betrayed, a feeling perhaps matched by their ineffectuality.[32]

The movement which brought the Gold Coast close to internal self-government was a curious one. The muddled action boundaries, the half-fearful demands, the shifts in allegiance, associations, and beliefs—all provided a fertile environment for a leader to come forward. Nkrumah provided the answers. If one did not know how to act, the answer was follow Nkrumah. If one did not know what to believe, the answer was follow Nkrumah. If one did not know what quite to hope for, the answer was follow Nkrumah.[33] They followed. Great hopes for a new society centered around his person, around the symbols of "Free-dom," the C.P.P. rallying

[31] At the time called "Leader of Government Business."

[32] For example, Akufo Addo, M. Dowuona, Obetsebi Lamptey, N. A. Ollenu are in the opposition. One member is the speaker of the assembly, Mr. Emannual Quist. One chief was destooled, largely, it is charged, at the instigation of the C.P.P., Sir Tsibu Darku. One man has returned to provincial politics and dropped out of party politics although he was a member of the assembly, Mr. Magnus Sampson. Two members were non-C.P.P. cabinet ministers in the last cabinet, E. O. Asafu-Adjaye, who is now a C.P.P. member and still a minister, and J. A. Braimah, who resigned from the previous cabinet after taking bribes and who represented the only Northern Territories cabinet minister in the first Nkrumah cabinet. Braimah, who is now a member of the assembly in the opposition party, is a chief (*kabachewura*). Some, like the Reverend Mr. Baeta, have dropped out of politics entirely and devote themselves to teaching at the University College. Of the forty members of the Coussey Commission, not one was prominent in the C.P.P. and all were members of the intellectual "middle class" which expected to inherit the political mantle when the British handed over a large measure of self-rule.

[33] It is a testament to Nkrumah's personal integrity that while he has used his popularity as a crucial political asset, he has taken on none of the attributes of a dictator. With responsibility he has been primarily concerned with translating public needs into a governmental program.

cry, and around the demand for "self-government now." "Forward
Ever, Backward Never" was the slogan of the party. Around the
slogans and the demands, around the green, white, and red of the
C.P.P. banners, around the almost mythical person of Kwame
Nkrumah there slowly emerged a faithful flock, shepherded by the
leader into the paths of nationalism and independence. We shall
call Nkrumah a *charismatic leader*.[34]

[34] See Weber, *Theory of Social and Economic Organizations*, Part vi, "The
Transformation of Charisma in an Anti-Authoritarian Direction," pp. 354-360. For
a more complete description of "charisma," see pp. 228 and 303, below.

CHAPTER 9

THE STRUCTURES OF SECULAR GOVERNMENT

THE Coussey Commission recommended a new legislature, increased in numbers and representative of "all sections of the community in the deliberation of national affairs."[1] It envisioned a more elaborate two-chambered legislative body than the unicameral assembly finally granted, but it modeled the entire structure upon the British parliamentary system, with an upper senate and a lower house of assembly. It proposed a responsible executive council or cabinet on which three members would be ex-officio.

Recognizing that the entire structure of indirect rule had been badly shaken, the commission, in effect, proposed to do away with it in substance. In addition, the commission advocated basic changes in local government structure, stating:

"The native authorities, through which local government is at present carried on, are virtually the old state councils vested with modern administrative powers. Their deficiencies include the restricted basis of their membership, their old-fashioned procedure, and their inadequate finance and staff.

"These deficiencies, despite the gallant efforts which have been made by the native authorities, efforts which have resulted in definite progress and solid achievement, have in general hampered their effectiveness as agencies of local administration, have made them unequal to the demands being made on them, and have prevented them from reaching the standard of efficiency required of modern local authorities.

"The complexity and stress of modern life, the desire for change and the progressive outlook, which are now pervading even the remote villages, call for more efficient organs of local administration. We therefore recommend entirely new councils, more democratic in composition, which should prove more efficient and effective in the discharge of greater responsibilities for the social welfare and well-being of their local communities."[2]

The effects of such a proposal, it was intended, would restore chieftaincy to its pre-indirect rule status, shorn of its political and

---

[1] Coussey Commission, p. 11.   [2] *Ibid.*, p. 4.

some other customary prerogatives. This, it was argued, was better than witnessing the destruction of chieftaincy entirely, through its failure to perform adequately in administration. Its destruction would wreck the community and increase the tension and aggressiveness of the younger elements, a situation full of unpleasant potentialities.[3] Although the Watson Commission, very prematurely, argued that chieftaincy was doomed, the Coussey Commission, a high proportion of whose members either were members of royal families or had been in long association with the outstanding chiefs under indirect rule, took issue with this point of view. They attempted to integrate chieftaincy into a new local government structure:

"Before going further, we must say a word about the role which we have assigned to the chiefs, particularly in the local government councils. The whole institution of chieftaincy is so closely bound up with the life of our communities that its disappearance would spell disaster. Chiefs and what they symbolize in our society are so vital that the subject of their future must be approached with the greatest caution. No African of the Gold Coast is without some admiration for the best aspects of chieftaincy, and all would be loath to do violence to it any more than to the social values embodied in the institution itself. Criticisms there have been, but none coming from responsible people whom we have known or met is directed towards the complete effacement of chiefs. We cannot, therefore, accept the status which the Watson Report would assign to them."[4]

We can sum up the intent of the Coussey Commission as follows. It envisioned a rational system of representative government with both elected and appointed officials at every level of formal organization. It sought to unify predominantly British forms of local and central political structures into a viable over-all government for the formation of a national state, meanwhile providing room for some of the basic symbolic and sentimental aspects of traditional social structures. It specifically did not want to see chieftaincy destroyed.[5]

[3] For an excellent discussion of the difficult position of the chiefs see the *Report of the Commission on Native Courts*, Accra, 1951.

[4] Coussey Commission, p. 4. Of the forty members of the commission, eight were important Gold Coast chiefs, some of whom had important positions under indirect rule. A considerable number of non-chiefs were related to royal families, or were spokesmen of chiefs.

[5] *Ibid.*, p. 9.

The various forms of councils proposed by the commission were directed at enlarging the scope of political institutional transfer. By using predominantly secular local and central councils, the range of effective recruitment would be automatically widened beyond the limitations imposed by traditional restrictions of lineage and age, a factor which limited the efficiency of the native authorities system. It was expected that the solid and respected members of the community would be chosen to fill these positions and that they would cooperate with the chiefs, allowing them to fulfill some of their crucial functions for the tribally oriented members of the community.

It is noteworthy that the members of the commission, entirely Africans, set the criteria for recommendations on efficiency. For the members, standards of British administrative practice had been entirely adopted. In addition the commission was concerned with enhancing the responsibility of Africans by granting greater access to crucial administrative and political roles, particularly to the intelligentsia who were obviously eager to participate. As such, the Coussey proposals, while far-reaching in effect, were still within the general complex of indirect rule. They did not call for a fundamental shift in the locus of authority. The primary target, rather, was a more secular foundation of rule, and the easing of maladjustments and authority conflicts perpetuated by indirect rule.[6] Its efforts were devoted to the multiplication of secular legitimacy roles, and to the recruitment of those who had received education and training under indirect rule, representing non-traditional solidarity groupings within Gold Coast society. The chiefs were to be preserved as local solidarity figures within traditional groupings insofar as they remained intact and could be utilized for fulfilling sanctional and structural purposes.

In one form or another, most of the Coussey Commission's recommendations were followed. On December 19, 1950, new letters patent were issued, and on December 22, 1950, the new constitution was put into effect.[7] It was the product of diverse inter-

---

[6] For an excellent discussion of the constitutional pattern of other parts of the British Commonwealth and Empire, see Wight, M., *The Development of the Legislative Council*, London, 1946.

[7] See *Letters Patent passed under the Great Seal of the Realm* constituting the Office of Governor and Commander-in-Chief of the Gold Coast Colony and Ashanti and making provision for the Government thereof, and *Statutory Instruments*, 1950, No. 2094, *The Gold Coast (Constitution) Order in Council*, 1950.

ests, segments of the population, and ideas. The hope which it inspired can perhaps be best summed up in a speech made by one of the members of the old Legislative Council. It is important to note the anti-political bias expressed in the speech since most of the intelligentsia viewed politics and political parties with some distaste, tending to think of a council as a deliberative body of educated gentlemen. The view, bitterly contested by the Convention People's Party, is common to what can be defined as conservative in the Gold Coast: government as the responsibility of an educational and traditional elect by representative means, on a conciliar basis: The speech which took place during the final session of the Legislative Council under the Burns Constitution stated as follows:

"Give the people the opportunity to show their initiative in order to evolve a system of government appropriate or suitable to them so that the world may know that Africans or the people of the Gold Coast, in particular, are capable of holding their own. We do not want that [sic] the elections be held at the end of five years, as contemplated in the Coussey Report, to be fought on a political platform or in agitation for political reform. We want a steady government that will cater for [sic] the needs of the people —a government that will be efficient enough to fight against the enemies of want, squalor, disease and ignorance and other disabilities which afflict this country; to raise the social and economic status of the people and ensure contentment and prosperity.

"We want faith and confidence in ourselves. Several years under colonial [sic] system of government have made us apathetic: our limbs have become atrophied through disuse, but they are not dead yet. We need Dr. Aggrey of revered memory to exhort us to action. We must remember that we are eagles and can fly; the sky is our natural habitat."[8]

While these gentlemen were occupied with learning to fly again, the Convention People's Party was scurrying around the Gold Coast in lorries teaching people how to vote. Electoral regulations were announced[9] and preparations were made to give effect to the new constitution.

As the preparations for the elections proceeded, Nkrumah and other important figures of the Convention People's Party resided

---

[8] Legislative Council Debates, Session 1949, Issue No. 4, p. 144.
[9] See the *Elections (Legislative Assembly) Ordinance*, 1950, No. 1 of 1951.

in jail, with Gbedemah stumping the country. The electoral campaign was identified with Nkrumah's suffering and his fight for freedom. Most of those who could not hope to achieve positions of political authority in an organization such as the United Gold Coast Convention flocked to the organization united by the struggle and "suffering" of its leaders. Others, seeing in the Convention People's Party an opportunity for social mobility, were quick to become little Nkrumah's in local areas, spearheading attacks on the chiefs. The Convention People's Party was a "radical" organization—it opened its membership to anyone who sought to change the system of effective authority, the people who were opportunists, idealists, those simply enamored by Nkrumah and the excitement of radical politics, and anyone who would follow the leader while shouting "Free-dom" with a good breath.

The widening of the electorate under the new laws was charged by the C.P.P. as insufficient. The new constitution was called bogus and fraudulent since it fell short of full self-government. But, for the youth, for the ambitious, for the frustrated, Nkrumah was the effective symbol of political life, and when he told them "seek ye first the political kingdom and all else will follow" they voted their approval.

The Transfer of Central Government Structures

"In embarking upon a new order of political life, we have chosen the British model and have sought to blend it with our traditional institutions," states the Coussey Report. The British Parliament, shorn of the House of Lords, has been reenacted, with some modification, in the Gold Coast. Unlike the British Parliament, however, the Legislative Assembly does not have full or complete local jurisdiction. For example, certain constitutional questions and changes are reserved to the Crown.[10] Nonetheless, the Constitutions of both 1950 and 1954 provided for greater representation and greater responsibility for Africans in the Gold Coast. The Legislative Assembly set up under the 1950 constitution adopted standing rules and orders which lay down a procedure

---

10 In actual practice the sphere of competence of the Legislative Assembly is very broad. It is not strictly correct that constitutional changes are reserved to the Crown. What is reserved is the Crown's right to revoke, suspend, or amend the Constitution—which it would otherwise lose, by virtue of the decision in Campbell v. Hall. See Jennings and Young, *Constitutional Laws of the Commonwealth*, Oxford University Press, 1952. I am indebted to Mr. Kenneth Robinson, Nuffield College, for bringing this point to my attention.

broadly similar to practice in the United Kingdom Parliament. The constitution provided for a general election at least once every four years. It empowered the governor, with the advice and consent of the Legislative Assembly, to make laws for the peace and order and good government of the Gold Coast.

Until June 1954 the Legislative Assembly was a unicameral body composed of a speaker, 34 members representing the Colony (made up of 4 municipal members, 19 rural members, and 11 territorial members). Nineteen members represented Ashanti (made up as follows: 1 municipal member, 12 rural members, and 6 territorial members). Nineteen members represented the Northern Territories, and 3 members, included in the Colony allocation, composed the representation from southern Togoland. Three ex-officio members who were cabinet ministers and 6 special interest members representing commercial and mining interests, only 2 of whom could vote, completed the composition of the assembly. After June 1954, an entirely British system of representation went into effect with members elected by direct election from 104 constituencies throughout the Gold Coast.[11]

The 1950 Constitution was a truly transitional medium. As such, we shall concern ourselves with its effect at some length, indicating the ways in which predominantly secularized behavior patterns were superimposed upon a system of representation which included commercial interests, chiefs, and territorial representatives, and thus provided for group representation rather than area representation on purely secular bases. The latter situation, which now prevails, has meant on the one hand an intensified use of political parties as electoral instruments, and on the other has excluded certain groupings from the assembly entirely, not without deleterious effects, as we shall see.

What was the assembly (which we can call the "old" assembly, lasting from 1951 until 1953) like in its treatment of government business? How did its organs help the development of the nationalist movement? How did the institution of chieftaincy engage itself with the more secular processes of debate and legislative decision-

[11] Representation by territorial membership, ex-officio, and mining and commercial interests was patently incompatible with the full secularization of government along the British parliamentary pattern. See *The Government's Proposals for Constitutional Reform*, Accra, 1953, and *Report of the Commission of Enquiry into Representational and Electoral Reform*, Accra, 1953.

making? Answers to these questions will preoccupy us for the remainder of this volume.

The Legislative Assembly, 1951-1953

The old Legislative Assembly was the first parliamentary body designed to act in the British pattern of parliamentary organization, i.e., its major function was to control the executive (the cabinet). As such its function differed sharply from that of the Legislative Council which it supplanted, since that body was essentially advisory, with its jurisdiction limited to the Colony.

Since the Legislative Assembly was the central parliamentary agency, control over the executive meant a genuine cabinet system. Cabinet ministers were responsible for the handling of government business and most of the powers hitherto reserved to the governor were delegated to the cabinet ministers as their jurisdictions were marked out. Again this process followed British precedent, i.e. the devolution of royal authority to parliamentary officers. Because of the transitional nature of the old Legislative Assembly, a complex but selective system of representation existed.

Qualifications set for membership in the assembly limited eligibility to: any person who was either a British subject or a British protected person; and was of the age of twenty-five years or upwards; and able to speak and, unless incapacitated by blindness or other physical cause, to "read the English language with a degree of proficiency sufficient to enable him to take an effective part in the proceedings of the assembly."[12]

Combined in a national legislature with members elected from rural constituencies by indirect election, and municipal members elected by direct election, were the representatives of the traditional society of the Gold Coast, given due recognition by virtue of their status as chief, or the agents of chiefs.[12a] Both the Joint Provincial Council, established, it will be recalled, by the 1925 Constitution, and the Asanteman Council, the traditional organ of the Ashanti Confederacy, were able to elect representatives to the Legislative Assembly from their own membership, or to select individuals whom they regarded as adequate spokesmen for their views. In this respect the chiefs, and the older intellectuals who had supported the chiefs, found a means to act as responsible

[12] See Regulations, *op.cit.* Para. 42.
[12a] *Ibid.*, The Second Schedule, Parts i, ii, and iv.

agents for groups having their affiliations to customary patterns of social life, rather than the more secular nationalism of the Convention People's Party. These representatives, called territorial members, included some of the more distinguished chiefs of the Gold Coast. The chairman of the Ghana Congress Party, the leading opposition party during the life of the old Legislative Assembly, was a territorial member.

In the north a special electoral college partly composed of the Northern Territories Council insured the representation of chiefs, and individuals favorable to chiefs from that part of the country. The highest agencies created for chieftaincy through indirect rule were provided for in the 1950 Constitution, and those members of Gold Coast society who were associated with custom and tradition, a large proportion of the population indeed, saw at least some of their views and grievances ventilated through the efforts of territorial members. On the whole, the territorial members opposed the Nkrumah regime on many fundamental constitutional issues. Today this form of representation is entirely abolished, and a large segment of the population finds itself without the kind of representation hitherto afforded. We shall discuss some of the implications of the present electoral pattern in our concluding chapter.

The commercial and mining members were chosen from representatives of the Chambers of Mines and Commerce.

Rural members of Ashanti and the Colony were chosen by electoral colleges. The electoral colleges were composed of members elected from each electoral subdistrict at a primary. Secondary elections for the assembly were held on the regular election day, the candidates having been nominated in writing by three electors of the electoral district for which he was a candidate, no candidate having been nominated for more than one electoral district.[13]

Following British precedent, every candidate deposited fifty pounds with the principal returning officer. The deposit was returned to the candidate if he withdrew his nomination, or if there was no contested election, or if in a contested election he obtained votes equivalent to not less than one-sixth of the total number of votes cast.[14]

[13] See Regulations, The Elections (Legislative Assembly) Ordinance, 1950. Part v.
[14] *Ibid.*

Elections were held for municipal representatives to the assembly according to direct election with candidates nominated by three electors of an electoral district. The same deposit conditions were required as in the case of rural candidates.[15]

The Legislative Assembly was empowered as follows: "Subject to the provisions of this order it shall be lawful for the governor, with the advice and consent of the Legislative Assembly, to make laws for the peace, order and good government of the Gold Coast."[16]

The general conditional proviso indicating the governor's reserve powers of veto and disallowance states that:

". . . if the governor shall consider that it is expedient in the interest of public order, public faith or good government (which expressions, shall, without prejudice to their generality, include the responsibility of the Gold Coast as a territory within the British Commonwealth of Nations, and all matters pertaining to the creation or abolition of any public office or to the salary or other conditions of service of any public officer) that any bill introduced, or any motion proposed, in the assembly should have effect, then, if the assembly fail to pass such bill or motion within such time and in such form as the governor may think reasonable and expedient, the governor at any time which he shall think fit, may, notwithstanding any provisions of this order or of any standing orders of the assembly, declare that such bill or motion shall have effect as if it had been passed by the assembly. . . ."[17]

The governor was further required to act on the advice of the Executive Council or, barring that, on the advice of the secretary of state's authorization, except in matters of extreme urgency.[18]

It will be noted that the legal framework still provided extensive powers to the governor. This was still a colonial constitution. In practice, a high proportion of the powers of the governor were delegated. Following British custom the unwritten parts of the constitution, as established by precedent through the office of the governor, have been the most crucial in transforming membership roles in the assembly and the cabinet into functionally responsible roles in the parliamentary structure.

The standing orders of the assembly provide for rules of debate,

---

15 *Ibid.*, Part vi.   16 Constitution, *op.cit.*
17 *Ibid.*, Para. 58 (1).   18 *Ibid.*, Para. 58 (2).

motions, and a parliamentary question period modeled after the British system.[19]

The speaker is provided with powers equivalent to the speaker of the House of Commons, and is the "sole judge of the propriety and admissibility of a question."[20]

The Legislative Assembly set up in the 1950 Constitution was designed to integrate British secular parliamentary structures with certain agencies created under indirect rule through which traditional structures could be represented. Those opposed to chieftaincy saw in it a reactionary document. Those who, along with Coussey, sought to blend British and traditional structures, were pleased. The 1950 Constitution widened the representation to rural areas via indirect elections, and the direct election of municipal members was maintained. The old assembly sought to be a widely representative body, both of tribes in territorial areas, individuals, by population, and special interests. It was not yet a fully responsible body, although in practice, as we have indicated, the governor's reserve powers were never used. In succeeding pages we shall discuss the operation of this assembly, which proved to have a crucial, if short, life as constituted.

In 1953 the prime minister sought greater independence via the mechanism of constitutional reform. A number of questions were again raised pertaining to constitutional structure, perhaps the most significant being that of the second chamber.[21] The prime minister called on public groups of all kinds to put forward their

[19] The parliamentary question period occurs in the morning after the opening of the day's session.

[20] See *Standing Orders of the Legislative Assembly of the Gold Coast*. It is worthy of note that the British procedural prescriptions are, in the main, followed.

See also, *The London Times*, March 3, 1952, as follows: "Today the Gold Coast Assembly received a British Parliamentary delegation which made the presentation on behalf of the British Parliament of a copy of Erskine May. The delegation consisted of Sir Edward Keeling, the Conservative member for Twickenham, and Mr. James Johnson, Labour, Rugby. They are members of a larger delegation which has been on a visit to Nigeria for the inauguration of the new constitution.

"The presentation copy of Erskine May was autographed by Mr. Churchill, Mr. Attlee, Lord Simon and the speaker. Sir Edward Keeling explained that the book enshrines the experience of 600 years of British parliamentary practice. He told the assembly it was popularly said that Parliament could do anything but change man to woman and vice versa, but in practice many things were not done. The sovereign's name was never brought in, the names of judges and magistrates were preserved, the Civil Service was never embroiled, and the rights of the opposition were observed."

[21] See the Coussey Commission Report, where the matter was originally discussed with two alternate plans laid out, one for a bicameral legislature and another for a unicameral legislature. The latter was followed.

proposals for constitutional reform[22] and the issues were debated in many different types of groups. In spite of the general support given to a bicameral legislature, the issue was resolved in favor of a single-chambered assembly. The nation was reconstituted for electoral purposes into 104 constituencies. The present "Nkrumah constitution" of 1954, therefore, represents the logical extension of constitutional development until the secular model is being followed fully.

The New Legislative Assembly

The present Legislative Assembly is much more strictly like the British House of Commons. Instead of the various groupings visible until 1954, there is a government bench and an opposition bench. The opposition, which is a regular party grouping, still remains a predominantly regional phenomenon insofar as the Northern People's Party forms the opposition bench. There was some question whether or not the N.P.P. should have been allowed to form the opposition since Nkrumah said only national parties should fill such positions. The Northern People's Party surely is not that.

The 1954 constitutional changes advancing public participation and the extension of universalistic criteria of eligibility have been radical, in the popular sense of that word. The parliamentary structure served as the means of widening public opportunities, much in the same fashion as the various reform acts in Britain, beginning in 1832, widened the electorate and brought the non-aristocratic public more and more into positions of decision. In the Gold Coast as well, privilege, whether due to special interests such as mining or commerce, elites, whether of an intelligentsia or tribal aristocracy, or role in the Colonial Service has been largely abolished. All these factions have been

[22] See *Despatches on the Gold Coast Government's Proposals for Constitutional Reform*, London, H.M.S.O., 1954, Colonial No. 302, and for an excellent discussion of the second chamber issue, Wraith, Robert E., "The 'Second Chamber' Issue in the Gold Coast," in *Parliamentary Affairs*, Vol. vii, No. 4. Nkrumah's invitation to all and sundry to submit memoranda on constitutional reform raised protest from older and more established bodies such as the Joint Provincial Council. Wraith indicates that "One hundred and thirty-one bodies of all shapes and sizes submitted memoranda on the Prime Minister's Statement. They included the obvious and powerful ones, but they included also, for example, the Cape Coast Literary and Social Club, the Kumasi Taxi Drivers' Association, and "O" Compound, Adiembra—a refreshingly new approach to the making of a constitution. The replies of the Territorial Councils, the political parties, the trade unions, and the Chambers of Commerce and Mines were published in full."

put into the position of competing for public favor, whether or not they like it, and the emergence of party politics of the secular kind is far more likely than before the recent changes.

However, the various groups who warranted special consideration in the Gold Coast for such a long time were, at the time this field research was done, part of the formal structure of government. They were allocated certain kinds of authority and represented segments of the population in terms of the cultural and historical groupings which existed in Gold Coast society. How these groups operated, what their members said and did, and the patterns of authority which they represented were articulated in the range of public business treated and in the relationships and groups to which members found themselves obligated. These groupings are still very much a part of Gold Coast society, although the patterns by which they operate are now shifted into less clearcut channels. For some, party politics will suffice to replace the position of privilege. For others, only sub-rosa activities remain. Almost everyone is locked in a basic struggle to capture the affiliations of those whose traditional or secular orientations make them potential political associates.

It remains to be seen whether or not, for purely Gold Coast purposes, and for the purposes Nkrumah has in mind, the British representational system is adequate to serve the representational needs of the Gold Coast. Certainly the present electoral system favors mass political parties, and it will be, no doubt, more and more difficult for independents to stand for political office. For groups constituted so that party organization is foreign to them, such as chieftaincy groups, the same can also be said. They will be barred from effective participation in parliamentary organs. Such a situation will, no doubt, be satisfactory so long as popular feeling remains with the Nkrumah regime, or with other groupings constituted on a party basis. If the public, however, should shift its affiliations back to the chiefs, even for a short time, *effective public opinion* will be removed from direct representation in central government. This eventuality would, therefore, endanger the entire process of political institutional transfer. It raises the entire question of the necessary formal degree of institutional transfer. Is it necessary to provide a mirror image of British practice in order for effective parliamentary democracy to work? If the answer is in the affirmative, then this means that the entire corporate structure of Gold Coast social and commercial life must also be made to conform to British patterns. If the answer is negative, it would seem that certain modifications in British practice would be necessary to fit the local Gold Coast conditions more adequately.

In spite of the implications of the new changes, therefore, an examination of the way in which various social groupings acted in parliamentary and wider social settings reveals much regarding the appropriateness of parliamentary structures as crucial instruments of cultural adaptation.

The Cabinet

The constitution provides for a cabinet to be the principal instrument of policy.[23] The cabinet was designed to follow the functions and procedures of the British Cabinet, except that the meetings were to be presided over by the governor. Ministers were chosen, however, by the governor submitting a list of those of the assembly members whom he proposed for membership of the cabinet, and the assembly resolved whether the governor's choice should be approved. Ministers chosen elected from their members a prime minister. The assembly may, by a two-thirds majority, request the governor to revoke the appointment of a cabinet minister.

In practice, the majority party in the assembly is called upon to help compose the governor's list, and the leader of the parliamentary majority party is selected as prime minister. This, of course, follows British precedent. Modified but similar procedures to that of English custom are evident, as an article in *The London Times* indicates, written at the time of the constitutional amendment of the office of prime minister:

"Dr. Kwame Nkrumah was elected first prime minister of the Gold Coast today. Under the amended constitution the governor is required to submit the name of his nominee to the assembly, who vote on it.

"When the session of the assembly opened, the governor's secretary was escorted to the bar of the house by the clerk of the assembly who announced that the secretary was seeking permission

23 The original title of Executive Council was changed to cabinet in Statutory Instruments 1952, No. 455, The Gold Coast (Constitution) (Amendment) Order in Council, 1952. At the same time the office of prime minister was created, with his title changed from "Leader of Government Business."

to cross the bar to present a letter to the speaker. Permission was granted, and after the letter had been handed over the speaker announced that the governor had nominated Dr. Nkrumah. The assembly then voted by secret ballot; the result was 45 for and 31 against, with eight abstentions.

"Later the speaker received a letter from the governor containing the instrument appointing Dr. Nkrumah prime minister, and another containing the nominations of the governor and the prime minister for the representative ministers. Mr. Botsio, Mr. Gbedemah, Mr. Casely Hayford, Mr. Braimah, Mr. Asafu-Adjaye, Mr. Hutton-Mills, and Mr. Ansah Koi were all renominated. The assembly voted in secret and all were elected."[24]

The governor's position relative to the Legislative Assembly is in procedural matters similar to that of the queen to parliament.

Cabinet practice in regard to minutes, memoranda, secrecy, etc., is patterned after British practice, and the Official Secrets Act. Until recently cabinet meetings took place in the governor's castle at Christiansborg, attended by the necessary permanent secretaries, who provided advice.

Just as the assembly has been presently modified to abolish special interest representation, so the cabinet has recently been changed to abolish the ex-officio ministries of defense and external affairs, justice, and finance, most of the functions of these posts now being open to Africans as are the other eight ministerial posts. This system went into effect in June 1954 subsequent to the new general election. The cabinet during 1952-1953, in addition to the three ex-officio ministers, consisted of a prime minister (who also held the portfolio of the Ministry of Development), Dr. Kwame Nkrumah. The Minister of Health was T. Hutton-Mills; the Minister of Agriculture and Natural Resources, A. Casely Hayford; the Minister of Local Government and Housing, E. O. Asafu Adjaye; the Minister of Commerce and Industry, K. A. Gbedemah; the Minister of Education and Social Welfare, Kojo Botsio. The Minister of Communications, Mr. J. A. Braimah, was the only representative from the Northern Territories. The Minister of Labor was Mr. A. E. Inkumsah. All but two of the members of the cabinet, except the governor and the ex-officios, were Convention People's Party members, with the life chairman of that organization, the prime minister. Ministerial

24 See *The London Times*, March 22, 1952.

secretaries were, in each case, Africans, members of the assembly, while the ministerial secretary to the Ministry of Justice, Mr. Krobo Edusei, was chief government whip until dropped from his position because of unseemly conduct.

The main business of the cabinet can be classified under eight main heads:
1. Legislation (bills).
2. Subsidiary legislation.
3. Exercise of statutory powers vested in the governor in council or in a minister with the prior approval of the governor in council.
4. Petitions addressed to the governor in council.
5. Power of pardon in capital cases.
6. Policy regarding the civil service.
7. Development and economic planning.
8. Questions of policy in spheres other than 6 and 7.[25]

Ministerial responsibility in the Gold Coast can be defined as follows. If a policy question relates exclusively to the sphere for which a minister is responsible, it is at his discretion whether he chooses to consult his colleagues; in the exercise of that discretion he may decide to act without previous reference to his cabinet colleagues. However, a minister knows that he will ultimately have to rely upon the support of his cabinet colleagues if political criticism becomes vocal, and he must temper his decisions by references to that consideration.

Proposed changes in approved policy or statements to be made in the assembly declaring the policy of the government are normal matters for consideration by the cabinet: for example, statements on import, lands, or housing policy. Matters affecting the economic life of the community as a whole are normally brought to the cabinet: for example, changes in price control. Under policy may also be included the setting up of commissions or committees of inquiry, their terms of reference and consideration of the ulti-

[25] Under the provisions of the Statutory Powers and Duties (Transfer to Ministers) Ordinance No. 2 of 1951, certain powers and duties conferred or imposed upon the governor or the governor in council have been transferred to ministers. In the exercise of these powers ministers may consult the cabinet. A large number of powers and duties remain, however, vested in the governor in council or the governor acting on the advice of the cabinet, and all orders, rules, and regulations made in the exercise of such powers are submitted to the cabinet before publication.

mate report and of the measures proposed to implement the recommendations.[26]

Strict British precedent in cabinet business is followed as much as possible, with due allowance for the special requirements of the structural and associational uniqueness of the Gold Coast. For example, the secretary of the cabinet had been seconded to Britain in order to study British cabinet procedure.

As distinct from the old executive council, there are no chiefs in the cabinet, and under the recent changes it is extremely unlikely that traditional qualifications will ever again carry weight in the secular structures of the Gold Coast government.

The Public Service

The Gold Coast Civil Service and Colonial Service are responsible to the governor.[26a] This is a temporary departure from British tradition in the United Kingdom, where, nominally, responsibility derives through the prime minister in his capacity as First Lord of the Treasury. Actually, the Gold Coast Civil Service is the responsibility of the prime minister. The various ministers are responsible to the assembly for the performances of their staff, whether Gold Coast Service or Colonial Service officers. While the passion for anonymity usually ascribed to the British Civil Service in relation to Parliament has been, at times, violated in the Gold Coast Legislative Assembly, disinterested public service is a recognized norm and violations are rarely made without negative comment.

At present most of the important senior positions in the administration are held by expatriate Colonial Service officers. In all cases, at present writing, the permanent secretary is a British official, as are most of the senior administrative secretaries. On the other hand, ministerial secretaries are in all cases African. A public service commission, advisory to the governor,[27] makes recom-

26 The information regarding cabinet business was received from confidential but absolutely reliable sources.

26a After August 1, 1955, all civil servants will be members of the Gold Coast Civil Service, responsible to the prime minister through the public service commission. This includes expatriate staff, who will then be employed by the Gold Coast government on a contract basis.

27 The public service commission, consisting of four members, is until August 1, 1955, purely advisory, although its advice is always taken. The chief secretary is the executive arm of the governor and takes the promotional, appointive, and other actions necessary to effectuate the decisions of the governor, acting on the advice of the public service commission.

mendations on the policy of the public services while an Africanization committee, headed by an African and responsible to the chief secretary, has been working out ways and means to increase the Africanization of the public service. Largely owing to a lack of trained personnel, versed in the ways of administration, and out of the range of politics, Africanization is proceeding more slowly than the Convention People's Party considers desirable.

It is of the utmost importance to note that through the predominantly expatriate staff, a high proportion of government business is handled by British officials, both in the secretariat and in the field.[28] These officials help to write the minister's speeches, do the spade work on most of the problems which the minister must handle, provide the answers to parliamentary questions, and, to a large extent, still make it possible for parliamentary institutions to operate while providing a framework of continuity and effective administration.

One of the most controversial symbols of colonial rule, the district commissioner, has been redesignated, however. Formerly the district commissioner represented the governor and the queen in the district area, and had almost plenary administrative and judicial powers. He has now been titled government agent, with predominantly advisory powers, although he remains the representative of each of the ministries in the field.[29] In addition, the chief

---

For top or senior staff, the public service makes appointments in terms of selective rather than competitive appointments. In the case of equally qualified applicants, Africans are given definite priority. Almost all recruitment of expatriate staff has ceased, although wastage has increased drastically.

The Africanization Board is an adjunct of the chief secretary's office and acts as a watchdog, seeing that no expatriate appointments are made in the event that a qualified African is available.

From an administrative point of view, the chief secretary was in effect two people: He was the permanent secretary of the Ministry of Defence and External Affairs, and the chief secretary or head of the civil service.

[28] Colonial officers are divided into four major levels as follows:

Secretariat	*Field*
Permanent secretary	Chief regional officer or regional officers
Permanent administrative secretary	
(Class I administrative officer)	Assistant regional officer
Senior administrative secretary	
(Class II administrative officer)	Senior government agent
Assistant secretary (Class III or IV	
administrative officer)	Government agent/or assistant government agent

[29] The following extract from the *Review of the Administrative Cadre of the Gold Coast* indicates their position:

"The administrative officer is the chief local representative of the central govern-

commissioner—the senior administrative officer in the field, generally in charge of a territorial area—has been redesignated the chief regional officer, and his powers are largely advisory at the level of regional administration and coordinative for the district officers within the region. There are three such officers, in the Colony, Ashanti, and the Northern Territories, who on ceremonial occasions play the role of lieutenant-governor, a position that they once, in fact, did have. They are, of course, responsible for regional law and order and are in charge of forces in the region.

The actual operating chief of the Gold Coast and Colonial Services was until June 1954 the Minister of Defence and External Affairs.[30]

The three chief regional officers have important advisory positions remaining in regard to the last political segments of indirect rule, the territorial councils. These councils—the Joint Provincial Council, the Asanteman Council, and the Northern Territories Council—have been preserved, although they will no longer be agencies for electing members to the Legislative Assembly. In most cases, these councils maintain a good working arrangement with the chief regional officer or his representatives, just as the new local councils, which have replaced the native authorities, maintain their relationship with the government agent. A new council has been recently set up, the Togoland-Transvolta Council with a regional officer in charge of its administration. A few government agents are African, more Africans are assistant government agents.[31]

The charge has been made, by the prime minister and others,

---

ment, and as such is responsible through the regional officer to the governor and to each minister in the appropriate sphere. In this capacity he is the chief co-ordinating officer in the area.

"He is responsible for the good order of the district up to the moment when a breach of the peace is imminent when it may be necessary to use force to maintain law and order. In this capacity he is expected to maintain contact with the people and the affairs of the district and especially to do what he can to guide and advise the traditional authorities without active intervention.

"He has special responsibilities towards the Minister of Local Government for the supervision of local authorities."

[30] Formerly chief secretary. The ministry has now been abolished, some of its functions being turned over to the governor and other functions provided for in a Ministry of Interior.

[31] It has been proposed that ultimately the position of government agent will be abolished if the district councils envisioned under the Local Government Ordinance of 1951 are ever set up properly. This information derives from personal communications in the office of the Ministry of Local Government.

that the presence of the British colonial officers in important administrative positions actually reduces the control theoretically exerted by the cabinet ministers.[32] Actually this points up the comparative helplessness of the African government in treating many of the problems of government with African personnel. The shortage of trained people is immense in the face of requirements, and the standard of efficiency and conduct demanded by British administrative policy is indeed high.[33] The importance of expatriate staff is well recognized by the government, and has recently been reaffirmed in a speech by the prime minister in which he assured expatriate Colonial Service officers safeguards on their jobs. This means that for some time to come many of the key decisions of Gold Coast political life will be made under the guidance of a British staff, with the governor's reserve powers as a temporary safeguard that the functioning of government will proceed, while the institutionalization of secular structures continues. It is by this means that supervision of institutional transfer by British officials takes place, with maximum permissiveness towards increasing African participation and control, and maximum control over the ultimate rules of the game—the substantive and procedural norms of parliamentary democracy.

The Transfer of Local Government Structures

Following the Coussey Commission recommendations, studies were made of the possible alternatives for local government that would be most in keeping with the new constitutional structure. Two select committees of the Legislative Council published reports and recommendations, and a special study of the regional needs of

---

[32] There is some merit to the charge insofar as the senior expatriate staff are in important positions. This point is discussed in Part IV.

[33] A report of the Africanization Committee, as prepared for the chief secretary's office, indicates that the number of Africans in senior positions does not correspond to the degree of Africanization since the number of expatriates in top posts has increased. It indicates that it is difficult for Africans to get promoted to these positions since they are already filled. The best that can be hoped for, it is indicated, is that directing and policy advising posts in all departments, ministries, and regions should be filled by Africans and the rate of Africanization should proceed on that standard.

In interviews with the secretary of the public service commission, it was found that the general policy is that when an African and an expatriate are equally qualified for a position, the African is given preference. In some cases, it was stated, even if the expatriate has a slight advantage, the post may be given to an African anyway.

the country was made under a regional commission headed by Sir Sydney Phillipson. Phillipson conceived of his task as advising on the best way of providing in the Gold Coast for the essential control inherent in a system based on the English model.[34] His recommendations were not followed, but the report is a classic study of the problems of local institutional transfer. Modifications of the structure of local government were, of course, politically important. The effect of secular structures at the local level would undermine the remaining system of chieftaincy and remove the local sources of revenue and power from the chiefs, power which they had retained through the native authority structure.

A non-Convention People's Party assemblyman (who has recently joined the C.P.P.), E. O. Asafu-Adjaye, Minister of Local Government, was in nominal charge of establishing a new local government system. In contemplating the structural changes involved, he stated that the recommendations made by the various committees on local government reform "may be said to represent great changes in the structure and processes of government." He continued as follows:

"The nature of this change is two-fold; in the first place, it contemplates a departure from the dominant influence of the traditional elements. In the second, it involves a breakaway from the existing centralized and official framework of the government. The pattern for the future is to be based, not upon either of these existing foundations, but upon popularly elected councils, which will in large measure assume the powers and discharge the administrative responsibilities now exercised by traditional authorities on the one hand or by officials on the other."

The statement goes on to specify certain principles laid down in the Coussey Commission Report as having special merit.

"a. The unitary nature of the constitution. The Gold Coast is not to become a federal state, but is to have one central government with final overall responsibility.

"b. Government is to be organized upon a regional basis, this being the best way of bringing the new local authorities into being, and thereafter of providing them with the necessary guidance, services and support.

[34] See *Regional Administrations*, Report by the Commissioner (Phillipson Report), Accra, 1951, p. 16.

"c. The British model of local government is to be followed, suitably adapted to Gold Coast institutions.

"d. The new councils, regional and local, are to be efficient, modern and democratic bodies, and are to have an origin and existence wholly distinct from the traditional councils. These, however, are to remain in being, exercising customary functions, and are to have the right to appoint one-third of the members of the new councils.

"e. The civil service should remain the service of the central government, and separate regional civil services should be established.

"f. The special position and present needs of the Northern Territories should be recognized."[35]

In the main, a revamped local authorities system came into being under the Local Government Ordinance of 1951. This ordinance removed local administration from the responsibility of the state councils (*oman*), returning to them only residual customary functions. The native authorities system was, as the instrument of local government, abolished. The powers of the government agent were made advisory. The new councils consisted of a two-thirds elected membership and a one-third traditional membership. The president of the council was the chief of the area, but he remained a figurehead. The operating head—the chairman of the council—was elected by the members of the council themselves. The local councils were empowered to hire necessary staff and to perform the functions hitherto residing in the native authorities system, with general responsibility to the Ministry of Local Government. A local government school was set up in Accra to help train efficient clerks of the local councils.[36]

For the most part, the local council authority areas utilized those set up under the native authorities system, although districting for local council elections and for representative purposes have caused bitter disputes in many areas. The burden of local taxation is often a cause for complaint, as is local jurisdiction.[37]

[35] See *Local Government Reform in Outline*, Part I, Introduction, Accra, 1951.
[36] See E. B. S. Alton, "The Local Government Training School in the Gold Coast," in *Journal of African Administration*, Vol. IV, No. 3, London, 1952, p. 108.
[37] See the Local Government Ordinance of 1951. For a discussion of the development of local government since 1947 see "A Survey of the Development of Local Government in the African Territories Since 1947," Supplement to the *Journal of African Administration*, Vol. IV, No. 4, London, 1952, Part IX.

Every local authority is required to appoint a finance and staff committee and may appoint other committees as well. The ordinance basically shifts the focus of local government from traditional to secular organs of rule in which the chief and his representatives are subordinate to popularly elected members of the council. The latter is phrased as modern and democratic; the former is phrased as autocratic and imperialistic by nationalists in the local areas, particularly during local government elections.[38]

The Territorial Councils

The territorial councils remain the last remnant of formal indirect rule. They act as a bridge between the traditional state councils, local government, political administration, and the central government. Since June 1954 their elective functions have been completely curtailed and they no longer can elect representatives to the Legislative Assembly, but for a long time, through this function, they provided to the assembly the bulk of the opposition to the Convention People's Party. Most of the chiefs, and the professional men and intelligentsia, came to the assembly not as popular candidates but as representatives of the territorial councils.

At one time, under indirect rule, the territorial councils and the Joint Provincial Council for the Colony had very high political status indeed and were the agency of recruitment of the important figures who dominated the political scene from 1926 until 1948.

The territorial councils are made up of representatives from the state councils (*oman*) and other selected people who might not be chiefs. They handle appeals on customary matters, as well as giving advice to government on the treatment of problems involving chiefs or customary law. Their objects are left purposely vague. The functions defined by ordinance regarding the Joint Provincial Council read as follows: "The Joint Provincial Council may meet from time to time for the purpose of deliberating upon matters affecting the welfare or interests of persons in the Colony, and may, for the purpose of any such deliberation, co-opt

[38] It is worthy of note that in the Northern Territories it makes little difference whether or not the members are elected. As yet opposition to the chiefs is small. Therefore, the members of the local councils still look to their chiefs as their rulers. When the council must decide on an issue, it is still the advice of the chief which is for the most part followed.

such additional members as it thinks fit."[39] Such vague terms of reference have helped to reduce the Joint Provincial Council to a significance more consonant with the new secular system of government. By law the council sends representatives to serve on various government advisory committees and boards, as well as recruiting assessors for constitutional disputes. It speaks for customary tradition and traditional constitutionalism.

The chiefs have recently repeated that they have no place in party politics. By this means they hope to avoid both constitutional problems regarding chieftaincy and the attacks of politicians. In their memorandum of the *Joint Provincial Council on Constitutional Reform*, the council stated:

"In pursuance of our appreciation of the position we have resolved that, in order to maintain the dignity of chieftaincy and to let the new constitutional machinery work unhampered, chiefs have no place in party politics. We have at the same time, during what we regard as an interim period, exercised some influence in the assembly through the election of territorial members and we have sought to exercise it responsibly and in the best interest of the country which we have served so long."[40]

Like the Asanteman Council in Ashanti, the memorandum from the Joint Provincial Council advocated an upper house of chiefs, a proposal which has not been followed. The Joint Provincial Council was a creature of the 1925 Constitution. The Asanteman Council has traditional precedent, and is the agency of the *asantehene's* authority. As such it still receives active support from tradition and exercises enormous influence in the affairs of Ashanti. We shall discuss the Wenchi case subsequently[41] in which a decision of the Asanteman Council retained a royal family which provided active parliamentary leadership against the Convention People's Party, as well as sending that leadership as territorial member to the old assembly.[42] The Northern Territories Council remains subservient to the chiefs, but dominates the Northern People's Party, the official opposition.

[39] The State Councils (Colony and Southern Togoland) Ordinance, 1952, Part VIII.
[40] See Memorandum of the Joint Provincial Council on Constitutional Reform, Dodowa, 1953.
[41] See the State Councils (Ashanti) Ordinance, 1952.
[42] See the State Councils (Northern Territories) Ordinance, 1952.

Municipal Councils

The picture of Gold Coast political structure would not be complete without a word on the municipal councils. Under the recent ordinance,[43] municipal councils are largely composed of elected members, with a proportion of traditional members varying with the size of the municipality. Its president, as in the case of the local government system in rural areas, is appointed from the traditional rulers, while the chairman is elected from the council. Its powers are modeled after the British municipalities and include law enforcement, education, licensing, road maintenance, etc. Generally speaking, it is alleged that the municipal councils are ridden with graft.[44]

These formal structures of government form the legal and administrative framework of the present Gold Coast government. Much of the pattern of today is under constant change, and the movement towards greater secularization has been hastened by the abolition of representation of chiefs and territorial members in the Legislative Assembly. Now all members will receive their seats by way of direct election. The structure of Gold Coast government more and more resembles its formal British counterpart. The structural framework, piece by piece, has been set up over a period of time, without a complete and paralyzing breakdown of the traditional pattern. The vitality and substance of this transfer in its behavioral implications will be a primary concern in the material which follows.

43 See the Municipal Councils Ordinance, 1953.
44 For example, the Kumasi Town Council built stalls in the market place in Kumasi and rented them to their relatives.

CHAPTER 10

THE PATTERNS OF GOLD COAST POLITICS

The General Election of 1951

FOLLOWING hard on the Constitution of 1950, the general election of 1951 was held in a climate of enthusiasm, excitement, and expectancy. In the Colony and Ashanti, a total of 663,069 voters registered, about 40 per cent of the eligible population.[1] In some rural areas apathy towards registration was apparent. An official report on the elections indicates that the attitude of the local chief was of great importance in this respect. In many instances no one would register until the chief had given his approval, and some were, for one reason or another, reluctant to support the elections wholeheartedly. Where they did give support, the registration rate was improved.[2] The opposition of local chiefs was vigorously countered by the apparatus of the Convention People's Party, which conducted local meetings, schools, and in general carried on intensive propaganda. The results were as follows:

RURAL PRIMARY ELECTIONS[3]

	Total sub-districts with registered electors	*Total sub-districts where no nominations were made*	*Total uncontested elections*	*Total contested elections*
The Colony including Southern Togoland	1,736	43	1,232	461
Ashanti	730	5	534	191
TOTAL	2,466	48	1,766	652

[1] See Price, J. H., *The Gold Coast Election*, Bureau of Current Affairs, London, (n.d.) p. 5.

[2] *Report on the First Elections to the Legislative Assembly of the Gold Coast*, 1951, Supplement to Appendix I of *Colonial Reports*, Gold Coast, 1951 (mimeographed document).

[3] From Appendix I, Colonial Reports, *op.cit.*, the report notes as follows: "The high proportion of uncontested elections (74 per cent) did not necessarily imply apathy on the part of the electorate since it is known that in the majority of cases the person to represent the subdistrict (often the normal spokesman such as the local headman, a leading farmer, etc.) had already been chosen at a village meet-

In the elections which followed, the Convention People's Party won 29 out of a possible 33 seats. Most of the non-C.P.P. candidates were independents rather than members of a political party. The United Gold Coast Convention, putting forward several candidates, won three seats. "Most of the independents were moderates in outlook, had little or no popular appeal and carried on virtually no campaigning."[4]

Territorial members were chosen as follows: the Colony put up 53 nominations for 11 seats; Ashanti put up 31 nominations for 6 seats; and Southern Togoland put up 6 nominations for 1 seat. Ten chiefs and 8 commoners were elected. Seven of these 18 had been members of the former Legislative Council, including 3 who had been members of the former Executive Council.[5] The Joint Provincial Council and the Asanteman Council indicated themselves as the strongest supporters of a political position associated with British rule, and were repudiated firmly in the rural and municipal elections.

In the Northern Territories, voting was carried out by an electoral college of 120 persons, composed of 16 members of the Northern Territories Council and 104 persons nominated on a population basis by six district councils. Six chiefs and 8 native authority civil servants were elected, of which 8 were trained schoolteachers.

The municipal elections indicated a clear C.P.P. majority. In the four municipal constituencies there was a total poll of 47 per cent of the registered electorate, as follows:

Electoral district	No. of candidates	No. of seats	Total electorate	Total poll	Percentage
Accra	6	2	48,773	23,122	47.4
Cape Coast	2	1	10,208	3,639	35.6
Kumasi	2	1	20,097	9,123	45.4
Sek.-Takoradi	3	1	11,647	6,912	59.3
TOTAL	13	5	90,725	42,796	47.2

ing in accordance with the usual custom and without recourse to the novelties of the ballot box." This rather revealing statement indicates the kinds of local adaptation of traditional practice to secular innovation which can be witnessed in many forms in the Gold Coast today.

4 *Ibid.*, p. 106.
5 *Ibid.*, pp. 108-109.

The Convention People's Party polled 58,858 votes against 5,574 for their opponents. The urban support for nationalism was by far the strongest of any of the major electoral areas.[6]

The results of the election indicated an overwhelming victory for the Convention People's Party. Its election manifesto, *Towards the Goal,* had charged that the "Coussey Committee let the country down by prolonging white imperialism, the C.P.P. will fight for self-government NOW." It had charged that "This country must send into the assembly men tried in the furnace of national tribulation and not found wanting. . . ."[7] Dr. J. B. Danquah, the leader of the opposition to the C.P.P., barely got himself elected to the assembly in the constituency which was his own home state. Prominent figures who opposed the C.P.P., like Dr. K. A. Busia, chairman of the Ghana Congress Party which was formed subsequently and the chairman of the Department of Sociology of the University College of the Gold Coast, lost the election to a C.P.P. candidate. Busia was, however, elected to the assembly as a territorial member by the Asanteman Council.

In a wave of exultation, the followers hoisted Nkrumah on their shoulders as he was released from prison along with other party leaders. Amidst the shouts of the public he stated:

"I desire for the Gold Coast dominion status within the Commonwealth. I am a Marxian socialist and an undenominational Christian. The places I know in Europe are London and Paris. I am no communist and have never been one. I come out of gaol and into the assembly without the slightest feeling of bitterness to Britain. I stand for no racialism, no discrimination against any race or individual, but I am unalterably opposed to imperialism in any form."[8]

The governor nominated Nkrumah as leader of government business. A cabinet was formed in which most of the top leadership of the Convention People's Party was provided with portfolios. Nkrumah's shadow cabinet, which he developed upon becoming active in Gold Coast politics, took on the substance of government.[9]

[6] *Ibid.,* p. 107.   [7] Quoted in Price, *op.cit.,* pp. 7-8.

[8] *The London Times,* February 14, 1951.

[9] The cabinet which was formed paid noticeably little attention to tribal affiliations. Such traditional criteria had little to do with appointment to ministerial rank. Rather, service in the party formed the main determinant, excepting for the selection of one Northern Territories representative in order that no major tribal group was omitted entirely.

The public had listened to the call of nationalism through the instrumentality of the Convention People's Party. The political kingdom was at hand.[10]

The Convention People's Party

The overwhelming victory of the Convention People's Party surprised most observers. There was little doubt that the C.P.P. would win the election, but their margin of victory came as a shock, particularly to the older participants in Gold Coast political life. The elections themselves had provided an effective organizing media for the C.P.P. One consequence of political institutional transfer, in its procedures, is the opportunity it provides for the organization of groups which utilize new structures for outlets in political action. Today, claiming over a million members, the Convention People's Party is the most effective mass political organization in Africa. It is highly organized. Nkrumah's years in the United States taught him a good deal about mass communications and effective political propaganda. In its largest sense, the party can be dubbed a Tammany-type machine with a nationalist ideology. In a more specific sense, it is composed of a militant elect who dominate and spearhead the nationalist movement, having their own highly disciplined nucleus.

[10] Of interest in this connection is a reporter's account of the election in an article entitled "Popular Hero of the Gold Coast" in *The Listener*, March 1, 1951. Robert Stimson writes: "At the elections too—this was just before Nkrumah was released—the voters showed their adoration in another way, by voting for him and his party. I went to a fishing village on the outskirts of Accra to watch the election there. The boats were drawn up on the beach and the idle nets were stretched in the sun. The fisher folk, most of whom could not read or write, but they were over twenty-one, some of them, and that was good enough to vote—they stood, these voters in a neat queue, in a sandy lane that ran alongside the village headman's house, and they were deadly serious. Each in turn, men and women, went up to the African official who was presiding over the election and gave his or her name. Each name was checked against the registered voting list and then a majestic policeman in a red fez took the voter's thumb and pressed it against a pad soaked in violet ink. This was to ensure that nobody would come back twice. The presiding officer then explained that when the voter got inside the polling booth —a dingy room of rough brick and beaten mud—he would find two boxes, one with a picture of an elephant on it, and the other with a cock. The elephant stood for Nkrumah's man and the cock for his opponent, who had been nominated by the conservative village headman. The voter had to drop his ballot paper in the box of his choice, and it was impressed on him with proper formality that his vote was absolutely secret.

"This village election was a model of correctness; partly because the colonial administration had worked so hard and partly because Kwame Nkrumah's party had told the people that the whole world was watching them, and they must not let themselves or the Gold Coast down."

Dr. Kwame Nkrumah is the life chairman of the Convention People's Party. Founded in 1949, its slogans, manifestos, and publications read like Marxist literature. Organizationally it is similar in structure to a communist organization and the British Labor Party, the composite allowing far more public latitude to members than the former, and preserving the structure of democratic control of the latter. The party has organizational unity, meanwhile allowing important members holding differing views to participate effectively. In this sense it is far more flexible than a communist party and is committed more to the form and discipline of unity rather than to any particular dogma or party line. In this last respect it is an empirically oriented party, very much in the British and Western tradition, rather than an ideologically oriented party in the sense of theory and purism.

The party has its right and left wings. It has its organizations within organizations. Its unity stems from its single aim as stated in the revised constitution of the C.P.P.: "Self-Government now and the Development of (Gold Coast) Ghana on the Basis of Socialism."[11]

There is little doubt that in the manipulation of its key symbols, and its commitment to clearly defined objectives, the C.P.P. has served as the only clear-cut orientational focus which excites the general public, gives a general opportunity to participate, and serves to reassure and define for the public a program of progress in which self-respect and income will be provided.

Ideology and Organization

The Convention People's Party divides its objectives into two categories, national and international. Under the former it lists the following objectives.

"To fight relentlessly to achieve and maintain independence for the people of Ghana (Gold Coast) and their chiefs.

"To serve as the vigorous conscious political vanguard for removing all forms of oppression and for the establishment of a democratic socialist society.

"To secure and maintain the complete unity of the people of the Colony, Ashanti, Northern Territories, and Trans-Volta.

"To work with and in the interest of the Trade Union Movement, and other kindred organizations, in joint political or other

11 Constitution of the Convention People's Party (revised ed. unpubl.), Part I.

action in harmony with the constitution and standing orders of the party.

"To work for a speedy reconstruction of a better Ghana (Gold Coast) in which the people and their chiefs shall have the right to live and govern themselves as a free people.

"To promote the political, social and economic emancipation of the people, more particularly of those who depend directly upon their own exertions by hand or by brain for the means of life.

"To establish a socialist state in which all men and women shall have equal opportunity and where there shall be no capital[ist] exploitation."

For its international objectives the C.P.P. constitution states:

"To work with other nationalist democratic and socialist movements in Africa and other continents, with a view to abolishing imperialism, colonialism, racialism, tribalism, and all forms of national and racial oppression and economic inequality among nations, races and peoples and to support all action for world peace.

"To support the demand for a West African federation and of Pan-Africanism by promoting unity of action among the peoples of Africa and African descent."[12]

Some of the antecedents of the constitution are manifestly clear. Yet it would be most misleading to mistake the document as communist-inspired in any sense. As one of the left-wing members put it, there is strong sympathy for this language. So far, however, the Nkrumah government has shown little evidence of preparing the groundwork for the socialist objectives of the C.P.P.

The combination of British Labor Party and communist party is a most interesting one. It ensures control at the top, with wide participation all along the line. The constitution states that "The National Annual Delegates Conference shall have the power . . . to lay down the broad basis, policy and programme of the party for the ensuing year. The decisions of the Annual Delegates Conference shall be binding on all members of the party, its constitu-

---

[12] I am particularly indebted to Mr. Kwame Afryea, former acting general secretary of the Convention People's Party, and Mr. N. A. Welbeck, its propaganda secretary. In addition, Mr. Kofi Baako, education secretary of the C.P.P. and now personal secretary to the prime minister; Mr. G. Amegbe, now chairman of the Cocoa Marketing Board; Mr. Boi-Doku, assistant propaganda secretary of the C.P.P.; and, finally, the prime minister and life chairman of the C.P.P., Dr. Kwame Nkrumah, all of whom granted liberally of their time and information.

ency branches and its affiliated organizations." This has, by its
actual operation, frequency, and organizational affiliates in the
constituency branches, the earmarks of Labor Party organization, including the annual Labor Party Conference. There is
little doubt that the actual procedures demanded by the parliamentary structures transferred to the Gold Coast have aided in
shaping the organizational structure of the C.P.P. The real difference with the Labor Party, in structure, lies in the degree of
conflict thrashed out in the party conference. In Britain it is extensive and in the Gold Coast it is indeed small. The annual conference is not exactly a rubber stamp, but it is not the arena of
group struggle for the factions within the C.P.P., and enthusiasm
and displays of esteem for the life chairman play a more significant part in the conferences than do the bloc maneuvering characteristics of a Labor Party conference.

While the National Delegates Conference is the plenary body,
the National Executive Council is the governing body. Its purpose
is "to carry out the policy and programme of the party as laid
down by the Annual Delegates Conference," and among other
things, it "initiates and undertakes all such activities as may
further the aims and objects of the party." In addition to the life
chairman of the council, it is composed of a deputy chairman, a
representative from each constituency, two youth representatives
from youth organizations, and two women representatives from
women's organizations. It also "co-opts" six other members, the
general secretary, the national treasurer, the national propaganda secretary (as ex-officio members), and the members of the
central committee.

The central committee is in fact the nub of effective authority.
The constitution states that "there shall be a central committee
of the national executive and other members of the party." It
further states that the central committee shall act as the "directo-
rate" of the national executive. An extremely important clause
states that "The central committee shall work in closest collaboration with all members of the party in the national Legislative
Assembly."

The actual field organization resembles the Labor Party. There
are regional organizations, constituency organizations, municipal
organizations, and the parliamentary party.

A national secretariat, consisting of the general secretary, assistant general secretary, national treasurer, and national propaganda secretary, forms the full-time administrative arm of the party.

The Convention People's Party is a peculiar combination. It is united in its devotion to the life chairman, Kwame Nkrumah. Beneath Nkrumah there is no one who remotely maintains the stature and power of the leader himself. There are other figures in the party who are powerful in local areas, such as Krobo Edusei, formerly chief government whip, whose following is among the youth associations in Ashanti. There is a certain aura of fame which surrounds the "P.G.'s," the prison graduates who served their time in prison for participation in the party leadership. The closest to Nkrumah in public esteem are Kojo Botsio, formerly the Minister of Education and Social Welfare and now Minister of State, and K. A. Gbedemah, formerly the Minister of Commerce and Industry and now Minister of Finance. These two are in somewhat "jealous" competition for the position of second-in-command. Apparently, as observed both in interviews and from a wide range of local experience, Botsio is a close confidante of Nkrumah, but Gbedemah is the organizational leader under Nkrumah. Worthy of some note is the fact that Gbedemah, the least ideologically oriented, is considered ambitious, and loyal to the groups who worked with him when Nkrumah was in jail and when the party was first effectively organized. Most of these groups consist of the extreme left-wing of the party. On the other hand, Botsio, considered far more left-wing than Gbedemah, does not seem to have a large personal following in the party, but rather receives his support from Nkrumah as a kind of ideological mentor of the party. There is little doubt that only the presence of Nkrumah has kept the left-wing from exerting overt and hasty actions, and a controversy between Gbedemah and Botsio from breaking out openly.[13]

The Convention People's Party as a Social Unit

Like most political parties, the C.P.P. is a combination of a hierarchy of offices, institutionalized roles, and personal controls.

[13] See below, p. 229, for a sociogram of the Legislative Assembly showing affiliational lines. The C.P.P. back bench opposition was destroyed in the June 1954 election and Gbedemah's independent following within the party eliminated.

Overshadowing both the offices and personalities is Nkrumah. The offices of the central committee and the national secretariat are hardly limiting factors in the role definition of occupants of these posts. Rather, definition comes from Nkrumah, and association with him provides legitimacy. Procedural convenience rather than the institutionalization of roles sets the operating mode of the party organs. This is of some importance. It means that so far the constitution and structure of the party are structures of convenience rather than legitimacy, and the legitimacy itself stems from the leader, Nkrumah. Not only is the C.P.P. flexible, but no organizational group at any level is assured of independent authority and power, except the life chairman. It means, further, that the precise ideological and structural definition of the Convention People's Party remains to be seen. As we shall indicate later, as long as this party maintains its power we can argue that as it goes, so goes the Gold Coast.

The leadership of the party is mixed. Nkrumah, holding degrees from American universities, is an "Achimota boy." That is to say, like many others who played a part in the national life of the Gold Coast, he received his secondary school education at Achimota School. Most of the parliamentary leadership of the C.P.P. is composed of journalists, lawyers, or youth leaders. Most are secondary school people, with a high proportion from Achimota, although many of those having cabinet rank have university degrees.

The nationalist movement in the C.P.P., as distinct from the more conservative nationalism formerly identified with the United Gold Coast Convention, is in its top leadership predominantly associated with the non-intellectuals. The high prestige which is accorded education, however, instead of redounding to the credit of the opposition, has been granted to Nkrumah, who is sometimes referred to as "The Doctor" (a B.D. degree having been granted him by Lincoln University in the United States). Such a state of affairs has accorded Nkrumah a monopoly of wisdom while other university graduates—like Busia, who are in the opposition—are charged with trying to be too clever, a most invidious charge indeed. Many of the marginal people, those having some elementary education, take vicarious pleasure in associating with "wisdom," partaking and expending of it through their membership in the C.P.P. In the local areas this has a second range of significance, insofar as the wisdom emanating from the leader and as expressed by his followers detracts from the "wisdom" of the chiefs and helps to undermine their position.

For many of the followers, the ideology of the party and of nationalism gives them an intellectual foundation, and a political education much as in communist movements. It gives them the "secret" of history and as such provides a superiority to the usually more pallid liberalism of the schoolteachers and the older educated gentry, and a feeling of knowledge which becomes all the more important because it does not truly supersede education itself.

In the structuring of action in the C.P.P., certain types of roles are formed at key organizational points which are reinforced and sustained by their links with Nkrumah. Observers often remark at the accessibility of Nkrumah in the party. Rather than accessibility, it is evidence of direct control, and direct and constant need by the member to receive his mandate from Nkrumah for role activity and support. Support, instead of stemming primarily from local units, comes from above; it is endowed as grace, which in turn is manifested through directives and personal contact. The highly organized C.P.P. maintains its discipline as a party through the personal allegiance to Nkrumah on the part of those who perceive their destiny as being achieved, ideologically and psychologically, through the leader and the party organization. All service to Nkrumah is the enhancement of local strength through organization, and his response, being non-doctrinaire, allows many diverse individuals and groups to identify their futures with him. At the same time, the local organizations are open enough so that public ideas, expressions of demand, problems of a local nature, and general discussion can be had, with lower level leaders depending upon local support as a requisite for Nkrumah's support. These local units admit of the widest membership, and not all of them are effectively under discipline. The Kumasi regional C.P.P., for example, has such an independent local following that its guiding light, Krobo Edusei, was treated with great consideration by Nkrumah, who made him chief government whip, although his qualifications were by no means clear.[14]

[14] Edusei was dropped as a ministerial secretary following the Braimah investigation. He was chosen, however, as the C.P.P. candidate in his constituency for the 1954 general election against the opposition of the local C.P.P. branch, and in spite of the availability of excellent alternative candidates.

Among some of the important administrative leaders of the party, there is a curious definition of roles in which service to the ideal of socialism is devoutly manifest. Such individuals as the former acting general secretary, the former propaganda secretary, and the former education secretary (the latter, Mr. Kofi Baako, now Nkrumah's personal secretary and chief government whip), are members of a curious party within a party, the League of Ghana Patriots. This organization, sponsored by Nkrumah, is conceived of as an elite formation, communist in type, organized on a cell basis, and having para-military "strong boys." They are "agit-prop" minded. The members of this elite are in charge of sending down to local party units many of the memoranda which are phrased as party directives and which must be followed.[15] They are the tacticians of the party, and their members are invariably with the prime minister on rallies, public occasions, and general public appearances. It is they who control the apparatus of the party and who press the ideological and militant revolution, thus according a deeper meaning to the popular doctrine of tactical action enunciated by Nkrumah. They have carefully provided the groundwork for a socialist organization not formally affiliated with the C.P.P. but in operation in the University College and under the leadership of the former education secretary of the C.P.P., Mr. Kofi Baako. A subsidiary organization, the National Association of Socialist Youth, is to form the nucleus for a future development of socialist consciousness. Such consciousness is most difficult to develop and, according to a personal interview with the prime minister, would be dangerous if premature.

The party directives often detail a local C.P.P. unit to capture a local council and enhance its organizing efforts. In fact, the party is alleged to dominate the *asafo* companies in areas where chiefs are openly anti-C.P.P., for purposes of bringing destoolment charges. An unseasoned nationalist with a respect for custom may balk at this, and some former C.P.P. organizers, particularly in the north, and Ashanti have turned bitterly against the C.P.P. because of such procedures.

These left-wing groups, including most of the administrative staff of the party secretariat, have been slated for the job of acting as ideological mentor of the party, if the circumstances appear

---

[15] Such directives are party memos which any disciplined member must follow. The resemblance to a communist organization is greatest in this respect.

ripe for a mass strengthening of socialism after the British leave. However, Mr. N. A. Welbeck, formerly the national propaganda secretary of the C.P.P., has indicated that the commitment to power comes first, while the commitment to ideologies comes second.

The right wing tends to have less sophisticated members but comprises most of the mass membership of the party. Actually, to call it a right wing is misleading, for it is composed of diverse groups of people who want independence and, on the whole, are not concerned about the form which independence will take. While for the left wing, whose members have read Marxist literature, parliamentary democracy is a useful adjunct of political power, for the right wing it is more or less expected in form, remote from personal conviction. For these groups nationalism is a far more pragmatic than ideological affair, and it is these groups who have little socialist consciousness and yet with whom it is dangerous to meddle along ideological lines. Their argument goes as follows: The British occupied positions of political authority. Under them the country was constrained. If they are forced to leave, then Africans will have more economic and political opportunity. Therefore, to get rid of the British as soon as possible is the goal. This view caters in the main to those who see in nationalist politics opportunities for personal advancement, reward, and prestige positions. There is little graft or corruption among the militant left wing, whose members, emulating Nkrumah, live in comparative simplicity, some of them in the slum areas in Usshertown in Accra.

While it would be unfair to charge most of the non-left leadership with being opportunistic, it is probably fair to say that they are less concerned with principles and ideologies, except for the demand for independence, which unites them all. From a functional point of view, the party as a whole is various in what it provides. It provides satisfactions to a diverse membership— status, position, power—satisfactions which, as in any political organization, can be misused. It must, however, be pointed out that the aspect of institutional transfer most difficult to achieve is the institutionalization of norms of political ethics. At present remuneration for services rendered within the political sphere is hardly considered bad,[16] particularly as such remuneration was

16 Such accrued satisfactions which we would call in more Western terms, bribery and corruption, raise a most complex series of questions which we shall discuss

in a sense institutionalized in the traditional pattern of authority.

Since the Gold Coast is not yet completely independent, the party has its common objective—self-government—intact. Its enemy is imperialism. Even when the C.P.P. was voted into office it continued to charge that the constitution of the country was "bogus and fraudulent" and it therefore evaded repudiation of its leaders and officials by the public. Final responsibility for the sins of political office can be to some extent shifted, by charging the British for the ills which beset the nation even under a Nkrumah government.

At the same time, the goals which ultimately unite party members in regard to purpose are to a large extent the more rational or objectivized purposes of large segments of the population of the Colony and Ashanti, even for those not actively participating in politics. The party is related to a larger structural framework which has been made tolerable, partly because of public acceptance of British constitutional changes (having little choice in the matter) and partly because the administrative structure of colonial government has been the only agency of politics. That is to say that the structure of parliamentary democracy as handed down by the British is the rational framework of politics which makes it possible for the Convention People's Party to be a party rather than a movement. As Weber indicates:

"Their action is oriented toward the acquisition of 'social power,' that is to say, toward influencing a communal action no matter what its content may be. . . . For party actions are always directed toward a goal which is striven for in a planned manner. This goal may be a 'cause' (the party may aim at realizing a program for ideal or material purposes), or the goal may be 'personal' (sinecures, power and from these honor for the leader and the followers of the party). Usually the party action aims at all these simultaneously. Parties are, therefore, only possible within communities that are societalized, that is which have some rational order and a staff of persons available who are ready to

---

further. It is no secret that the party as a vehicle for social mobility attracts many followers for idealistic nationalist reasons, but it also attracts others who see an identity of private good with public gain. Most observers agree that "dashing" or giving presents or bribes is common throughout the Gold Coast, and the political parties are no exception to the practice.

enforce it. For parties aim precisely at influencing this staff, and it possible, to recruit it from party followers."[17]

Yet while the C.P.P. as a political party developed within a framework of political organization which gave it subsidiary rules and modes of operations—elections, seats in the assembly and on local and municipal councils—one crucial element in this development must be pointed out. The party, before it was a party in the sense of integration with parliamentary structures of government, was a movement. As a movement it did not define the structure of government-to-be, nor did it specify the terms of such a government. Rather, it reacted against existing structures and their control. In doing this it found a popular cause and an effective source of recruitment. Insofar as it was successful in attaining a mass following, even while some ·of its leaders were in jail, but did not have effective opportunity at the time to act as a lawful political party, *it formed a major element in the societalization of what was a predominantly localized and fragmented set of tribal and regional areas, but hitherto without social cohesiveness beyond the tribal purview, excepting in municipalities and excepting a small educated minority of the population.* The C.P.P. activated public orientation towards central government structures which were in the parliamentary structural pattern, identifying the achievement of popular ends with the framework of parliamentary democracy, as controlled by the Convention People's Party.

In this respect the party and the structures of government form concrete membership units which are indices of national solidarity. The legitimacy of Nkrumah—that which he bestows—has been granted to the norms around which secular role behavior within the government must conform (since the British are overtly present to insure functional conformity). The problem for the C.P.P. has been to achieve this object, allaying the suspicions of the British officials and maintaining a well-functioning administration to insure that government does not break down with the achieving of political independence, meanwhile retaining a freedom of action which will seek out, create, and be responsive to changes in support by the public. The first job, Nkrumah stated in personal interview, and the first responsibility, is to the party.

[17] Weber, M., *Essays in Sociology*, translated by Gerth and Mills, New York, 1946, p. 194.

The Convention People's Party creates agencies in its local and regional units, for non-tribal social action, integrating with the structure of local government. It does the same thing at the national level. It reinforces its solidarity through maintaining the orientational aspects of the "cause"—which is possible because the Gold Coast is still a colony. It can maintain its organization since with political office, it has the sinecures, power, and honor of official and party posts. It has plenty of patronage. At the center is the leader.[18] From him the effective legitimacy of governmental parliamentary structures flows. Through the C.P.P. *effective public support* and *effective authority* converge.[19] In this respect, through Nkrumah and the C.P.P., legitimization for secular political roles continues to stem from non-secular—charismatic—sources.

The Party as a Tactical Weapon

The party is open, radical in the populist sense of the word, and democratic in many crucial respects. Ultimately its strength indicates the effectiveness of the weapon which Nkrumah holds in his hands, whether as a liberator of West Africa, as an instrument for control of the machinery of government, or for whatever other purposes he defines. The immediate problem of tactics is to avoid public disillusionment with the Nkrumah regime, to keep the "revolution" alive, to provide for organizational foundations in the system amenable to party control (such as elective local councils), and to operate an effective government. Most of these objectives run head on into one another.

Not for a moment is the country allowed to forget that the final objective is not yet achieved. Anything which is done has an interim quality. No one can judge the government, except by its successes. For example, in December 1952, after Nkrumah had been prime minister for almost a year, the C.P.P. magazine stated:

"Need we remind ourselves that the struggle is not over? The struggle still continues and it intensifies as the end approaches. We have India, Ceylon and Burma to draw inspiration from. Ours therefore at this hour of our struggle is to keep on organizing and disciplining our forces for the final blow against imperialism in

18 Charismatic.

19 The first objective is expanding the party to increase its effectiveness in making the public more socialist conscious, indicated Nkrumah in personal interview.

our country so as to make Ghana take her rightful place among the comity of nations."[20]

Recognizing, however, that collaboration with the British once the decision was made to participate in the government would make necessary some compromises which a fickle public might view as a repeat performance of the precedent established under indirect rule when the older nationalists and the chiefs became identified with the British administration, Nkrumah organized the doctrine of Tactical Action, as distinct from Positive Action which he utilized when out of power. Tactical Action has been described to the public as follows:

"Kwame Nkrumah has now launched another political bomb— Tactical Action. As usual the reactionaries, the die-hards and the unimaginative cannot see the outcome. Many say Tactical Action is a washout, but the imperialists are more cautious this time. They do not want to be found naping [sic] at the psychological moment so they are bringing all their wits to bear on the situation. Unfortunately for the people of the Gold Coast the reactionaries have a fine flow of choice words and the reactionary newspapers are even more intelligent now than in the days of Positive Action so the old campaign of sabotage is on.

"Kwame Nkrumah now sitting with the imperialists in power is for ever vigilant; he knows he is there by the will of the people and his work is to see their welfare. The Imperialists lynx-eyed, and ever on the qui vive, bland, courteous, tactful, diplomatic are as vigilant as the sea surrounding their little island."[21]

This picture of Nkrumah watching every move of the "Imperialists" is probably the closest one can come to finding a definition of Tactical Action. It indicates that certain actions which seem to many loyal C.P.P. members as eating cake with imperialists are only a tactical maneuver on Nkrumah's part. Whatever collaboration occurs is phrased as tactics; whenever collaboration breaks down, the vigilance of Nkrumah is reaffirmed. Under this system, Nkrumah is able to utilize effectively the services of the British

[20] *Freedom*, C.P.P. monthly magazine, December 1952, no. 1. It is interesting to note that one of the members of the magazine committee of this organ, Turkson Ocran, former general secretary of the Trades Union Congress, has been expelled from the C.P.P. for alleged communist affiliations. This is a most interesting development in the light of Tactical Action enunciated by the prime minister, considering that expulsion came hard on the heels of the British Guiana affair.

[21] *Ibid.*, "Towards Freedom via Nkrumah," Yaa Asantewa.

colonial staff without substantial diminution of party integrity.

It is clear, however, that to maximize Nkrumah's alternatives and freedom of action, the party must serve up bases of support various in their kind, which provide him with a variety of blocs which he can control and which, taken together, can undermine a major opposition which might emerge in the party. For example, the left-wing organization group within the party is the nucleus of a more formalized non-democratic structure which could control the party, if Nkrumah so desired, and, in the event of self-government if Nkrumah's power should wane, could dismiss parliamentary structures as British and imperialist while instituting a more totalitarian system modeled after Marxian practice. This is not to say that Nkrumah would do any such thing, but it is a practical alternative which at least one member of the party high command indicated in personal interview.[22]

At present the party follows the precept of democratic centralism. Yet it would be wrong to conclude, as the Watson Report did so prematurely, that the C.P.P. and its internal structure are communist. Its present major tenet is Tactical Action. Tactical Action is a unique political program because it makes possible a combination of ideological purity and pure political opportunism, the former deriving its very intensity from the latter. The alternatives open to Nkrumah, so long as he retains his charismatic authority, are enormous, in his capacities and roles as life chairman of the party and prime minister of the Gold Coast. If it seems politically wise he can get rid of avowed communists, or proclaim the need for keeping the British around, the latter course perpetuating the conditions which demand and keep alive revolutionary exercise. *Tactical Action, as used by a charismatic figure like Nkrumah, allows the very conditions which would destroy a lesser revolutionary movement to intensify support for the leader.*

Meanwhile, Nkrumah does not overtax the limits of acceptance of his charismatic authority by the public. The secular organs of government at the central and local levels, as well as the party units throughout the country, serve as excellent sounding boards for public response and attitudes. In addition, Nkrumah tours the country almost every weekend, going to first one village and then another where any signs of disaffection occur. These rallies, which

22 Who cannot be named here because it would violate certain confidences.

are well-staged affairs, do great honor to the village and remain an event to be remembered in the quiet of the ordinary rural environment. After such a rally, the local C.P.P. politicians usually have gained considerably in stature and the strength of the party is enhanced.

The language of the party is partly Marxian. Its practice is essentially empirical. In this it resembles the British Labor Party far more than any other. The C.P.P. is disciplined, but Nkrumah is not a party dictator in the usual sense of the word. The national executive and the central committee meetings are often bitter and stormy. Personal acrimony is often great. The leadership is by no means divorced from its membership. Nkrumah himself seems to have an infinite capacity for listening. He is too good a politician to be doctrinaire.

Some insight into the way the various factions are organized for party purposes can be gained by viewing the levels of personal authority and the ideological subscription of the individuals on these levels, which to some extent do not conform to the organization plan of the party.

In general, top leadership of the C.P.P. involves three levels. In the top level there are the old guard who are primarily in positions of ministerial or near-ministerial rank. Gbedemah, the Minister of Finance, and Botsio, the Minister of State, are the most important of these.

When not involved in ministerial duties, these old guard cooperate with the second rung, which revolves around the permanent officials of the party: the propaganda secretary, the education secretary, and the acting general secretary. N. A. Welbeck, formerly national propaganda secretary and now Minister of Works, is probably the most important organizationally, while Kofi Baako, the education secretary and personal secretary to the prime minister, as well as chief government whip, is the most important ideologically.

At this level, major rallies are planned, the needs of the party apparatus, the formation of party directives, and the control of party discipline are manifested. Very often, for example, Welbeck coordinates the work of the C.P.P. field staff. Party officials see Nkrumah constantly on both a formal and informal basis. They are close to the field units and constantly on the alert for strains in the party apparatus. They are party zealots: tough, resourceful, tireless, and sincerely nationalist.

The third level refers to the organizational people directly under Baako, Welbeck, and Afryea. They are constantly in the field and keep in personal touch with most of the local party headquarters, forming a resource group which can be called upon to perform certain activities from fomenting a riot if necessary to heading government boards, such as the present chairman of the Cocoa Marketing Board. Others like Boi-Doku, assistant propaganda secretary of the party, control those who are not adverse to a bit of violence if occasion demands it.

There is little doubt that the second level is in constant touch with Nkrumah and that the third level is constantly in touch with the second. These two form the disciplined hard core of the party. They put out the *Evening News*, the C.P.P. newspaper which states on its masthead "Go to Bed with the Accra Evenews and Wake Up with the Spirit of CPP." They know how far they can push the ideological aspects of party work, and how much depends on the deification of Nkrumah.[23] For Nkrumah they are a constant source of advice on party matters and represent, with the possible exception of Botsio, his closest confidantes.

These groups can be counted on to provide support where necessary and to oppose the prime minister when tactics demand. They carry out the instructions of the prime minister to the C.P.P. back bench. If a measure is unpopular and the prime minister wants it dropped, but as government must table it in the assembly, the C.P.P. back bench may be counted on ostensibly to desert the party rather than allow the real parliamentary opposition to take credit for reform or change. If some advantage is demanded which the British are unwilling to give, Nkrumah can have his supporters make a major issue of it, possibly forcing the hand of the governor. If the British want something unpopular done, Nkrumah can go to the party and indicate that Tactical Action is

[23] A short questionnaire elicited from the general secretary of the C.P.P. the following information, to be taken with considerable question:
1,000,593 estimated and paid up members of the party.
103 full-time party organizers.
6 regional officers as follows: Colony 3, Ashanti 1, Northern Territories 1, Trans-Volta 1.
2,885 local offices in the country as follows: Colony 1,136, Ashanti 1,043, Northern Territories 204, Trans-Volta-Togoland 502.

required and that some accommodation must be made. In this situation a good deal of freedom to maneuver is left in Nkrumah's hands.

The Functioning of Government

The government of the Gold Coast, as set up in the Order in Council of 1950 and amended in 1953, and operated by the Convention People's Party, has both diffuse and specific sources of legitimacy, and complex systems of authority roles. Its specific legal legitimacy derives from the Crown. Its diffuse effective legitimacy derives from Nkrumah. From the specific legal legitimacy of the Crown, the governor, through his reserve powers and through the military forces, exerts a control on the process of institutional transfer. By endowing the roles and structures of secular government with diffuse effective legitimacy, via charisma, the institutionalization of these roles and structures has begun.

The differing groups in the assembly derive their sanctions from differing sources, welded into a decision-making body by the network of functions and procedural rules to which members must orient their action. If, for example, concepts of representation are confused, the functions of the parliament as laid down in the constitution are not. The scheduling of business under the constant guidance of the British officers, who are in the background as permanent secretaries in the office of the prime minister or advising the clerks of the assembly, promotes consistency of role and procedure through the orderly process of debate, committee, vote, enactment of bills, and ordinances. Around the flow of business, the cabinet, the assembly, and the administrative service have achieved functional coherence, while role definition for the Africans is by no means clear nor, if defined, thoroughly institutionalized. The non-procedural norms to which different individuals adhere, dealing with the sources, expression, and limits of authority, are often different in focus depending on whether or not an individual is governed by the traditional normative pattern, the charismatic normative pattern, or the predominantly secular normative pattern.

Even so, the procedural norms have wide implications for political institutional transfer insofar as they have become legitimized by their acceptance as regulations by some members. The criteria of rational activity following norms of logicality have been subsumed under procedural norms governing the flow of public business in which efficiency, for example, is a most pronounced objective.

In the course of assembly business, the larger norms of a parliamentary democracy are raised again and again, first with the idea that the world is watching, and secondly because of the individuals who have accepted the norms and others who must give them lip-service. Such concepts as free choice, freedom of action, representation of the major segments of the population (however defined), majority rule, the integration of the opposition into an integrally compatible political framework providing for peaceful social change, are all but by no means exhaustive aspects. Essentially these latter norms refer to the terms of order set by British requirements.

While it was impossible to examine such questions from the point of view of public opinion, we can view public representation as it appeared in the assembly.[24]

The Legislative Assembly, as it was constituted prior to June 1954, represented certain associational groups in the country at large. The actual membership, responsible to the associational group whence they came, maintained certain affiliational ties with significant segments of that associational group in order to receive cooperation and support.

Clusters of members around parliamentary leaders, in parliamentary association over a period of time, as distinct from a coalition for immediate purposes, indicated complementarity of objectives and larger association of groups in the country. For example, the Ghana Congress Party opposition often united with the chiefs in the assembly, not only on important issues but in planning strategy. Evidence indicates that the chiefs looked with a good deal of favor on the Ghana Congress Party while looking upon the Convention People's Party with contempt—a fact which foreshadowed cooperation between the conservative opposition parties. Most of the chiefs in the old assembly were elected from the territorial councils, as was Dr. Busia, the chairman of the Ghana Congress Party.

---

[24] See below. However, the general public is interesting to watch in participation in rallies. These are often grand affairs, with everyone participating; women dance, drums beat, the C.P.P. colors are everywhere, prayers are offered, and the imperialists are heavily castigated.

In the main, the various groups in the 1952-1953 assembly could be categorized by the way they were elected. There were those who were chiefs or representatives of the territorial councils who could be identified with the interests and position of the traditional authorities.

There were the Northern Territories members who were closely tied up to the extreme traditionalism of the north; the activities of these members indicated the limited participation which they were willing to accord central governmental operations. They have since formed a separate Northern People's Party, now the leading opposition party in the assembly.

There were rural and municipal members whose overwhelming sentiments were in favor of the Convention People's Party. Not the least element of these was the increasing number of urban voters and youngmen who sought to evade the pattern of tribal-agricultural life and use nationalism as a means of achieving economic as well as psychological satisfaction.

Each of these groups of representatives tended to have somewhat differing notions of political norms, while their integration was procedurally achieved within the limits of parliamentary rules and standing orders, as well as the rationalized work flow of government business.

Some members found their roles in one social pattern conflicting with their roles in another. For example, one chief, in answering a questionnaire distributed among all the members of the Legislative Assembly, claimed that the chief should be above politics. In effect, his position as a chief abolished his representativeness as a member. He could act only as a guardian of the interests of traditional leaders and vote accordingly. He, like other chiefs in the assembly, became a special member, a watchdog, seeing in most secular measures a new threat to chieftaincy, forced to resist those bills which promised to destroy the old structures of authority. On many issues the chief found himself on the wrong side as far as popular demands were concerned. Otherwise he had to abstain from debate or division, or sustain the wrath of the Convention People's Party, both on the floor of the assembly and back home in his tribal area where C.P.P. youngmen might find a pretext for instituting destoolment proceedings. Many such chiefs, such as the *konor* of Manya Krobo, who sat on the old Legislative Council and subsequently as a territorial member from the Joint Provincial Council, bore this sort of attack continuously.[25]

The formal requirements of membership and participation set one pattern of role prescriptions in which procedural factors which bound all members for a common purpose—legislation— were paramount. The place of origin of the members, whether Northern Territories, Colony, or Ashanti, set some patterns of representation and responsibility. The Northern Territories representatives were responsible to the Northern Territories Council, while Colony and Ashanti rural and municipal members were responsible to the public.

The affiliations which members held determined the dominant reference groups to which they belonged, the criteria by which they made decisions on important issues (other things being equal), and the parliamentary groups which they formed in the assembly. In formal terms, regionalism, legitimacy affiliation, reference orientations, group affiliation, and interest representation appeared to be the crucial factors in guiding the members' decisions, insofar as these issues affected the decisions of the parliamentary party as a whole. Each of the major groups had its party whip who imposed discipline with various success.

The parliamentary system therefore imposed structural and procedural bases for integrated action at the most general political level by wielding diverse elements into a procedural chamber in which the decisions made are considered binding upon the members of the entire Gold Coast population. Open normative conflicts at the central government level were avoided by the participation of various significant sub-groups, such as chiefs, political parties, etc., and by the overwhelming parliamentary majority of the Convention People's Party in which *effective public support* and *effective authority* have been combined.

We shall make some attempt to cast more light on this process by examining these various groups in relation to the business of the assembly.

During the sessions of the assembly which lasted from February 9 to March 6, 1953 (which were all observed in the course of this research), the government consisted of eleven cabinet ministers

25 See the Manya Krobo Case below, p. 257.

and an equal number of ministerial secretaries. The prime minister held the portfolio of Minister of Development.[26]

The general composition of the assembly during this session can be described as follows.[27] Facing the speaker, the table, and the mace were the main benches. On the left sat the government in the front row of seats. On the right on the other side of the table sat the front row of the opposition. The most active members of the opposition bench, which sat eight members, were William Afori Atta, Dr. J. B. Danquah, Mr. Kwesi Lamptey, and Dr. K. A. Busia. Behind them sat the bulk of the chiefs. The Northern Territories members sat on the government side of the house. Scattered throughout were the C.P.P. regulars, the C.P.P. back bench, the special interest members, and the territorial non-chief members.

Comparing the ages and education of the members of the Legislative Assembly, we get the following breakdown from Price:[28]

AVERAGE AGES AND EDUCATION OF THE ASSEMBLY

	ASSEMBLY						GOVERNMENT		
	Municipal representatives (5)	Rural representatives (38)	J.P.C. and A.C.C. members (18)	N.T. members (19)	Europeans (9)	Total (assembly) (84)	Ministers (11)	Ministerial secretaries (11)	Total (government) (22)
Average age*	43	38	46	34	45	40	44	35	40
U.K. univer.	3	5	3	—	5	16	8	2	10
Extra-mural students	2	10	1	1	—	14	—	4	4
U.S.A. univer.	1	2	1	—	—	4	1	—	1
Exter. degr.	—	1	1	—	—	2	—	1	1
Teach. cert.	—	3	1	4	—	8	—	1	1
Senior Cambridge	—	2	2	—	1	5	—	1	1
Post-standard VII	1	5	1	—	—	7	1	4	5
Standard VII†	—	16	9	11	—	36	1	4	5
Sub-stand. VII	—	—	—	4	—	4	—	—	—
Achimota	3	3	1	2	—	9	3	1	4

* The average age is computed as at February 28, 1951, but as is common in countries where birth certificates are a rarity and where there is a high percentage of illiteracy, there may be a tendency on the part of some members to overestimate their age.

† Standard VII is the normal primary school leaving age in the Gold Coast. Those marked "Post Standard VII" have varying degrees of attainment between Standard VII and degree standard.

[26] Having high patronage implications. The cabinet consisted of the prime minister and Minister of Development, Dr. Kwame Nkrumah, M.A., M.Sc., B.D., LL.D.,

The most significant groupings were, of course, the proportion of university and Standard VII people, both in the assembly and the government. Professions are listed below, following the above breakdown.

PROFESSIONS OF THE 1951 ASSEMBLY

	Municipal representatives (5)	Rural representatives (38)	J.P.C. and A.C.C. members (18)	N.T. members (19)	Europeans (9)	Total (assembly) (84)	Ministers (11)	Ministerial secretaries (11)	Total (government) (22)
Carpenter	–	–	–	1	–	1	–	–	–
Chief	–	–	9	6	–	15	–	–	–
Civil servant	–	–	–	–	4	4	3	–	3
Engine driver	–	1	–	–	–	1	–	–	–
Farmer	–	3	–	1	–	4	–	–	–
House agent	–	1	–	–	–	1	–	1	1
Journalist	2	1	–	–	–	3	1	2	3
Lawyer	2	1	1	–	1	5	3	–	3
Letter writer	–	1	–	–	–	1	–	–	–
Medical practit.	–	–	1	–	–	1	1	–	1
Merchant	–	7	2	–	3	12	–	–	–
Native auth. employees	–	1	1	5	–	7	1	2	3
Pharmacist	–	4	1	–	–	5	–	2	2
Postal agent	–	–	–	1	–	1	–	–	–
Professional politician	–	6	–	–	–	6	2	1	3
Retired army officer	–	–	–	–	1	1	–	–	–
Schoolteacher	1	6	2	5	–	14	–	3	3
Stenographer	–	1	–	–	–	1	–	–	–
University lect.	–	–	1	–	–	1	–	–	–
TOTAL	5	33	18	19	9	84	11	11	22

[*Note 26 continued*]

Minister of Defence and External Affairs, R. H. Saloway, C.M.G., C.I.E., O.B.E., ex-officio; R. P. Branigan, Q. C., ex-officio; Minister of Finance, R. P. Armitage, C.M.G., M.B.E., ex-officio; Minister of Health, T. Hutton-Mills, barrister-at-law, C.P.P.; Minister of Agriculture and Natural Resources, A. Casely-Hayford, M.A., barrister-at-law, C.P.P.; Minister of Local Government and Housing, E. O. Asafu Adjaye, B.A., LL.B., barrister-at-law, independent; Minister of Commerce and

It is interesting to compare this data with the table given by Price for the 1950 Legislative Council as follows:

THE 1950 LEGISLATIVE COUNCIL PROFESSIONS AND BASIS OF MEMBERSHIP

| | *Official* | *Nominated* | ELECTED | | | |
			Munic.	*Col.*	*Ashan.*	*Total*
Chiefs	—	—	—	5	1	6
Civil servants (including retired)	8	1	—	—	—	9
Ex-servicemen's welfare officers	—	1	—	—	—	1
Lawyers	*	1	1	3	1	6
Lecturers	—	—	—	1	—	1
Medical practitioners	—	—	1	—	1	2
Merchants	—	2	2	—	1	5
Ministers of religion	—	1	—	—	—	1
Schoolteachers	—	—	1	—	—	1
TOTAL	8	6	5	9	4	32

* One official member (the attorney-general) could be counted either as a civil servant or as a lawyer.

According to one account, the C.P.P. controlled a bloc of disciplined members numbering thirty-four.[29] The main group of party supporters following the lead of Nkrumah were, however, by no means thoroughly disciplined. Some of them maintained an independence commensurate with their signal failure to hold important party or ministerial posts. One prominent member of the back bench, finding it a political misfortune not to be a "Prison Graduate," threatened a magistrate, spent nine pleasant months

---

[*Note 26 continued*]

Industry, Mr. K. A. Gbedemah, C.P.P.; Minister of Education and Social Welfare. Kojo Botsio, B.A., dip. ed. F.R.G.S., C.P.P.; Minister of Communications and Works, J. A. Braimah, independent, N.T.; Minister of Labor, A. E. Inkumsah, C.P.P.

[27] The pattern varies from that of the House of Commons, inasmuch as representation differs.

[28] Price, J. H., *The Gold Coast Election, op.cit.*

[29] This estimate was made by K. A. Gbedemah in personal interview and had reference to the hard core of members relied upon to vote with the government. Other estimates by high-ranking British officials placed the effective C.P.P. bloc at 42. In any case, party discipline had to be maintained and the Northern Territories generally voted with the government, having at their disposal 19 votes. Discipline was hard to maintain, however, and in some cases the chief government whip ignored his party commands. For example, on the Lidbury Report

(by his own account) in jail, and returned to the assembly with his prestige greatly enhanced.[30] (Yet as a party man he was not considered reliable, and it is noteworthy that he was dropped by the C.P.P. as a candidate in the 1954 elections.)

Questionnaires sent to the members of the Legislative Assembly revealed the C.P.P. opposition back bench in support of Gbedemah and an extremely left-wing member, Anthony Woode.[31] Gbedemah, apparently amenable to maintaining an independent party support within the C.P.P., was considered right wing. Woode, on the other hand, an avowed left-wing individual, was the man most frequently named in the C.P.P. opposition back bench as a parliamentary guide. It is noteworthy that in the questionnaires answered, the C.P.P. back bench members in general were willing to define their position as extreme left wing.[32] In the main, the C.P.P. opposition back bench objected to the moderate position taken by Nkrumah on many issues.[33]

The C.P.P. opposition back bench was important because it appeared to be in close connection with the second and third levels of the C.P.P. leadership in orientation or ideology, and because it represented a potential basis for a party split if doctrinal issues became larger than they are at present. The youthful sincerity of some of them was probably one of their greatest assets.[34] It was demolished in the June 1954 election.

The major opposition tended to consist of the Ghana Congress Party under the uneasy leadership of Dr. Busia. (A Northern People's Party and a Moslem Association Party have emerged as more significant opposition contenders than the Ghana Congress Party since this research was undertaken.) According to Busia, who did not want to enter politics at all, the "dictatorship" of

---

the chief government whip opposed the government motion after the cabinet had approved of it. The motion had to be withdrawn. On another occasion, the cabinet decision had to be withdrawn when it was repudiated by the Parliamentary Party of the C.P.P. (the income-tax bill).

[30] This information was related by the member in question.

[31] Since expelled from the C.P.P. as a communist.

[32] 58 per cent of the members of the assembly returned the questionnaire.

[33] See the Volta Debate below.

[34] In the debate on the Volta Scheme, for example, which tended to be acrimonious, the back bench opposed the government motion in many details. While the prime minister tended to get angry at the opposition, he said to one of the back-bench members who was trying to speak but was being shouted down by the regular C.P.P. members, very quietly and with a smile, "Speak your mind, boy, speak your mind."

Nkrumah is intolerable in a democratic system. He has little regard for Nkrumah, calling him "showboy" and feeling that his is an inferior intellect and that he is a dangerous demagogue. Busia feels strongly that there can be no democracy in the Gold Coast until there is an effective opposition to the C.P.P.

Busia, a graduate of Oxford and one of the first African district commissioners before he returned to Oxford for his doctorate in sociology, has affiliations to tradition which are both intellectual and customary. He is the brother of a tribal chief. He represented the Asanteman Council in the assembly. As a sociologist, the integrative aspects of secular and traditional patterns of authority are paramount in his mind. Peaceful change under a legal institutional framework and a deep respect for traditional social structures seem to characterize his position. He is scarcely a political adept and is regarded as an aristocrat and snob. Shortly after he helped found the Ghana Congress Party several of the other leaders attempted to remove him from the chairmanship. The attempt failed. One officer, Mr. Obetsebi Lamptey, left the party and set up a splinter group, the Ghana Nationalist Party. Busia found this introduction to politics somewhat disillusioning.[35]

Some of the other opposition leaders in the old assembly were directly traditional, and/or "old intelligentsia," oriented by their lineage ties and their intellectual associations, and having chieftaincy or United Gold Coast Convention antecedents. One of the cleverest parliamentarians in this category was William Ofori Atta, a lawyer, who was the state secretary of Akim Abuakwa.[36] His uncle, Dr. J. B. Danquah, the former leading member of the United Gold Coast Convention, was one of the important figures in earlier Gold Coast nationalism, while the chief of Akim Abuakwa, Nana Ofori Atta, a cousin, also sat in the assembly. The latter's predecessor, a classificatory brother of Dr. J. B. Danquah, Nana Sir William Ofori Atta, was one of the titled chiefs of the period of indirect rule.

---

[35] Most of the information stated here comes from personal interview with Dr. Busia. It is of interest that while Dr. Busia lived in the same place as the author under conditions which would have made it easy for him to attempt to influence the research going on, he scrupulously avoided making his presence felt. It is noteworthy, however, that in the 1954 election Dr. Busia, standing in his home constituency, Wenchi, was elected to the assembly by only eleven votes. However, Busia was in the United States during the election campaign and was not able to participate personally in the campaign.

[36] A "customary" post under the native authorities system.

Other members of the opposition included Mr. Kwesi Lamptey, a former C.P.P. ministerial secretary, and Dr. Ansah Koi, an ex-C.P.P. minister. As a group they tended to be erratic and undisciplined, the integrity of some not being too highly valued. Ansah Koi attempted to splinter the opposition even further by starting his own party, the Ghana Action Party.

To the main core of the opposition, the C.P.P. government was anathema. Particularly for those whose orientations were similar to those predominating during indirect rule, the C.P.P. government represented a violation by the British of their commitments to the chiefs and to the intellectuals who, it was assumed, would take over the reins of government.

Some, like Busia, argued for a climate of secular rationality in the parliament, with opportunities for the chiefs to participate, but not the rabble-rousing (as they regard it) of Nkrumah. Some of the chiefs felt betrayed by the British. One Ashanti chief, a brother of the *asantehene*, indicated his feeling that people would become weary of parliamentary government and return to the chiefs.[37] There is some indication that in rural areas at least part of the population now views the government by the C.P.P. in almost the same way as they regarded previous governments— remote and no concern of theirs. After the excitement of the elections had worn off and the villagers found the same conditions in the village the day after as the day before the Nkrumah victory, some return to traditional association was to be expected. Not many of the chiefs would share the view stated above, however, and some like the *asumejahene* indicated in interview that the sooner the chiefs completely removed themselves from politics, the better it would be for them.

A pro-chief position was clearly manifested among the Northern Territories group. In questionnaires, these members indicated, in the main, a devout disassociation from the Convention People's Party, or from any party, while indicating Dr. Busia as the "man for whom they had the highest respect." They looked with disfavor upon the rapid growth of self-government, particularly under the C.P.P., which is primarily composed of southerners, whom they

[37] This feeling has been intensified recently by the growth of an Ashanti separatist movement, the National Liberation Movement, which, protesting against the pegged price of cocoa, has pressed for a federal system of government. This is a direct thrust at Nkrumah and is supported by the Asanteman Council.

do not like. "We are proud of our chiefs and these C.P.P. boys show them no respect," said one assembly member from the Northern Territories.[38]

Until recently, the Northern Territories bloc as a parliamentary group met under the leadership of Mr. Braimah, formerly the Minister of Communications, who resigned from the cabinet after taking bribes. Actually, it was directly responsible to the Northern Territories Council, the chairman of which was a member of the Legislative Assembly (the *tolon-na*). In this respect it was directly related to the traditional authorities since the Northern Territories Council was under the control of the chiefs, although it had about three C.P.P. members, one of whom was a regional secretary of the C.P.P.

Since only a few of the Northern Territories public are literate, most of their representatives in the old assembly tended to be young, with such occupations as schoolteachers, letter writers, and clerks, rather than lawyers or professional men, or professional politicians like many of the young elements in the C.P.P. They had little sympathy with nationalism in its present form. There had been talk in the north of petitioning the Crown for a special relationship based upon the old treaties of protection, rather than participating in an independent Gold Coast dominated by C.P.P. southerners.

Parliamentary business flowed around the figure of the prime minister, who endowed that role with a very special significance. Immunity from his influence was impossible in the assembly. He evoked admiration and excitement without being either pompous or remote. He would have been a unique figure on any political scene. His leadership went beyond the structural confines of his office, from his charisma, to use Weber's term.[39] He chose to work within the parliamentary framework, although it is questionable whether or not his commitment to the norms of parliamentary democracy was basic to his performance. He was able to maintain allegiance from a multiplicity of sub-groups in the C.P.P. and wield them as an effective instrument of policy, as indicated in the following diagram:

[38] Northern Territories groups have formed the Northern People's Party, which is now the formal opposition in the new assembly.

[39] Weber says charisma rests "on devotion to the specific and exceptional sanctity, heroism, or exemplary character of an individual person, and of the normative patterns or order revealed or ordained by him (charismatic authority)," *Theory of Economic and Social Organization, op.cit.*, p. 301.

A SOCIOGRAM OF THE OLD LEGISLATIVE ASSEMBLY

February 1953 Session*

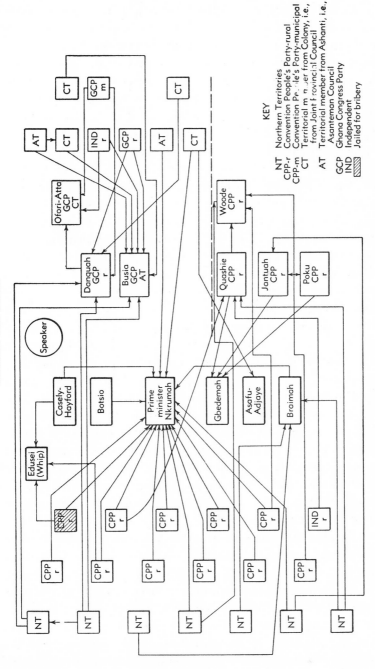

KEY

NT	Northern Territories
CPP-r	Convention People's Party-rural
CPP-m	Convention People's Party-municipal
CT	Territorial member from Colony, i.e., from Joint Provincial Council
AT	Territorial member from Ashanti, i.e., Asanteman Council
GCP	Ghana Congress Party
IND	Independent
▨	Jailed for bribery

*This sociogram is based on questionnaires circulated among all the members of the assembly. A return of 56.1% on the questionnaires was checked by personal interview with members of the assembly as well as observation of voting patterns, apparent informal groupings, party allegiances, and other factors. On several occasions it was possible to participate in caucusing sessions in the assembly refreshment lounge, and key roles and figures were demarcated by several independent checks.

The diagram is an image of the assembly in the February 1953 session. At the far left we find the Northern Territories members. Between them and the government sat the regular C.P.P. back bench. To the right of the speaker of the House sat the opposition, composed of territorial members, chiefs, ex-C.P.P. members, and Ghana Congress Party members. They formed a bloc which was by no means well amalgamated and which had little group cohesiveness. Below them, divided by the dotted line in the diagram, sat those C.P.P. back benchers who, unrewarded by official posts, maintained a spirit of party independence. Only one member of this group, and he not a very ardent C.P.P. opposition back bencher, was a ministerial secretary. They constituted a sub-unit within the C.P.P. parliamentary party, often opposed governmental policies, and often refused to submit to party discipline, bucking the party whip. The C.P.P. back bench opposition tended to support Gbedemah, who therefore had an independent following within the party. Some of the members of the C.P.P. back bench opposition were followers of Anthony Woode, an extreme left-wing assemblyman.

In the diagram, the lines and arrows point to those who the member in question felt provided the personal leadership for him in the assembly. They indicated the leader to whom members looked for guidance on a division, and they show the cross affiliations and groupings in the Legislative Assembly.

The observed closeness of Botsio to Nkrumah is interesting in the light of the lack of independent support accorded to Botsio, therefore reducing him as a potential danger in the party, as distinct from Gbedemah. It is noteworthy that out of a total of three people who indicated their closeness to the chief government whip, Mr. Krobo Edusei, one of them was convicted of bribery and sentenced to two years in jail.

We note also the potential alliances between chiefs, territorial representatives, and the Northern Territories, i.e. a potential opposition composed of regional, religious, and customary identifications, each with a large support in the society as a whole. Of importance, too, is the fact that much of the opposition or leadership of the opposition to Nkrumah came from the territorial councils, a factor not to be minimized insofar as much of this leadership is now cut off from the assembly under the new electoral regulations. The territorial councils, until recently so important a source of recruitment for central government, now remain a "headless" fourth branch of government, having vaguely defined functions, and a displaced leadership with no outlet for responsible action.

With the image of the 1953 Legislative Assembly in mind, the popular support from the public and the internal party maneuvering to strengthen discipline and control is revealed in the June 1954 elections. Launching its "Operation 104" (to capture all 104 seats in the new Legislative Assembly under the revised direct election system) the election results were as follows:

JUNE 1954 GENERAL ELECTION*

Party	No. of Seats
Convention People's Party	71
Independents (including C.P.P. expellees)	16
Northern People's Party	12
Togoland Congress	2
Ghana Congress Party	1
Moslem Association Party	1
Anlo Youth Organization	1

* These figures are adapted from Reuters dispatches of June 18, 1954.

Of the registered electors 59% voted. The Convention People's Party vote was 391,720. The total vote for all other candidates was 324,822. The latter vote was surprisingly strong, since most observers felt that Nkrumah had reached his peak in popular appeal.

The results of the June 1954 election, in light of the above information, are interesting. The Ghana Congress Party opposition was almost entirely eliminated, with Dr. Busia the only representative of the G.C.P. elected. He, of course, was put there by Wenchi, where his brother is chief. A good portion of the opposition was eliminated under the 1954 Constitution which excludes all candidates from territorial councils or chiefs except as individual candidates competing with other candidates.

The C.P.P. back bench opposition was virtually eliminated. Quashie was placed in a shaky constituency and lost. Anthony Woode had been expelled from the C.P.P. as a communist. Bediako Poku was not allowed to stand as a C.P.P. candidate. Jantuah won in his constituency but was made a cabinet minister. Meanwhile, some of the hard-core party leadership previously outside the assembly was now brought into the assembly. N. Welbeck, the former propaganda secretary and later acting general secretary of the C.P.P., became a cabinet minister (Minister of Works) and Mr. Kofi Baako also joined the assembly. The possible independent threat of Mr. Gbedemah was entirely eliminated while his talents were retained. He is now Minister of Finance.

An entirely new opposition developed centering around the figure of Mr. Braimah, formerly the Minister of Communications and Works who had resigned from the government because of bribery. As an independent, he represents the senior member of the Northern Territories group, now represented for the first time by an opposition political party, the Northern People's Party. The problem of the new party is to gain local support from presently apathetic groups, particularly if new educational and welfare measures for the north are thereby gained. The new Minister of Education is a Northern Territories C.P.P. man and former ministerial secretary in the old cabinet.

The diagram indicates how systematically the elections and the new electoral regulations combined, demolished the old representation in the house, and, equally, how the authority of the Nkrumah group has been consolidated. The only major loss has been from South Togoland, an area with which we have not directly concerned ourselves here, but which is assuming great significance as the question of whether or not British Togoland will join the Gold Coast on independence day merits the attention of the Trusteeship Council of the United Nations.

Finally, the election results, taken in conjunction with the diagram, indicate the development of political parties in the Gold Coast as the only effective means of representation, a significant departure from the previous assembly. The abolition of several important membership groups found in the old assembly indicates the further procedural integrity of the assembly in following the practice of the House of Commons, while the activities incumbent upon political parties in functional terms are manifestly clearer in the political arena. The new opposition is based upon regional, and to a lesser extent, religious associations in which the historical differences between north and south, aggravated by differences in development, are now given recognition in party terms. It is possible that a coalition of Ghana Congress Party remnants having intellectuals and chiefs among its supporters, Moslem Association Party remnants, having religious supporters, and the solid body of the Northern People's Party, all in coalition, could provide a possible alternative government—a genuine opposition—although such a possibility seems limited at the present time.[40]

Nkrumah remains many things to many people. As a parliamentary leader, he has been able to use the legitimate organs of political rule as a vehicle for nationalism, and use the British Colonial Service to strengthen the efficiency of his government. More than anyone else, he has endowed the parliamentary structures with *effective legitimacy* by demanding role performances from members of the cabinet and assembly, as well as in the Gold Coast Civil Service, which conform to the institutionalized pattern of their British counterparts. The problem, as we shall indicate later, *is to reduce the charismatic source of such legitimacy, and give it an independent normative basis.*

Before closing our discussion of the functioning of government in the Gold Coast, we shall examine the old assembly in respect to two bills. The first, the Volta Development Scheme (Preparatory Commission), is concerned with the preliminary stages of a vast T.V.A.-type developmental project having wide implications for the economic and political future of the Gold Coast. The second, the Local Government Ordinance of 1951, strikes at the heart of traditional authority, but was envisioned by the Coussey Commission prior to the C.P.P. victory in 1951. The latter ordinance not only indicates the attitudes of differing groups in the old assembly, but leads us to some of the most fundamental authority conflicts going on in the Gold Coast at present, the local council difficulties, where traditionalism, charisma, and secularity manifest themselves in complex and difficult ways.

[40] For an excellent account of the 1954 general election, see Bennett, George, "The Gold Coast General Election of 1954," in *Parliamentary Affairs*, Vol. VII, No. 4, Autumn 1954.

THE LEGISLATIVE ASSEMBLY
IN ACTION[1]

The Volta Debate

THE Volta Debate indicates some of the general attitudes held by members of the old Legislative Assembly in regard to control, foreign capital, and concepts of imperialism, as well as some of the problems of the C.P.P. leadership in pushing a "capitalistic" venture after preaching socialism.

Under the proposed Volta Scheme, an attempt will be made to lift the Gold Coast from its economic dependence upon only one crop, cocoa, and allow a more diversified income-producing production schedule. With large reserves of bauxite and with the Volta River as a source of hydroelectric power, the plan is to develop a large-scale project which will ultimately involve the production of aluminum, the construction of a new harbor at Tema, the extension of a railroad to the new port from Accra, and irrigation of the Accra plains,[2] now unexploited because of the vagaries of the water supply.

In political terms, the consequences for the Gold Coast are large. The largest man-made lake in the world is contemplated, which would inundate tribal areas along the Volta. New towns involving an industrial working force would be one of the major developments. Ultimately the power reserves created could serve as a source of light industry, and the port nearby would be an economic center. Some of the larger political directives of the C.P.P. would be fulfilled, namely to strengthen the development of a proletariat instead of what is now almost entirely a rural population, since the former is considered the most effective way to awaken socialism i.e., promoting the "capitalist revolution" first. This is Tactical Action, in action.

As it stands at present, the plan is to attract outside investors, particularly British and Canadian, who would control 90 per cent

---

[1] The debates discussed in this chapter occurred in the "old" Legislative Assembly, i.e., prior to the assembly as presently constituted. See Chapter 9 for clarification of this point.

[2] Which is alternatively flooded and arid.

of the shares of equity capital and assume responsibility for the operation of an aluminum smelter. The British government, through loans, would build the required hydroelectric station. The Gold Coast government would be responsible for the new harbor and railroad.[3]

The program immediately involves "capitalistic" enterprise. A good deal of sentiment was expressed against the scheme, but the British were devoutly in favor of it. "Anyone who is opposed to this scheme is crazy," said the prime minister in a personal interview. "We have no other sources of power. How can we expect to develop the country without power?" Others charged imperialism and most of the opposition was against the scheme as constituted in the government White Paper.

The White Paper[4] called for the establishment of a preparatory commission to examine the terms and explore the possibilities of the Volta Scheme. On February 23, 1953, the following motion was tabled in the assembly by the prime minister:

"Mr. Speaker, I beg to move the motion standing on the order paper, namely: That this house, in the light of the further stage reached in the negotiations on the Volta River Project as set out in Her Majesty's government's White Paper, Command 8702, and having regard to the terms of its resolution on the development of the Volta River Basin made on the 25th April, 1952, approves the continuation of the negotiations and the establishment of a preparatory commission with a view to arriving at a final agreement which will be in the best interests of the Gold Coast."[5]

In an effort to ward off criticism of the scheme as imperialistic and to make it clear that the assembly was not being asked to approve the White Paper but only the setting up of the preparatory commission, the prime minister stated:

"As I said to you on a previous occasion—and here I am quoting myself—'we are determined to obtain for this country the maximum possible benefits from the development of our natural heritage' and also—I am quoting myself again—'we shall agree to nothing which will endanger our economic independence,' and I have also made it clear in the past that I will never put my name

---

[3] See *Development of the Volta River Basin*, A Statement by the Government of the Gold Coast on the Volta River Project and Related Matters, Accra, 1952.
[4] See *The Volta River Aluminum Scheme*, London, 1952, Command 8702, hereinafter referred to as the White Paper.
[5] Legislative Assembly Debates, Issue No. 1, Vol. i, Accra, p. 460.

to any agreement until I am fully convinced that it is in the best interests of the country. I have not lost and will never lose sight of these aims."[6]

After a supporting speech by Mr. Botsio, the Minister of Education and Social Welfare, Mr. Bediako Poku, a part-time member of the C.P.P. back bench, proposed an amendment adding two members to the commission, to be nominated by the assembly. In support of his motion, Mr. Poku added that an influx of expatriates should be avoided and Africans trained to perform the technical jobs. He indicated that: "since this scheme might be the basis of our expanding economy, the government should endeavor to avoid a second Abadan, that is, a possible Anglo-Gold Coast-Canadian dispute. The country should own the scheme, but if that proves difficult, at least more than half of each section of the entire scheme. Since, if the whole capital should come from foreigners, it might mean economic enslavement."[7]

The C.P.P. back bench immediately viewed the scheme as imperialistic. Confusion was engendered over the propriety of putting the amendment at that point in the schedule, and Dr. Danquah suggested consulting Erskine May.

A number of speeches from the opposition followed. Dr. Danquah charged that the scheme paved the way for control by the capitalists and imperialists. He proposed the use of Cocoa Marketing Board reserves to finance the scheme.[8] He asked for an "independent commission, not one dominated by foreigners."

Rising next, Dr. Busia, chairman of the Ghana Congress Party, criticized the general scheme. He questioned the amount of electric power left over from smelter needs, and the use to which any left-over might be put. He warned that "the sociological implications of the scheme" must be looked into, indicating that "the breakdown of traditional sanctions, the movements of populations, the submergence of old towns on the Volta, the creation of a great lake, all these are things at which we ought to take a second look." He stated:

"We are accepting the principle that the government have laid down, but our anxiety is that we should look at it carefully, because we are inexperienced in dealing with experienced people and I think it is quite fair to assume that they will try to get out of

6 *Ibid.*, pp. 461-462.   7 *Ibid.*, pp. 471-472.   8 *Ibid.*, p. 484.

us the most they can, and our responsibility to our own country is to make the most we can; and I do not think that we are in any way delaying or obstructing when we ask for this kind of second look."[9]

Continuing that the scheme would be at the operational mercy of the Aluminum Company, Busia indicated that the control of the economic life of the Gold Coast would be outside the Gold Coast. "I am saying that there is here, the problem of ultimate control . . . it is against our interest as a nation to mortgage our entire economic future between the benevolence of the British and the restraint of the Aluminum Company (Hear! Hear!)"[10]

After a speech by another opposition member, Nene Azzu Mate Kole, a chief, from Manya Krobo, a former member of the Legislative Council, a person subject to attack from the local C.P.P. branch in his area, stated:

"Mr. Speaker, I am very happy that today's debate has been placed higher, in the field of our parliamentary discussions, above party politics and has been on the level of the Gold Coast as a nation for us all. . . .

"I would like to pay a special tribute to Governor Sir Alan Burns.[11] If he did nothing at all for the Gold Coast one thing he did was to have the foresight to know that a scheme of this magnitude was not to be entrusted into the hands of one private company."[12]

The debate adjourned for the day with the following exchange:

"Dr. Ansah Koi: Mr. Speaker, on a point of order, honorable members should not attack personalities when they are speaking.

"An honorable member: You did it.

"Dr. Ansah Koi rose—

"Dr. Danquah: Mr. Speaker, this debate is a big one and I beg you to stop these boys from being personal.

"Some honorable members: Who are these boys?

"Mr. Speaker: The debate on the Volta River Project will continue tomorrow."[13]

In the subsequent debate, other ministers, including Casely Hayford, the Minister of Agriculture and Natural Resources, and Mr. Armitage, the expatriate ex-officio Minister of Finance, spoke in favor of the motion. Asafu-Adjaye, the non-C.P.P. Min-

9 *Ibid.*, p. 496. 10 *Ibid.*, p. 498. 11 Formerly governor of the Gold Coast.
12 *Ibid.*, p. 504. 13 *Ibid.*, p. 511.

ister of Local Government and Housing, spoke in favor, while William Ofori Atta charged that "the British are not devils, they are English and imperialist angels (laughter)." When the prime minister objected, Ofori Atta said, "Mr. Speaker, I am ashamed of the Prime Minister, that in a debate like this he should try to irritate me in order to put me off my point and to tell me in soft tone (interruption)." Nkrumah, getting angry, charged:

"On a point of order, Mr. Speaker. When this debate started and when the second rural member for Akim Abuakwa [William Ofori Atta] started to speak he made a promise . . . that he would regard the scheme as an issue and therefore he was going to be very careful not to weaken any of the participants. In fact, he made it plain that since most of the participants are British companies the arguments would be so carefully worded that we should not in any way prejudice those who are going to be participants; but the whole of the speech was a diatribe against the British government. As far as I am concerned when the national movement started in this country, I was one of the principal soldiers against imperialism. All my acts have had this purpose. Go through the whole history of the United Gold Coast Convention and you will see that my arguments have always been against imperialism. Yet you say here that Kwame Nkrumah is selling out to the imperialists. . . . We are not boys! Do you think I am a fool to enter into a project like that blindly? If I were a fool do you think I would have been able to organize the country to this stage. I am not so damned silly as to put my nose into something that is detrimental to the interest of this country. Nobody says we are going to discard your criticisms.

"Mr. Ofori Atta: Mr. Speaker, after this brilliant interruption, I shall proceed."[14]

When Mr. Gbedemah attempted to sum up the government position, thereby winding up the debate, the C.P.P. back bench called for more time. The request was granted and Mr. Anthony Woode (recently expelled from the C.P.P. for alleged communist affiliations), stated:

"Although self-government is hazily in sight, yet we must not lose sight of one fact that the ultimate goal is socialism. We also want to socialize this country; we cannot make any mistake about

[14] Legislative Assembly Debates, Issue No. 1, Vol. ii, Accra, 1953, pp. 566-567.

that fact. The prime minister himself is a great Marxist socialist, yes, and we strengthen him in that, and when some of us in this house get up to say, or when we are compelled to say nationalize the mines for reasons we know, we are told no! That will place the government in a very difficult position as far as national implications are concerned. . . . I am no economist, I am no authority on this issue, but the feelings of my common nature, taking all these things into consideration, rebel strongly against how these things are going now."[15]

When the motion and amendments were put to a division, the opposition amendment lost 51 to 14. The C.P.P. back-bench amendment was tacked on the original motion and passed, the C.P.P. back bench voting with the government. Only the hard core of the opposition voted against the amended motion.

There is little doubt that the debate was vigorous and that each position was thoroughly ventilated. The prime minister by no means escaped abuse. The British ex-officio cabinet ministers who were members of the old assembly were looked upon as fellow members of the government and when insinuations were made against them the prime minister became angry. In this debate, the British and the C.P.P. were on the same side, a common situation. At the same time, the clear-cut problem of development was never lost sight of by the prime minister, and no amount of talk about imperialism shook him from the object, not even appeals to his "Marxism."

The opposition sounded superficially "radical," warning of the "imperialist" threat. Not opposed to the scheme itself, they were in a weak position. In effect they were charging Nkrumah himself with being a dupe of the "imperialists." For most of the C.P.P. members this was a laughable charge since by definition Nkrumah could not possibly be a dupe of the "imperialists." Rather, there was the feeling that advantages were to be gained in cooperation. In effect, this was part of Tactical Action. In case anyone was to be misguided on this score, Nkrumah himself affirmed his history of nationalism. Only a few of the left-wing members in the C.P.P. back benches saw intervention by foreign capital as part of a sinister plot, and they cautioned the prime minister on these grounds.

[15] *Ibid.*, pp. 598-599.

For the most part, the chiefs said little. Their comments followed those of the Ghana Congress Party unless they were one of the few C.P.P. chiefs. The Northern Territories group said next to nothing, in the main taking the side of the government.

In the debate, which was phrased as a national rather than party issue, 36 speeches were made. Of these, 17 were in favor of the government motion, and 4 were opposed until an amendment which they proposed was accepted. Ten speeches by the C.P.P. regulars were made entirely in favor of the government, of which 6 were made by C.P.P. cabinet ministers. Non-C.P.P. cabinet ministers who spoke in favor of the government motion totaled 3, of whom 1 was an independent, 1 a British ex-officio minister, and 1 a minister from the Northern Territories. Seven speeches by members of the opposition were heard, including some of the longest in the debate. Five chiefs spoke, 3 tentatively opposing the government and 2 supporting. Six Northern Territories members were heard, including the cabinet minister, 2 being opposed and 4 in favor of the government motion.

In the main, therefore, the Northern Territories voted for the government, the chiefs were split,[16] and all the back bench voted for the government. There is some reason to believe that for reasons of strategy it was decided to have the C.P.P. back bench modify the original motion, rather than incorporate the desired amendment in the original motion itself, since in this way the government appeared to modify its views in the face of strong pressures and present a façade of sweet reason.

The Volta Debate was the focus of a good deal of public interest. Long articles appeared on it regularly in the press, both pro and con. It was found, on a very impressionistic basis, that even in the bush the issue was known.

By Western standards, the parliamentary organ was utilized very effectively. The debate involved a major decision: whether or not to proceed in investigating the possibilities, terms, and arrangements for a large-scale development program. It did not, however, represent a direct attack on chieftaincy or involve fundamental questions of legitimacy.

From the standpoint of institutional transfer, the Volta Debate indicates the effective use of the assembly as a parliamentary

[16] One abstained and one was absent from the opposition when the division was taken.

organ. It indicates the extent of discussion, within the rules of parliamentary procedures, in which diverse groups expressed their feelings and voted in accordance with party discipline, or occasionally in accordance with their beliefs. Although it was a tense, often angry debate, the attacks on imperialism never extended to the structure of government within which the debate was organized. There was no question but that the most powerful organized political bloc was in charge of the government, and therefore had no reasons to disagree with the conditions of power. In this sense, parliamentary structures were being utilized for their primary functions—the orderly representation of opinion and the enactment of decisions considered binding upon the members and the population at large. In this process the position of Nkrumah, his responsibility in organizing parliamentary government and endowing it with effective legitimacy, has been central. He serves as more than an orientational focus in government; he is also a source of sanction.

A more fundamental debate, in regard to basic forms and conflicts of authority, was manifested in the Local Government Ordinance of 1951. As such it deserves more than cursory reference.

The Local Government Ordinance of 1951

The Coussey Commission, as well as other authorities, had indicated clearly that the future of parliamentary structures depended in part upon the establishment of a firm secular base throughout the country. This entailed a direct threat to the traditional authorities, whose positions were legally entrenched under the Native Authorities Ordinances, at a time when youngmen had engaged in widespread revolt against them. When the Coussey recommendations were made, however, the Convention People's Party was not an immediate power. Rather, it was expected that most of the people having prominence under indirect rule would continue in positions of political importance and maintain their good relations with chiefs.

Nonetheless, almost everyone agreed that "something had to be done about the native authorities," regardless of the C.P.P., even after Nkrumah's victory.

For some members of the C.P.P. this meant an opportunity to break the political effectiveness of the traditional rulers and, at the same time, of the district commissioner. The first represented obstacles to C.P.P. control on the local level. The second represented, to the C.P.P., an evil influence. The alliance between the chiefs and the district commissioners had been considered unholy and imperialistic.

The new Local Government Ordinance, as it was launched in the assembly, was the product of months of party and cabinet discussion. It provided:

1. A chance to create local C.P.P. organs for local council elections, thereby increasing both the effective membership and income of the party.

2. A chance to put C.P.P. members into office in the local areas, thereby providing a reorientation away from traditional and British authorities and towards the party.

3. The control of both central government and wider party units provided greater and more expeditious channels of communications, more effective patronage, and more effective C.P.P. responsiveness.

4. A chance to remove anti-C.P.P. chiefs.

5. The use of governmental organs to promote the effectiveness of the party, making it difficult for widespread opposition to arise.

To most of the chiefs, the new ordinance meant the loss of many of their sources of revenue, as well as their effective control. To the opposition in the old assembly, it meant at least in part the fulfillment of the Coussey Commission recommendations, which they had supported and been instrumental in fashioning. At the same time they realized what had not been apparent to them when the Coussey Commission had been in session: that the ordinance gave the C.P.P. a tremendous political advantage, both in recruitment of new members and control, while it cut down the effectiveness of their own allies, the chiefs.

We shall examine the debate which occurred on the Local Government Bill in some detail, since it illustrates the complexity of authority conflicts in political institutional transfer. It indicates clearly that institutional transfer is not a mechanical or legal creation of political structures in which Africans are substituted for Europeans. Rather, institutional transfer, by shifting the norms of political action on all levels, including the arena of parliamentary organs, which have, themselves, been transferred, takes place in the most fundamentally political atmosphere possible, that of defining, with public consensus as voiced in effective public opinion, the norms of the society.

Under indirect rule local areas were governed by the traditional authorities who were given substantive grants of power by ordinance.[17] In the sphere of tribal customary affairs, and in other items of a more non-traditional nature, such as maintenance of roads, repairs on government buildings, the administration of finance and courts, the chiefs and their elders ruled the local area. They ruled, however, subject to certain discretionary powers of the district commissioner. A proportion of income from tribal lands and court fees was reserved for the state council, which financed a variety of local affairs. In addition, they had control of the native treasuries and employed clerks and administrative assistants paid from the native treasury. The state council (*oman*) continued to be the major unit of local rule, with the *asafo* Companies, the chiefs and elders, maintaining some customary social patterns in village and rural life. The state officials, including the chief, his household staff, and extended family, were all on the payroll. For administration, the country was divided into 108 native states, or native authority areas.[18]

There was little question but that the system had through the years become considerably debased as the more substantial normative controls lifted. Aside from secular pressures against traditional authorities, graft, corruption, and other non-traditional behavior on the part of the chiefs had further shattered the operating efficiency of the traditional system. It was not capable of maintaining itself intact under the revised functions of a more secular social structure which was becoming more and more the public demand.[19]

In the Colony and Ashanti, destoolments were common while chiefs often abused their functions. Comments on the moral decline of the nation were common. Only in the Northern Territories had the integration of traditional authorities and British district officials worked out well. There the pattern of tribal authority was more absolute, and disintegrating social forces had not played havoc with the traditional structures of roles and role limitations.[20]

17 See Native Authorities Ordinance of 1935.

18 See *Native States Map and Code*, Survey Department, Accra, 1946.

19 With such responses, for example, as chiefs taking bribes, playing favorites, etc.

20 Two valuable documents which taken together provide an interesting com-

As we have indicated, British support tended to give chiefs powers to which by customary law they were not entitled, and this was a continuous source of contention. In addition, old disputes concerning the stool survived for years, affecting the relations between the states and often inhibiting the development of the area.

On November 21, 1951, the Local Government Bill was tabled in the assembly. The ministerial secretary to the Minister of Local Government led off with the government's position:

"First, that local government means the administration of local services by local people. Secondly, that there must be a definite separation of the authorities responsible for ceremonial, ritual, constitutional, and customary functions from those responsible for the administration of local government services. Thirdly, that the traditional element so closely connected with local administration in the past has still an important role to play in the future structure of the government in this country.

"Hitherto, the administration of local affairs has been undertaken either by the central government or by authorities not democratically elected. By introducing the principle of democratic elections the government is giving the people a very great measure of control over their own local affairs. At the same time, by reserving one-third of the total membership of the new local authorities for representatives of state councils or other traditional authori-

---

mentary on local government in indirect rule are *Enquiry into the Constitution and Organization of the Dagbon Kingdom*, Accra, 1932, and Gass, Irving, M.D., *An Essay on the Traditional Native Authority in Urban Administration in West Africa*, 1948 (unpublished manuscript).

The latter piece, written by a district commissioner in the Northern Territories, indicates that under indirect rule local government meant the full use of traditional organization. He states: "Such a policy could not however be implemented in a vacuum and so in its working out the traditional authorities have been constantly subject to modifications in character. The removal of the sanction of armed revolt and the inevitable backing of British imperial power has given many chiefs an authority which they could not have otherwise attained." He goes on to indicate that "in general the traditional native authority evolved in purely rural surroundings and was based on the existence of a homogeneous society in which all members lived similar lives in a state of social and economic equilibrium." In all areas such "equilibrium" as we have has been upset radically. This kind of social change should have a concept of "multiplier" or "acceleration" which, if it did not imply a specious precision, would be appropriate in discussing the rate of change in these local areas. In the north, where the rate is low, the old administrative system worked efficiently. Where change has taken place, particularly along the coast with its centuries of contact with Europeans, the administrative system was held together more by the district commissioners than by its own structure.

ties, the government recognizes the valuable contribution which they can make to the proper conduct of local, as well as national affairs."[21]

This was the government statement on the bill. However, before it had reached this stage, it had been the subject of careful cabinet discussions. During the cabinet sessions devoted to local government, the permanent and senior administrative secretaries were in attendance, the latter having been the secretary to the Coussey Commission as well as to the Minister of Local Government. The problem of local government reform was viewed at the cabinet level in these terms:

1. The relationship between the state councils and the new local authorities. It was recommended that the functions of local and state councils be clearly separated, and that the functions of state councils in regard to customary law be defined by statute.

2. Problems of land. Stool land would remain with the stool, and local councils should collect the revenues and divide them between the stool and the local authorities. In addition, the local councils would make grants to the state councils towards administration and toward the maintenance of chiefs and their retinues.

3. Problem of general framework of local authorities and their duties. Whereas the Coussey Commission had recommended local government areas defined by community of interest, population, resources, and geography, the ministry proposed maintaining the existing state or native authority areas with district councils as the overlapping links between local and urban councils.

4. Problem of establishing local authorities.

5. Problem of establishing limits on the committee system of the local councils.

6. Problem of regionalism.

7. Local government service.

8. The control relationship between local authorities and the central government. The central government is responsible for the enactment of legislation and, with the courts, for the maintenance of the law. The government therefore recognized the obligation of insuring that local authorities act only within the limits of their

[21] Legislative Assembly Debates, Session 1951, Issue no. 4 (volume 1) Accra. See pp. 52-53, speech by Kwesi Plange, one of the most brilliant of the young C.P.P. parliamentarians and the only C.P.P. member of the old Legislative Council. Unfortunately, he died in 1953 at the age of 27.

legal powers. This is the main expression by central government of legal and judicial control.

In addition, since the central government would be obliged to provide financial assistance to the local authorities, financial control was to be insured.

Finally, general responsibility for government was recognized as sufficient cause for asserting control.[22]

The draft bill, prepared by the law officers, was submitted to the cabinet, which went over it clause by clause, amending, correcting, and discussing until agreement was reached on the bill to be presented to the assembly.

It is noteworthy that the criteria of decision in the cabinet were non-political in the partisan sense of the term. A rational structure of local government was envisioned, using three reports and one special regional survey as a basis for its decisions. The problems raised were in terms of the promotion of efficient government with the least possible disturbance, within a context of secular, conciliar democracy. Assessment was made of the kinds of difficulties expected and there was a conscious realization that institutional transfer was involved. Where the cabinet saw conflicts arising between traditional authorities and elected members of the councils, the cause was defined as arising from failures to define carefully the division of responsibilities between the two councils. They attempted to insure a more efficient integration suited to the more complex needs of modernity. The motives of the ministers may have been political, but the criteria used in cabinet discussion were Western, rational, and secular, in keeping with the role definition of British Cabinet practice. At the end, the bill was turned over to the law officers to be written. When finally decided by the cabinet, it had 170 clauses. Approximately 103 of these were taken over from Nigerian ordinances and adapted, 2 were taken from Kenya, 1 was taken from a Northern Rhodesian ordinance.

When the bill was made public, opposition arose immediately from certain forces opposing the part of the ordinance regarding stool lands. The issues were taken up by the Joint Provincial Council, which in turn registered its protest against this section. The territorial councils, therefore, had a chance to examine the

[22] A considerable amount of this material comes from confidential sources.

bill before it came up in the Legislative Assembly for debate. The Asanteman Council, in turn, took up the cudgels, stating:

"The council is of the opinion that the provisions in the ordinance affecting stool lands as they stand pay only lip service to stools being the owners of stool lands. If stools are to retain the rights of ownership which they have enjoyed from time immemorial they, and not the new urban or local councils, should control the use of and disposal of interests in their lands. The only limitation to this should be stool lands acquired by the urban or local councils for public purposes."

The reference to "time immemorial" is by no means a casual one. It signifies the basic violation of what the council considered legitimacy. The opposition of the territorial councils considered that he who controlled the land is the sanctified ruler, holding in trust the people's and ancestor's birthright. Furthermore, land meant revenue, and revenue meant the means to power. Land and revenue losses could not be abided in spite of the façade of legal formalism.

The territorial councils had no effective outlet to give impact to their views. They saw the new definition of the chief's role as a figurehead, president of the local council, but having no authority, while a secular chairman would have priorities in the administration of the state. They saw clearly that the long process of modifying the chief's authority which had begun such a long time ago ended with the chief left as the residuary legatee of nobility.

After the first reading of the bill in the old Legislative Assembly it went into committee.[23] Opposition developed immediately. One opposition member immediately raised the question of the land prerogatives given to the central and local authorities under the provisions of the bill. Indicating the successful resistance of the chiefs, he cited the history of attempts by the British to make Crown lands out of tribal lands. He stressed the fact that even the British government was finally forced to recognize that the customary law forbade the assertion of willful prerogative over stool lands and that to assert such prerogative was contrary to the maintenance of traditional institutions. "Stool Land," said the member, "does not belong to one person in this country. It does

[23] Committee of the Whole House.

not belong to the chief. Never has it belonged to any chief in this country; never at all. It belongs to all of us. . . ."[24]

The next speaker charged that "when a man who is not a subject of a Stool . . . is allowed to control Stool Lands, then the Stool does not exist."[25] In an impassioned address he went on as follows:

"Mr. Speaker, I want to remind this house of the pledge of the government to the people of this country, that this government has not come to destroy but to fulfill. But what is it going to fulfill? What this government pledges itself to fulfill is to encourage and to allow chieftaincy to remain. This is the thing. If chieftaincy is not going to be wiped out, then why are we trying now to take the powers of the institution itself? The stool is the institution itself (Laughter). Do not laugh! I am very serious—no amount of interruption will stop me."[26]

For many the laughter from the government side seemed tragic. For them the fulfillment of self-government was to have been the privilege of reaffirming the dignity and expression of traditional life without the intervention of alien authorities. Now the government appeared in the guise of young malcontents, far more dangerous to chieftaincy than the British ever were.

The secretary of the Joint Provincial Council, Mr. Magnus Sampson, indicated that the recommendations of the council had been accorded short shrift in the phrasing of the bill:

"With the introduction of the British administration into the Gold Coast by means of the Bond of 1844, the British government adopted the right policy of administering this country through the chiefs and their councillors. In other words, the British government based its administration on native institutions or local conditions. Let others say what they may, for a hundred years, indirect rule has done much to advance this country economically, educationally, socially and otherwise. We admit that the spread and advance in educative democratization of native institutions has become imperative and the chiefs have gladly accepted the position with commendable spirit. They are prepared to adapt themselves to the changing conditions and that is why they accepted the Coussey recommendations. The chiefs as custodians of our

[24] Legislative Assembly Debates, Session 1951, Issue No. 4, Vol. I, p. 66.
[25] *Ibid.*, p. 69.
[26] *Ibid.*

heritage and as responsible men realize that they and their people are one and therefore their interests are interwoven."[27]

An Ashanti chief, a territorial member, got up proposing the amendments advocated by the Asanteman Council. He argued:

"If I am the owner of my cloth, is it for somebody to tell me 'if you do not sell this property within two days I am going to sell it for you.' Is this reasonable? So we are going to sit down in Ashanti and allow urban or local councils which will be composed of perhaps Syrians or other foreigners to control stool lands. We do not know who are going to be members of the local councils. It may be, excuse me to say, Syrians, it may be Indians, it may be Japanese, or any persons. And if these people come on this council and they tell us—say the *asantehene*—'clear out from this land' what have we to say? We shall have to go, and so, I say, Mr. Speaker, it will be a serious blow to the dignity and prestige and the authority of our stools, if stools are to be deprived of their control over stool lands."[28]

A Convention People's Party member arose to answer:

"By peaceful revolution, a judicious attempt is being made to democratize our institutions now without due regard to the traditional importance of chieftaincy. From my own estimation, the bill is an innocuous reformation calculated to promote a more salutary relationship between the people in some states and the elevated chiefs. . . .

"In the good old days the administration of stool lands was vaguely left in the hands of the chiefs. Although the provision was made in the Native Assembly Ordinance to the effect that revenue accruing from stool lands would be paid into the native authority treasury, this in most cases was never done. . . . There is going to be no compromise on this issue, and we do not care what form of positive action chiefs in the assembly will take. They may even go to the extent of petitioning Mr. Churchill and his cabinet, but I would point out one thing to them.

"In the 19th century, when the people of this country agitated against the acquisition of land by the government it was an agitation organized by the people and the chiefs jointly and not by the [chiefs] alone for their own selfish ends. At this moment I would also make the chiefs understand strongly that we are not going

[27] *Ibid.*, pp. 70-71.
[28] *Ibid.*, pp. 74-75.

to allow them to continue a day further with the misuse of stool lands."[29]

In his speech opposing substantial portions of the bill, Dr. Danquah, at that time the leader of the opposition and related to the royals of Akim Abuakwa, charged that stool funds were not necessarily misused. He referred to a ritual murder which occurred at the death of the Akim chief, Nana Sir Ofori Atta, indicating that no stool money was used on the case.

"A local government must be a self-governing entity. We must ensure that we have elasticity; we must have democracy; we must have responsibility, and we must have efficiency. I want to give myself time to examine that aspect of the bill but before doing so, I hope members will give me the indulgence to answer the allegations against my state, namely that there was a ritual murder and that monies of the state were used to defend those concerned. I stand here to say categorically that there was not a penny of the stool fund or the state fund used in defense of that alleged ritual murder case. . . . My friend here, the second member for Akim Abuakwa has got figures to show you what we do with our revenue in Akim Abuakwa State. . . .

"Now it seems to me unfortunate that the paramount chief of Akim Abuakwa has been made the butt of so many attacks; Akim Abuakwa is one of the biggest states in the Gold Coast. If you take Ashanti, Kumasi Division, or you take the Northern Territories, Mamprusi, yes, Akim Abuakwa is the biggest, therefore, it can afford to make monarchs, grand monarchs, of its rulers. It can afford to make a grand monarch of our *okyenhene* not because we are wasting the money but because he is entitled as a ruler of the state to hold up dignity and importance."[30]

The second member from Akim Abuakwa, William Ofori Atta, stated categorically:

"They have introduced their own ideas and chieftaincy has not had the chance to demonstrate what chieftaincy can be. And there I would like to suggest—and this is purely political—that the most important thing for the Gold Coast people to do is first to

[29] *Ibid.*, p. 99. The speaker, Mr. Ohene-Djan, the ministerial secretary to the Minister of Finance, is at present under indictment for bribery and was sentenced to two years in jail.
[30] *Ibid.*, pp. 106-107.

get self-government. Who in 1948 could have said that we must have local government before we have self-government?"[31]

Meanwhile, the chief of Akim Abuakwa, Nana Ofori Atta, a territorial member of the assembly, stated:

"But I would not leave you with the impression that chiefs are the only people who will be adversely affected by some of the obnoxious sections in the bill. For example a public pronouncement was made by the most responsible member [Nkrumah] of the government at one of the far too many rallies held in my state that a bill will soon be introduced which will not only upset the traditional authority of Ofori Atta over his people but will leave him no ground to stand on.

"To all those who may be led into the trap that this bill seals my doom, and for that matter the doom of any chief, I say, do not be deceived."[32]

In this open struggle between the legitimate authority as traditional or as secular the chiefs lost. The bill was gone through clause by clause, with the opposition getting in word changes, minor amendments, and small deletions. In substance the Local Government Ordinance was passed as the cabinet, in the main, had approved. From this time forward there was no question of the strength of legal secular authority. A more formidable threat to secular authority than opposition by chiefs remained. The threat came from what was in practice the operational source of government—from the charisma of Kwame Nkrumah.

Conclusions

In the Local Government Ordinance an issue of fundamental strength was tested, and the formal associations and reference orientations of various parliamentary groups were demarcated. This was an issue regarding basic legitimacy. In the field, the issue was phrased by the Convention People's Party as the downfall of the power of the chiefs, the district commissioner, and imperialism.

The C.P.P. government, however, both in the cabinet and the assembly, phrased the issue in purely secular terms. They sought to develop democracy in local areas and the issue, they argued, was a compromise since it left the chief with his pre-indirect rule powers while stripping him of the new secular functions which

---

31 *Ibid.*, p. 121.
32 *Ibid.*, p. 183.

had been provided him by the British colonial system. The chiefs were therefore being restored.

More important, however, was the fact that democracy was phrased as a justification of itself. The C.P.P. phrased the arguments for democracy as the degree of representativeness of the structure within which recruitment was by election, and qualifications universalistic. No one was barred from responsible office at the local level because of lineage or other factors stemming from traditional criteria of availability.

Most of the opposition non-chiefs, who accepted the sanctity of democracy, were hard put to deny this position. It was essentially in accord with their views in regard to democracy in central government, but they had strong visions of the C.P.P. sound trucks, the free spending, and the aggressive activity of C.P.P. commoners in the local areas, waving the red, white, and green of the Convention People's Party, and they saw the solid advantages, organizationally, which the ordinance provided the C.P.P.

The predominantly conciliar and elective framework at the local level has been pursued for some time. One after the other, the native authority structures have been replaced with local councils having a two-thirds elected membership. In many areas elections have been held after bitter disputes over boundaries, jurisdiction over stool property, and local struggles for power. The setting up of wards, for election and representation purposes, has substantially changed the old clan and lineage basis of social organization, and the growth of secularization has reached down into the most local and rural communities. The remaining authority of the chiefs is supported by affective bonds attached to ceremonial or religious aspects of social life, and the functional requisites of chieftaincy are being diminished, as is the role and office itself.

It is quite clear from the debates on the Volta Scheme and local government that certain types of action criteria and role structures are in effective operation at the central government level. Except for the definition of parliamentary roles held by the nineteen members of the Northern Territories bloc in the old assembly (now formally abolished, with Northern Territories candidates for the assembly standing for direct election on a party ticket or as independents), there was a conscious acceptance of the procedures and terms of the British parliamentary model. Where the chiefs, for example, referred constantly to the uniqueness of chieftaincy as an indigenous system of rule—a position which seems to them as fundamental as the position of the stars—they found little support for their convictions in the more secular atmosphere of the old assembly. Prestige attaches to different roles and structures than chieftaincy.

The opposition in the form of the now largely defunct Ghana Congress Party tended to evaluate items such as finance, local government, and development in terms of efficiency. Their normative position, their commitment to the values of secular democracy, particularly in regard to their self-image as a responsible opposition, was exacerbated by the fact of their comparative helplessness in the assembly. In some instances they manufactured issues with which to harass the government. They tended to regard the supremacy of the Convention People's Party as dictatorship. Since their party organization had few funds and small public support, they attempted to be more nationalist than the C.P.P., but with signal failure; their position was generally accepted to be extremely conservative by the public. For example, when they charged, in the old assembly, that the Nkrumah regime had sold out to imperialism or reneged on its promises of self-government, their position was identified as a false one, while Nkrumah's was regarded as tactical.

The opposition leaders indicated, however, that they accepted a position of loyal opposition, thereby establishing a firm precedent. They did not, prior to the 1954 constitutional changes, overtly attempt to convert the parliamentary Northern Territories bloc, for example, or woo them in such a fashion as to confound the government and break down its ability to perform, although association between the new Northern People's Party and the Ghana Congress Party was likely. For some of the opposition leaders, a well-developed sense of parliamentary propriety prevented them from attempting to use parliamentary organs for purely diversionary tactics.

Most of the Convention People's Party members appeared to take their cue from the government, although a considerable difference in behavior was observed between those occupying cabinet posts and those who did not. The ministers tend to conduct themselves along the lines of British front-bench precedent. They argued issues on cogent grounds from speeches generally prepared at least in part by their British permanent secretaries. Having access to information which their parliamentary opponents did not, they used this advantage rather than less dignified ones. For the most part they acted the part of occupants of high political office. There is no doubt, as well, that the high standards of performance set by their British predecessors made them wary of a bungling performance.

On the whole, the ministerial secretaries at the time research was done were not nearly of the stature of the cabinet ministers. Some of them, like Krobo Edusei, were perhaps too conscious that their position was due to the votes they could control in the party and were contemptuous of the rules of parliamentary procedures.

In almost all cases among the C.P.P., including its back bench, the attempt to translate all party activity in the assembly into a position of independent merit was noteworthy, if sometimes shallow. The repeated comment in the assembly that the eyes of the world are upon the Gold Coast, and a consciousness of the hostility of other groups in south, east and central Africa, let alone across the borders in French territories, helped to stimulate performance along parliamentary lines.

During one occasion when discipline in the assembly broke down—the names of civil servants were being mentioned invidiously and members were calling one another names—a speech entitled "Parliamentary Etiquette" was prepared for the prime minister. It stated, among other things, that if the Gold Coast was to respect its constitution it must approve the way its legislature conducted its business. The need for certain formalities in the assembly was emphasized because of its essential formal status. The speech added that even if the electorate had been a bit misguided in the choice of its representatives, all members were entitled to an equal amount of respect; it stressed that all were honorable members, although some were honorable friends and others honorable gentlemen. The proprieties were to be observed even in the climax of debates, and the speaker must in all cases be in control. The speech pointed out that the convention of the house ruled out such terms as "those wicked men" and "imperialist stooge" when referring to members, and "political bed-bugs" when referring to district commissioners.[33]

---

[33] The speech was actually never given. It has therefore not been possible to quote directly, since to do so would have been a violation of confidence.

There is little doubt that the persuasiveness of the parliamentary roles—and for the cabinet, the cabinet roles, as defined by British criteria—has exercised a powerful influence over the political leadership of the Convention People's Party as well as the secular opposition. They are institutionalized to the extent that effective performance outside the parliamentary structures has no other legally possible structural outlet. This is backed up by the courts and the police. In a more affirmative sense, these roles have been the objects of goal-directed behavior for a considerable number of years, having a sustained standard of prestige and a recognized set of performance demands. The knowledge that the performance of parliamentary roles is one criterion by which Westerners will judge them, stimulates the Africans in the performance of such roles until the initial novelty has worn off and they become part of a structure and orientational network having its own vitality as a social system.

As we leave the sphere of central government, however, role definition in Western secular terms is less effective. The struggles at the local level perhaps indicate most effectively the threads of relationship, differing orientational constructs, and the interplay of local and central politics at the level where conflicts over substantive authority are by no means resolved. Such conflicts indicate the more widespread public affiliations in the Gold Coast, and can be taken to mean that where the chief is strong (assuming he is not a C.P.P. chief) the members of his area still provide traditional supports and sanctions, since they now have alternatives to chieftaincy and traditional authority which they can select. *It is only after the substantive issues of legitimacy have been fought out to the level of consensus that a sustaining and institutionalized system of political roles appears. Equally, it is only when effective public support and effective authority are in organizational identity that legitimacy is possible.* The presence of traditional authority in significant measure at local levels indicates that the substantive issues of legitimacy are still being fought out, and that consensus has not been achieved, as yet, throughout the system. Therefore, a sustaining and institutionalized system of political roles in the secular pattern has not yet been fully achieved.

We shall briefly examine two cases at the local level. The first, Manya Krobo, is a state in the Colony area about fifty miles from Accra, surrounded by Akwamu and Akim Abuakwa (Akan), while the Krobo people themselves are Adangme. The second case, Wenchi, is a state in the Ashanti Confederacy, from which Dr. Busia, the chairman of the Ghana Congress Party, comes; the *wenchihene* is his brother.

It is our purpose, in discussing these two cases, to show the many facets of institutional transfer, its ramifications on the local as well as central levels of government. If we view these cases as a struggle for power we dismiss the whole range of issues which form the substance of political institutional transfer. Rather, we can, if we can handle the discussion properly, view this transfer as the resolution of basic consensus throughout the society.

CHAPTER 12

NATIONAL ISSUES AND LOCAL
POLITICS

The Manya Krobo Case

MANYA KROBO is a small area lying near the Volta River. It is a collection of villages and towns, largely constructed of "swish," like most of the other towns and villages of the Colony. Nearby Akuse, on the Volta River, was once a flourishing trade center which declined when a major road was put through the area. For a time cocoa was a main industry, but the swollen shoot disease decimated the cocoa trees and Krobo income has seriously declined. Emigration to neighboring states like Akim Abuakwa, which is less affected by swollen shoot, has proceeded rapidly and the Krobos have been buying land from Akim and farming in areas adjacent to Manya Krobo itself.

There is no tradition of destoolment in Manya Krobo, and the matrilineal system of descent does not strictly apply. For example, the father of the present *konor* (chief) was the previous *konor* and a well-known figure in the days of indirect rule who was decorated by the British government.

Behind the government agent's bungalow in Akusi, the Krobo Hill rises sharply out of the plain, a grim reminder of the recent past when condemned prisoners were led up the steep slope on one side of the hill and thrown to their deaths over the sheer cliff on the opposite side.

Much of the area is unsuitable for farming because of flooding during the rainy season and drought during the dry season. Its principal towns, Odumasi and Kpong, are small trading centers athwart the main road leading to the Senchi ferry across the Volta, a principal lorry route.

The present *konor* of Manya Krobo is a strikingly handsome figure. Educated at Achimota, he is well-spoken, a member of the former Legislative Council, a member of the Joint Provincial Council from which he was elected a territorial member of the old Legislative Assembly. The Convention People's Party regards the *konor* as an opponent. He is one of the group which cooperated with the British during the period of indirect rule with the "Achimota elites." The *konor* prides himself on being an enlightened chief, a moderate, and his Achimota affiliations tend to support more traditional claims to being a member of the aristocracy.

The rural member of the old Legislative Assembly for the constituency which included Manya Krobo was a staunch C.P.P. follower. A Krobo who had considerable differences with the *konor* and his followers,[1] the member, Mate Johnson, was a former post office clerk and had a strong C.P.P. retinue in the area.

On May 1, 1952, the instrument setting up a local council in Manya Krobo was posted, but not before a series of bitter debates and recriminations occurred between the traditional authorities and the commoner groups.

The main headquarters of the council was to be Odumase, and the council itself was to be composed of twenty-four representative members and twelve traditional members. The traditional members were recruited by the Manya Krobo State Council in accordance with customary procedure.[2] Twenty-four wards and seventy-four subdistricts were set up. Manya Krobo itself is within the Volta River electoral district.

On the surface, the procedure seemed a rather simple one. Wards were established, representatives were nominated, and an election would take place, all according to instrument. However, a number of problems were immediately raised.

Problem 1. The wards established by the instrument were charged as being contrary to tradition.

One of the divisions of Manya Krobo opposed the ward setup, stating in an emergency meeting that there were six tribal divisions (*wetsoi*) with their divisional chiefs (*wetsoi-matsemei*), and that these tribal divisions were all natural wards of traditional

[1] In interviews with people in the area it was stated that the old *konor*, father of the present *konor*, had had the father of the M.L.A., Mr. Mate Johnson, beheaded. The family is said to have sworn vengeance. Some of the people interviewed, both C.P.P. and non-C.P.P., claimed that much of the antagonism of Mate Johnson and the *konor*, both members of the old assembly, can be traced back to this affair. Whether or not this is actually true it was impossible to estimate.

[2] In case there is confusion on this point, a state council is a traditional body which has its traditional functions. During the native authorities era, it expanded its concerns. The arguments of the secularists are that the Local Government Ordinance of 1951 returns both the chiefs and the state councils to their traditional functions. Actually, of course, it changes their functions radically, since in spite of the fact that chiefs amassed considerably more authority under British rule, they had been sovereign before the British came. The factor of sovereignty is crucial to the functional evaluation of their job.

society. A clear distinction was made between the artificial wards proposed under the instrument and the natural wards of traditional society.[3] Since the former cut across the latter, it was held to be a violation of tribal prescription and authority. The *konor* supported this position publicly. While the ministry of local government attempted to deal with the problem, those who opposed the *konor* argued that the artificial wards were more in keeping with democracy and free choice. The issue has never been entirely settled.

Problem 2. The area in question happened to be disputed land undergoing extensive litigation with the neighboring state of Akim Abuakwa. The inclusion of disputed land in the Manya Krobo local council area would give support to the konor's claim to the disputed territory.

The *konor* advocated keeping the jurisdiction of the Manya Krobo native authority as the basis of the new local council jurisdiction. The jurisdiction of the old native authorities extended over the Krobo people who had bought farms in the Akim area. The Akims claimed that selling land did not give other than usufructuary privileges, in keeping with tribal law, since the land belonged to the Akim ancestors and could not, in any final sense, be sold. They argued that although the land in question was almost entirely populated by Krobo people, the ultimate sovereignty was Akim.

A host of petitions from individuals and native authority councils to the minister of local government stated that the abolition of tribal wards meant the abolition of chieftaincy, of tribal and divisional rights of custom and inheritance, and the destruction of the natural order. In effect, the new ward system would break up the patterns of internal allegiance through which the larger tribal organization was integrated. It meant different authority units, with different foci of leadership orientation.

Attempts to resolve the problem went as high as the cabinet level, with efforts to find borders which would minimize disputes and give people with some uniformity of interest a viable local unit of government.[4]

---

[3] The terms "artificial" and "natural" were those used and are not mine.

[4] Again, much of the material contained here comes from sources which cannot be revealed. It suffices to say that they are documentary and reliable. The remainder comes from personal interviews with the people involved. In the course of my research in this area (which was visited on three different occasions) the gov-

Problem 3. The differences in custom between Akim Abuakwa and Manya Krobo, particularly in regard to sensitive traditions, intensified the conflict over land, in the problem of deciding the jurisdictional area of the new local council.

The customary leaders argued that the Manya Krobo State differed in customs from Akim, and that to be placed under Akim sovereignty would make a division in the integrated Krobo society. In particular they mentioned *dipo* and *bobum,* having to do with female circumcision and puberty rites, which drastically differ from those of Akim Abuakwa, as well as the burial of the dead in Manya Krobo cemeteries. They charged that it would be unnatural and a very gross injustice on the part of the central government to partition a state, placing part under "foreign" rule.

Problem 4. The disputed area was a prime source of revenue which both Akim Abuakwa and Manya Krobo wanted.

The Krobo groups stated that since the schools in the area were Krobo schools, maintained by the Krobo native authority, and because the area had been a source of revenue for the Krobo native authority, the precedent should be written into the new instrument.

Problem 5. The interest of the C.P.P. as opposed to the interests of the traditional authorities.

The member from the Volta River electoral district, Mr. Mate Johnson, intervened on the side of the youngmen. He claimed that delays in setting up the instrument were caused by a controversy between the chiefs of Manya Krobo and Akim Abuakwa, that the people had no interest in such a problem, that the local council was what the people wanted, and that the instrument establishing the local council would free them from the chiefs.

C.P.P.-dominated local groups like the Manya Krobo State Improvement Association and the Manya Krobo Farmers Union wrote petitions, sent telegrams, and deputations to the ministry of local government. They claimed that the days when chiefs decided the fate of the people had passed.

Problem 6. Intervention by the member of the Legislative Assembly against the chief.

Mr. Mate Johnson began to use his prestige as a Nkrumah man

---

ernment agent, Akuse, provided every convenience in locating people, providing quarters, and information.

to rally those who were opposed to the *konor*. In this he had the support of the C.P.P. in Accra.

Problem 7. C.P.P. dissatisfaction was expressed in charges of inefficiency against the administrative authorities within the ministry.

A large number of charges of delaying were leveled at the administration. It was discovered, however, that telegrams to the prime minister, the governor, and other authorities coming from the C.P.P. actually were from fictitious persons.

When a date of election was finally fixed, it was discovered that it fell on the Manya Krobo state annual festival, a customary rite necessitating the further postponement of elections. In the heat of charges and countercharges among the participants, some old and hitherto abolished customs were revived, these symbols of the past taking on a fresh and more immediate reference.

When elections finally were held, however, the C.P.P. majority was clear, with even some C.P.P. sympathizers among the traditional members on the local council. Pressure was immediately stepped up to make the *konor* abdicate. The local council elected a chairman bitterly hostile to the *konor*, and the chairman was careful to surround himself with anti-*konor* elders who had grievances against the *konor* and were therefore willing to ally themselves with the C.P.P.

The new local council immediately fired the native authority employees, regarding them as pro-*konor*, while new ones were hired almost immediately, those selected being pro-C.P.P. For some this was an example of patronage, and for others a demonstration of C.P.P. supremacy.

A series of indignities was then begun by the youngmen and the member of the Legislative Assembly against the *konor*. The *konor's* chair, a "chief's chair," was removed from his house, and it was alleged that Mr. Mate Johnson held a rally while sitting in the chair and told the public that he had overthrown the *konor* and was now occupying his chair.

The youngmen began to "beat Gong-gong"[5] which is the pe-

---

[5] While I was doing research on this area, a special meeting of the local council was called by the Ministry of Local Government to try to resolve some of the difficulties. At this meeting, the ministry took up the charges made by the *konor* against the council and tried to promote greater harmony. The meeting was a distinct failure. The British and African officials from the ministry were received

culiar prerogative of the chief, announcing local matters by this means. When the *konor* protested, the chairman of the local council was alleged to have said that he would interpret the objection as a deliberate effort to create disharmony between the president (the *konor*), and the chairman of the local council.

In the meantime, the member of the Legislative Assembly sat in on local council meetings, although not supposed to do so, and directed strategy against the traditional members who remained loyal to the *konor*.

The general background of this case is not untypical: a strong chief associated with indirect rule, but exhibiting local vulnerability. The *konor* had participated in politics and was identified with the British authorities. Although he had done a great deal to bring about improvement in the local area, some of these improvements, such as schools, weakened his traditional hold over the younger groups. In many respects the *konor* was arbitrary with his people, all the more because of the support given him by the British. He had violated the traditional limits of his office.

Although the native authority ordinances were supposed to separate the police, judicial, and customary functions by law, in practice this failed and in Manya Krobo, as well as in other areas, the *konor* could prefer charges, judge, prosecute, pass sentence, and collect fines. Of course these functions were a prime source of revenue and open to abuse. Sometimes a series of provocative acts would go unpenalized until one unlucky offender would bear the accumulated wrath of the chief. There was no formal codification of customary law, although the general public was aware of the broad limits of penalties and offenses.

Occasionally the most ardent C.P.P. proponents were unscrupulous. In the Krobo area literate small-time former civil servants who had retired or been discharged used their experience in order to gain a following. In some cases, on the other hand, C.P.P.

---

politely and courteously, but the charges made by the *konor* were rejected, and countercharges were made instead. When one traditional member, claiming that he would probably receive some violent action for making the statement, charged that the wool was being pulled over the eyes of the officials by the council chairman, and tried to forward to the official a petition by the anti-*konor* faction demanding his abdication, as evidence, the chairman got very upset. He tried to find out where the visitors had obtained their information, and the general feeling was that the officials were on the side of the *konor*. Feeling ran far too deeply for these issues to be settled without a fundamental decision over the ultimate burden of authority. With the *konor* as a figure still to be reckoned, the bitter fight went on.

supporters were people who had served time in jail, masquerading as "Prison Graduates" and thereby raiding the prestige of the C.P.P. for their own advantage. Sometimes unemployment was a major reason for joining the C.P.P. and attempting to gain political authority and turn it into personal gain. Some individuals with a smattering of education, when they saw the rise of the C.P.P., became party zealots. They would claim to "be the government" and announce that the chiefs were "finished." Occasional visits from a C.P.P. leader would give them the opportunity of acting as host or making speeches and becoming identified with top political figures as far as the local public was concerned. Sometimes they made grandiose promises, saying that when the C.P.P. came to power in the local area only those who cooperated would receive benefits.

All this is part of the stuff of which a political party is composed. In an environment where people are dealing with a set of structures which undermine what they have considered inviolate and with which they are familiar, all kinds of abuses are possible. In the local areas, tension is all the greater if the public knows that some of the C.P.P. or other party zealots are false or irresponsible or rogues. Where such is the case the fight is dirtier and more intensive; the larger party leadership, not knowing the local situation, continues to provide support to C.P.P. personnel.

To set up a new type of authority system, particularly a secular democratic one, demands the utmost in self-imposed behavioral restraints. The shift releases the most fundamental conflicts over substantive authority. Opportunities are provided for all sorts of behavior to arise before new institutionalized controls manifest themselves, and the larger legal framework of the courts exerts controls only after there is proof of crime.

Resentments come into play which may go back twenty-five years and which are released as motives or as suspicions of motives, as a situation of normative flux occurs within the non-institutionalized structural reference of conciliar government. Very often the sincere and ardent young C.P.P. nationalists are regarded as upstarts while the desire of the youngmen for a newer and different way of life in line with Western counterparts helps to recruit a C.P.P. membership which regards the chiefs with little affection.

Because the local areas are the foundations of the strength of the Convention People's Party, they receive specialized attention in the mixture of local and central government. In the case of Manya Krobo, the member of the Legislative Assembly had a long-standing vengeance dispute with the *konor*, which coincided with the *koncr's* general unpopularity and the C.P.P. interest in removing him from the position he held.

In the substance of political institutional transfer, the achievement of new patterns of role limits and role definition within the normative and membership structures of conciliar government is indeed complex. Without it a reintegration of social life is impossible if the society is to maintain itself. If the allocation of power and responsibility is not institutionalized within the structural requirements set for it, then a self-sufficient society cannot develop. Needless to say, so long as it remains in colonial status and is catered to from outside sources, such maintenance is an open question.

In the Manya Krobo case, the problems which present themselves are both inherited and new. Problems of land dispute and sovereignty emerge involving another state and carrying attendant implications for customary issues and revenue as well. The case involves the incitement of the youngmen against the chief, with the political opportunities raised by authority conflict of this kind. It was a case that reached cabinet levels in which the minister of local government, a non-C.P.P. man, came under criticism since he did not belong to the party.

Yet, since these issues touched upon things sacred, the level of affect, of guilt, and fear, and bravado made a cooperative and rational solution to the problem difficult.

The Manya Krobo case indicates some of the grassroots aspects of institutional transfer, the kinds of issues which disturb men as they move from one institutionalized frame of reference to another.

The Wenchi Dispute

Whereas the Manya Krobo case deals with predominantly local conflicts consequent upon the establishment of secular authority in which the incidence of central politics is comparatively indirect, the Wenchi dispute takes place in an environment of old conflicts and new, in which central politics is directly relevant.

Wenchi is a small state in Northern Ashanti, bordered on the west by the Kumasi Division,[6] on the east by Techiman, and on the south by Offinso. Techiman and Offinso are Brong states, composed of an earlier Akan group which settled the area prior to the main waves of the Ashanti peoples. Techiman is a center of anti-Ashanti Confederacy activity, having attempted on numerous occasions to break away from the Ashanti Confederacy and form an independent Brong Confederacy. In a recent effort, the *wenchihene*[7] refused to go along with the *techimanhene*[8] and remained within the Ashanti Confederacy. This earned him the affection of the *asantehene* and the enmity of the Brong nationalists, including the *techimanhene,* who now support the C.P.P. and are supported by them. The Asanteman Council has plenary powers in regard to customary powers and is still an important predominantly political structure in Ashanti social organization.

Dr. K. A. Busia was supposed to have become *wenchihene,* but he declined because of other duties, and his brother was enstooled in his place. Busia was the most important territorial member of the old Legislative Assembly, and was elected by the Asanteman Council. Having tremendous influence with the Asanteman Council and the *wenchihene,* he was regarded by some of the local people as the power behind the throne. Having been a district commissioner at one time, he was widely felt to have a large influence with the British authorities.

There are two royal families in Wenchi which have had disputes going back over many years.[9] The dispute has been marked by conflict over the stool, litigation, and indebtedness.

The various issues which converge in Wenchi indicate some of the possible relationships between traditional matters and national politics. At the same time, the member of the Legislative Assembly from the area which includes Wenchi was Mr. Bediako Poku,[10] a former schoolteacher, and a Brong from Techiman. He

[6] The Kumasi Division, in addition to being one of the most powerful of the Ashanti Divisions, is the center of the Ashanti Confederacy. The paramount chief of Kumasi is the *asantehene.*

[7] Paramount chief of Wenchi.

[8] See *Commission of Enquiry into Wenchi Affairs,* Accra, 1952. This report attempts to trace the background of difficulties from the turn of the century. Field work for this material was possible through the cooperation of the government agent, Wenchi, the *wenchihene,* and the ministry of local government.

[9] *Ibid.,* p. 8.

[10] The C.P.P. refused to support his candidacy in the 1954 election.

had little use for the Busia family and was a staunch Convention People's Party man. The Wenchi State is predominantly Ghana Congress Party and was the only state in the constituency which did not vote in favor of Mr. Poku in the general election of 1951. As such, the Wenchi State was the main source of operations for the Ghana Congress Party.

The two royal families are perpetually in dispute over the stool. The Busia family is firmly in possession at present. The alternate royal family claimed that the Busias were originally only the cooks[11] of the *wenchihene*, a position which never entitled them to the stool.. The present *wenchihene*, a Busia, says this is nonsense and argues instead that the other royals were in fact royal strangers who had once done a favor for the Wenchi queen-mother and who had been awarded the stool for lack of a male heir, many years ago, but this was by no means a prerogative granted them in perpetuity.

The Asanteman Council supported the Busia family in their case, and since the ultimate power of decision lies with them, this should have concluded the case. Needless to say, it did not. Rather, in 1953 the member of the Legislative Assembly, using the customary issues involved in the dispute, received the support of the alternate royal family now constituting the core of the C.P.P. bloc within Wenchi. Their position was argued as false by the brother of the *asantehene*,[12] which only served to heighten the resentment of the C.P.P. royals against the Asanteman Council. They charged that the council was dominated by Dr. Busia, the *wenchihene's* brother. In addition, they claimed to be Brongs, and stated that the *wenchihene*, in failing to join up with a Brong Confederacy and break out of the Ashanti Confederacy, was a traitor. Apparently public opinion supports the Busia family and the *wenchihene*. When Nkrumah came to Wenchi to make a speech, he was booed and stoned.

There is a large stranger population in Wenchi. The strangers hold their land at the pleasure of the *wenchihene* and therefore do not directly participate in the dispute between the royal families. Since they do not have the proper membership qualifications, they are barred from genuine participation in the dispute. However, there is a local council in Wenchi in which one of the leaders of

[11] Not entirely a menial position in Ashanti.
[12] In personal interview.

the C.P.P. sits, having been elected as councillor from the ward in which the strangers live. The C.P.P. is a minority on the local council, and hence the strong position of the *wenchihene*. If the C.P.P. could capture the local council, the *wenchihene* would be in serious trouble. The C.P.P. leader, Donkoh, is bitterly opposed to the *wenchihene* and to the Ghana Congress Party, in favor of the opposing royals, and a man of large disappointments and some bitterness. Donkoh served as an interpreter for several anthropologists both British and American, but he has been forced to watch his former pupil, Busia, find a secure status in the academic world, while he, Donkoh, is only a small shopkeeper in the stranger area of Wenchi, having been removed from his post as teacher in the Methodist School in Wenchi at the demand of the Busia family.[13]

The present *wenchihene* was enstooled in January 1950. Shortly thereafter it was found that a treasury clerk had appropriated over a thousand pounds.[14] A large number of persons on the native authorities staff were implicated.

The arrangement whereby disputes over the stool were to have been patched up (one royal family was to occupy the chief's stool while the other family was given the stool of the queen-mother) was, it has been alleged, violated. "The Wenchihene's sister was elected Queen-Mother in December, thus giving the Busia family both the Paramount and Queen-Mother Stools. This has caused the long standing feud between the two Royal Houses to flare up again. The feud has taken the form of underground political intrigue which has caused a considerable uneasiness within the division and is having an adverse affect on the administration."[15] When the financial malpractices involving the finance committee of the native authorities came to light, charges of all kinds were leveled by the newly chagrined alternate royals.

A petition handed to the district commissioner by some of the youngmen requesting a commission on enquiry into Wenchi finance was turned over to the *wenchihene*. When a commission was finally established, it found the *wenchihene* guilty of incurring debts and lowering the prestige of the stool. The chief commis-

---

13 A position he had occupied for over twenty years, hence his sense of grievance and bitterness.

14 From the Wenchi native authority.

15 *Commission of Enquiry, op.cit.,* p. 12.

sioner came to Wenchi shortly thereafter and "publicly announced that he accepted and confirmed the findings of the Commission of Enquiry and found that the charges did not justify the destoolment of the *wenchihene* but that the Finance Committee[16] be disbanded at once." This, it seemed, tied the Busia family to the authority of both the British and the *asantehene* even though the opposition felt that adequate grounds for destoolment, in line with customary issues, were presented. They protested to the governor in a petition, and some of the youngmen gained the support of some elders, particularly the *kyidomhene*. They were summoned by the Wenchi Native Authority and, when they did not appear, warrants were issued for their arrest.

Then the *wenchihene* swung into action. The district commissioner was appealed to for help in capturing the malcontents in order that they make their "customary" reconciliation with the Wenchi traditional authorities. The state council destooled several sub-chiefs for "rebelling, breaking their oath of allegiance to the Omanhene," and refusing to appear before the state council (*oman*). Five malcontents were put on trial before the Asanteman Council and were sentenced as follows: One day's imprisonment, a fine of £100 or six months' imprisonment with hard labor in default of payment. They were ordered to renew their allegiance to the *wenchihene*, and to enter into a bond for the sum of £200 each, to be of good behavior to the "*wenchihene* and his loyal supporters" for a period of five years.[17] In addition, the *wenchihene* was awarded one hundred and fifty pounds as compensation.

After the decision in favor of the *wenchihene*, rejoicing on the part of the *wenchihene* and his followers took place for some time. Under customary law, those who brought unfounded charges against a chief were liable to death penalties. In this case, those who had proceeded against the *wenchihene* were firm Convention People's Party members, while the *wenchihene* was a brother of the Ghana Congress Party leader. It directed the attention of the C.P.P. against the Asanteman Council, long disliked by many Brongs, as Ashanti imperialism, a cry which goes back long before British intervention. The guilty persons were made to "eat dirt" and drag their faces on the ground as punishment, all legitimate

[16] *Commission of Enquiry, op.cit.,* p. 13.
[17] *Ibid.,* p. 14.

under customary tradition, and by customary standards mild punishments at that.

The disputes by no means ended here. Concerted efforts by the member of the Legislative Assembly, Mr. Poku, to organize an effective Convention People's Party organization capitalized on the resentment caused by the *wenchihene's* behavior, although it seems as if the general public in Wenchi is on the side of the Busia family, considering the opposition royal's arguments to be false or at least distortions of customary tradition and lineage history.

The *wenchihene* indicated in interview that the feeling was that if the Convention People's Party stopped mixing in Wenchi affairs, the difficulties between the two royal families would soon clear up. He admitted being a staunch Ghana Congress Party supporter and felt that the Wenchi State must remain a center of Ghana Congress Party activity. He argued that the C.P.P. was therefore out to destroy him and was exploiting the difficult situation in Wenchi for that purpose.

An opposition royal, who most probably would have been queen-mother, was interviewed in the courtyard of her house. She felt that many ills had fallen on Wenchi which she laid at the door of the Busia family.[18] She said that the "Convention People's Party had opened the eyes of the people."

The C.P.P. defeat in this matter is by no means final. On May 5, 1953, the Asanteman Council heard charges that the *wenchihene* was subject to mandatory destoolment since he had once been convicted and fined by the authorities. The Asanteman Council ruled that under tradition or customary law, the *wenchihene* would not have been fined at all or found guilty; therefore the charges were dismissed. Immediately, Mr. Poku, in the Legislative Assembly, called for a commission of enquiry of the Asanteman Council. For the first time secular government under the Convention People's Party was to strike at the stronghold of Ashanti tradition, a pattern contrary to the separation of customary law and secular law in British Crown Colonies.

[18] It must be noted that the severe penalties, death or exceedingly heavy fines and imprisonment, are awarded under customary tradition when the destoolment proceedings fail and the charges are found to have been without just cause. This is to prevent malicious and irresponsible destoolment proceedings. Such irresponsible action is defined as rebellion.

In this dispute, customary issues served as the focus for matters of central politics. In larger perspective the dispute is a fight between rival political parties. Yet, it distinguishes some of the substance of party politics in the Gold Coast, pointing up the kinds of issues which, remote from the sphere of Western politics, provide a source of recruitment, orientational sub-foci, and which impinge upon political institutional transfer when tribal organization still survives.

Conclusions

In this section on the development of secular structures in the Gold Coast, it is manifestly clear that a wide gap persists in the definition of roles, and the normative requirements of action between central and local levels of government. At the same time, we have tried to indicate some of the problems attendant upon pursuing the secularization, via structural reforms, of predominantly political sub-structures throughout the society. The criteria for action at the central level are predominantly secular on a procedural basis. Membership within the parliamentary structures carries norms, which, however, are not necessarily institutionalized either in the political parties or in local affiliatory groups.

In the Manya Krobo case, we have tried to indicate how substantive conflicts over the nature of authority, whether traditional or secular, tend to objectivize and define role patterns, structures, and norms of secular democratic conciliar government in the move to discredit the old by Convention People's Party groups, regardless of their motives for doing so.

In the Wenchi dispute, we find the C.P.P. involved in a customary dispute in order to recruit members in an area having a strong opposition party majority. The first represents political institutional transfer in a more direct sense, but indicates complexity of motives for such transfer. The second represents a struggle over an essentially secular problem, political party struggles against one another, but almost entirely within the purview of traditional matters or customary issues.

Both of these aspects of conflict came into central perspective at the assembly level in the Local Government Bill debate, where the issues were defined by both sides as between chieftaincy, tradition, and customary prerogatives against the youngmen, the secularists, interested in rationalizing the political structures of the country in keeping with the structural demands of political democracy on the British model. Yet, at the same time, the essential element in secularity—rational criteria devoted to generalized objectives—was vitiated by the feeling of the opposition members that secular structures were being used by Nkrumah for his own devious purposes and that a wide gap between the reasoned terms of the bill and the motives of the Convention People's Party Members did in fact exist. In this respect, the advantages given the C.P.P. in the furthering of political institutional transfer at the local level detracted from its desirability.

Yet, in the debate on the Volta Scheme the present capabilities of both the government and the opposition in effectively examining an important proposed development project was demonstrated in the assembly. Here issues of substantive authority did not directly arise. Rather, within the procedural confines of the Legislative Assembly, the subject matter of the bill allowed the parliamentary roles to operate at a high level of efficiency. In this respect one index, admittedly a rough one, of the institutionalization of Westernized political roles is determined by the substance of the issues involved. *Where the issues do not directly involve problems of basic consensus in regard to norms, role performance is procedurally effective. Where it is effective, however, it is remote from the orientational universe of the general public. Where issues of substantive authority arise, however, conscious role definition may occur in the efforts to strengthen a position, as in the case of the C.P.P. group in the Manya Krobo area, or the issues may be fought out within a context of traditional roles, while serving the larger purposes of ultimate secularity, as in Wenchi.*

The attempt has been made to illustrate some of the complexities of political institutional transfer on both the local and central government levels and the impact of general social factors upon the process. Such a process involves the multitudinous efforts of widely differing groups and peoples, working out huge problems of structural and orientational reconstruction. We can now begin to indicate some of the features of control in this process. We have tried to indicate some of the sources of role definition, the functionally defined positions which plot the structural and behavioral requirements of political action in the newly established secular organs of government. We can now examine the critical institutionalization of newly developed secular roles attendant upon institutional transfer in the Gold Coast today. Finally, we can explore the nature and functions of the forms of legitimacy which can be observed, making for the institutionalization of the secular roles which have been both defined and structured into decision-making units of government.

CHAPTER 13

CONTROL FACTORS IN INSTITUTIONAL
TRANSFER

WE have attempted to indicate some of the processes of politics which occur when a colonial area is simultaneously moving towards economic and social development and towards greater political integration around political structures made available to the indigenous population. We have tried to indicate some of the basic kinds of conflicts which become manifest in such a process, and how they are worked out at the levels of central and local authority. In viewing the traditional system first, we made an effort to define some of the crucial factors which maintained that system. Subsequently, we indicated the progressively complex impacts of new norms and structures of politics upon the traditional. Such impacts can be likened to the *accelerator principle* of which some economists speak, in which the input of a unit compounds its consequences.

The outside polar limits within which the success of such a process must take place are apathy and anarchy. For the Gold Coast as the general concrete unit of analysis, the word "system" is coterminous with "order." Order refers to the authority equilibrium at the most generalized hierarchy of social systems within the limits of apathy and anarchy. To maintain the Gold Coast as a political system—a unit within which political or predominantly political sub-structures serve as an action reference for the members, and as a decision-making set of organizations in such fashion as to prevent apathy or anarchy—institutional transfer deals with the reintegration of localized predominantly tribal sub-systems composed of concrete membership units into a national membership unit by using predominantly political structures. *The acceleration of impact at the local level which is disruptive of the traditional pattern of social organization must be counterbalanced by the acceleration of integrational opportunities at the central level and provide for a shift in public orientational focus from local to more general affiliations.* The consequences of acceleration at the central level cannot, of course, provide an integrative base for problems which are inherent in the local situation, but once a central integrative focus has been established with a functioning government at this level, provision can then be made for local integrative systems.[1] To put this in more technical form, *political institutional transfer, involving secular parliamentary structures, requires and achieves disruption of traditional societies and is in fact composed of elements some of which are dysfunctional to the maintenance of traditional systems. To avoid the breakdown of order possibly consequent upon such dysfunctionality, generalized structures must replace localized structures, initially, and then provide localized structures institutionally compatible with the more general ones.*

A too sudden authority shift, in which entirely alien rules and roles are imposed, runs into the danger of apathy when drastically unfamiliar patterns of behavior are demanded from a population geared to more limited objectives, modes of behavior, and localized affiliations. Or, the consequences of immediate and drastic interjection of secular politics would mean drastic orientational upheaval, in which new roles have not yet been defined and, without definition, have no institutionalized boundaries. Such a situation, coincident with high levels of subsistence expectations, is in danger of breaking down into anarchy.

In the Northern Territories of the Gold Coast, where little impact was made upon traditional institutions until very recently, some of the indigenous groups (such as the Konkomba and Fra Fra) are to a considerable extent apathetic, their system being the least articulated in Western terms and having almost no formal indigenous predominantly political structures. To bring such a group into the processes of modernized Gold Coast social organization is extremely difficult at best. The growth of the Northern People's Party presents one possibility for such reintegration, although it remains to be seen whether or not control of the N.P.P. by Dagomba, Mamprussi, and other "conqueror" groups will serve to deter membership of Northern Territories indigenes such as the Konkomba and to represent purely a regional phenomenon. Certainly the present position of the N.P.P. as the official parliamentary opposition in the assembly is encouraging at this level.

[1] A situation contrary to the general program of indirect rule.

By the introduction of behavioral alternatives in the form of Western type roles within predominantly political structures such as the Legislative Assembly, when these factors were coupled with the effects of a widening educational base, new religious patterns, and new economic alternatives, opportunities for mass behavioral shifts were made available to Gold Coasters. Judged by their acceptance of these new standards and their consequent action responses and sequences, Africans were forced to play drastically contrasting roles, shifting from one to another, depending upon which significant group was dominant for the moment. Even the modern chief who had accepted Christianity and held office in a secular council had to perform ceremonial obeisance to the stool and to the ancestors, and to respect the *ju-ju* of his people. Many traditional beliefs were less undermined than incorporated with the new. Individuals shifted from institutionalized traditional roles to partially institutionalized non-traditional roles, gradually to work out some sort of composite which allowed such shifts with increasing facility.[2]

Such shifts found reference in larger segments of the population which frequently cut across local boundaries. Some of the new roles developed in a context of nationalism. Some of the role opportunities served as motivating factors in nationalism. Insofar as a mass nationalist movement was concerned, marginal Gold Coast Africans found new structures of expression and solidarity in moving towards symbols of prestige and positions of authority within the exciting framework of nationalism. One of the important contributions of indirect rule was the creation of this marginal group. By failing to turn over substantive authority to these newly created segments of the population in advance of their expectations, and by allowing them to coalesce into an effectively organized national organization, indirect rule created an awareness of national membership which overrode the limits of local traditional affiliation.

2 For example, in going to a formal dance and subsequently dinner at a hotel in Kumasi with a member of the Legislative Assembly and his wife, I found that the pattern of behavior was entirely European. There seemed to be no difference between the behavior of the member and his wife and that of any European in a similar situation. Shortly afterwards, on being invited to a dinner with the member in his house in Accra during a session of the Assembly, I came upon the wife in the courtyard, clad only in a waist cloth, pounding *fufu* with a large stick, like rural women everywhere. She did not eat with her husband. The traditional family pattern was maintained.

The Constitution of 1950 was the first major recognition of the demands of the nationalists, perhaps less by intent than by consequence. In dominating the assembly and the cabinet, the British-type roles built into the organization of the Gold Coast government were made available to them in a procedural body having almost plenary powers. By the time Africans were given this substantive grant of authority, enough of them were available who had been educated, both in the schools and in the struggle for independence, to become politically sophisticated in a Western sense, at least to the extent that structures of secular government had some sense, some meaning, even though endowed with authority from charismatic rather than legal-rational sources. Misunderstandings along these lines, so far as operations were concerned, were cleared up by the actualities of office, which set out prescriptions according to law and precedent. Both the precedent and the law were British.

Transfer Control

There is little question but that nationalist aspirations were directed towards taking over the government and driving out the British authorities. Taking over the government, however, meant for the most part government as set up by the British authorities. There was also little chance of the British being driven out. If necessary, they would have engaged in military operations, even at large cost. There were few British officials who would not have thought such a course undesirable, but necessary. The symbols of British authority, therefore, have been maintained throughout the transfer process. The governor is still the commander-in-chief of the armed forces, and army units are established in major depots all over the country. Most of the soldiers are from the Northern Territories and have little love for the Colony or Ashanti peoples, where most of the nationalists come from. They are considered reliable troops.

It can hardly be forgotten, however, that the Gold Coast is still a British colony. The picture of the queen is found in government offices. The secretariat is still full of an expatriate complement. On the opening day of the Legislative Assembly, full pomp and ceremony is observed in the tradition of the opening of Parliament in London. The governor drives to the hall in his Rolls Royce, wearing a plumed helmet. Troops in full dress are lined up with their colors in front of the George the Fifth Memorial Hall. Preceding the governor's car, mounted troops on black horses canter down the processional route carrying plumed lances, wearing green or red Zouave jackets, while a military band drawn up on the green strikes up "God Save the Queen."

Such symbols are viewed, more and more, with equanimity by Africans. To some they impart oppression, but to others, now that Nkrumah is prime minister, a feeling of impartiality and disinterested justice.

It is impossible to measure just what meaning such symbols do have upon Gold Coasters in any wide numerical sense, but there is little doubt that they have helped to maintain the prestige value of British and parliamentary authority. They help to make clear that nationalism will not be allowed to deteriorate into rebellion. At the same time, the use of British authority by Nkrumah has been of value in clearly demonstrating to non-nationalist groups that the parliamentary structure is the fundamental form of political organization in the Gold Coast and that potential opposition to the party or group in office does not include drastic modification of the political structure.

In addition, the sharing of authority has been a most sobering experience for most of those members of the C.P.P. who participate in authority roles or who influence them via the party. The struggle is increasingly difficult to maintain when African nationalists themselves are in most of the key political positions. It is difficult to abuse that from which they receive support.

In the background is the residual authority of the Crown, which serves a useful function both as a symbol of support and of alien domination. So long as the Gold Coast is technically a colonial area, within the reference of the Colonial Office, the Convention People's Party can maintain the fiction of revolutionary appeal, meanwhile providing an opportunity for the greater institutionalization of new secular role patterns and clusters of authority.

The Role of the Governor

The governor has characterized the shift in his position since the Order in Council of 1950 as fundamental. He described his position before the shift as that of an autocrat, a representative of the Crown who ruled with the advice of the Executive Council, but under no obligation to follow its advice. In effect, he ruled by decree. His present position is a cross between a constitutional monarch and a prime minister. He sits in on cabinet meetings, but he does not vote. All members of the 1952-1953 cabinet interviewed indicated a very high regard for the governor. His rights of veto and disallowance are never used, but residual controls insure action by the cabinet that will preclude their use. Apparently the governor is not taken casually. His important addresses, particularly to the assembly, are written by the majority party.

The significance of a respected British governor, with the full consciousness of his rank, is perhaps of paramount importance in the determination of cabinet role definition. An African cabinet secretary prepares the order of business and takes the minutes of the cabinet while present at the meetings, the effect of such recording probably being salutary in the preservation of calm and dignity. There is little doubt that the cabinet discussions take place in such an atmosphere. Standards of rational calculation prevail in the presentation and adjustment of cabinet business. The splendor of the room, the fact that until recently meetings took place in the governor's castle, and the official presence itself create an environment of disinterested justice and impartiality. Entering the cool high-ceilinged cabinet rooms of the palace, party politics and controversy were left outside with the tropical heat.

The presence of the governor helps make it difficult for the emergence of the kind of bitter and recriminating partiality which often marks party and Legislative Assembly meetings. Cabinet issues are discussed until general agreement is reached. The sub-identification which may occur within a group with formalized voting procedures and which tends to promote splits is not tolerated in the cabinet. Rather, the climate is one of a working group in which a decision made is the joint responsibility of all. Once the decision is made, it is a government decision, which has the full backing of the entire British and African administrative staff, only then going before the guns of parliament. In this process Nkrumah as prime minister and the governor as constitutional monarch are in close touch.

Some of the members of the prime minister's office are expatriate officials. They meet with representatives of the governor, while as British Colonial Service personnel they are still responsible to the governor. They work in much the same fashion as they would work in England. The consciousness of difference in race, the particular party affiliation of the prime minister, the historical background attendant upon the achievement of an African government tend to lose pertinence as the normal processes of parliamentary government guided by the governor and the British staff demand role prescriptions of impartiality and secular formality as the norms of official conduct.[3]

The British Colonial Service

Whereas the governor acts as a symbol of the queen and as a reminder of British residual authority, the Colonial Service personnel, soon to be incorporated into a unified Gold Coast Service, act much as their equivalents in the Home Civil Service in Great Britain. Occupying most of the senior posts in the administration, they work closely with the ministers. In most cases, the ministers would be lost without the permanent secretaries, who write up the reports and propose the alternatives for the minister to decide. In most cases one of the staff proposals for a source of action will be initialed by the minister. Action is therefore very often initiated and effectuated by the European staff. Thus not only are the experience and modes of thinking and conduct of the Europeans made available, but few drastic differences in administrative practices would be possible without throwing the entire system into chaos.

The ministers, no matter how nationalist they are, are in the position of holding an office which has a pattern of routine that is their salvation in the performance of their duties. Obligations to learn the routine, and find out what the problems, issues, and decisions of government are about, tend to orient the minister in his ministerial role rather quickly. Suddenly he learns that the degree of nationalism is not necessarily the standard for judging performance. Suddenly he is faced with answering parliamentary questions. He finds he must keep his diplomatic skirts clean. He has to make decisions which meet with the approval, tacit or otherwise, of his British subordinates and increasingly of Africans who take their cues from the British. He has chosen to play the roles which they have provided, with which they are more familiar than

[3] The recent Korsah Commission investigating the Braimah resignation has certainly underscored these standards, and the new cabinet, chosen after the C.P.P. victory of June 1954, is of considerable stature.

he is. The British expatriate staff represents, in varying proportions, judge, teacher, and dependable subordinate.

Under the circumstances, the working relationship between most of the ministers and their staff is rather close, in office; outside of office they tend to be more remote. Usually it is on formal occasions or at more public parties that the ministers and the staff mix socially. What would have been observed as snobbishness and arrogance on the part of the British only a short time ago has become the acknowledged impropriety of ministers and their staff having close personal relationships outside of business hours. However, African and British members of the administrative class[4] of the civil service do tend to meet at parties, and to entertain one another.[5]

The presence of the British administrators has, in action terms, defined the ministerial role on the British model. The same standards and limitations both procedural and substantive apply. The general evaluational criteria in regard to budgetary matters and revenues, taxes and local disturbances, health or housing, crime and delinquency, all apply as in the United Kingdom, excepting only in regard to the means of solution available and a judgment of the relevance of the problems in accord with local conditions.

The procedural processes of handling problems of this nature, and the formal relation of the work flow, both in regard to parliamentary responsibility on the one hand and administrative treatment on the other, integrate the total governmental process. Problems arise for ministerial and administrative treatment through the formal organs of government, and are dispatched within a normative climate of secular rationality, intermediate means and ends, and procedural integration.

The prime minister, as we have indicated, has decried the British administrative staff as a powerful influence group which exerts considerable control over the content and direction of governmental processes. Yet by so doing, the staff has kept the formulation and resolution of political problems within the taxable limits of the structure for which they are designed and within the resources of the Gold Coast. The political objectives of a relatively

---

[4] Although not enough, and there is the element of consciousness in it. Certain Africans are accepted more than others in the social circle of the Colonial Service.

[5] The old system of senior and junior service has been abolished and the British system has been adopted.

inexperienced political party have thus been tempered by practical considerations of cost assessment, resource evaluation, weighing of alternatives in keeping with realizable potentialities; the nationalist government has not been submitted to burdens which it could not shoulder. Yet by providing the administrative means within a procedural framework of British structures, the British have insured a deepening regard for the limitations and obligations incumbent upon participants in parliamentary processes. While they may be a hindrance to Nkrumah, they help to insure his success via the widening of institutionalized roles and through an effective problem-solving mechanism, and by this means are instrumental in promoting political institutional transfer.

That such a process has to be subject to certain time limitations is taken as given, assuming that the objectives of the Convention People's Party continue to be independence or self-government within the British Commonwealth. The major factor which makes British intervention tolerable is the conclusion, by all parties, that as soon as an African is available to replace a British civil servant in a vacant post, he will fill it. Replacement is occurring and the Africanization Committee of the Gold Coast Civil Service has sought to maximize African recruitment and training. Yet the qualifications for service remain by the regulations of the service the very criteria of action which are built into the institutionalized British roles. For the most part only university-trained personnel are qualified for administrative class positions. The recruits come in under the aegis of the British administrators, who are replaced only when the recruit becomes qualified in British role and procedural terms.

One immediate problem which has resulted, however, from efforts to speed up Africanization, has been the rapid advancement of Africans who never go through the long process of promotion, persistent work, and discipline imposed upon their European counterparts. The Africans coming into the Gold Coast Civil Service, in addition to the fact that they are less well trained, for the most part, than the expatriates whom they replace, tend to get promotions rather more quickly than is normal in the British Colonial Service, and tend also to regard their positions as preludes to more active parts in politics. Thus, there is neither the full internalization of certain types of norms regarding civil service roles, nor the need to be concerned with a maximum level of performance. Qualified Africans are still at such a premium that they can, in some respects, write their own ticket.

Not only does this not bode well for the future of the civil service, but it will undoubtedly contribute to the lowering of standards, once self-government is achieved. With the British staff, then, on purely a contract basis, and members of the Gold Coast Civil Service responsible directly to the prime minister and the public service commission (their Colonial Service ranks retained on the lists, however), they will be in a position to do little about such matters. Today, British officials still can report directly to the governor (over the heads of their ministers), whose responsibility it remains to see that the Gold Coast government operates properly. After independence day, this outside check on the African regime would be over. The governor (as a governor-general) could exercise only moral suasion.

The maintenance of the relational, procedural, and substantive norms of the British administrative apparatus directly proceeds to the institutionalization of the central governmental process.

Administration in the Field

We have indicated the formal pattern of European control through the use of the government agents and regional officers as part of the network of regional and local organization, and their position relative to the new conciliar organs of local government. Although the administrative officers in the field have undergone a similar transition from autocratic authority to more advisory supernumerary authority, they fulfill important control and role prescriptive functions. Particularly since the new local council system has been put into effect, the government agent acts as a field administrator and advisor for the Ministry of Local Government, as well as the agent of all the other ministries in the field. In reference to the development of secular structures under the Local Government Ordinance, the advice of the government agent has proved for the most part salutary. In matters of capabilities and resources, the government agents have served to ease the difficulties engendered by the setting up of a new, and often suspected, system of local secularity. They have provided sources of information on such items as building materials and where to locate them, labor requirements and costs for local projects, maintenance of local roads, building and maintenance of schools. In addition, as the representatives of the Ministry of Defence and External Affairs (now the Ministry of State), the government agent, in collaboration with the police commissioner, has charge of the local security and police forces within his area, as well as power of magistracy in certain cases.

It is the official view that it is in the local areas that one finds the training ground of democracy. This view, which follows closely upon the traditional notions of indirect rule in its stress on local units, is shared by many of the government agents interviewed. The effectiveness of the process is, however, undermined by the fact that usually the most alert and capable young Africans tend to leave the local areas if such areas are predominantly rural, and try to settle in more urbanized places. Often men of lesser caliber remain and if anti-traditional in their orientations they are occasionally of considerably lower repute than the traditional authority members themselves, particularly those having a high sense of traditional moral purpose. We have indicated some of the kinds of struggle which can ensue under these circumstances. The government agent is usually in the middle of all this, and by defining the functions of the local councils time and time again tends to channel local activities into the role prescriptions created under British local government conditions. Particularly where substantive authority conflicts persist he is a dreadfully unpopular figure. In this respect, the government agent is often in a more crucial and more demanding spot than his secretariat colleagues.

The government agent has been able to make manifest the latent secularity built into the formation of the local council structure. A particular ally in this process has developed around the office of clerk of the local council. Often the clerk is the sustaining influence in promoting the development of more rational normative boundaries in regard to conciliar behavior. Many of the clerks come from the local government training school, which, under its very capable former director, Mr. E. B. S. Alton, was providing a source of well-trained, reasonably honest, and competent local government clerks. One of the primary factors of success in this area will depend upon the prestige attached to the role of clerk as an impartial figure who handles most of the daily business of local administration which falls within the purview of the local councils.⁶ Local institutional transfer on the procedural level has been profoundly influenced by the government agent and the clerk, often in collaboration with one another, once basic authority consensus has been established within a procedural network of conciliar action.⁷

The effort to reconstruct Western-type bureaucratic and political roles within the limits of a procedurally precise, functionally specific pattern of relationships serves many purposes both on central and local governmental levels. The network of administra-

⁶ See Chapter 11.

⁷ In one area the clerk of the local council had saved the situation from degenerating into an open battle. The clerk who was trained in the local government training school wrote the following memorandum:

"The Aftermath of the Supercession of a Native
Authority by the Local Council

"After the publication of Coussey and the Select Committee's Reports on local government, the talk became a necessity of the local councils taking over, in the near future, the reins of local administration from the native authorities. Several people, even some of the chiefs who constituted the native authorities, became anxious to see the dawn of the transfer of the local power. I wonder whether any of the aspirants properly visualized the consequences of such a change.

"The death of a native authority is a latent resurrection of a 'cold war.' As soon as a new local council authority [is set up, it offends the traditional leaders] who automatically cease to take part in the proceedings of its meetings, made to feel that they have lost a hereditary right. It requires a statesmanship and mental alertness of the highest degree to obliterate the bitter feelings of such a disgruntled people. In most cases a member of the former native authority tries to assume his old role of power in his locality, or otherwise, looks on the activities of the new council with a certain amount of apathy.

"Some of the new councillors, who had been aggrieved by some acts of the former native authority, fall under the impression that the council chamber is the best place to plan for vengeance. It is not easy to convince councillors with such intentions that they have conceived a wrong idea. Certain councillors, obsessed with power, go to the extent of interfering with the work of the officials. But it is usually observed that such a situation arises more from the councillors' ignorance of their duties than a deliberate display of power over officials.

"Many taxpayers have been so optimistic about the local council to such an extent that they think their needs would be met immediately the council is established, even without paying any taxes at all. You can, therefore, imagine their utter disappointment when the new council, as is almost usually the case, increases taxes to enable the needs of the people to be effectively met.

"In these circumstances, the place of the clerk of council as an advisory official cannot be too strongly stressed. There is, in fact, the tendency on the part of the clerk of the council being too much heard at meetings in the execution of his duties as the Council's Chief Advisor. This may sound a discordant tune to the principles of English local government system—or model—but it seems almost inevitable at least in the early stages of the council's establishment, when the trained clerk is looked upon not only as a servant but also as a teacher.

"In the face of these problems the student of local government quickly realizes that knowing the principles of local government is quite a different thing from putting them into practice. The problems are, however, not insuperable, if only they are tackled with tact, patience, and skill."

tion which blankets the country has both the force of law and the prestige of British judgment. The administration is functionally integrated with the assembly and the cabinet, making possible an effective government. Individuals who occupy the roles within the administration are forced to operate in terms of standards approximating the European, and these standards have developed in Great Britain out of the traditional pattern of her own indigenous social organization. One of the key factors in political institutional transfer in regard to the role occupants and their self-identification, and their own role modalities, remains the successful Africanization of posts now held by the British.

Sources of Role Conflict

In the definition of British-type roles, both in the government and in the Colonial Service, peculiar difficulties are faced by some Africans with regard to the maintenance of a plurality of role systems required by multiple membership affiliations. The African civil servant, or member of the Legislative Assembly, or, to a lesser extent, political party official, deals with a wider range of significant subgroups than his British counterpart. Patterns of social organization are far more fragmented and polarized during the period of institutional transfer than in the more homogeneous place of origin of the transferred structures. The problems of control are great, particularly since the maintenance and further development of institutionalization must not be inhibited by the consequences of controls. The control factors overtly used are varied and sometimes not recognizable as controls since their effects and ostensible purposes might be divergent.

Three general types of controls which can be found operating can be roughly categorized:

1. Predominantly *legal and judicial*: these include the use of law, the agents of law and adjudication, such as magistrates, courts, etc., and the governor's reserve powers, including the use of the armed forces.

2. The *procedural* requirements within any governmental structure: these include the civil service standards, the standing rules and orders of the assembly, manuals of instructions regarding ministerial or sub-ministerial responsibilities, regulations, as well as immediate standards of efficiency and comportment within a particular post.

3. The endowment of *legitimacy* for the secular structures: such legitimacy derives in practice from two sources, first from the Crown for those so oriented, and secondly from Nkrumah.

For members of the Legislative Assembly, performances are controlled by parliamentary procedures, while judgments, at least overtly, tend to be predominantly secular and rational in normative mode. While public sanctions in this regard are not sufficiently articulated, the sanctional supports for such role definition as exists are partly culled from the standing orders, partly because of the prestige associated with effective parliamentarianism and partly because of the serious promotion of such roles by the direction of Nkrumah and the C.P.P. leadership.

The observance of formalities is of major importance: the dignity of the house enhancing the dignity of its members; the dignity of its members enhancing the institutionalization of the parliament and its role structures as the central decision-making body in the Gold Coast, and giving it sanctional priority as the source for internal law.

Nevertheless, the members of the assembly must return to their constituencies. They may find themselves locked in a bitter struggle at home with the local Convention People's Party opposition, such as attends the *konor* of Manya Krobo. They may find themselves bombarded by special requests and favors, particularly if they are rural or municipal members where the feeling of public participation in the party is conducive to extracurricular pressures from small-time party members. In any case, members leaving the comparative procedural safety of the house enter into an environment of widely differing cross-behavioral pressures including conflicts between traditional and secular demands raised sharply in primary group associations of the member himself.

For example, a member who belongs to the Convention People's Party may have effectively "partaken of Nkrumah's grace" insofar as the members of his constituency are concerned. He may have promised that when he got into office, the local area would receive certain benefits associated with the power of Nkrumah and the ascendancy of the C.P.P. He may face demands that more government funds be allocated to the area for development. Equally he may receive deputations from the various primary and secondary groups with which he is associated, asking him to intervene in a struggle between the chief and the local party unit.

Meanwhile, members of his family may belong to some of the traditional authorities. A local contractor might wish to have a favor shown in a bid, with a promise of financial help to the member in return. Members of the family may need employment and ask the assembly member for help. The assembly member might be given gifts, some tokens of esteem which under the traditional system were a form of customary respect. Now the gifts might contain an obligation. What represents graft and corruption within the normative pattern of secular democracy may well be responsible community social relations under the traditional system. At the same time, the member must conform to widely fragmented patterns of norms so that he does not promote local conflict and alienate the voting population. He must be able to provide tangible evidence of the power of his office and of the benefits which he can provide. As yet, he rarely can find the strength of his office and the dignity of the parliamentary role as effective as his association with the authority of Nkrumah, or even with the British, so far as the more tradition-minded members of his constituency are concerned. For the most part, members of the assembly have indicated that the people in the constituencies failed to understand the position and responsibilities of the members.[8]

Very often severe orientational conflict faces African members of the administrative service, or of municipal councils, or other secular bodies. Some of the African participants, whose families may have spent considerable sums to put them through school, are obligated under the traditional pattern of social life to support the family. Since family in this usage mostly involves the extended family, a great deal of pressure to find additional sources of income to augment salary is not uncommon. To resist bribery and corruption is to avoid the responsibilities of customary citizenship. Insofar as the customary patterns in this respect are very much alive in the primary associations of the civil servant or other governmental employee, he is caught between conflicting behavioral demands. Regarding the general public, there is small doubt that little real disapproval of bribery in high places exists. Rather,

---

[8] Almost all the members of the Legislative Assembly interviewed who took their parliamentary roles seriously and with some degree of genuine purpose, found that "the people" didn't understand the problems facing them, and that they could not act as independent agents even though Nkrumah ran the government.

it is expected that those in public office will have their price. A singular lack of public indignation is evidenced in the not infrequent exposures of graft and corruption in places both high and low. Often, to escape from such pressures, African public servants request assignments in areas far from their homes and families.[9]

In the Gold Coast the impact of primary group associations is more significant than in Westernized systems. The primary associational groups are strongholds of non-political traditionalism. Those who may be bitterly opposed to the chiefs, and to the entire structure of traditional authority, may conform to very traditional behavior patterns in his immediate family environment. The family remains for the present a stronghold of solidarity. For example, one of the bitterest opponents of the traditional leaders and a powerful C.P.P. leader conforms to the respect and obligations demanded in the Ga mother-son relationship, including respect, support, and an accounting of his activities. One tough young Kumasi C.P.P. official proudly introduced his "wife," a baby of some two years of age, while showing great deference to his future mother-in-law, giving her presents for herself and for his "wife." The closeness of such ties is real, and the individual who attempts to follow the Westernized family model is under grave injunction.

By comparative Western standards, the Gold Coast is a comparatively open society but lineage and clan membership, and even tribal membership, promote a kind of fraternalism conducive to special favors. Almost everyone is "related" to everyone else.[10] Friendship is a highly articulated intimate relationship in which recognition of reciprocity carries almost as many obligations as familial ties.

Under such circumstances the primary or face-to-face groupings within the Convention People's Party are important building blocks of non-traditional affiliation, out of which solidarity grows, and through which social pressure is brought to bear on party members. The Gold Coast primary group is the building block of membership and orientational integrity of far greater functional significance than in Western countries.

As we have indicated, in the Legislative Assembly itself, as well

---

[9] See Busia, K. A., *Social Survey Sekondi-Takoradi*, Accra, 1947, passim.

[10] Assuming totemic affiliation as the widest extent of "relatedness" as perceived by the members.

as in other organizational units of authority throughout the system, participants are strongly affected by the diversity of behavioral demands structured around primary groups of one sort or another. The action-results, insofar as the secular role performances by Africans are concerned, often appear to Western observers as dilatory and inconsistent.

For Africans to examine the differing norms and standards imposed is difficult since they themselves must first enunciate them conceptually. This requires a self-conscious awareness by Africans of the substantive content, and behavioral consequences of secular and non-secular norms and sources of legitimacy. It is one thing to prescribe a procedural course to follow; it is another to comprehend or enunciate norms of secular legitimacy since, for the most part, those who must enunciate them cannot separate them out of the action references in which they themselves are at home. For example, the British Colonial Service officers know what the limits of sanctioned role behavior are. Yet, if asked to enunciate those limits in normative terms, they cannot do it. They can say, "This is the right way to do things and that is the wrong way." The behavioral code is substituted for the normative code. In this respect procedural organs work out fairly well as functioning instrumentalities in government, but the very Africans who can operate within a procedural unit often cannot maintain consistent behavioral standards beyond the limits of that unit. Whereas traditional roles had internal sanctional support within the social unit, secular roles have, for the most part, only procedural sanctity which does not range systematically throughout the structures of central and local politics.

From a control point of view, the basic malintegration of the Gold Coast during the lengthy period of political institutional transfer can be stated as resulting from conflicting sets of generalized moral predispositions and notions of obligation, some of which have internal supports within the sub-systems in the Gold Coast and some of which are enforced by external supports, particularly those set by British officers and enforced in the courts. *Procedural integration on the level of central government has been achieved. Substantive integration of the significant sub-groups of the society around the norms and structures of secular democracy has not yet been achieved.*

The various roles which the individual may play are now diverse indeed. The political roles are clustered into prescribed authority units such as political party units, the Legislative Assembly, and the cabinet. The roles subsumed under each of these authority units derive sanctions and legitimacy from various sources, with effective legal authority deriving from the Crown (hence the enforcing power of the police and the courts), and effective internal legitimacy stemming from Nkrumah. Secular warrants as such seem to have little vitality in any independent sense.

One of the factors in the creation of internally supported secular legitimacy warrants, expressed in institutionalized secular roles, will involve the diminution of role affiliations in widely differing sub-groups. This means that the role prescriptions held by an individual will be less widely dispersed in sanctional terms. It means a growth of consensus in regard to compatibilities in behavior. It means the sloughing off of a variety of affiliations still maintained in the system. Until the range of sanctional sources, expressed in widely differing primary and secondary group affiliations, is narrowed, and made more coherent, consensus and reintegration of society around norms of secular democracy remain a considerable distance away.

The establishment of parliamentary democracy in the Gold Coast rests in final analysis upon a shift away from the controls exerted by the British as a "demand group" exercising judgments in regard to behavior. What is required is a shifting of the sources of legitimate authority into secular modes given normative prescription and sanction by the significant sub-groups of the public. It is in this light that our original hypothesis takes on increasing meaning: *some of the factors which were most crucial to the maintenance of traditional society tend to be dysfunctional for the development and maintenance of secular society.*[11]

[11] One final factor in control has not been discussed but deserves attention. The armed forces remain under the discretion of the British in a West African defense command. Aside from the obvious implications in terms of minimizing armed rebellion from nationalists, it has also meant that attempts to dominate politics in the Gold Coast have not resulted in the struggle for control of the armed forces which characterizes other nations. The military does not become the scene of the struggle for political domination, which remains in the elective and legislative systems. Only after independence has been achieved and, presumably, political structures of the secular type have been institutionalized, will final disposition over the armed forces be granted to the Gold Coast government. I am indebted to Professor William Bascom of Northwestern University for bringing this point to my attention.

CHAPTER 14

PROSPECTS OF GOLD COAST
DEMOCRACY

In this study we have attempted to trace the impact of one set of social stimuli upon another in order to shed light on the predominantly political aspects of this kind of process. We have phrased the problem as political institutional transfer. We have examined the traditional environment of the Gold Coast, and tried to abstract significant variables which emerged when alien structures were superimposed upon those that came before.

In particular we singled out the Ashanti for special attention and indicated some of the crucial social and political structures which gave meaning and vitality to the lives of the Ashanti peoples. We saw certain factors in the Ashanti Confederacy, for example, which were aids in the shift in social orientations from a traditional to a more secular world, factors such as the traditional separation of the individual from office, the limited functions of authority, the hierarchical pattern of bureaucracy, and the centralized pattern of government. These tended to promote a certain resiliency, helping to prevent a drastic cultural depression in which apathy rather than reintegration might have been the consequence.

But deeper than the more formalized aspects of the Ashanti system, we saw the limiting factors of lineage controls and barriers, totemic and tribal definitions of social exclusiveness, highly ritualized religious and political patterns, with beliefs legitimized from the past. Such structures required diffuse and intimate patterns of social and political relationships. The sources of authority were remote, and the limits of sanctioned behavior narrowly circumscribed. These factors were the cement which bound traditional society together. The impact of secular political structures tended to dissolve that cement, and to strike at the most basic features of social organization, those pertaining to orientations and political beliefs.

The very factors which helped to sustain and support traditional society became the agencies of its downfall, largely because such sustaining elements were now regarded as restrictive. New generations had different horizons which put the village and the tribal grouping second to the idea of national membership—not entirely, but enough to provide fertile ground for nationalism. Indirect rule, in changing the source of legitimate authority from internal tribal support to the foreign system of Great Britain, helped to bring this about. These changes ranged from the breakdown of Ashanti authority (always incipient in that largely reluctant Confederacy) to encouraging a repudiation of traditional allegiances in favor of a more secular pattern of social values. In its turn, too, indirect rule, which helped to liberate[1] certain groups from traditional responsibilities and restrictions, became essentially too limited for the very goals and objectives to which it attached high premium.[2]

Both of these authority systems, the traditional and that characterized by indirect rule, were increasingly divorced from the goals and aspirations of the youngmen. For them Kwame Nkrumah appeared as the fount of authority, once the ground had been readied. He was the new source of goal-directed behavior. Under his leadership the electoral procedures set up by the British, bearing the dual impress of education and sanctity, the one procedural and the other normative, became weapons of mass revolt. But mass revolt in turn followed both the procedural and normative paths which the British symbolized themselves. The organs of secular government became, simultaneously, symbols of "progress" and "achievement" and a means to further the nationalist goal of independence.

Today, the Convention People's Party is the major expression of nationalism in the Gold Coast. Its ideologies may be confused, but its overwhelming purpose is clear: it demands self-government within the British Commonwealth. It has by no means fixed the terms under which its domestic political system will finally take shape, i.e., just what kind of institutional transfer will ultimately emerge.

The party gains its strength from some of the following sources:

1. Resentment against racial and cultural domination by Great Britain.

[1] As used here the term "liberate" carries no invidious connotations regarding traditional society.

[2] See Busia's excellent discussion and summary in the chapter on "The Ashanti," in *African Worlds*, International African Institute, O.U.P., London, 1954, ed. by Daryll Forde.

2. Psychological disabilities suffered by Africans when judged by non-indigenous standards.

3. Hostility on the part of increasing segments of the local population to tribal and rural life, which are increasingly viewed as obstacles to Western patterns of behavior and Western standards of subsistence.

4. Limited access by Africans to publicly perceive roles and symbols of prestige and success.

5. Tensions and malintegration deriving from value conflicts and changing goal orientations.

At the same time that these sources of recruitment have filled the Convention People's Party ranks, *the party itself has chosen to use the structures of parliamentary democracy as a means of achieving its political objectives.* At a rally on a Sunday, Nkrumah may damn the "imperialists," but on Monday he sits down to work with them in the sleek modern offices of the secretariat.

Imposed upon those playing both party and governmental roles is a system of neutrality imposed by the norms of secular government and controlled by the British authorities. In the cabinet itself, as distinct from party meetings, the atmosphere is one of calm deliberation rather than of personal recrimination or anger. The same issue may be handled in bitter and angry terms in the party secretariat, even though some of the same participants as in the cabinet might be involved.

The presence of the British officials in all the major organs of British parliamentary structures has helped to promote general evaluational criteria for action, neutrality, and a sense of a larger purpose for politics than wrangles over formal controls. The governor has become a symbol of impartiality, and the major aggressive focus of the nationalists has in many respects shifted away from the British and against the secular opposition. The British are used as symbols of imperialism on the one hand, and as standards for behavior on the other. The former attitude toward the British is for the arena, for the crowds, and for the political rallies; the latter is in the daily routine of government business.

Conflicting sets of behavioral requirements increasingly belong to separate and isolated spheres of activity. Yet, there remains a large gap between the behavioral requirements of parliamentary government as directed by the British, and the self-sustaining and internally supported extension of sanctions to the parliamentary framework by the general public. The full impact of parliamentary business and administration, as well as the structures of conciliar secular rule in general, have struck only a comparatively few people in the Gold Coast, although the changes promoted by the Local Government Ordinance of 1951 are drastic. The sanctional limits of behavior are by no means well defined, aside from those educated few, or those inducted into governmental processes. As long as the gap remains, subject to the kind of internal decisions which the government will have to make, the institutionalization of parliamentary government remains incomplete.

Yet major steps towards such institutionalization have taken place. The local orientation and political boundaries of tribalism have been partly shattered. The shattering has been uneven, both in area and degree, but it continues nevertheless. At the same time, except for certain places in the Northern Territories, the result has not been *anomie*. Rather, an aggressive national community has been outlined around the central figure of Kwame Nkrumah. He has, for the time being at least, endowed the structures of parliamentary democracy with legitimacy so far as public sanctions are concerned. His decision to do so has been aided by the legal authority of the Crown and the controls provided thereby to the colonial authorities. Nkrumah has limited his overt field of action to the framework of parliamentary structures; and to the extent that the vision of independence, soon to be realized, is a vision of achievement through parliamentary processes, he has at a minimum related these essentially alien structures to the very vitals of political change in the Gold Coast.

Legitimacy and Transfer Efficacy

Three sources of legitimacy have reference to one another around the secular structures of parliamentary government. For the British colonial officers, the system of parliamentary democracy is legitimized by itself, as part of a generalized value hierarchy, defined for purposes of colonial rule in the letters patent, orders in council, and bills and ordinances, and in behavioral terms by norms of disinterested service, mutual deference, self-imposed limits of action current in the United Kingdom environment. Limited themselves by these norms, they have imposed the same limitations upon those seeking to use the structures of parliamentary government. By recreating a parliament, the Legislative Assembly, they have transferred a structural mechanism capable of translating radical objectives into a progressive program requiring responsibility from those who participate.

A second source, a rapidly growing group of well-educated Africans who have either been abroad for university work or have come from the University College of the Gold Coast, tend to fit into the British pattern.[3] Particularly those educated abroad have a sense of mission, full of enthusiasm for the benefits which they can bestow upon their people. Many have been in touch with West-

---

[3] Both the University of the Gold Coast, which grants the London External Degree, and Achimota College, one of the best secondary schools in West Africa, have played and are playing parts the significance of which it is difficult for an American to appreciate.

Achimota School, founded by the government in 1924, supplied many of the individuals most prominent under indirect rule, as well as those in the present government. Nkrumah himself is an old Achimotan, and most of the Gold Coasters having higher degrees from European and American universities are Achimota graduates. The characteristics of secular roles are stressed in Achimota education much as in England at Winchester or Harrow. The graduates form an elite which has been sustained to the present time. This educational aristocracy has been partly deliberate (not in any malicious sense) in the preparation of an intellectual reservoir, schooled in the British secular tradition of social life and education, capable of performing responsible tasks in much the fashion as in England.

Equally, the University College is expected to do the same for the Gold Coast today. The principal of the University College is developing a university closely and consciously modeled after Cambridge. The proper and fit subjects for university education are deemed those about which a tradition and philosophy have developed over many generations, not the specific requirements of the Gold Coast today. For instance, traditional tribal drumming, increasingly regarded as a significant art form, is held to be a manifestation of primitivism having no place on a university campus. The university, therefore, has its standards set according to the traditions and customs of Cambridge (even the new buildings at Legon Hill reflect the Cambridge "college system") and the university graduates, particularly if they have first gone to Achimota for secondary school, have the close equivalent of the education of a British civil servant or colonial service officer. This fact has important ramifications for institutional transfer, particularly as Africanization of the civil service proceeds. The chances are that the most "British" of the available educational elite will be those educated through the Achimota-University College system since many of those who go to Oxford, Cambridge, or American Universities come back with initial biases against the government, at least in the short run. In fact, whatever theoretical Marxism is found in the Gold Coast, and there is very little, probably resides with the African expatriates. Many of them are therefore in the "conservative" position of having an English intellectual's supposed contempt for the traditional way of life, a British democrat's dislike of "irrational" social movements, such as they charge Nkrumah with, and a British Marxist's interpretation of the association by Nkrumah with British authorities as "selling out." There is much less likelihood of these attitudes cropping up in the graduates of the University College of the Gold Coast, who are close to the actual situation in the Gold Coast and often have less visionary expectations about the part they will play in the working life of their country, than their European-educated compeers.

ern radical ideas, and have had communist affiliations. Yet, on their return to the Gold Coast, often after five or six years as students in England or the United States, they find to their dismay that they are rarely welcomed with open arms into the policy-making ranks of the Convention People's Party. They are not made cabinet ministers. They do not replace the less educated ministerial secretaries. There is little room for most of them in the C.P.P.

On the other hand, they are badly needed in the administrative services so that Africanization can proceed. As a result, many of these educated individuals become increasingly embittered at Nkrumah, charge him with dictatorship, take increasing pride in the British-type association within the administrative service, tending more and more to judge the nationalists by British standards. As graduates of British or American universities, they tend to support the climate of secularity and restraint which they may have ignored while abroad but have nevertheless absorbed.[4]

Legitimacy, for such a minority, tends to derive from the framework of British parliamentary precedent, including the sanctity of the conciliar foundation of law. Those most associated with this view have either traditional affiliations or a past associated with indirect rule. To individuals possessing such views, the charisma of Nkrumah is considered dangerous, and they tend to ignore the crucial role Nkrumah has played in creating a system whereby an integration of public sanction and secular norms is now possible.

It is true that for most of the members of the Convention People's Party effective legitimacy does not flow from British political

---

[4] The charge was made by one of these people, a Cambridge-educated economist, that the nationalists made a conservative out of him and everyone he knew. By refusing to accept these young educated people into the Convention People's Party, Nkrumah keeps the loyalty of those who are most in touch with the general public, as well as keeping prima donnas from destroying the organizational integrity of the party. Nkrumah, part of whose charismatic role derives from the "monopoly of brains" with which he has been endowed by large segments of the public, does not need these intellectuals, who might prove difficult to control and organizationally unreliable. The experience of the Gold Coast with intellectuals in politics has demonstrated the difficulties these people have in getting along with one another in a political party. In this respect, psychological self-interest plays more havoc in an organization than financial self-interest with which some of the members of the C.P.P. are endowed. The opposition is constantly splintering, with each major opposition figure attempting to establish an independent following.

However, the young intellectuals, particularly those who have been intensely wrapped up in the independence movement while abroad for study, identify their lack of acceptance in the C.P.P. as an indication of Nkrumah's selling out or dictatorial policies or his lack of political scruples.

norms, behavioral restrictions, or procedural limitations, although these intervene in increasing fashion. Rather, legitimacy remains the prerogative of Nkrumah, stemming from the charismatic aspects of his leadership. Yet, as we have indicated, Nkrumah has chosen to endow the parliamentary structures with his "gift of grace." He did so in such a fashion as to give instrumental vitality both to his program and objectives, and to the structures of secular government as well. To the extent that the Convention People's Party is committed to parliamentary structures, it organizes its activities and focuses attention on the warrants of secular political life. Perhaps the most important testament to this fact has been the heightened popularity of Nkrumah and the C.P.P. when the Legislative Assembly adopted the new "Nkrumah constitution" which fixed more firmly the pattern of secular politics. Almost immediately, in the ensuing elections in 1954, party discipline was strengthened, while the caliber of the C.P.P. candidates was in many instances greater than in the past. Candidacy depended a great deal on party loyalty, it is true, but also upon an appreciation of parliamentary responsibility, and secular criteria of responsibility and training.

With the Nkrumah constitution the C.P.P. has set its objective within the limits of parliamentary structures to such an extent that it would seem almost impossible for any leader to disengage from such a political pattern. Immediately, therefore, party government with all the local factionalism, attention to popular demands, and dangers in the form of local splits and rivalries becomes part of the tussle over who shall form Her Majesty's government—not what form the government will take.

The many issues over traditional versus non-traditional norms and structures which have characterized this transitional period in the development of the Gold Coast are gradually being decided. Having played their part in the integration of parliamentary and subsidiary concrete political structures, the chiefs, the representatives of the territorial councils, the special interests, have departed from the scene of national government, at least in formal terms.

The General Election of 1954

The Nkrumah constitution and the Legislative Assembly election in 1954 perhaps mark the truly transitional aspect of the shift from traditional to secular social and political life. This is not to say that secularity has finally been achieved on a national scale; such a judgment would certainly be premature. Yet even in the last two years, the political picture in the Gold Coast has been substantially altered. In June 1954, as we have indicated in Chapter 10, the first general election on the basis of the revised system of representation was held. Preparatory to the election, the C.P.P. had launched its Operation 104 to gain all the seats in the new assembly. It suffered defeats, however, in the Northern Territories and in Southern Togoland, the latter of increasing significance in view of recent United Nations reevaluations of the status of Togoland and of its possible integration with the Gold Coast.

The Northern People's Party emerged as a powerful bloc, and is now the official opposition in the Assembly. The old opposition parties disappeared, Busia being the only representative of the Ghana Congress Party to be reelected, and he by 11 votes. The Convention People's Party is clearly the majority, with 71 seats. The Northern People's Party, the Moslem Association Party, the Ghana Congress Party, a new Anlo Youth Party (formed on purely local issues) and 16 independents of whom some 5 affiliate with the Northern People's Party make up the new house. Regional and separatist tendencies were thus manifested both in the north and in Southern Togoland, the latter showing less votes for the C.P.P. than for the Togoland Congress and other opposition.

Meanwhile, the opposition of the old Legislative Assembly which carried over from indirect rule and the days of the Legislative Council was entirely wiped out, such leading figures as J. B. Danquah and William Ofori Atta having lost their seats. It is reported that when Danquah was told that he had been repudiated by the electorate in his own home state of Akim Abuakwa, he could scarcely believe it.

In many cases individuals who had associated themselves with the C.P.P. for reasons of local politics, yet who did not receive party backing, set themselves up as C.P.P. "rebels."[5] Meanwhile,

---

[5] Bennett says "one of the most interesting features of the campaign was the emergence of the C.P.P. rebels. The party had received over a thousand applications from prospective candidates for the 104 seats in what the C.P.P. called 'Operation 104.' The choice and endorsements were made in the party's Accra headquarters. In some cases the C.P.P. flouted local feelings as part of its struggle against tribalism—but not always with success. For these and personal reasons, some of the disappointed aspirants insisted on standing. On Whit-Sunday, 6th

whether or not by design, Nkrumah has smashed the C.P.P. back bench in the assembly. The potential leadership of Anthony Woode, the pro-communist member of the C.P.P. back bench, has been ended with his expulsion from the C.P.P.[6] Mr. Bediako Poku, who figured so prominently in the Wenchi dispute, was not given C.P.P. backing and did not run for office. An Ewe, Mr. C. K. Quashie, a close associate of Woode, was given an uncertain constituence in Togoland where Antor and the Togoland Congress was strong, and he lost his seat in the assembly. The net effect has been the abolition of a possibly dangerous independent left-wing group in the back bench, which supported Gbedemah and looked to him almost as much as to Nkrumah for party leadership. At one stroke, Nkrumah has strengthened his control over the party groupings and reduced the potential rivalry of Gbedemah, while retaining the latter's services in the new government.

The Northern Territories group of the old assembly is now represented by a new political party, the Northern People's Party under the control of Mumuni Bawumia, a former secretary of the Mamprussi Native Authority, and more recently a clerk of the Mamprussi District Council, who has close ties to Braimah, Yakubu Tali, the *tolon-na*, the President of the Northern Territories Territorial Council. The tacit opposition of the north to the south has been replaced by a formal party opposition.

The potentialities for cooperation between the Moslem Association Party, the Northern People's Party, and the Ghana Congress Party appear to be good. Many of those in the N.P.P. have strong sympathies with the Ghana Congress Party which has so far confined its activities to the south and central areas of the Gold Coast. The attitudes against Nkrumah on the part of the northerners have probably been stiffened by the charges against Braimah during the corruption scandal of 1953. Charges of corruption by Braimah against other C.P.P. ministers were unsubstantiated by the findings of an investigating commission, and considerable resentment must have been felt in the north that Braimah was forced to resign, and left holding the bag for sins which they felt all the cabinet ministers were guilty of on a larger scale.

The new cabinet is of considerable quality. Some of its weaker

---

June, sixty-four of these rebels were formally read out of the party by the prime minister. . . ." See *Parliamentary Affairs, op.cit.,* p. 431.

[6] See Chapter 10 and the Sociogram of the old Legislative Assembly on p. 229.

figures, like Hutton-Mills, have been dropped. Mr. Asafu-Adjaye, the former independent Minister of Local Government and Housing has joined the C.P.P. while Mr. Inkumsah, the former Minister of Labour, has been reduced to the rank of ministerial secretary. The former Minister of Finance, an expatriate official, has become the economic advisor to the new government and in that capacity will apparently continue to exert almost as much influence as previously.

The new cabinet has ten ministers, all of them African, as follows: Mr. Gbedemah, former Minister of Commerce and Industry, has become Minister of Finance. A new Ministry of State has been formed headed by Botsio. A former ministerial secretary, Mr. J. E. Jantuah, has replaced Casely Hayford as Minister of Agriculture, the latter becoming head of a new Ministry of Interior. Mr. Ako-Akjei has become head of the newly set up Board of Trade, while the former propaganda secretary, and more latterly acting general secretary of the C.P.P., Mr. N. A. Welbeck, newly elected to the assembly, assumes the position of Minister of Works, a post of crucial patronage implications. Mr. Aaron Ofori Atta, a C.P.P. cousin of Dr. Danquah whom he defeated, has become the Minister of Communications, while Mr. Asafu-Adjaye remains in his post of Minister of Local Government. The Ministry of Health is run by Mr. Igala, replacing Mr. Hutton-Mills, while a Northern Territories C.P.P. stalwart, Mr. J. Allasani, is in charge of the Ministry of Education—a move designed to placate the pressing demands of the Northern Territories for more educational facilities. In the cabinet, five are university graduates, three hold four-year teacher training certificates, and two hold inter-arts certificates.

Nkrumah has stiffened party discipline. In local areas those C.P.P. men who would set themselves up as "C.P.P.—Independent," i.e., run without party backing, were removed from the C.P.P. and as has been indicated, approximately 64 members were dropped in this fashion. A severe blow against the left wing in the Parliamentary Party was struck, resulting in the virtual elimination of that group, while the left wing of the party organization has been brought closer to Nkrumah himself, with the former education secretary of the C.P.P., Mr. Kofi Baako, now a member of the assembly and chief government whip. Meanwhile Nkrumah has been able to enforce his statement that affiliation to "foreign" beliefs and political associations will not be tolerated.

From the point of view of tactics, the old opposition has been smashed, to be replaced by a new one. If Nkrumah can successfully win over the Northern Territories people, he may be able to keep that group from being anything but a temporary regional association with no firm roots throughout the Gold Coast. It remains to be seen whether or not, after an increase in education and social mobility in the Northern Territories, more popular public affiliations will appear in moves to the Northern People's Party, with its strong affiliations to chiefs, or towards the C.P.P., which still poses as the radical party. Perhaps even more important will be the sub-ethnic groupings in the north. At present the Northern People's Party seems dominated by the Mamprussi and Dagomba groups —those who tend to have Moslem chiefs—and are in some respects the traditional enemies of indigenous groups such as the Fra-Fra, still bent under the weight of an enormous political apathy. Thus the north has suddenly assumed a crucial significance in the future of the Gold Coast.

Structurally, the government has been made to conform even more closely to the British model. Formal representation of chiefs in the assembly having been abolished, all people stand election on a popular basis, a fact which tends to strengthen the role of political parties in the Gold Coast. The new parties seem to have a more deeply rooted basis than the splinter groups which used to characterize the opposition. With an all-African cabinet, the responsibility for full internal self-government has been achieved, but the British expatriate staff has been assured that it will not be removed for a long time to come. The process of role definition and institutionalization has therefore gained considerably, both in structural terms and in the kinds of associations which have been perpetuated both in the administrative and conciliar organs of government. It will be only a few years before the Gold Coast takes her place beside India, Pakistan, and Ceylon as an independent member of the Commonwealth, with Dr. Nkrumah as its responsible queen's first minister.

So long as the general economic situation does not suddenly deteriorate, as is always possible in mono-products nations, and no immediate threats to the leadership of Prime Minister Nkrumah appear, it would seem that the slow process of the institutionalization of parliamentary democracy will proceed. Dangers to such a process exist insofar as some members of the Convention People's Party have predilections towards a structure of authoritarianism which could conceivably be imposed after the British leave. Whether such an alternative is utilized will depend largely upon whether the free world can contribute effectively to the needs of the Gold Coast, so that widespread domestic demands will not place an impossible burden on the new government. A widespread disenchantment with Nkrumah might extend, as well, to the parliamentary system. In other words, if needs, both psychological and economic, are not met, then the possibility increases of the entire structure of parliamentary and conciliar government being branded as part of an "imperialist" plot to subvert the cherished ends of Gold Coast leaders. Such a possibility imposes a responsibility upon the United States as well as the United Kingdom, to continue to supply technicians, equipment and investment funds which will be needed in increasing quantities if the standards of life which the Gold Coast people have striven for can be supplied. In the long run, only if subsistence demands can be met will the Gold Coast be able to "afford" the luxury of parliamentary political organs. Only if development continues can parliamentary organs serve as reintegrative foci for a democratic national society in the Gold Coast.

Yet political institutional transfer is well on its way. Its final achievement in the Gold Coast will be one indication that democracy and social change can proceed simultaneously.

As far as genuine institutionalization is concerned, such a start is important. As secular rules and roles are accepted, no matter how tentatively, the participants begin to operate a system from which it is increasingly difficult to disengage, if any kind of effective government is to be maintained. In addition, the general public has been activated to expect from government—particularly a government operated by Nkrumah—a large range of benefits. What began as grudging and limited support by members of the Convention People's Party brought them into a network of orientational and behavioral controls and forced them publicly to identify their objectives within the parliamentary pattern. Yet the acclaim which they have received has helped to make the C.P.P. a group giving highest priority to parliamentary practice. While charisma was a major source of public endowment of sanction to parliamentary structures, it has given major stimulus to the development of a situation whereby "charisma can wither away." *Charisma is initially dysfunctional to the maintenance of traditional systems of authority, and initially eufunctional to the development of secular systems of authority. In the long run, however, maintenance of charismatic authority is dysfunctional to the maintenance of secular systems of authority.* Operationally, as has been indicated earlier, *specific legal legitimacy* of the Crown has been endowed by Nkrumah with *diffuse effective legitimacy* via charisma.[7]

The Functions of Charisma

The question that assumes importance in this stage of our discussion relates to charisma itself. Charisma has developed out of a mass support to Nkrumah. As such it has provided a source of orientational and organizational unity, tending to break down the local separatism and lack of consensus which so often is characteristic of newly emergent states. In the development of a national state, charisma appears to be of immediate value in channeling and vitalizing latent political propensities into conscious or manifested activities.

We can examine some of the complex functions which charisma performs with the following prefatory statement: *As charisma has worked in the Gold Coast as a newly accepted source of legitimacy, it has provided for the public extension of legitimacy and support to new types of social structures in keeping with the objectives of nationalism, meanwhile retaining sub-relational aspects of the traditional system, and integrating these aspects in different relational and behavioral modes permissible by Nkrumah's sanction. Out of this last it is possible for secular institutionalization to emerge.*

[7] This proposition would be in full accord with Weber where he indicates as follows: "A charismatic principle which originally was primarily directed to the legitimization of authority may be subject to interpretation or development in an anti-authoritarian direction. This is true because the validity of charismatic authority rests entirely on recognition by those subject to it, conditioned as this is by 'proof' of its genuineness. This is true in spite of the fact that this recognition of a charismatically qualified, and hence legitimate, person is treated as a duty. When the organization of the corporate group undergoes a process of progressive rationalization, it is readily possible that, instead of recognition being treated as a consequence of legitimacy, it is treated as the basis of legitimacy. Legitimacy, that is, becomes 'democratic.'"—Weber, Max, *The Theory of Social and Economic Organization*, translated by Parsons and Henderson, William Hodge and Co. Ltd., 1947, London, pp. 354-355.

Such conflicts as we examined in Wenchi and Manya Krobo do not simply represent struggle between differing groups within the same general normative system; they are not a simple struggle for power. The essential issue here is the terms of eventual establishment of secular legitimacy which does not derive from traditional sanction.

Local followers of the C.P.P. flaunt traditional authorities. Insecurity and guilt are often manifested in the furtive dealings of some local C.P.P. members. Charisma, as wielded by Nkrumah, becomes the means of absolving sin, of removing the vengeance of the ancestors, and of striking out against the more subtle powers of the chiefs. At the same time, the groups of youngmen find a close personal and intimate expression of solidarity through the charisma of Nkrumah, as close perhaps as that prevailing in traditional society. The Convention People's Party is fraternal and open, intimate and tolerant. It is particularistic in its loyalties and universalistic in its recruitment. It rewards its friends and removes its enemies. It has diffuse purposes with as many different groups of people finding in it social, economic, or political succor as is necessary to provide a mass following; yet it is specific in its political objectives. It is responsible in its local groups, tightly unified, a society of the elect to which many are elected; yet it is individualistic insofar as general norms of responsibility of action are not required by members.

The intimacy is an intimacy of participation, in face-to-face relationships with other members, all partaking in the endowment of support and psychological comfort provided by Nkrumah. Confusions over choice of evaluative criteria in political action have become identified with faith in the wisdom of Nkrumah himself, whether expressed as Tactical Action, or, as one rural villager put it: "I am for Nkrumah. Nkrumah is for the people."

Yet it would seem that most of the effective sources of Nkrumah's charisma have the identical functional counterparts as chieftaincy. *The efficiency of charisma lies in the fact that it satisfied the same functional requisites of leadership as did traditional leadership in the past. Nkrumah's charismatic authority has replaced the chief's traditional authority by meeting the same functional requirements, but by introducing new types of structures for their satisfaction.*[8]

[8] See above, p. 104.

1. *Sanctional Source.* Whereas the expression of sanction stemmed from the chief acting as trustee for the ancestors, Nkrumah has become a sanctional source in and of himself. He has become a source of norms which, having been made explicit, become a standard for his followers.

2. *Symbolic Referent.* Where the chief was the central orientational symbol of local tribal unity, continuity, and integration, through which members of the system related in social and political intercourse, Nkrumah has become the symbolic referent in which widely differing social groups find orientational identity with one another.

3. *Integrational Integer.* Where the chief was the central figure in the pattern of traditional authority through which legitimized power was expressed in institutionalized role structures within hierarchical patterns, Nkrumah has become an independent central figure expressing charismatic authority for groups in the system within a dependent party structure, integrated within a legal framework of British governmental units.

4. *Sub-ethnic or Ethnic Definition.* Where the chief was the central figure expressing membership and group-interrelation based upon blood, clan, and lineage in traditional society, Nkrumah has become the symbol of Ghana and African membership based upon nativity and racial definition transcending localized cultural limits[9] to a more generalized African Gold Coast definition.

It is held here that this functional set represents the requisites of non-secular leadership. The structures which follow from these requisites, identical to those under chieftaincy, are expressed, however, in totally differing concrete membership organizations such as the parliament, cabinet, administrative services, and the like.

In other words, the functions of charisma have been phrased against the functions of chieftaincy in traditional society. The assumption is made that for the general public, the indigenous associations surrounding chieftaincy have been transposed in kind via charisma to the larger social membership around the symbol of nationhood or *Ghana*. The assumption is made specifically because in the course of investigation it appeared that the basis of association and participation in the nationalist party and the

[9] Such as Akan, or Ga, or Adangme.

government, the relationship aspects of social life were modified but not destroyed around the new structures of political parties and secular parliamentary structures. At present, the wider supporting relational aspects of membership associated with industrialized countries and found in secular political parties—universalism, functional specificity, individual responsibility, etc.—have not emerged as sanctioned relational criteria in the Gold Coast.

In addition, charisma permits new social and political groupings around a central ideological symbol, "Free-dom," so far applied to the secular parliamentary pattern. The individual discretion regarding the choice of political systems open to a "charismatic carrier" is considerable, precisely its danger in the short run as well as its greatest strength. *Provided that it is used and controlled within the structural model of parliamentarianism, in which role definition and substantive norms of a different kind from those of charisma—norms of critical rationality, secularity, political representation via conciliar decision-making structures, public responsibility—are actually operative, charisma tends to make possible a viable central political system in what was hitherto an artificial territory.* Such a process involves the procedural and orientational institutionalization of norms of parliamentary democracy as a highly structured system of roles, controlled by legal safeguards and directed by the residual powers of the British authorities. It is the assumption here that charisma is ultimately used against itself, so long as there is an effectively operating parliamentary system, with an opposition whose rights are protected, and with role structures sufficiently limited to secular democratic precedent. In this process, charisma is potentially totalitarian. Any colonial power engaged in such a pattern of institutional transfer is faced with a most difficult problem of timing. It cannot be too permissive so that the regime is identified with imperialism, making more real a left wing right wing split having even more dangerous consequences. It cannot pull out of the area until an efficient government is handling the business which people are accustomed to expect, lest a mass disenchantment cause extreme responses from any charismatic leader who seeks to preserve his leadership, or else result in public apathy in which no government can operate effectively. The situation required, it would seem, is one in which processes of national integration around norms and procedures of parliamentary democracy partake less of an educative quality than that of a set of generalized moral predispositions. In such a process, a colonial government must exert very careful controlling provisos, if democratic structures are not to be replaced by more authoritarian ones when independence is granted. *Within our two polar extremes of apathy and anarchy within which political institutional transfer can take place, are succeeding limited factors, including disenchantment with charisma premature to secularism, or repudiation of secularism as associated either with charisma and/or imperialism.* One major safeguard against such extremes is provision of the means for effective governing, gradually turned over to Africans, by insuring economic stability and providing funds for development. It means also that a colonial power must be willing to relinquish control, meanwhile serving as an object of aggression displacement.

The British authorities are willing to be referred to as imperialists in the nationalist press. They recognize the ideological discipline which Nkrumah has imposed on large segments of the Gold Coast population. They recognize that to many Nkrumah equals the political kingdom. At the same time, the British have insured that within the political kingdom, parliamentary practices will prevail. By this token they have given Nkrumah the use of a legal-rational framework to service his political objectives and permit the utility of the framework to serve a wide range of political ends. The public is increasingly sharing in political democracy, and provision for a truly secular, non-charismatic pattern has been made.

The operational effectiveness of the parliament framework has been secured through the services of the British Colonial Service, and the Africans that have been trained within it. Rather than allow the new system to break down, they have sought to enhance Nkrumah's efficiency in such a way as to make it impossible for him to shift to an alternative political system. The thousands of daily operations of government are handled and have been handled in a particular fashion, by men well trained in the arts of administration. If *effective public opinion, effective authority,* and *effective administration* are combined within the parliamentary structural pattern, the assumption is, other things being equal, that pressure for totalitarianism will be minimal, particularly as

British roles and behavioral restraints among citizens become publicly acceptable and supported.

One problem facing any colonial power is when, in these terms, it is the proper time to take leave. Time itself seems to make the problem unimportant. In the Gold Coast, the assurances given to Colonial Service personnel—that they might remain at their posts on a contract basis, in the predilections made for procedural parliamentary norms, in the publicly stated normative assertions of the C.P.P., and in the new "Nkrumah constitution"—make it appear that the process of political institutional transition is very much under way and make formal leavetaking by British authorities an administrative affair. In other words, it appears possible to grant the Gold Coast independence now, while recognizing that in regard to institutional transfer *the shift from traditionally to charismatically defined norms has occurred for effective public opinion, but the shift from charismatic to norms of secular rationality on a public level is only now beginning,* strongly enhanced by Nkrumah himself.

Dilemmas of Success

We have indicated some of the conditions which served to refocus Gold Coast social life and membership around larger social organizations than those of traditional society, and around political structures represented in secular decision-making organs, e.g. cabinet, parliament, Gold Coast civil service, local and district councils, etc. The speed and efficiency with which such structures have been adopted by the C.P.P. as instruments of achieving self-government have at the same time posed crucial problems which it would be unwise to ignore. The very degree of success creates certain dilemmas for the government. These can be listed as follows: (1) excessive centralization in the government in Accra; (2) increasingly limited party recruitment for top posts; (3) inadequate representation of traditional units of society (particularly as the territorial councils still exist); (4) inadequate local development; (5) continuing conflicts over legitimacy (particularly when fought out on local levels in the councils), which appears, finally in (6) heightening rural-urban conflicts where, for example, youngmen from urban areas are sometimes considered traitors by their age-grade compatriots in *asafo* companies in the rural areas.

In addition, the orientational problems incumbent upon such drastic social change have been heightened by tensions which might have worked themselves out in more pragmatic fashion if the process had been more leisurely. It cannot be concluded that since the functions of charisma stem from their requisite status, and since requisite status of charisma is the same as that for chieftaincy, that chieftaincy itself no longer performs its functions. Its structures have been under attack, but they are very much alive, and just as charisma draws its strength from non-secular "reserves," so does traditionalism. In that sense the struggle over legitimacy is by no means over. The very fact that non-empirical factors remain primary means potentially great pitfalls in political institutional transfer.

One possible difficulty results from the fact that political office prior to the actual day of independence has given the fruits of victory to the C.P.P. almost prematurely. That is to say, the responsibilities of office, while they help to indoctrinate and teach nationalists the processes of government, also by the very demands of parliamentary and bureaucratic roles require a kind of purging in the party. Some of those who made the "revolution" are no longer appropriate to consolidate its gains. More and more, access to top positions demands a kind of training which bars many of the radical, dispossessed, partially educated young C.P.P. members from important political posts. Some such individuals, like Krobo Edusei, have proved hard to get rid of. But the important factor here is that one of the major appeals of the C.P.P. was its provision of new roles, new jobs, new sinecures for those barred by lineage or clan ties from positions of importance, and for those from rural areas whose ideas, expectations, and desires had gone beyond the local purview. Now a closing down of political awards, a more stringent set of demands on behavior, and the very requirements of government itself, tend to undermine the fruits of political victory. A situation almost like Michel's "iron law of oligarchy" has occurred. What began as a populist, radical, open-ended process attracting thousands of people has gradually closed down. Irresponsibility is often punished with expulsion and party discipline begins to appear more and more as governmental chastisement. Freedom of action has become tempered by the exercise of legal authority via decision-making structures of the state. At the very top levels of government (in particular those which are the symbols and substance of achievement and success), allocation of political offices among a comparative few automatically reduces the chances for others in the C.P.P. to achieve the sinecures and positions which they might have expected. Rather, many of the people now most available for such positions are those having a far better education or stronger commitment to standards of parliamentary behavior, and a greater amount of political sophistication, than those who "made the revolution."

A temporary palliative has been found in "pensioning" off formerly important figures in the party or potentially aggressive but unsuitable candidates by providing chairmanships of committees, statutory boards, etc. Giving some important figures positions of prestige in an organization where a European official or effectively trained staff will prevent major blunders (while policy decisions remain in the cabinet) has been quite successful. The chairmanship of the Cocoa Marketing Board is a specific example of this process in action. Individuals given such positions remain loyal to Nkrumah and remain his agents. They can prelude their ultimate downfall with positions of high honor and if they make a mess of their jobs can be more successfully removed from the political arena, and, finally, if they should prove to be superior figures in these posts, they might then come into the "inner circle" once again (if they originally had such a position). To some extent, however, such positions have been immediately useful as a prelude to downfall for an individual—an "up and out" system prefaced by high honor.

But this is not only temporary; it suffices for only a few individuals. The greater mass of the C.P.P. and the stronger claimants for political recognition had seen their horizons and their expectations widened dramatically through their participation in the nationalist movement. Many of them remain deeply disappointed. Not only does the horizon remain in the distance, but the image has proved a mirage. This means that at the height of its success, and almost by virtue of its success, the Convention People's Party is weakened even before self-government has been achieved. The crusade against imperialism has been vitiated by the obliging behavior of the imperialists, and those who see the C.P.P. operating the government in cooperation with the British can look either to left or right, over the shoulders of the C.P.P.

leadership, to a more pristine anti-Europeanism, e.g. to the left, where some individuals charge that Nkrumah has sold out to the British, and to the right, where those chiefs who have been removed from contact with the government ever since the downfall of indirect rule can now claim a more fundamental right to nationalism, e.g. the pre-European past.

As a result of these factors, there is a danger that the party will be thus less and less satisfactory as a social unit. Limited access to top positions has reduced the prospects for social mobility (and intensified the pressures on African civil servants and party officials to partake in "extra-legal" activities), tending to reduce the effective bases for further recruitment among the youth in the Gold Coast. Finally, the objective, the mission, and the almost religious quality to "Free-dom" and "Self-Government Now," are weakened by the sureness of success.

As a social unit the C.P.P. achieved much at the expense of the membership of other social units in the Gold Coast. We have indicated how the C.P.P. has been a product of urbanism and revolt against the rural agricultural pattern of life, of youngmen against elders, i.e. of a youth in revolt against both a traditionalism perceived as restrictive, and authority from which they were barred. But, as we have indicated, shifts from traditional life to that of nationalism have not been without grave personal conflict and guilt. It is because of these factors as well as several others that charisma is possible, and that Nkrumah can perform certain functions hitherto reserved for chieftaincy. To remove oneself from the traditional sphere of life, the full weight of the religious sanctity of traditional life had to be fought, and such weight was not only a matter of belief and conscience, but also involved friends and family, father and mother, lineage and division, and the ancestors whose nearness was manifest in the network of social relationships of daily life. The very intensity surrounding the nationalist movement was both a product and a source of exacerbation of the conflicts exhibited in individual and group behavior. The almost furtive and sometimes flaunting disrespect exercised against traditional authorities by some youngmen in the new-found support and solidarity of the C.P.P. scarcely passed unnoticed by the chiefs and elders, particularly in Ashanti, where the system of chieftaincy, the pride in the Confederacy, and the aristocracy of the Ashanti vis-à-vis other inhabitants of the Gold Coast did not brook such changes with equanimity.

The strains set up by the very degree of success, and the sharpness with which Nkrumah emerged as a charismatic figure, have tended to be blurred by the formal development of government, while other more fundamental changes in society have been piling up. For example, many of those who joined the C.P.P. when the party was still largely a movement, when its leaders were either in jail, or just out and enjoying high office, regarded the rural areas with contempt, and sought to escape the prescriptions and obligations of traditional life. Many of them, holding high hope of political and social status, now face a return home with their ambitions unrealized. In much the same fashion that the colonial regime accelerated wants and desires beyond its ability to satisfy, the nationalist movement too must shoulder the same burden. Its main accomplishment, independence, is soon taken for granted. Revolutionary fervor can easily be dissipated in the difficult tasks of governing. Nkrumah not only faces the danger of public disenchantment as he achieves his goal, but a disenchantment all the more pressing because of the lofty heights which so many of his followers had envisioned for themselves. Many of the Gold Coast chiefs, particularly in the Northern Territories and Ashanti, are aware of such feelings. The very slings and arrows which the C.P.P. directed at them, and the very indignities which they have had visited upon them in the rapid, buoyant development of the Convention People's Party, may ultimately prove to be a powerful factor in the revival of support for chieftaincy. Those whose commitments to the C.P.P. are by no means wholehearted may well find that the chiefs still serve as more satisfactory media for social needs. It must be recalled that in this analysis the functional requisites of charisma and the functional requisites of chieftaincy are the same; the former arising in a new context through dissatisfaction with the membership structures (the concrete structures of traditional society) through which they were achieved in traditional society. If dissatisfaction with the membership structures by which charismatic functions are achieved should become widespread (e.g. local party units, the Legislative Assembly, the Cabinet, etc.) then not only will secular government be endangered, impaled on an immediate struggle over legitimacy, but chieftaincy might well regain a large measure of its status, at least for a short time. Traditional life and the membership structures of indigenous social organization, and the norms governing social life in that society, are far from dead. The chiefs and elders still perform many of their roles, and the attack upon them may prove to serve as a rallying ground for those who become disillusioned with Nkrumah and the C.P.P.

The greatest dilemma posed by success for the nationalists, therefore, remains success itself, as far as its immediate objectives are concerned. The very conditions which brought the Gold Coast youth into a movement, which disciplined the movement into a party, and finally which made the party a government operating secular structures of government, can still serve as the undoing of nationalism even before self-government has been achieved. A movement based on a charismatic leader has as its leading characteristic a kind of religious fervor out of which legitimacy stems. It is a reformation and a crusade. Yet the counter-reformation waits in the wings. As the C.P.P. metamorphosed into party government, particularly of a centralized sort, some of its appeal was lost through the closure of public access to authority positions and failure to carry through some of its multi-various purposes on local levels. Since the demands of office carry heavy responsibilities which the C.P.P. has, on the whole, faced squarely, the religious character of charisma itself has been undermined. The hour of victory is in that sense the hour of greatest danger. Solidarity decreases in intensity, finding outlets in more fragmented groupings than a large-scale unified movement, and the personalization of authority, and the central orientational characteristics surrounding charisma tend to be less and less significant.

A leadership as politically aware as the C.P.P. will no doubt find two major alternative paths of action presenting themselves if such disenchantment should come before parliamentary government is institutionalized, i.e. before the C.P.P. politicians themselves would rule out certain kinds of activity as unsanctioned and improper. Either they can seek to promote a new movement dedicated to a new "revolution" (and it is in precisely these terms that some left-wing individuals evaluate the events and developments in the Gold Coast) or seek a religious or revivalist kind of movement such as Islam, or a neo-traditionalism. The possibility is real that the first will be used against the second. The Convention People's Party has developed its organizational nucleus: disciplined, militant, ideologically minded, tactic-minded, and' capable of carefully manipulated violence for self-conscious socialist objectives. The core is fostered by Nkrumah himself, with members on most of the key boards, councils, and other agencies of both central and municipal government. It could never show its teeth until after the British formally turn over final power to the Gold Coast government. But if need arose, self-government could increase once again that range of maneuverability of the Nkrumah regime, now limited within the parliamentary context of secular government. There is little doubt that Nkrumah wants desperately to have parliamentary government succeed, but equally there is little doubt that if faced with a loss of authority, the possibility of alternative political practices to those of parliamentary democracy would be utilized.

But is there a danger that an opposition which looks to the past as its source of inspiration, around the chiefs and the intellectuals, the rural groups, and the Islamic groups might find a common inspirational weapon and split the pattern of political institutional transfer apart? The National Liberation Movement is perhaps one warning that such a coalition is possible. The recent rout of the Ghana Congress Party at the polls might perhaps look more conclusive in terms of fundamental issues than it really is. Too many groupings who have in common more than a simple dislike of the Nkrumah regime are slowly taking their bearings in the sea of Gold Coast politics. The moves towards alliance between Northerner and Ashanti groups might perhaps herald a new kind of association where traditionally oriented groups themselves under the common guise of a reformed chieftaincy might activate large numbers of individuals who now only dimly realize that self-government and freedom are at hand, and that the changes taking place in the Gold Coast mean changes in their own lives. If such a movement is to succeed, however, it must serve to refocus a disgruntled population around significant symbols having indigenous meaning, while serving up more tangible satisfactions. It is difficult to see how such a coalition would be able to accomplish such objectives over a long period of time. Yet certainly in the short run such possibilities are real. Their reality endangers the entire process of political institutional transfer.

The very centralization which has allowed the Nkrumah government to exert discipline and control, and has integrated a far-flung range of communications and authority, has made both the Northern Territories and Ashanti more remote, almost as back provinces of Gold Coast politics, almost indeed like colonial areas. That the Ashanti do not greet such goings-on with equanimity has been marked by their demand for more seats in the Legislative Assembly and, more recently, their demand for a federal constitution. For many Ashanti who joined the C.P.P. out of opportunism, or other reasons which they no longer find telling, the appeals of the C.P.P. have been temporary. Ashanti greatness in the immediate past, the chiefs who are the living personifications of the ancestors, and the callousness of the C.P.P. when dealing with Ashanti and Northern Territories traditional leaders, have revived the functions of the *asantehene*, and the Asanteman Council has emerged in a crucial position in rallying dissidents against the government itself. The Asanteman Council is thus in the peculiar position of achieving major effectiveness as a political force just as it has lost all central governmental functions. It no longer sends its representatives to the Legislative Assembly.

Centralization, meanwhile, has appeared more clearly than hitherto partly because the new electoral system favors the election of individuals coming from a party background rather than a traditional background. The relationships which existed under the old Legislative Assembly between different social groupings, and more particularly between representatives of chiefs and party politicians have been abolished, with the traditional groups entirely cut off from the formal processes of decision-making. The activities which they hitherto could support in the Assembly can no longer be supported in legitimate fashion. The territorial councils are now simply vestiges of indirect rule. The advice and strength which came from these organs, and their meaning for many people in the Gold Coast, have been frustrated by the new constitution. Either the groups represented by these organs must work underground, or they must watch their influence wane, their importance demolished.

Some of the advantages of the old highly centralized political administration of colonial government have been ignored by the present government, i.e. the dual range of traditional and non-traditional structures of authority which allowed maximum use of local authorities and agencies has been too easily dismissed. The new local councils with their two-thirds secular majorities have proved in the main successful in removing the chief from his sources of income and control, but have not yet been successful in unleashing new and richer sources of belief and ideas with which to prelude purposive action.

With the calendar or time-table of self-government almost complete, traditional groups see their former supporters, the British leaving them at the mercy of the youngmen, the secularists, the C.P.P.—hence the anguish with which many Northern Territories and Ashanti groups have greeted the time-table of independence. They are perhaps less sanguine about the Nkrumah regime than the British are. They fear the youngmen, and they are for the most part convinced that the C.P.P. is a movement of immorality and irresponsible self-interest whose commitment to impartiality and disinterested justice is less than the taking and holding of authority. Many of the chiefs fail to see the real promise which the nationalist movement has brought, and their own lack of faith in it might well prove to be an important consideration if the Nkrumah regime should fail, either through a continuing revolution or in succumbing to a revivalist movement of the past.

The authoritarian potential of the C.P.P. remains unknown. There is little reason to feel that it will do other than remain latent unless the entire regime is threatened by disorder and local rebellions. The long-term possibilities that an anti-C.P.P. coalition opposing charisma with religious revivalism would be able to accomplish much where the C.P.P. fails seem poor. The intellectuals having their commitment to the secularity of democratic institutions would soon be opposed by the chiefs, while regional and local loyalties would assume new proportions. Even today, as we have indicated, the Brong areas (such as Techiman, Bechem, and Wenchi) all have strong secessionist leanings against the Ashanti Confederacy.

One procedural factor which might prove of major importance would be an upper house for chiefs and their representatives. So long as the traditional system of state councils and territorial councils co-exist alongside of secular councils, cutting off their participation in central government and channels of legal activity would seem only to provoke them to illicit aggressive behavior. An upper house would give the territorial councils a representation they have enjoyed ever since the constitution of 1925, even if their position should be largely honorific. Traditional society needs an outlet for expression qua traditional society. Groups now ignored by the elected members of the Legislative Assembly need representation. Given the fact that a parliament is much more than simply a lawmaking body, but a body which provides means of adjusting conflict and mediating differences as well, a parliament which excludes large numbers of the Gold Coast population almost by virtue of the way in which elections work, runs the same risks that the old Legislative Council did under the 1946 constitution. Given the historical context and indigenous background of the Gold Coast, it is not adequately representative in terms of the peculiar structuring of significant groupings. Indirect rule at least had the virtue of recognizing that one could not destroy without fashioning something new. Equally, the Gold Coast government needs to be aware of the dangers which result when in refashioning something new it destroys something traditional. The tenaciousness of social habits makes the consequences of such destruction most difficult to predict and unless what is newly created serves to satisfy the needs of the traditionally oriented population and bring them via their chiefs into the role structures of secular government, political institutional transfer will be hard-pressed. The social atmosphere thus remains charged with aggression and the possibilities for local separatism. Riots over ostensibly minor issues, and perhaps even ill-fated rebellions, could only be matched by the need for the new government to take repressive measures. Indeed, under such circumstances political institutional transfer may appear in the guise of threats to various established orders. It might well be used to establish repressive roles in a bureaucratic state apparatus rather than instrumental roles in a parliamentary democracy.

The Nkrumah regime, in widening its struggle to include chieftaincy as a target, is now in danger of paying a heavy price for its success. Yet, having broken the hold which chiefs had in the early days of nationalism, and removing the inhibitions which they presented, Nkrumah has much to gain from the chiefs. If one way of satisfying their needs and demands is through an upper house, another is to utilize their functions in support of local governmental activities through the framework of the state councils (*oman*) and local councils.

Nkrumah needs the chiefs insofar as they are still well-springs of traditional sentiment. He needs them to activate local groups to self-help projects. If the central government is to devote itself to larger matters requiring over-all planning, requiring balancing of priorities, and evaluating needs and requirements of many different areas and sectors of the country and the economy, then it cannot be at the mercy of constant local demands, which in the long run can well subvert the larger objectives of the government (given the shortages of all kinds which beset the government). If immediate demands in local areas are acceded to because of the votes at stake, the nation's developmental future might be jeopardized.

So long as the local councils remain the scenes of fighting over legitimacy, and so long as the attack against traditional authorities proceeds at all levels, central and local, the greater the chances that the chiefs will be able to rally newly disillusioned groups back in the comfortable folds of family, belief, and ancestor. The Nkrumah government, with its recruitment gradually closing down, its movement having fulfilled its primary purpose, might well begin to lose its party membership. The prophecy which some of the chiefs voiced—that the people would someday return to their "natural rulers"—might appear to be not entirely incorrect.

On the other hand, if the local areas can cease to be the scenes of bitter fighting, then the chiefs can ease the pressures which the Nkrumah government has created for itself by the very ambitions it has for the Gold Coast. The rural areas still look much the same as when the old district commissioner plied on shanks' mare through his district. To get people to dig wells, to build rice paddies, to irrigate their fields, and to build out of their own labor and indigenous materials both a new physical and social environment is difficult. If the government should, in its need, turn to authoritarianism and coercion, parliamentary democracy will be doomed. If nothing else, the experience of the Soviet Union demonstrates the futility of "forcing people to be free," of using coercion (and the consequent process of compounding coercion) as resistance rises. So long as the chiefs hear themselves labeled as reactionary and diversionary, so long as they are denied representation, and so long as they are made to bear the onus of backwardness and irresponsibility, so long will they remain dangers rather than assets for the government. They remain a possible focus for resentment against the Nkrumah regime. Indeed, if charisma should wither away before institutional transfer has been achieved for large sections of the population, the dangers to this struggling young democracy remain great.

Where does the Nkrumah government have its greatest potential for successfully achieving parliamentary democracy? In its ability to solve problems posed by the ambitions of the leadership itself, to capitalize on its boundless confidence, and to achieve projects such as the Volta Scheme, the Accelerated Plan for Education, the new road-building and rural development programs all envisioned for the near future or actually underway. Having served successfully as the instrumentalities of nationalism, the structures of parliamentary government must do equally well as instrumentalities of problem-solving. If local problems could be solved at local levels, the chiefs could well help fulfill Gold Coast political requirements without either vitiating their traditional prescriptions (as occurred under indirect rule) or gaining too much secular-style authority. Serving in their local capacities as significant figures in the village, in the territorial divisions, and in their symbolic and integrative capacities, chiefs could help to satisfy the needs of traditional elements in Gold Coast life, relieve the pressure on the central government, and in fact decentralize the operations of governmental activities. For this the present constitutional framework would appear entirely suitable, federalism entirely unnecessary, while an upper house could serve as the outlet for those whose importance in the culture and organization of the Gold Coast is an important part of its heritage. An almost entirely honorific upper house would still serve to ventilate the attitudes and contributions of large groups in the population of the Gold Coast, and if the functions of charisma should be taken over by a more secular set of structures, the same might also be said for the functions of chieftaincy.

Removing the chiefs and representatives of traditional society would, therefore, appear to be one of the more dangerous turns taken under the Nkrumah constitution and one which promotes the greatest obstacles to the diminution of charisma via democratic secularity. It enhances the conflict between rural and urban areas, between youngmen and elders, between Colony, Ashanti and the Northern Territories, between government and the governed, and it poses "revivalism" against "messianicism." The foundations of consensus in a parliament, and the expression of new norms of secular legitimacy would thereby seem to be endangered.

These are some of the problems which face the Nkrumah regime as it stands on the threshold of independence—its central purpose almost accomplished in a matter of six or seven years. The very rapidity of its success under a brilliant leadership has perforce meant the by-passing of stubborn problems of ordinary day-to-day living. In the daily lives of the people, Nkrumah as the life chairman of the Convention Peoples Party and the prime minister of the Gold Coast, vies with the chiefs, the elders, and the *asafo* for ultimate allegiance. The local party unit vies with the kin group and the territorial divisions. Yet the traditional family and the sense of tribal membership still play their part. The undeniable success of the moment hides some of the age-old customs and characteristics which have been and remain a part of the traditional heritage of the Gold Coast. It is against such a complex of factors that the control features imposed by the British assume greater significance, while the problems awaiting solution leave many of the larger questions of political institutional transfer unanswered.

Legitimization of Secularity

At present, we can conclude that the use of parliamentary structures has provided the means of satisfying a multiplicity of national ends. The authority of the man has been substituted for the authority of the chief, and the form through which the authority of the man has been expressed is parliamentary.

Since the functions of charisma contain crucial transfer value, unifying the membership of the system around key national symbols and structures, such a process, once occurred, supports a system having an elaborate role and normative structure of its own, a structure having been endowed with a high degree of utility. The new solidarity units in the system are geared to the operations of the new structures. As such, they are secularized reference groups. They become the sanctional source for secular political behavior. The degree of local reference in all parts of the Gold Coast to secular political structures and behavioral prescriptions is the degree of institutionalization of parliamentary processes in the Gold Coast.

These sanctions deal not only with observable behavior, but

with criteria regarding forms and types of decision-making. Such criteria involve norms of rational choice.

Rational choice as a predominant criterion for decision-making can wholly displace charismatic factors, as long as objectives are within a secular field rather than non-secular and within a parliamentary structure. In its widest implications, however, the question of political institutional transfer in the Gold Coast remains open: Can sanctional allegiance to the parliamentary form include limitation of sanctions to "critical rationality" in parliamentary decision-making?

All underdeveloped areas have certain similar problems in lesser or greater degree. They are troublespots of disease, of ignorance, of confused beliefs, and a partially shattered culture. If their peoples are not to remain apathetic, quiescent, and fatalistic, or seek violent means of removing their disabilities, they need to find a reunification of hope, desires, and beliefs around social structures through which achievement can be registered. If their goals cannot be realized by the structural pattern of democracy they may seek alternatives. These alternatives do not involve a careful process of selection and evaluation of what forms of social and political systems are most efficacious for democracy.

For the West, the problem is gearing democratic processes to the needs of sorely troubled peoples in such fashion as to promote the enhancement of new objectives while the resources of the local population are in short supply and bitter demand. The potentialities of communist ideology and organization in this kind of complex are great, since the language of Marxism and the language of nationalism often sound alike. In crucial respects, both stem from the same sources: a disadvantaged class, or group, or nation, seeking to control the means of government and the means of subsistence for the benefit of a group formerly barred from such means.

Equally, charisma, in preserving the "sacral" characteristics of the nationalist movement, at the same time points up the crucial role it plays in the formation of a national solidarity, i.e. a national membership tied together with common bonds of social consciousness. The party cannot become a predominantly *representative* organization, so crucial in American concepts of functioning democracy. Nor can it become simply one among several alternative groupings operating the government in which parliamentary controls over the executive become a predominant feature, as in British cabinet government. So long as the solidarity element is crucial, the societal functions of a political party like the C.P.P. go beyond their more normal functions as in Great Britain, because it is engaged in satisfying a large scale of social wants. To the extent that it promotes such satisfactions, the nationalist party itself is torn by its procedural responsibilities in government, and the needs to which it must cater in the larger social environment. Its ability to get votes may depend upon the latter, but until a large range of subordinate social supports lift the main burden off the C.P.P. it is caught between retaining its popular characteristics as a movement, and its functional responsibilities as a participant in cabinet government.[10]

The pluralism of democracy, which provides for so many levels of integration around institutions of choice, makes it difficult to establish both broad tolerance and behavioral limitations in areas where key symbols, key leaders, and key slogans tend to extremism. Nationalism and other movements of mass revolt tend to "eat their young," and leadership to be as potentially vulnerable as the leaders are formidable. If nationalism in the Gold Coast can provide the motive force for an integrated society in which representation, rational choice, secular law, and decision-making via debate and conciliar organs can subsume regional differences, divided loyalties, and conflicting norms, meanwhile depending less and less upon charismatic authority, then the peoples of Africa will have witnessed political institutional transfer in action.

In the process economic development is required, coincident with political transfer, so that a steady measure of domestic secu-

[10] For the implications of solidarity upon political parties, see the informative discussion in Duverger, Maurice, *Political Parties*, London, 1954 (North translation), p. 122. Duverger, in addition, points to the appearance of "totalitarian" parties or parties having sacral characteristics as coming with the decline of organized religion, an additional reminder of the functional equivalence of the "movement-party" of which we have been speaking.

In addition to Duverger's discussion, Ernest Barker's distinction between the state and society, while promoting as many theoretical difficulties as it solves, at least illuminates the problem of coordinate and separate functions performed by "voluntary" associations which he claims belong to "society," as distinct from the agencies of government and their private adjuncts like political parties. Barker indicates in his discussion, although indirectly, that private associations in integration with the public governmental are necessary requirements for a democratic national state. Where the political party performs the functions of the private and the governmental, the social and the legal, the national state itself tends toward totalitarianism. See Barker, Ernest, *Principles of Social and Political Theory*, Oxford, *passim*.

rity will appear in widely discrete parts of the country. The development system must be responsible to differential demands by various groups. It must serve the interests of diverse individuals and groups whose consensus regarding the fundamental patterns of parliamentary government may be those of expediency rather than of disinterested service.

It has been stressed here, perhaps unduly, that charisma and its functions has been the central motivating feature by which men have responded in the Gold Coast, so far as authority shifts are concerned. The control authority has seen to it that charisma was not destroyed while the alternatives granted the charismatic leader have gradually been narrowed by the effective public derivation of consensus around approved patterns of role activity and behavior within structures of parliamentary government.

Charisma and its consequences have been varied, both in the formation of a national society and in the structuring of role and authority systems throughout Gold Coast life on both central and local levels. Its crucial role in the changing social life of rural Gold Coast can scarcely be underestimated. With all its special difficulties, and the problems it poses for democracy, charisma remains an important device by which political institutional transfer is effected. Because of the functions it performs we might very well question what other functional equivalents there might be for the process of institutional transfer in other parts of Africa. Is charisma and its functions a prerequisite of political institutional transfer where the process involves the development of secular political societies within a traditional indigenous environment?

Meanwhile the prescriptions and roles of secular government are increasingly part of the Gold Coast pattern of social life and government. It is true that under the new constitution of 1954 some of the conflicts between traditional and secular are now pushed underground, out of the arena of central politics. Nevertheless the achievements of African administrators, educators, and politicians are remarkable. They are changing their society as they learn to operate alien structures.

Equally impressive have been the accomplishments of the Gold Coast people who are developing the economic and human resources of their country by peaceful means. Their ability to adapt and create their own social environment is an achievement of heroic proportions.

It is often pointed out with a certain degree of smug compassion that a little over fifty years ago some of the people of the Gold Coast were cutting off each other's heads. What is perhaps more important is to remember that a little over fifty years ago these people were living in a complex and difficult world. They managed to survive under often incredible conditions. As a perceptive universe, the Gold Coast is a place into which no educated person, African or European, can enter without feeling a sense of humility and drama in observing old wisdom and new knowledge clash.

CHAPTER 15

GHANA AS A NEW NATION

Introduction

"A REVOLUTIONARY Government, that is a government anxious by word and proven deed for rapid changes in the interests of the mass of the people, has been set in Ghana over the past few days by His High Dedication Osagyefo the President."[1] With these words the *Evening News* commented on the government formed after several senior members including the Minister of Finance of Ghana, Mr. K. A. Gbedemah were removed from office and stripped of party membership. A new political generation had arrived, militant, angry and determined. The *Evening News* was their newspaper as was the *Ghanaian Times*. They desperately desired to be revolutionary—for "to be revolutionary is to be completely dedicated to the objective of serving the true ends of the people, ending exploitation of man by man, believing absolutely in the rule of the majority and ruthless predominance of the interests of the ordinary people over the interests of all others; a belief that such interest is completely married with the existence, the very essence, of the State—and, above all, intimate understanding of the ideological force that socialism represents with criticism and self-criticism as a cementing and consolidating force."[2]

The "cult of personality" also emerged. "To millions of people living both inside and outside the continent of Africa, Kwame Nkrumah is Africa, and Africa is Kwame Nkrumah. When the question was asked: 'What is going to happen in Africa?' it is to one man that everyone looks for the answer: Kwame Nkrumah. To the imperialists and colonialists his name is a curse on their lips; to the settlers his name is a warning that the good old days at the expense of the Africans are coming to an end; to Africans suffering under foreign domination, his name is a breath of hope and means freedom, brotherhood and racial equality; to us, his people, Kwame Nkrumah is our father, teacher, our brother, our

[1] The *Evening News,* October 3, 1961.
[2] *Ibid.*

friend, indeed our very lives, for without him we would no doubt
have existed, but we would not have lived; there would have been
no hope of a cure for our sick souls, no taste of glorious victory
after a life-time of suffering. What we owe him is greater even
than the air we breathe, for he made us as surely as he made
Ghana."[3]

"The Convention People's Party," said Nkrumah, "is a powerful
force, more powerful, indeed, than anything that has yet appeared
in the history of Ghana. It is a uniting force that guides and
pilots the nation, and is the nerve center of the positive operations
in the struggle for African irredentism. Its supremacy cannot be
challenged. The Convention People's Party is Ghana, and Ghana
is the Convention People's Party. There are some people who
not only choose to forget this, but who go out of their way to
teach others to forget also. There are some persons, both staff and
students, who mistakenly believe that the words 'academic freedom'
carry with them a spirit of hostility to our Party and the Government, the same Party of the workers and the farmers, and the
same Government whose money founded the University and maintains it, and who provides them with their education in the hope
that they will one day repay their countrymen by giving loyal and
devoted service to the Government of the people.

"The Convention People's Party cannot allow this confusion
of academic freedom with disloyalty and anti-Government ideas.

"In the future we shall attach the greatest importance to the
ideological education of the Youth. The establishment of the
Young Pioneers will be a step further in this direction. The Youth
Section of the Party will be fully mobilized under the close guidance of the Youth Bureau of the National Secretariat. We shall
make our party ideology fully understood in every section of the
community."[4]

These quotations represented the goals of an independent
Ghana. In terms of political control and ideology, and the monopolistic quality of its party, Ghana was to be transformed into a
society mobilized for internal development while demanding the

[3] See Tawia Adamafio, "A Portrait of the Osagyefo Dr. Kwame Nkrumah."
Accra: Government Printer, 1961.
[4] Kwame Nkrumah, "What the Party Stands For," in *The Party*, Vol. 1,
No. 1, 1960.

fullest loyalty of its citizens. Like Guinea and Mali, it represented the militant left in the politics of contemporary Africa. The result in Ghana was an often ugly pattern of development which had many confusing and dramatic aspects to it. Hundreds were jailed without trial (no one was executed). Sycophants surrounded Nkrumah.[5] If there was a great discrepancy between "theory" and practice, compared to the more puritanical (and more modest) socialism of Mali or Guinea, Nkrumaism and its political practices nevertheless represented more than shrewd, hard, power politics (or, as one observer in Africa called it, "Nkrumaism, the highest stage of opportunism").

The situation in Ghana was still fluid, despite the harshness of government acts, and the sometimes flamboyant misuse of political power. The real issues remained to be fought out.

That is even more true today.

Originally I stated that democratic institutions in the Gold Coast, operated by the C.P.P., were at their onset strengthened by being endowed with the charismatic authority of Nkrumah. I also said that charismatic authority and secular authority were opposed to one another. An assumption was made that democratic institutions rest on the public acceptance of secular values. Hence, the contradiction—charismatic authority both strengthened and weakened parliamentary government.

The contradiction was never resolved. It is true that parliamentary institutions are not themselves the values which support them. Charismatic authority did give to parliamentary institutions a liveliness and vitality which would have otherwise been lacking in an alien set of government structures. Comparative colonial experience clearly shows that. Nevertheless, for institutional transfer to succeed would have required charisma to decline in favor of non-traditional secular authority. This clearly did not occur.[6]

---

[5] Some of them have been jailed, such as Tawia Adamafio, the author of the "Portrait" of Nkrumah quoted above.

[6] The term "political institutional transfer" was deliberately chosen despite its ungainliness. It referred to the transfer of roles and through them, values, associated with secular authority. It was the role which had to be institutionalized rather than organization in government. Hence, for purposes of analysis, unless governmental forms of democracy were supported by roles institutionalized in terms of secular democratic values, then political institutional transfer had not taken place.

My original assumption was that active use of parliamentary structures of government would have the effect of restricting charisma so that it would increasingly decline in favor of secular authority with democratic values. The other alternatives I posed were a lapse into neo-traditionalism, or the growth of "totalitarian democracy."[7] What began in tactics, i.e. the use of parliamentary institutions by the C.P.P. to wrest power from the British would either end in the use of parliamentary institutions in a meaningful sense or not, depending upon a number of factors: tradition, religion, the ability of the party to "generalize" itself into a new society, and the importance of charisma as a "balancing element between all these and other forces." When the C.P.P. and Nkrumah were voted into office, they were required to restrict their political activities to a system which recognized the primacy of parliamentary government and procedures. It remained to see whether, after independence, charismatic authority would gracefully disappear to be replaced by secular authority in a suitable modified parliamentary framework—a system composed of a network of roles reinforcing the parliamentary framework itself. If one deterrent to this outcome was charisma, as I suggested, so was its premature decline.

Two questions appear when the matter is put in this fashion. What is premature? Would any real threat to Nkrumah's authority have been defined as premature? Secondly, did charisma really decline? To answer the first we must consider the second.

Events moved very quickly after independence. The opposition attack on the government was sweeping and fundamental. Even in Nkrumah's own constituency the Ga Shifmo Kpee, a Ga nationalist movement, swept up large numbers of former C.P.P. zealots. By the summer of 1957 bitterly anti-Nkrumah groups could be found everywhere. In Ashanti the Ashanti Youth Association went over to the National Liberation Movement. Backbenchers of the C.P.P. threatened to bolt to the opposition. These and many other examples of the decline in charisma could be

---

[7] See J. L. Talmon, *The Origins of Totalitarian Democracy*. London: Secker and Warburg, 1955, *passim*. See also the remarkable discussion in Alexis de Tocqueville, *The European Revolution*. New York: Doubleday Anchor Books, 1959; and Karl Jaspers, *The Future of Mankind*. Chicago: The University of Chicago Press, 1961, particularly Chapter 6, "The End of Colonialism."

cited. In Ghana there was a recognizable drift away from charismatic authority back to traditional authority, the representatives of which called for decentralized parliamentary government. The chiefs used the "national" organization of the tribe to fight the C.P.P.

Perhaps this would have been a good solution to the problems of Ghana right after independence, but it is not very likely. Traditional authorities and their secularized representatives were not only divided along ethnic lines, they also had very little of a positive nature to offer the population. Essentially, their campaigns were against Nkrumah. Despite a small number of lawyers, educators, and civil servants, both in government and opposition, who accepted the basic values and roles of secular democracy, the reality behind the battle between parties and as well, as over constitutional forms (i.e. federalism and unitarism) was less in the spirit of constitutionalism than in a conflict of charismatic authority with traditional authority. These were the circumstances under which charisma began to decline. The C.P.P. defense of the unitary constitution was a way of preserving power for the party and for Nkrumah just when the latter's ability to manipulate the public was weakened. What was premature about this decline becomes clearly understood if one accepts the notion that the attachments of the people to their chiefs and the authority which the latter represented had not yet been replaced by an attachment to Nkrumah.[8]

However, even if charisma had been capable of shifting belief away from traditional authority, it does not follow, of course, that charisma would have disappeared in favor of democracy. Several years more of resident colonial authority standing outside both tradition and charisma might have helped, but I doubt it. The confrontation between tradition and charisma was inevitable.

The country remained parliamentary in form. In practice there was established a *mobilization system* which had as its object the

[8] Nkrumah's popularity was not at issue here. He remained a popular figure. But charisma implies the ability of a leader to transform public values. It is a rare, not a common, phenomenon. Hence charisma has declined before public values had been transformed away from tradition.

See D. E. Apter and R. A. Lystad, "Bureaucracy, Party and Constitutional Democracy," Carter and Brown (eds.), *Transition in Africa*. Boston: Boston University Press, 1958.

transformation of the society.[9] The mobilization system recognizes certain secular values—those dealing with equality, opportunity, and the unfolding of the individual personality in the context of the unfolding society—but it downgrades other secular values, such as individual liberty, popular representation, pluralism and the like. Within it, however, can be found many of the properties of the traditional system. It seems to me that Ghana politics makes little sense unless one appreciates that what occurred was a new relationship between traditional and secular politics in the *form* of the mobilization system. At the top of this system was a Presidential-monarch—a kind of chief.[10]

The Evaluative Propositions

I propose to take some of the general statements which were developed in the original study and examine some of their implications in the contemporary setting of Ghana politics. Ten have been selected. They fall into the following categories: (a) propositions about the "party of solidarity" as distinct from the "party of representation" (as these might be termed); (b) propositions about charisma and its significance for the development of secular government; (c) propositions about the rise of charisma and its

[9] Proponents of mobilization systems assume that division between men is due to unnatural causes: colonialism, neo-colonialism, classes derivative of objective differences in relation to property. Once these causes have been removed, then harmony in the political sphere will result. The charismatic leader reflects the "one" and underwrites the essential monistic quality of the system.

Mobilization systems begin by politicizing all social life. As a result, politics as such disappears. This is in keeping with monistic political belief. Conflict is not only regarded badly, it is counter-revolutionary, i.e. against the natural evolution of human society and thought. The counter-revolutionaries thus must be dealt with symbolically, since by injecting a political element into what becomes a non-political situation, they menace the legitimacy of the government and particularly authority of the leader.

Mobilization systems are characterized by what Durkheim called "repressive law." They are humorless regimes. Their model is an organic one. It is for these reasons that Marxian social theory appeals to them both for its organizational convenience, i.e. as a form of Leninism, and for the emphasis on modern forms of puritanism. Progress is its faith. Industrialization is its vision. Harmony is its goal. Political religion is most commonly found in the mobilization state. See Edward Shils, "The Concentration and Dispersion of Charisma: Their Bearing on Economic Policy in Underdeveloped Countries," in *World Politics,* XI, 1958.

[10] I put the matter this way, even though many will argue that Ghana is confusing enough without a complicated theoretical superstructure. However, without the latter, the confusion is easily glossed over. What is going on in Ghana is, in my view, a very profound political process. Too often the flamboyance of personality and political style appears to detract from the significance of the events.

relation to traditional authority; (d) hypotheses about the consequences of the decline of charisma in relation to the authoritarian potentiality of the C.P.P.

The propositions are as follows:

1. The C.P.P. formed the nucleus of a new society. This required the party to "generalize" itself into society. (p. 212)

2. The growth of Cabinet government during the last period of British rule prior to independence was dependent on charisma. How the cabinet and parliamentary government could be given independent popular support was the central question behind the problem of institutional transfer as defined. (pp. 9, 233)

3. Only after substantive issues of legitimacy have been fought out to the level of consensus is a sustained and institutional set of political roles possible. This emphasizes the unsubstantial nature of authority based on charisma, and implies a struggle over the nature of legitimacy, the resolution of which is a precondition of stable political structures. (p. 255)

4. To maintain Ghana as a political system—a unit within which political or predominantly political sub-structures serve as an action reference for the members, and as a decision-making set of organizations in such fashion as to prevent apathy or anarchy—institutional transfer deals with the integration of localized predominantly tribal sub-systems (composed of concrete membership units) into a national membership unit by using predominantly political structures. The acceleration of impact at the local level (which is disruptive of the traditional pattern of social organization) must be counterbalanced by the acceleration of integrational opportunities at the central level, and provide for a shift in public orientation from local to more general affiliations. (p. 273)

A new set of dynamic local institutions needs to be established which, without paralyzing local life, would provide for the acceptance of central government authority. The problem is not one of a simple changeover in affiliations from local to central authority however, because a chain-reaction is set off which requires government to provide an elaborate network of agencies and institutions to serve a more complex political situation.

5. Procedural integration on the level of central government had been achieved, but substantive integration of the significant

subgroups of the society around the norms and structures of secular democracy had not been achieved. Originally, this referred to the previously prevailing relationship of parties, voluntary associations, traditional ethnic and other groups with government. No philosophy of pluralism in relation to democracy and the representative principle emerged from these groups. (p. 289)

6. Some of the factors which were most crucial to the maintenance of traditional society were dysfunctional for the development and maintenance of secular society. (p. 290) This proposition had to be taken in two different contexts. First, it referred to the great difficulties placed in the way of secular political development by traditional societies which continued to play an important part in the social life of a country. Second, it referred to charisma as the functional equivalent of chieftaincy.

7. Charisma is initially dysfunctional to the maintenance of traditional systems of authority and initially eufunctional to the development of secular systems of authority. In the long run, however, maintenance of charismatic authority is dysfunctional to the maintenance of secular systems of authority. (p. 303)

8. Charisma in Ghana was a newly accepted source of legitimacy. It provided support for new types of social structures in keeping with the objectives of nationalism, meanwhile retaining subrelational aspects of the traditional system and integrating these aspects in different relational and behavioral modes permissible by Nkrumah's sanction. Out of this last it is possible for secular institutionalization to occur. (p. 303) On the whole this proposition was meaningful only during the last stages of colonialism. Perhaps it will be true in the very long run, when nationalism is itself more a memory and spent force than it is today. Events, however, proved this proposition wrong. The mixture of "subrelational" aspects of the traditional system quickly came in conflict with the party branches and auxiliaries run by Nkrumah. Conflict in Ashanti, local separatism, and demands for a federal constitution, were all evidence of this.

9. The efficiency of charisma lies in the fact that it satisfied the same functional requirements of leadership as did traditional leadership in the past. (p. 304) This meant: (a) that Nkrumah might have come to be regarded as a chief; (b) that people could easily be diverted from loyalty to Nkrumah and return to their

chiefs; or (c) that both would cancel each other out, hence, providing opportunities for secular democracy.

10. Within the polar extremes of anarchy and apathy within which political institutional transfer can take place are succeeding limited factors, including disenchantment with charisma premature to secularism, or repudiation of secularism as associated with charisma and/or imperialism.

Political efforts of the Nkrumah regime were to stimulate local activity and training through schools, party groups, and revised local administrations. There were, as well, virtually anarchic situations in Ashanti right after independence, leading to the break-up of the region into two (the Brong areas were formed into the new Brong-Ahafo region). Secular government had been brought into some contempt by the sometimes arbitrary use of parliamentary institutions and sometimes by the claim that new forms more in keeping with the African personality are necessary.

Following these ten prepositions were a set of inferences. I originally suggested that while a party acting as a social movement is essential in the development of a national consciousness, it cannot become a representative body or tolerate alternative parties. (p. 321) Either the party had to become invisible, i.e., blend with the state itself, or it had to monopolize political life within the state.

With all that has transpired in Ghana, if we ask whether or not the functions of charisma are needed for successful transfer of alien political institutions, the evidence is confused. Today the sources of alien values and practices include Soviet, Chinese, Israeli, and Yugoslavian models. Political institutional transfer has not ended. On the contrary its base is widened, undigested and more complex. No longer does the British model serve as the exclusive one. Given such institutional confusion, one might make the case that charisma is more essential than ever.

In the final discussion of the prospects for democracy, I pointed to the dangers to democracy inherent in charismatic government. One set of possibilities suggested was that either a new, more revolutionary movement would emerge from the C.P.P. or else there would be a revival of chieftaincy and religious groups. The latter did not occur. The government made it clear that religious politics would not be tolerated. It attacked the Muslim Association

Party, and more latterly the Christian churches which opposed the government on the matter of youth training and indoctrination. It was therefore not the church but the chiefs who struck back. As a result authoritarian elements in the C.P.P. emerged. Disorder and conflict in the immediate post-independence day period brought these to the fore, with the result that the structures of secular government were used in repressive acts. (pp. 316-17) Disorder followed, as I suggested it might, beginning with the effects of the 1954 Constitution which denied chieftaincy a central government medium of expression (such as an upper house), and drove it underground. The direct attacks on the political role of chiefs by the C.P.P. helped to polarize the issue between "revivalism" and "messianicism" as I suggested. (p. 319) Yet in 1957, despite all this, the prospects for parliament appeared quite good.

At the point of transition to independence, the ingredients of authority were shared between legislative bodies at the center based on British parliamentary practice, and local authorities. The latter, limited in scope, remained focal points for ethnic and traditional activity after 1954. Constitutional government in a popular parliamentary form did help provide a relatively smooth transition to independence. The development of electoral constituencies throughout the country, and the expansion of local and district councils also served to give point to party work so that the local, regional, and constituency parties had work to do at all levels of government. With opportunities opening up everywhere for new local cadres of leadership in government and party, a seedbed was laid from which sprouted a new political awareness and participation.

This was in turn reflected in wider opportunities to practice the arts of government in a local setting. Out of this came the new political recruits for higher office. The recruits brought with them a spirit of novelty and a willingness to experiment with government. This "potential elite" put heavy pressure on the central government with the result that many local organizations were altered and new ones created. Civil administration in the districts was changed. The Government Agent disappeared to be replaced by a District Commissioner, who was a political appointee and therefore a party man (Nkrumah's representative in the districts). The Chief Regional Officer, hitherto the senior administrative officer in a region, was replaced by the Regional Commissioner, a political appointee with ministerial rank. New groups appeared, sometimes political ones under administrative auspices like the Workers Brigades, or the newly remodeled Cooperative Movement under the control of the Farmers Council, a C.P.P. auxiliary group. Others were frankly political, such as the Young Pioneers which came to replace the Boy Scout Movement as the main youth organization of Ghana. Once these changes had been introduced, however, the result was revolution from above. Government took it upon itself to transform society in its own image, even if political leaders were unclear about what that image ought to be.

Institutional transfer did not disappear. It broadened its source, with a corresponding confusion and dislocation in political roles and the relationship between governmental groups. Socialism was to be an integrative ideology. But socialism even in its simplest form has many variants and in practice is an extremely complicated system.[11] As a result it failed to re-integrate Ghanaian society successfully.

Instead, local systems of social and political organization were revised and new party organizations established alongside and often in competition with the older ones. These not only sharpened antagonism, but often put cross-pressures on individuals, families, and friends. The result was increasing intervention by government in all aspects of life, whether land, law, custom, or community development, the use of leisure, and the rearing of children.

To prevent chaos, the party attempted to monopolize life within the state. By 1961 a one-party system was established with Nkrumah as the symbolic leader, the President, as well as the actual executive force. Although his charisma had declined sharply after 1954, he remained popular for a considerable period afterwards, partly because few could then see a positive alternative to his rule. Many had faith that he would have more discretion and wisdom than his immediate followers. Stability and control existed in the state and society, but a fluid political condition remained at the top which was characterized by manipulative politics. Yet the

---

11 Nkrumah's view is that "capitalism is too complicated a system for a newly independent nation. Hence the need for a socialistic system." See his book, *The Autobiography of Kwame Nkrumah.* Edinburgh: Thomas Nelson, 1959, p. vii.

roles established under British practice were by and large retained at the senior levels of government. Procedural integration continued in some measure as a result. Substantive integration was achieved by the ritualization of charisma into a peculiar mixture of socialism and neo-traditionalism. It was a uniquely Ghanaian blend and the new, non-charismatic role at the top took the form of a Presidential-monarch, increasingly backed by force.

Ghana After Independence

By 1958 political control was consolidated. Politics pervaded everything. The opposition was effectively smashed, partly because of its own ineptness and partly because in its reliance on traditional authorities it remained ethnically divided. The National Liberation Movement, demanding a federal constitution prior to independence, afterward continued with its demands in a situation of rising violence. To establish law and order the government was able to employ measures against the opposition in conjunction with local C.P.P. forces so that the organized opposition was obliterated.

However, opposition did not disappear. Many of the constituency and branch units of the C.P.P. now began to take on the characteristics of an opposition inside the party. As a result, the functional auxiliaries of the party, the T.U.C., the women's and farmers' associations, the youth movements, were built up at the expense of the regional, branch and constituency parties. These developments were accompanied by an increase in militant ideology and the effort to shape the meaning of African socialism under the name of Nkrumaism.

The civil service, and other outposts of resistance to the C.P.P., such as the University College, were brought into line in the first instance through obligatory membership in the T.U.C. The university was curbed through a slow series of steps culminating in termination of the University of London connection.

Nevertheless, the Civil Service continued to function well; so did the University under its vice-chancellor, Dr. Conor Cruise O'Brien. Efforts were made to establish C.P.P. groups in church congregations, to open Young Pioneer branches in all the schools. Achimota College, which resisted the Young Pioneers, was made a prime target for attack and its headmaster resigned to take a post with the United Nations. No potential centers of resistance to party control were left untouched.

Constitutional monarchy was changed to republicanism in a constitution which provided exceptional autonomy on the part of the first President, i.e., Nkrumah.

A series of bills, enacted to assist the government in dealing with opposition and subversive elements, eliminated many of the legal safeguards customary to Western legal practice, including special courts for treason and the suspension of *habeas corpus* for political crimes, whether committed or anticipated.

The unity of state, party and president more and more became the order of the day, culminating in parliamentary resolutions in favor of making Nkrumah the Life President of Ghana and to recognize Ghana officially as a single-party state.

Industrialization and development replaced independence as the basic political objective of party and state, to be pushed along the lines of a socialist-mixed economy (i.e., a mixture of government, cooperative and private enterprise).

An entirely new dimension was added by Ghana's role in foreign policy and pan-Africanism, with Ghana in a political position for the African independence movements analogous to that of U.S.S.R. and communism after the Russian revolution, i.e., independence in one country as a base for the liberation of other African territories.[12]

[12] The events which accompanied these major changes in the development of Ghana were often magnified in the press. Ghana underwent the most intensive political scrutiny which a developing area has had to bear. When people were put in prison for political "crimes" in Senegal or Ivory Coast, no one remarked this. When it happened in Ghana there was a worldwide public reaction. Ghana continues to have an interesting and special role in Africa. Not only was she the first to become independent, but the world continues to look to her as the model for all the rest of Africa. Richer than most, carefully groomed for independence, with trained cadres exceeding those of far larger countries, without racial minority problems, having inherited a good and expanding educational system, Ghana is regarded as having the resources, manpower, and moral and spiritual qualities to set the pace and tone of political development in all of Africa. That is one reason why there is a worldwide public opinion about Ghana as about no other African country.

It is also one reason why Ghana, although a small country, remains important. Unfair though this may be, Africa as a whole remains on trial in Ghana. If people become widely disillusioned with Ghana, it will be most unfortunate for Africa as a whole. Only respect and strength will prevent Africa from becoming a pawn in the cold war, to be manipulated and curried in half-hearted fashion. The blunt fact is that unless Africa is important to the West in moral as well as political terms it will become pretty much irrelevant to westerners, whose phenomenal growth and

Three main trends emerged after independence. The first was characteristic of new nations generally, the "politicization" of the country. Every aspect of social life now took on a political value: marriage, land, tradition, schools, or development. A second related to the first showed the political re-socialization of the population. Thus the emphasis on ideology, socialism, political obligation, and civic responsibility. A conscious political program, at times indistinguishable from indoctrination, was carried on by party organs, trade unions, youth movements, and other organized voluntary associations, not to speak of churches, schools and universities.

A third characteristic, prompting political re-socialization, was caused by the "premature" decline in the charisma of Nkrumah. Charismatic leaders can ritualize their offices and by this mean traditionalize them, or they can establish alternative and substitute mechanisms of government such as those represented by parliamentary government. Caught in a maze of organizational politics after independence, with local and ethnic sectionalism, party factionalism, not to speak of personal conflict within the bureaucracy of the party, Nkrumah became less a source of charisma than a party manager, holding one group at bay, pacifying another, threatening still a third. Finally the "ritual" aspects of his role, which before independence were located in the party, were now transferred to the state. It was not surprising that a republican solution was formed. The formal and symbolic qualities of Nkrumah's role could clearly not be ritualized when shared with a Governor-General. The Ghanaian form of republican and parliamentary government provided for an active political manager, while "ritualizing" the role of national leader.

Patterns of Political Change

With this discussion of events and propositions in mind we can now turn to the evolution of party and government in Ghana to

---

development since 1952 trivialized "decolonization," at least in their own minds. Europe has also become independent of Africa! A danger then is that Africa's main relevance to the West will be a sentimental one, or possibly a negative one— preventing Africa from moving into the Soviet orbit. Such a situation would be sad with divisive implications within the sub-continent. Tweaking the lion's tail is only useful when it is attached to the lion. Once the tail is detached, the lion licks the wound a bit and bounds away, but he who holds only the tail finds it a useless instrument. It is not even a good whip.

see if they substantiate the more general theories about authority put forward in this book.

The party as society

Stephen Dzirasa, the former Resident Minister of Ghana in Guinea, and subsequently Deputy Minister of Foreign affairs, explicitly pointed to the C.P.P. as a moral instrument. He regarded religion and politics as "God's ordained instruments of moral and social adjustment always at work bringing into being a new world in which all men shall dwell together. . . ."[13] This view brought him into party politics and a political career. If his pamphlet is not distinguished for its intellectual contributions, it nevertheless represented views commonly held among party men. To belong to the party was to identify with a new society in which all virtue could be realized.

However much the moral dimension of the party needed to be realized, the concrete role of a party needs to be tactical and practical. As defined by George Padmore: "The C.P.P. has not only to explain the Government's policy and plan to the masses, it has the task, above all, to mobilize the support of its main allies, the T.U.C. and the United Ghana Farmers Council, the youth and the working women to back the economic revolution at which we are aiming, just as they did in carrying through the national revolution which has brought us independence. Both revolutions —the National Revolution and the Economic Revolution—are interrelated, the second being dependent on the first. . . .

"The Colonialists, having been forced to concede the political power which automatically gives them control over the economic resources of our country, are concentrating upon the economic counter-revolution in an effort to restore their absolute control over us by economic means. It is for us, therefore, not only to be vigilant but to reinforce our strength by building up our economy on a socialist basis, firmly keeping under State control the basic means of production."[14]

The most central role of the party in independent Ghana was

[13] See Stephen Dzirasa, *Political Thought of Kwame Nkrumah*. Accra: Guinea Press, n.d.

[14] See George Padmore, *A Guide to Pan-African Socialism, A Socialist Program for Africa*, printed in William H. Friedland and Carl G. Rosberg (eds.), *African Socialism* (Stanford: Stanford Univ. Press, 1964), pp. 223-237.

an economic one. However, from the point of view of building a socialist society, all other social relations come to depend on the new economic relations to be established. Hence the party becomes the crucible for forging new patterns of social behavior, associations, and attitudes. From this follows the central role of the party in society and the oft-quoted remark made by Nkrumah that "the party and the nation are one and the same, namely: the Convention People's Party is Ghana and Ghana is the Convention People's Party."[15]

Although the C.P.P. effectively consolidated its power and tried to live up to Padmore's conception of its role, this does not mean that it was successful. The opposition, fragmented though it was, became increasingly embittered at what was clearly the issue of survival. Shortly after independence it appeared as if civil war would break out, particularly in Ashanti. For a time few C.P.P. political leaders dared appear in Kumasi. The opposition tapped deep wellsprings of feeling. The National Liberation Movement had been formed in 1954 under the patronage of the Asantehene and with the support of the Asanteman Council. Its chairman, Bafour Osei Akoto was a prominent cocoa farmer and the Asantehene's chief linguist. It was claimed that the N.L.M. was a national movement of Ashantis, not a political party. Similarly in the case of other ethnic parties.[16]

In October, 1957, a United Party was finally formed. The United Party had considerable voting strength. The traditional forms of social organization were a kind of "natural" mechanism for mobilizing voters in the rural areas. Traditional government was thus a ready-made party machinery, which had been falling into disuse. Moreover, it was a relatively inexpensive machinery. It could utilize traditional methods to maintain solidarity. Hence many of the opposition parties which combined in a coalition in the United Party, were in reality also social units posed against

[15] See Kwame Nkrumah, "A Message on the Twelfth Anniversary of the Convention People's Party, June 12, 1961" (Accra: Government Printer, 1961), p. 1.

[16] Many attempts were made to unite such ethnic groupings. In 1954 a Volta Charter was prepared which was to have united the Togoland Congress, the Ghana Nationalist Party, the Ghana Action Party, the Gold Coast Muslim Association Party, the All Ewe Conference, and the Ghana Congress Party. The representatives of the parties could not agree on even minimal terms of association and the Charter was stillborn.

the C.P.P. Their strength as well as their weakness was thus in their localism.

How strong sentiment was for these groups is indicated in the 1956 election, the so-called independence election. Despite a full-throated campaign by the C.P.P. the opposition received 299,000 votes while the C.P.P. received 398,000. Moreover, the opposition was centered in key areas such as Ashanti, the richest cocoa-growing areas of the country. With Ashanti nationalism success-ful all the other separatist groupings in the country would also have been stimulated.

It was thus not too surprising that government and party, combined, should mount a joint attack on the opposition. This attack took many forms. Leading members of the N.L.M. party executive were implicated in a plot on Nkrumah's life. Dr. K. A. Busia became Ghana's first major political exile. The parliamen-tary party organization was smashed, with so many former opposition members crossing the floor that the government, wish-ing for the moment to avoid the appearance of a one-party state, refused to accept any more.[17] Punitive legislation was set up under which opposition leaders were exiled, jailed, or intimidated. Altera-tion was made in the character of agricultural marketing boards. Perhaps most important of all, a modification in the structure of local government was made so that local authorities no longer conformed to the old State Council (Oman) jurisdictions. The one-third traditional members were removed from the local councils; government agents were replaced by political party representatives known as district commissioners. The local coun-cils were regrouped into more adequate population centers and resource clusters in favor of more rational resource potentials. The country was divided into eight regions instead of the previous four with Ashanti divided into two by the creation of a Brong-Ahafo Region.[18]

The revision of the older pattern of local government, while logical and necessary from the point of view of more efficient local government, also served the political end (as did the earlier

---

[17] Cited in Donald S. Rothchild, "On the Application of the Westminster Model to Ghana," *The Centennial Review*, Vol. IV, No. 4, 1960, p. 473.

[18] See the Greenwood Report (Accra, Government Printer, 1957); see also A. F. Greenwood, "Ten Years of Local Government in Ghana," in *Journal of Administration Overseas*.

ordinance in 1951) of dismantling local opposition organization where these were centered in traditional organization and the power of the chiefs. To do this required a strong build-up of party strength.

In order to strengthen its national position to accord with its larger social objectives, the C.P.P. went through major re-organizations after 1957. These occurred in three stages.

The strengthening of the regional, branch and constituency organizations

This first phase of the development of the C.P.P. was merely an extension of the organizational work which had already been underway. Regional organizations were, particularly in Accra and Kumasi, the nerve centers of the party, reaching out to the local areas where pockets of resistance were to be found. The party directives of this time had a military flavor about them. Certain strongholds were to be "attacked," key individuals to be "removed," etc. The local branches carried the "battle" against tribalism, feudalism, and reaction, and other aspects of neo-colonialism. The opposition was the "enemy" to be ruthlessly "eradicated." The constituency parties were to make sure that every electoral "campaign" was completely successful, and for this they were provided with "ammunition." The entire press was mobilized at Government expense in favor of the C.P.P. The only opposition newspaper, the *Ashanti Pioneer* was censored, gradually curbed and became a government supporter.

This first post-independence day phase of party organization ended in 1959 when the rout of the opposition was virtually complete. In 1960 a plebiscite over republican status offered the voters a choice between continuing the system of constitutional monarchy or adopting a republic (and voting for Nkrumah or J. B. Danquah as first president). The pro-republic vote was 1,008,740 to 131,425 against.[19] The opposition, with many of its leaders in jail, was impotent. The victory was so complete that in some of the local branches, the Ashanti regional organization

---

[19] Nkrumah received 1,016,076 votes against Danquah's 124,623. A year and a half later the latter found himself in jail on Preventive Detention. He was released to be elected President of the Ghana Bar Association, and subsequently imprisoned once again, to die, tragically enough, in jail.

of the C.P.P. began to take over grievances which hitherto had been the hallmark of the opposition. Local factionalism in the party resulted. Opportunism, and a breakdown in party discipline, threatened the party from within. Having won its battles with opposition the enemies now appeared within the ranks rather than outside the party.

The building up of the party auxiliaries

To counteract these separatist and opportunistic tendencies in the party, the party auxiliaries were now built up at the expense of the local organizations. The state was a republic. The party had to be rebuilt. Moreover, the auxiliaries were to be representative of the new organizations of society. Not local branches of Ashanti, or Fanti, or Ewe, or Strangers, but farmers, workers, youth. Not local women's organizations fitting into the older forms of political and social life of a locality, but C.P.P. women concerned with national problems.

The building up of the party's auxiliaries was thus designed to have two effects, namely to reconstruct the significant groupings in the society along lines conducive to and representative of modern economic growth, modern education and national discipline. As well, the auxiliaries were a new counterpoise, taking local strength at the regional, branch, and constituency organizations.

The first auxiliary to be put in this central position was the T.U.C. Its ties with the International Confederation of Free Trade Unions were broken. Its internal structure was revised by statute, the number of unions reduced, automatic check-off introduced, and the national executive strengthened. Its leader, J. Tettegah, was made an Ambassador Extraordinary and Minister Plenipotentiary with offices in the splendid new building of the C.P.P.

The second auxiliary to be strengthened was the cooperative movement. The farmers had attacked the Cocoa Purchasing Commission, and the Cocoa Marketing Board. The cooperatives were charged with mismanagement and corruption. Eventually the C.P.P. abolished the Boards and many of the cooperatives, but their first response to attack was to eliminate the National Farmers Union (an opposition group) and constitute the United

Ghana Farmers Council. A new cooperative movement was set up
under the U.G.F.C. and its leader, Mr. Martin Appiah-Danquah,
was also made an Ambassador Extraordinary and Minister
Plenipotentiary.

The third auxiliary was the youth organization. The Young
Pioneers were established under a national organizer (Z. B.
Shardow). The Boy Scout movement dwindled in membership to
a few thousand although it was not abolished.[20]

It is of some interest that when the Bishop of Accra objected
to indoctrination in the Young Pioneers during a speech, he was
forced to leave the country.[21]

[20] The aims of the Ghana Young Pioneers were as follows: "To train the mind,
the body, and soul of the youth of Ghana; to train them to be up to their civic
responsibilities so as to fulfill their patriotic duties; to train their technical skills
according to their talents; to foster the spirit of voluntaryism, love, and devotion
to the welfare of the Ghana nation; to inculcate into the youth, "Nkrumaism"—
ideals of African personality, and economic reconstruction of Ghana and Africa
in particular, and the world in general." The pledge reads as follows: "In the
cause of Ghana and Africa we are ever ready. We sincerely promise to live by
the ideals of Osagyefo Kwame Nkrumah, Founder of the State of Ghana, initiator
of the African personality.

"To safeguard by all means possible, the independence sovereignty and territorial
integrity of the State of Ghana from internal and external aggression.

"To be always in the vanguard for the social and economic reconstruction of
Ghana and Africa.

"To be in the first ranks of men fighting for the total liberation and unity of
Africa, for these are the noble aims guiding the Ghana Young Pioneers.

"As a Young Pioneer, we will be a guard of workers, farmers, cooperators and
all other sections of our community." See *Nkrumah Youth*, Vol. No. 1, November
1961, p. 7.

[21] Although there was considerable discussion of this issue in Ghana, the following letter was perhaps the clearest statement of pro-government views:

"Perhaps, it might serve a good purpose to explain that in all countries aspiring
to achieve socialism, political indoctrination is the best form of education. If the
masses are not indoctrinated how can they cast their votes and serve the Government loyally? For the Bishop to maintain that Ghana has been tramping on free
speech is really confusing. Let us remind ourselves that there is a limit to any
allowance. If a country allows freedom of speech, that does not infer that any
sane person can just mount a platform or pulpit and vilify the Government in a
way likely to incite the people to act violently.

"Why should not the Government of Ghana be ruthless, when ruthless people are
aiming at overthrowing it by bombs? Africa needs strong governments. Ghana is
not the only country that is getting tough. In Nigeria, the Opposition are in trouble.
In Tanganyika there is the new detention act, while in Sierra Leone, the first
deportations were made recently.

"Nobody doubts that the peace of the world hangs on the spin of a coin. I
think the Bishop could help mankind by trying to pontificate on world problems,
thus, helping to put an end to the nuclear race, rather than engaging in internal
politics which is perilous at this stage when Africa is full of unknown enemies."
See *West Africa*, October 13, 1962. Letter by Kwesi Yalley.

Perhaps the new emphasis on youth was the most important feature of the reorganization of Ghana. If social life was to become disciplined, then it was with the youth that such discipline must begin. It is easy to see in this more than mass methods of education, but doctrine as well. This was particularly so since the oath of the Young Pioneers deified Nkrumah. There was, of course, a rationale behind it in addition to indoctrination. If modernization was to affect the population along the lines of a militant mobilization system, then the need for managerial personnel became immense. The educational system on which this managerial system was to be based was expanding rapidly and showed the signs of rapid growth. Quality of work was uneven. Many schools were inadequately staffed. The impact of education was often less than it should have been. Movements such as the Young Pioneers served the purpose of raising the level of motivation and aspiration among the youth, and making the contact with modernity by a total immersion in new associations which had a training side as well as an ideological one. That such a system would stifle local initiative and managerial capacity was not foreseen.

Nor were the objectives too different with regard to the women. Women's organizations were affiliated with the Council of Ghana Women. The women were exceptionally well organized in Ghana in local organizations including dance societies, lending and thrift societies, marketing associations, and the like. The women's organizations were singled out for special ideological treatment particularly in a system where so much of the education of the youth rests with the mother. As well, it is the women who are the hard core of the consumer goods distribution system. The market women could paralyze the major towns and cities by closing their markets. If they should associate with a key transport group like the lorry drivers, they could paralyze Accra (as they once nearly did in strike called over third-party risk insurance).

These new elites were to be served by an ideological center to create a philosophy to be carried to the schools through the Young People's League and the Young Pioneers, to the women through the Council of Ghana Women, to the civil servants and workers through the T.U.C., and to the farmers through the United Ghana Farmers Council, and finally to the University by NASSO (until the dissolution of the latter).[22]

The point is clear. The party built its regional, branch and constituency organs as the backbone of the party. These were to win electoral victories and secure C.P.P. government in the local governments as well as the central government. Once the opposition had been more or less smashed, the regional branch and constituency organizations began to change their character. Discipline for winning elections gave way to a desire for an accommodation and reconciliation with those formerly associated with opposition. Families wanted to repair long-standing breaches. C.P.P. stalwarts wanted better relations with chiefs. Particularly in those areas where conflict had been most bitter, the traditional forms of healing splits, from kinship and lineage association to Asafu Companies, worked to restore balance and health to the community. Rather than militant organs of revolution, the branches became opportunistic and friendly. Moreover the "right wing" of the party, which both in the National Assembly and in the party organizational hierarchy had roots in the local branches, formed the largest part of the party as such, and with the new relaxation in the branches they were a dead weight pulling back the socialist militants in the auxiliaries. The party then became ready for overhauling.[23]

*The reorganization of the party in the new
party structure*

Overhauling the party to counteract the conservatism of the rural rank and file and to purge the party of its opportunists became an important political object after the Republic was established. The new structure established a closer link between

[22] The University of Ghana nevertheless remained constituted substantially along much the same lines as before, even after severing its London connection. Some important new developments were long overdue. An institute of African studies was set up. Thomas Hodgkin, one of the most distinguished scholars in the African field, served as Director of the African Institute. Meanwhile, the former Kumasi College of Technology became the Kwame Nkrumah University of Science and Technology, and a new University College of Cape Coast was opened.

[23] For a full statement of the party program see *Program of the Convention People's Party for Work and Happiness* (Accra: Government Printing Dept., 1962).

the party and its affiliate bodies. The auxiliaries now were given representation on the National Executive. As such they were able to participate in the Central Committee, the most significant policy-making group of the C.P.P.

The party bureaucracy was also strengthened. Nkrumah, in addition to being Life Chairman of the party, also became General Secretary. The National Secretariat expanded. The socialist militants were particularly strong in the Secretariat, which now had the following composition: the General Secretary, Administrative Secretary, Bureau of Information and Publicity, African and International Affairs, Local Government, Functions, Education and Anti-Corruption, National Propaganda, Youth, Finance, Women Organizations, Membership, Trade Unions, Cooperatives and Farmers, Disciplinary Control, and a Director of Ideological Studies.

It was with the National Secretariat that much of the task of "social reconstruction" of the society rested. Moreover the National Secretariat, composed of paid officials, was the central body to which the Branch, Regional, and Constituency secretaries reported. It was the link between the Central Committee and the National Executive, on the one hand, and the local party administration, on the other. The day-to-day conduct of political affairs rested with the party administration.[24]

In tightening up the party, ideology was applied to organizational reform. The chief ideological organ was *The Party*, which laid down the principal line for the party to follow (though it scarcely obtained for itself the central position which *L'Essor* occupied in Mali). As militant was the pan-Africanist organ, the *Voice of Africa*, published in English and French by the party's Bureau of African Affairs. *Ghana Labour* linked the T.U.C. with the ideological line of the party and exhorted the trade unionists to exercise their vigilance in building a socialist Ghana and to work harder. *The Co-operator* did the same for the Cooperative movement. Its editor was Dorothy Padmore, the wife of the late George Padmore. *Nkrumah Youth* was the official organ of the Ghana Young Pioneers. In addition, a steady stream of government publications reported the President's speeches

24 See "The New Party Structure," in *The Party*, Vol. 1, No. 1.

while the most widely read newspapers were directly under party auspices or relatively non-political in their emphasis.[25]

The general reorganization of the party brought the social militants into a very strong position. They formed the intellectual backbone of the party. Leaders drawn from these top cadres formed C.P.P. study circles in Marxian theory. (Some took place at Flagstaff House, the residence of the President.) The socialist militants tried to work out ideological differences between themselves to define more adequately the meaning of socialism in the context of Ghana. Many sought a new ideological devotion, a faith so strong that it would prevent corruption and increase public energies. Under the prompting of the socialist militants, Nkrumah made his famous "dawn" broadcast in April 1961 in which he threatened dire penalties for corruption. Perhaps the greatest victory of the socialist militants was in forcing Nkrumah to part company with his two most important colleagues in the party and government. Both Gbedemah, who although a "rightist" had for long flirted with the militant left without taking up leadership among them, and Botsio, whose personal following was never very great, were removed from their posts and thrown out of the party.[26]

The reorganization of the party gave the socialist militants exceptional opportunities. It also caused a split in their ranks. This split found the social militants divided between what could be called the "moderates" and the "puritans." The moderates were far more opportunistic and personally more politically ambitious. Some of these were removed by Nkrumah and put in

[25] The "Socialist puritans" included among themselves Charles Heymans, Secretary of African Affairs in the T.U.C.; C. A. Addison, Administrative Secretary of the All-African Peoples Conference and supervisor of Radio Ghana; Kofi Batsa, the editor of *Voice of Ghana;* T. D. Baffoe, editor of the *Ghanaian Times;* Eric Heymans, editor of the *Evening News;* Kwaku Boateng, Minister of Interior; Z. B. Shardow, National Organizer, Young Pioneers; Kwaku Acquei, Ideological Secretary of the C.P.P.; A. M. Quaye, Rector, Kwame Nkrumah Ideological Institute; George Magnus, Deputy Secretary-General of the T.UC. and former High Commissioner to Nigeria; and Deputy Governor of the Bank of Ghana, Kwasi Amoako-Atta.
[26] Party purges and attacks have so weakened the C.P.P. that there are few on whom Nkrumah could rely for efficient and sensible administration and government. He asked Gbedemah to return but was rejected. Gbedemah wrote an attack on Nkrumah and the party program, "For Work and Happiness." See K. A. Gbedemah, *It Will Not Be Work and Happiness for All, An Open Letter* (1962, n.p.).

jail under Preventive Detention, the two most important being Tawia Adamafio and Ako Adjei, the former Minister of Foreign Affairs. But when the puritans became too powerful the study groups were dissolved, NASSO (the National Association of Socialist Students Organization) disbanded, and the power of the puritans at least temporarily checked.[27] The general trend in the party was, however, clear enough. A buildup of the party membership was followed by its reorganization. The reorganization raised the new auxiliaries to the status of party nucleus. The party itself represented national "discipline."

Nkrumah's comments are interesting here. After describing the various auxiliaries, he says that what is basic to them is membership in the party. "Whatever they do, the character of the Convention People's Party must be clearly manifested for all to see. They all have a single guiding light, the guiding light of our Party ideology. This light must constantly be kept bright and full of luster and must on no account be allowed to dim, for, as soon as this happens, we are bound to find ourselves in difficulties.

"Let all Comrades remember, whether we be Trade Unionists, whether we be Farmers, whether we be members of the Women's Council or the Young Pioneers, that the dominant character which should take precedence in all that we do is the character of the membership of the Convention People's Party. *This character is the guiding force of our Ghanaian life and existence and constitutes the bulwark against national treachery, intrigue, subversion, and other un-Ghanaian activities* (my italics).

"The next category of Party organization includes the Workers' Brigade and the State Construction Workers, which also indirectly but nonetheless effectively, bolster the Party structure. Why shouldn't the workers of the State, who are composed mainly of the laborer group, be put into uniform? This would give them an added incentive to serve the State, a reason to feel proud of their service and a sense of belonging. . . .

"The Asafu Companies also, the members of which are almost all members of the Party individually, will come within this category. *They should be properly uniformed and perform their traditional role in a modern manner* (my italics).

[27] See Kwame Nkrumah, "Guide to Party Action," Accra: Government Printer, 1962.

"Another group of workers whom we now call 'Watchmen' will have a new orientation and come under this category. And why shouldn't they also be dressed in a smart uniform and be renamed 'Civil Guards'?

"All this will lead to one useful result—discipline. *The whole nation from the President downwards will form one regiment of disciplined citizens* (my italics). In this way, we shall move forward with great confidence, stepping ahead ever firmly with a keen sense of purpose and direction."[28]

There is, of course, a great difference between theory and practice, between ideology and action, and between rhetoric and meaning. Ideology in Ghana lacked the conviction which obtained for it in Guinea or Mali, her erstwhile political partners.[29] Ideology did not prevent intrigue between the socialist moderates and the socialist puritans. The latter divided between the socialist militants and the socialist opportunists. The socialist opportunists were down-graded. Some of them were put in jail. Moreover, the exceptional position of the functional auxiliary organizations was, once again, offset by building up the constituency parties as a check on the functional bodies. In place of the study groups, NASSO, a new group was developed. These were the Party Vanguard Activists. The PVA's functions were as follows: (a) perpetual preparedness in the service of the party; (b) maintenance, propagation and defense of the party, its aims, objects and purposes; (c) maintenance of eternal vigilance within the party. They were similar to the *Brigades de Vigilance* in Mali. The reasons for their organization were given in the new party constitution.

"The Convention People's Party has developed from a small organization to a nationwide mass movement which embraces within its ranks and among its sympathizers the overwhelming majority of the nation. As a consequence of the phenomenal growth of the Party, the politically conscious leadership is faced with the danger of being swamped by tribal, regional and other communal ideological influences which are penetrating the ranks of the more backward Party membership.

28 *Ibid.*, pp. 7-8.
29 See *The Charter of the Union of African States, Ghana, Guinea, Mali.*

"These dangers are some of the biggest which other national movements have had to face after the attainment of independence. Defections in our moral standards divorce us from the masses, who look up to our Party not only for the political leadership which it gives, but as an example to set them correct standards for building up an egalitarian society in the new Ghana. To combat ideological menace and factional rivalries, the Party will adopt certain inner organizational measures to safeguard its socialist aims and unity of program during every phase of the post-independence period of national reconstruction.

"To achieve 'ideological purity,' emphasis must be placed upon quality rather than quantity. Quantity has been achieved by the nationwide following which the Party enjoys. What is needed is quality personnel: the Party needs a vanguard of consciously dedicated activists and propagandists ideologically trained."[30]

The Vanguard Activists were to attend and graduate from the Party School, to be directly responsible to the Central Committee of the party and serve as the educators of the public. Their role was to be equivalent to members of the Communist Party in a communist system including agitational and organizational work, recruitment of new members, formation of study circles, leading self-criticism sessions, leading the struggle against political opponents of the party, and in general the Party Vanguard Activists were to be the "eyes and ears" of the Party.[31]

Despite the new emphasis on discipline, unity, and the new ideological cadres such as the Vanguard Activists, Nkrumah was never able to fasten down discipline upon the state. If anything, people talked more freely than ever before. The ease with which the public translated stern political directives into something quite different from what their founders intended was a superb Ghanaian talent which drove the socialist puritans to distraction.

30 See *The Constitution of the Convention People's Party* (Accra: Guinea Press, Revised, 1962), Part 4, p. 22.

31 *Ibid.*, p. 24. The oath of the Vanguard Activists was as follows: "I solemnly swear true allegiance to the person and office of the Leader and Life Chairman of the Convention People's Party, and promise solemnly always to obey and abide by the rules and regulations of the Party; and I shall at all times, in duty bound, observe all commands of the Central Committee of the Convention People's Party." It might also be noted that in addition all party members took an oath to be faithful and loyal to the party and to its "Leader, Comrade Osagyefo Dr. Kwame Nkrumah."

Indeed, Africans from Mali or Guinea on more than one occasion commented on how much wider the disparity between rhetoric and action political life was in Ghana than in their own countries. An openness of outlook, and much of that fundamental pragmatism which characterized the C.P.P. from the start remained. But there was no doubt where the party stood in the state. In August 1962, motions were tabled in the National Assembly to proclaim Nkrumah Life President, with Ghana to be made a People's Democracy with a single party system. In his speech to the National Assembly, Nkrumah rejected the first and supported the second. Thanking the Parliament for its congratulatory message after his narrow escape from a bomb-throwing at Kulungugu in Northern Ghana on August 1, 1962, Nkrumah said, "I thank you, Mr. Speaker, Members of the National Assembly, for your motion which is a mark of the confidence you have in me, and a unanimous expression of solidarity behind my person and office. I would, however, remind you, Mr. Speaker, that we have adopted a People's Democracy in which the sovereign will of the people is exercised through Parliament, a President and a Party. We are guided by a unique Republican Constitution which states quite clearly that elections for the office of President shall be held once every five years.

"It is essential that the people shall freely exercise their sacred right and duty of self-expression through voting; that once every five years they shall have the opportunity to renew their faith and confidence in the Party and its leader.

"Therefore, while I thank the House for the faith and solidarity expressed in the motion to confer a life Presidency on me, I submit, and most humbly, that the most conclusive way to demonstrate this singular support and confidence is by securing the return of me and my Party, the Convention People's Party, to power at the five yearly elections of Parliament. The objective which you sought in your motion can be attained if the nation does this."[32] The people shall vote—for Nkrumah.

Ghana As a People's Democracy

If Ghana became a People's Democracy the form of it was distinctively her own. A Soviet-style People's Democracy is

[32] *The Ghanaian Times,* October 3, 1962, p. 4.

technically distinguishable from a communist state. A People's Democracy is a "mixed system" which, as in the case of Eastern Germany or Poland, "tolerates" several parties although one is obviously in control. It allows greater economic diversity and particularly broader categories of private property and enterprise. People's democracies are socialist and therefore, in theory at least, less communist. Technically, too, People's Democracies are a stage in the fuller development of socialism and therefore in transition to a communist state.

Ghana did not, however, follow "theory" with "practice." Her institutions were still a curious blend of alien and new through which she sought her political personality. In the Republic, Nkrumah had the title of Osagyefo the President. The constitution was itself a continuation of the parliamentary system. Ironically enough, if one were to look for formal parallels in Europe, the constitution which most resembled Ghana's was that of De Gaulle prior to the September referendum on a popularly elected president.

The alteration of government

In their excellent analysis of the constitution and government of Ghana, Rubin and Murray remarked that the constitution was not ratified by popular vote. Rather a draft was approved in a plebiscite in April 1960 binding the government to carry out the main provisions of the constitutions along the lines approved in the plebiscite. However, a number of changes introduced after the plebiscite raised the question of the validity of the constitution itself, since key provisions inserted afterward and not specifically approved by the public substantially altered the meaning and construction of the constitution itself. As Rubin and Murray pointed out, "On the one hand, there are provisions which, though embodied in the Constitution, cannot be said *in fact* to have been put to the people *at all*. On the other hand, in the case of provisions contained in the draft Constitution but absent from the Constitution, their omission cannot be said to have been passed upon by the people."[33]

The most important discrepancies between the draft constitu-

---

[33] See Rubin and Murray, *The Constitution and Government of Ghana*, London: Sweet and Maxwell, 1961, p. 16; Chapter 2 has detailed comparison of the draft constitution approved by the people and the final constitution enacted.

tion and the final document raised questions about the validity of the constitution. Article 20 of the constitution clearly laid down the principle of parliamentary sovereignty along the lines of the British system. Article 55 expressly contravened the principle for the first President of Ghana. "Notwithstanding anything in Article Twenty of the Constitution, the person appointed as first President of Ghana shall have, during his initial period of office, the powers conferred on him by this Article." Among the powers granted was the provision for the first President to "give directions by legislative instrument" if he considered it in the national interest. And, to make sure that the initial period was not restricted to the first five-year term in office, "For the purpose of this Article the first President's initial period of office shall be taken to continue until some other person assumes office as President."[34] Since Ghana had become a single-party system, and the President was to be elected in future by the Parliament, it was unlikely that the first President of Ghana would have ever been voted out of office.

The first republican constitution was an ingenious document which recognized in law what existed in fact, i.e., the need for strong government in Ghana. On the other hand, it also contained democratic values which, although not entrenched as legal *rights*, were recognized as important. The *spirit* of the constitution was democratic, and while it had no bill of rights, its "fundamental principles" included the following: that the powers of government spring from the will of the people, that freedom and justice should be maintained, that the Union of Africa should be striven for as in Guinea and Mali; there was provision for a sharing of sovereignty in the interests of African unity. As well, there were principles laid down against discrimination on grounds of sex, tribe, religion, or political belief, and for the preservation of chieftaincy, the nation of fair shares in the proceeds of development, and against unnecessary restrictions on freedom of religion, speech, assembly, access to the courts, and deprivation of property except as dictated by the public interest. The President, on taking office, swore an oath to uphold these principles.[35]

[34] See Part X, Article 55, Constitution of Ghana, *op. cit.*, Special Powers for First President.
[35] See *Ibid.*, Article 13.

These remained principles. The President could not be impeached for violation of the oath, and the principles were not enforceable in the courts. The President could ensure their observance or not, depending upon his inclination.

The ambiguity of the constitution was perhaps a good reflection of the genuinely mixed feelings maintained by members of government toward Western democracy, and as well, wider segments of the population. To a very large extent the Constitution was a compromise between genuine representative government, and a desire to strengthen the sense of national purpose and unity by mobilizing the resource of the entire community for development. It clearly allowed Nkrumah to continue on in his role, but this peculiar Presidential-Monarchy role which Nkrumah established for himself was not to extend to his successors.

At the same time every effort was made to restrict the activities of those who might oppose the regime. Punitive legislation in this regard became unnecessarily restrictive.[36]

Hence the usual guarantees of limited government and a liberal constitution were embedded in the theory of the constitution, while they remained uncertain in their practice. The pull of other principles rooted in the party became dominant. These treated the state and the society as an organic community forged in a heritage of racial discrimination and colonialism and seeking radical transformation in human personality. The emphasis was on loyalty and unity rather than individualism or localism.[37]

[36] In July 1958 the Preventive Detention Act provided for imprisonment for up to five years without trial. The investigations of Crimes Act, 1958, broadened the Attorney-General's authority to compel any subject to supply information where crimes against the state were involved. The Offenses Against the State Act, 1959, gave judges the authority to sentence up to fifteen years persons convicted of making false reports about Ghana. The Sedition Bill of 1960 provided for imprisonment for up to fifteen years of persons found guilty of intentionally exhorting the overthrow of the government by illegal means or inciting contempt of the government or judicial branch. The Criminal Procedures Act of 1961 provided for Special Courts to enact the death penalty for political crimes without trial by jury. The Emergency Powers Act of 1961 gave the President the right to declare a state of emergency by legislative instrument and with the approval of the Cabinet. In 1962, after the attempts on Nkrumah's life, emergency regulations came into force which, among other things, suspended habeas corpus (see The Criminal Code (Amendment) (No. 2) Act, 1962, 20th September 1962).

[37] The habit of writing constitutions, especially by those trained in the Western legal tradition, encourages the incorporation of individual rights and safeguards,

The interest of the militants was in maintaining solidarity and cohesion in the society. They intended to make such cohesion a joint concern of party and state. The leaders of both were in effect *political entrepreneurs* using political power to mobilize and transform the conditions of material life, to develop the country, and to reach out to other African nations in some form of association.[38] Political power was used also for economic ends. Emphasizing a kind of economic solidarity, Ghanaian socialism or Nkrumaism was a blend of moral values which emphasized many of the puritan qualities: thrift, hard work, honesty, sacrifice, devotion to duty. It was, in addition, a doctrine of state enterprise in which political leaders used the state and the resources of the community both for development and in increasing measure, ownership.

These objectives extended to all aspects of the internal economic and also well into pan-African affairs. Domestically a five-sector economy was called for which included: (a) state enterprises; (b) enterprises owned by foreign private interests; (c) enterprises jointly owned by the State and foreign private interests; (d) cooperatives; (e) small-scale Ghanaian private enterprises. That private enterprise on a large scale should be foreign rather than Ghanaian, and acceptable only with a first option by Ghana to buy, was an indication that private enterprise was acceptable as long as it was expedient. The long term objective was a socialist society, linked to other African countries in an African common market.

Nor was this restricted to the industrial sphere. State farms were slowly being introduced. Nkrumah in a speech to the conference of African farmers in 1962 pointed out that the "major task is the creation of a complete revolution in agriculture on our continent—a total break with primitive methods and organizations and with the colonial past which tied the African down to subsistence farming, cultivated monocultural crops all

particularly in a written constitution, the original purpose of which was to limit government and assert the sovereignty of the people. This spirit was perhaps present. But it was not very strong among those responsible for running the government.

[38] See D. E. Apter, "Nationalism, Government and Economic Growth," in *Economic Development and Cultural Change,* Jan. 1959, for a fuller discussion of the concept of political entrepreneurship.

over the continent, created scarcity in the midst of abundance and kept our masses at a very low ebb of nutritional and subeconomic standards."[39]

In its new party program, the party called for the establishment of State Corporations or Agricultural Cooperatives for marketing of livestock and livestock products as well as various marketing boards and public corporations for major products. The Soviet government agreed to help manage the new state farms under the Ghana State Farms Corporation, administered by the Ghana Farmers Council, a C.P.P. auxiliary.

Party and government then emphasized a new socialist state in which every aspect of economic and social life was to be utilized, mobilized and transformed, whether banking, marketing, or overseas trading. Socialist planning was the goal. Its enemies were imperialism and neo-colonialism.[40]

Paradoxically enough, despite all the emphasis on socialism, economic policy was most successful in the private sector. The single most important achievement was the decision of the aluminum consortium to go ahead on the Volta dam and aluminum scheme. This private venture in cooperation with the Ghana government was largely directed by Kaiser Aluminum. A number of other private firms also participated in Ghana's development.[41]

Between April 1, 1959 and June 30, 1960, 64 factories were established, bringing their total to 519. These included cosmetics, fiber products, aluminum roofing, drugs, towels, soap, enamel goods, matches, milk processing, sawmills, etc. The list was impressive. But Ghana proved to be neither a model of socialist endeavor nor a monument to African enterprise. Planning created an extremely grave organizational problem which put unanticipated obstacles in the way of development. Ghana depleted her reserves in showpiece projects, public buildings and other costly endeavors, particularly in the large towns. The

[39] See Kwame Nkrumah, "Africa Needs Her Farmers," Accra, Government Printer, 1962.
[40] See "For Work and Happiness, the Program of the Convention People's Party, Accra": Government Printing Department, 1962.
[41] On the other hand, the socialist sector was expanding. A Ghana National Construction Corporation was set up. Many other examples could be cited, few of which proved to be economically profitable. As a result the volume of indebtedness increased dramatically.

surface was hardly scratched in the smaller towns and villages although there were some notable achievements such as the new town and harbor at Tema.

Authority, Ideology, and the Routinization of Charisma

To what extent did Ghana become a stable, autocratic, socialist regime?

Nkrumaism, although clearly directed toward the establishment of a socialist state using modern rational means of planning in order to move rapidly toward modernization and economic development, failed.[42]

The nation replaced the ethnic community. The Presidential-monarch replaced the chief. The authority of charisma ritualized into the special role of the warrior-priest.[43] Ideology became a political religion increasingly intolerant of all other religions, monopolistic, expressed through the militant elect of the party. The writings and speeches of Nkrumah took on the quality of sacred texts, to be interpreted in slogans and revolutionary

[42] In a very interesting paper entitled, "On Assessing a Development Plan," W. Arthur Lewis has argued that most underdeveloped countries are, in this sense, incapable of executing large-scale development programs. "The larger the program the less preparation is given to each project and the greater is the number of incompetent people appointed to public service. Programs fall into arrears, are overcostly and are badly executed." Lewis, speaking from the experience of Ghana's development plan, argues that in planning economists pride themselves in their techniques. "They make mathematical exercises estimating the growth of demand. They speak of the need for consistency between public and private intentions, and they even use input-output tables to demonstrate appropriate relationships. Actually this is the area where precise estimation matters least because mistakes find themselves out rapidly. If the planner neglects to provide adequate services a bottleneck develops, people fuss and the mistake can be corrected quickly. Fortunately, too, if the planner provides too much service, he is not in error for long, since rapidly growing populations and productivities soon produce enough extra demand to catch up with overcapacity. The difficulty arises not in matching public supply to the needs of private commerce, but in deciding how much service to provide for domestic consumers, how high a priority should one accord to order supplies in the village, to rural electrification, to providing good road services even where road traffic is small, to hospital and medical services, to broadcast rediffusion, to decent prisons and to such other consumer facilities. These are matters for political decision." See W. Arthur Lewis, "On Assessing a Development Plan," July 1959 issue, *The Economic Bulletin,* p. 7, Accra, Ghana.

[43] The following description is illustrative. When Nkrumah arrived at the Parliament to give a speech, he was greeted by "the blowing of horns and rolling of drums as well as a 21-gun salute, and members in white robes and kente cheered and clapped as he was led into the Chamber. In attendance and flanking him as he spoke were the Heads of Ghana's armed forces, a standard bearer, and eight State linguists." See *West Africa,* No. 2366, October 6, 1962, p. 1095.

symbols and to be taught to the women and children. Around Nkrumah were socialist militants, both the moderates and the puritans. Some of them took a long view. Others, impatient with the ritual, manipulated it. Some were sycophantic and anxious for power.[44]

Others associated with Nkrumah from the beginning, for whom charisma and ritual meant little, were purged. So were virtually all other would-be claimants for political power. Gbedemah, the man who built the C.P.P. in its early days, went into exile. Botsio, for long Nkrumah's chief confidant, was stripped of his ministry and purged from the party, to crawl back later.

Meanwhile, Nkrumah more or less confined himself to Flagstaff House. A huge estate and palace built for Nkrumah in Aburi, outside Accra, was never used.

Inside Flagstaff a few able civil servants tried to patch together the party directives and put them in some kind of order. A handful of expatriates remained in the inner court. Around Nkrumah, it was like a court built around the figure of the Presidential-monarch. There was intrigue within; highly placed government officials were accused of complicity in plots against the Presidential-monarch. Old associates like Ako Adjei were placed in jail without trial. Others like John Tettegah, who fancied themselves as the possible heirs-apparent, were picked up for police interrogation. As in the courts of earlier monarchies, there were personal and ideological factions each vying for the favor of Nkrumah. Few could be trusted to give adequate advice save Kofi Baako and Krobo Edusei. Nkrumah could control his court, but not rely on it.

Nor could he trust outside advisers. Some of his civil servants, well trained and loyal, continued to perform their work doggedly and sympathetically. Many of them, including the army officers, were simply patient. Theirs was the politics of aloofness, even while they were deeply engaged in the machinery of government. Some around Nkrumah who did not accept the ritualization of charisma, demeaned themselves by giving it lip-service. Others saw in ritualization a new form of an understandable and ancient system of government. Thus real conflict was between those forces

---

[44] The case of Tawia Adamafio is in point.

which were impatient to build the mobilization system—modern, technical, and industrial—when confronted with traditionalism, not its old form, but in the new one. The ideological fare of the militants was diluted into more comfortable but traditional terms in the villages.

What kept the system going was the quiet alliance between two often hostile forces, the party bureaucracy and the civil service. If they had mutual contempt for one another, both recognized that they were essential for the running of day-to-day affairs. If the "steel-frame" of the administrative service had not been so well organized and capable, and if the party bureaucracy had not been so effective, it is doubtful whether the regime could have withstood the many political tensions and shocks it faced from independence to the coup, not the least of which were economic difficulties leading to extremely high taxes.

As in India, what the British endowed was of inestimable importance in a new state, a civil service capable of serving even under conditions hostile to it. The political framework, too, though twisted far out of shape, having been forced to serve tasks to which it was ill-adapted, also remained.[45]

Nor was parliament meaningless. Criticism of government was often intense. The C.P.P. backbenchers were as anxious to embarrass a Minister as the opposition had been formerly. Members raised issues for the attention of Ministers. Moreover, debate often raised fundamental matters. Mr. S. D. Dombo of the United Party was still able to say in the debate on the Preventive Detention Bill, "Any member of this House who still feels that this is a good piece of legislation which must remain permanently on our statute book is only fooling himself, and fooling the country too. (A Member: 'The U.P. is dead!') The Member may say that the U.P. is dead. Why is it dead? It is dead because anyone who attempts to organize it is branded as being subversive and is charged and arrested. Even belonging to that party is considered to be an act of subversion. But as far as I am concerned, the United Party is not dead! All our members may be detained, but the U.P. is not dead. Give us the change; grant us permits to organize rallies and see whether or not people support our cause. But you have restricted

[45] See Kenneth Younger, *The Public Service in New States,* London: Oxford University Press, 1960, pp. 53-60.

our activities; you have tied our hands; and how do you expect us to organize?"[46]

How they organized and what the consequences were would form the appropriate subject matter for a new book. A brief review will conclude our analysis of Ghana in transition.

[46] See Parliamentary Debates, Ghana, Vol. 27, No. 15, Wednesday, June 6, 1962, p. 556.

◻◻◻ | CHAPTER 16 | ◻◻◻

GHANA IN TRANSITION: A RETROSPECTIVE VIEW[1]

Introduction

ONE OF THE intriguing problems confronting anyone who wishes
to understand Ghanaian political life is how to determine what is
shadow, rhetoric, or fantasy, and what is substance—concrete,
and fundamental. What makes this question even more confusing
is the openness which, more than in most societies, characterizes
the political and social aspects of Ghana life. All appears available to public scrutiny. Such openness has its pitfalls because
even well-articulated events defy easy evaluations. Clear evidence
of ethnic conflict such as prevails between the Ewes and the Akan
or Twi-speaking groups does not necessarily mean "tribalism."
It may, but then again it may not. Observers disagree over the
terms and characteristics of a phenomenon which seems at first
glance to be perfectly obvious. But what is called tribalism may be
localism, class cleavage, ruralism, religious antagonism, and many
other forms of conflict.

Similarly in politics: Ghana's governments have passed from
a liberal democratic form with a dominant political party at independence to a single party state, overthrown in a military coup.
The military regime restored liberal democracy, with a dominant
political party which was thrust aside by a second military coup.
At each turn of the political screw some obvious priorities were
altered, as well as methods of development. What happened below
the surface is not so clear. The predominant political emphases
changed from the desire to mobilize around predetermined goals
to the desire to reconcile diverse interests, only to focus again on
urgent economic priorities. These have affected the degree of individual autonomy possible in work, education, and family life,
as well as bigger issues of major public interest such as pan-
Africanism, anticolonialism, and appropriate relations with the

[1] The research for this chapter was made possible by a grant from the Council on
African Studies, Yale University. The author also wishes to acknowledge the help
of Professor Jon Kraus of the State University of New York at Fredonia for a
critical review of an earlier draft of this chapter.

rest of the world. No matter how substantial such changes have been, it is also true that many specific social and political practices remain unaltered. Certain constants can be found which carry on, despite changes in political style and emphasis. There is a characteristic way in which Ghanaians work. There is a durable network of obligations and responsibilities which reaches back into the history and culture of the country. A good deal remains from the period of British rule. Certain roles which arose then remain embedded in such specific institutions as the Ghanaian army or the civil service, both of which many observers regard as essentially "British." There remains, too, a body of beliefs and practices created during the heady days of mass nationalism, the "charismatic period" when Nkrumah first came to power with a larger political "morality," a sense of a pan-African mission, and an emphasis on racial and political rebirth. This reached its nadir in the official party ideology, which claimed that Nkrumah could do no wrong at the very moment when he was committing error after error and appeared to be unable to do anything right.

Whatever the period selected for scrutiny, however, there stands behind every positive descriptive statement of fact a counterfactual, qualifying shadow. Tribalism is not a characteristic of Ghanaian politics, but ethnic competition looks strongly like it. Nkrumah never built a monolithic party or state, but he attempted it. The Ghanaian army is not at all like the British army, but it shares many characteristics (not the least of which is the regimental mess which shares British characteristics with other ex-colonial armies from the Sudan to India).

The special problem of a modernizing society as distinct from an industrial one is that few roles finally and utterly disappear. Nothing becomes completely obsolete. Despite the progress of change, an amazing quality of many roles is that, like snakes, they shed their skins while retaining their forms, and they slide about effortless in a new terrain. This "slithering" of roles, or more properly, role ambiguity, affects the institutional structures which incorporate them and makes organizational life far different in practice than even their most familiar counterparts in industrial societies. Similarly in government: for all its qualities as a British-style administrative class, the Ghanaian civil service is only superficially similar to its counterpart in Britain (or India) despite a common set of originating roles and somewhat similar educational structures. The same point could be made about any institutional pattern in Ghana. This is one reason why the more facts we have, the more research is necessary. Indeed, the reason why intensive study of a single case is extremely valuable is precisely because this interleaving or layered quality of life does not reveal itself quickly. Of couse, Ghana is hardly unique in this respect. All societies share these complexities, and to articulate the meanings of each level becomes a nice task of both the theory and practice of contemporary research.[2]

Here we can only claim a surface sensitivity to the multifaceted quality of Ghanaian life. Such a sensitivity comes from long observation at a level best described as comparative rather than intensive. A less charitable interpretation is that such a perspective is necessarily shallow or superficial. It is, of course, very difficult to do both the comparative and the intensive simultaneously. Each requires different theories and methods and involves different types of research. We have applied a comparative perspective to a single case and hoped, despite the obvious inadequacies of this approach, to reveal a political perspective of constant and variable factors in Ghana's political life. Our method has been a comparison within the case. We are exceedingly conscious of the pitfalls of that approach.[3]

Two Men and Two Regimes

There is another dimension, a more dramatic one, which lies behind the periods covered here. That is the conflict between two men, each of whom represented an entirely different tradition in Ghanaian life, whose personalities, life styles, and fundamental beliefs were completely different, and for whom politics was a struggle of life and death. The Nkrumah regime lasted for a little more than fifteen years, the Busia government only two and a half. But for a great deal of the time it was Busia who formed

[2] See the discussion of such matters in Alfred Schutz, *Reflections and the Problem of Relevance* (New Haven: Yale University Press, 1970). See also Peter L. Berger and Thomas Luckman, *The Social Construction of Reality* (New York: Doubleday Anchor Books, 1966).

[3] For an exposition of my own method of comparative analysis, see D. E. Apter, *Choice and the Politics of Allocation* (New Haven: Yale University Press, 1971).

the principal opposition to Nkrumah in parliament as the leader of the only party which could challenge Nkrumah's authority. If it was a party of ethnics, elites, and reformers, it also included some of the best brains of the country. To a considerable extent then, in the hatred or perhaps contempt that each of these men had for the other, there is symbolized the two prevailing coalitions of Ghanaian political life. The one is urban, populist, and autocratic. The other is rural, elitist, and democratic. The problem in Ghana has always been to transpose the last terms.

Before going on to a more detailed description, several contrasts may be drawn between the Nkrumah government (particularly in the last years prior to the coup), and the Busia government. Each had a claim to legitimacy. The Nkrumah government, for example, entertained the hope that one day a more socialist economy would come to dominate, while the Busia government saw socialism as a form of bureaucratic stagnation.[4] Both failed.

Nkrumah saw his regime as an evolving system—a political shape that had not yet taken substantial or final form. For Busia, the government was in its final form, a perfected constitution serving as the basis of legitimate rule.

Each suggests different criteria of evaluation. A finished political system can be judged by its results. An unfinished one claims exemption because only "history" can be its judge. Those who favored the Nkrumah methods and principles of rule can argue that he was unable to complete the job because those who were his enemies were responsible for the anomalies which appeared during his period of office. To this there can then be no final answer. A critical review of this period would point to a growing list of errors in judgment and plan which themselves were intrinsically faulty or products of the system and not the whimsies of Nkrumah the man. An ever-widening gap between theory—the theories of socialist society (no matter how ephemeral and vague)—and its practice was perhaps not a matter of error, but built into the political dogma. How else can one account for socialist principles, which relied on capitalist support? Indeed,

---

[4] For an excellent review of Ghana's economic experiences see Elliot J. Berg, "Structural Transformation versus Gradualism, Recent Economic Development in Ghana and The Ivory Coast," in Philip Foster and Aristede Zolberg, *Ghana and The Ivory Coast* (Chicago: University of Chicago Press, 1971).

during the most socialist years of the Nkrumah government, roughly 85 per cent of all investments came from Great Britain, West Germany, the United States, and France. New programs of expenditures for developmental and political purposes, which were designed to enhance Ghana's independence, resulted in a dramatic increase in external indebtedness, making the country more rather than less dependent on capitalist countries and their money markets. By the time the Nkrumah government was overthrown, economic chaos could not be avoided. One major handicap of the Busia government was this "capitalist" inheritance from a "socialist" government.

There are many such paradoxes which constitute the substance of Ghanaian politics today. Behind its practices are the living shadows of other men and other times. The officials who surrounded Busia wanted to draw a clear distinction between what they symbolized in Ghana and what Nkrumah represented. If the latter was a populist in the sense that he drew the young, the urban poor, and those people who looked for a better deal under independence than colonial rule, many of the men around Busia had the longer record of nationalism. Their roots were in the nationalism of the elites, the ethnics, and the reformers, or more specifically the chiefs, the lawyers of the John Mensah Sarbah and Joseph Casely-Hayford variety and men of the United Gold Coast Convention and the Coussey Commission. Those who continued this liberal conception of politics brought it to fruition in the Second Republican "lawyer's constitution." But, if theirs was not a populist tradition, it nevertheless had much popular support.

The Nkrumah generation was rude, upthrusting, and challenging to chiefs and elders, the educated, and above all the British. There has always been an alternative tradition in Ghana, deferential to authority, respectful of tradition, education, and superior wealth. For its followers the Nkrumah period represented an "unnatural" phenomenon. Many people looked up to their educated men with pride and trust. Busia, who in his life, work, and demeanor was perhaps the best representative of this persuasion, was elected to office with a greater majority than Nkrumah received in the last free election in Nkrumah's Ghana (the so-called independence election of 1956). Though he was clearly no populist, one could nevertheless hardly argue that Busia was unable to win wide-scale public support. Indeed for Busia populism had been the cause of much of what had gone wrong in Nkrumah's Ghana and had led to stringent methods of rule and political brutality when ill-conceived projects failed. It was the basis of "group-think" and ideological institutes. It produced widespread corruption and political cynicism.

Indeed, so strongly did Busia's supporters feel about such matters that they tried to make the contrast between the two regimes as complete as possible. Nkrumah they would have preferred to see as a mere aberration in the national life, an interruption in the longer process of building a liberal democratic polity. Thoughts and ambitions for parliamentary rule did, after all, begin far back in Ghana's history (as did capitalism and the development of commerce). Private enterprise at the commanding heights of the economy and parliamentary competition replacing cabinet dictatorship and one-party rule now seemed the fulfillment of a national evolution, a process interrupted by Nkrumah. Hence the post-Nkrumah government leaders dedicated themselves to policies based on rational compromise and the intelligent reconciliation of various interests. It is in the light of those policies, and their ultimate consequences for liberal democracy, that the failures of the Busia government need to be judged.

As we shall show, the record was mixed. The Busia government soon became liable to many of the same charges as were leveled at Nkrumah. There was growing unrest over unemployment. Charges of corruption at high levels were heard in responsible quarters as well as the opposition newspaper.[5] If there was little overt sentiment for bringing Nkrumah back from his exile in Guinea, the Busia government quickly lost its appeal. The memory of Nkrumah exists. His period of rule continues to take on a certain nostalgia. Especially among the youth and the urban workers there is remembrance of past significance in world and pan-African affairs and a renewed curiosity about the man, made all the more compelling because of the period of debunking which, during the National Liberation Council period, represented an at-

---

[5] The most hard-hitting opposition newspaper was *The Spokesman* which, under a most politically astute editor, managed to locate one weakness of the government after another and caused it considerable embarrassment.

tempt to lay the Nkrumah myth to rest once and for all.[6] Whether that was accomplished, or whether the regime went too far so that its efforts to root out all vestiges of loyalty to Nkrumah have backfired, remains to be seen. Under the leadership of Colonel I. K. Acheampong, the new National Redemption Council, which overthrew the Busia government on January 13, 1972, is hardly taking a pro-Nkrumah line.

Taken together, the complex layering of Ghanaian life, the memories—ethnic, social, and political—the contrasts in political methods and styles, the remarkable variety of political experiments all suggest the need for a deep study of Ghana today. Virtually every group has experienced some sense of the political, whether through direct participation or in feeling its effects. Even the chiefs and elders, who seemed to be dramatically reduced in importance during the Nkrumah period after having participated in politics under British rule, formed stubborn nuclei of resistance and opposition.[7] Under Busia they came back as instruments of local government. Such contradictions are intrinsically fascinating and sometimes ironic. The efforts to build socialism during the Nkrumah period generated commercialism by expanding the world of petty traders, whose ruthless pursuit of self-interest was as capable as that anywhere in the world and helped to corrupt local officials, and provided splendid opportunities for friends and family; thus socialism at the top became capitalism at the bottom. The return of liberal democracy resulted in radicalizing those who had been prim and conservative in the past, such as university students (who were wholeheartedly against the Nkrumah regime). They became estranged from the Busia government, which initially they had helped to form.

The Busia government had all the weakness of a fragile democracy. It could not blame all its deficiencies on the legacy of Nkrumah. In a parliamentary system, a prime minister and his party must accept the responsibility for prolonged failures in

[6] The Busia government amended the criminal code to make it a felony to promote the revival of the Convention People's Party or the restoration of its leadership as head of state.

[7] This is not to say that there were no pro-Nkrumah chiefs. There were. But mainly their support was based on obtaining government support against another chief or royal house, i.e., in local disputes of a traditional nature, as in the case of some of the Brong areas against the Ashanti Confederacy.

policy. Long before the Busia government was overthrown, rhetoric had replaced action. Although Busia's style was less flamboyant than that of Nkrumah, it was in its own way as inflated. Where the one spoke of revolution and liberation, the other spoke in the voice and sentiments reminiscent of ancient Greece. Its ideals of rational participation were classic, its concept of service Christian. But such lofty expressions, desirable though they might be, are not substitutes for the more pragmatic political skills which democratic government also requires, even when employed by political leaders with exceptional education and knowledge. Nor were such credentials as having suffered, having been in prison and exile under Nkrumah sufficient in the long run to sustain support. At least some political ambitions needed to be put into more practical actions. The democratic leaders of Ghana opposed populism with principle, but they also needed to practice a democracy which "allows experiment and innovation." They "questioned whether the single party experiments provide adequately for criticism and opposition." They failed to render opposition into constructive cooperation. They recognized that "all men, including party bosses and rulers are fallible and, consequently, that there should be effective institutions for the expression of criticism, and for a constitutional change of rulers." But they paid less attention to the issues raised by the opposition than this statement would suggest. "Intolerance of opposition often stems from the conviction that the party bosses are always right, and that only they understand and interpret the will of the people; so that whatever they say should be accepted without challenge. Such an attitude is very dangerous for democratic life."[8] The Busia government affirmed this view many times. But it demonstrated its own intolerance. It smashed the trade union movement, expelled foreigners, dismissed civil servants, and became increasingly hostile to criticism. The Progress Party, which formed the government of the day during Busia's period, while not studded with party bosses (a fact that may have been partly responsible for its grave organizational weaknesses), failed to show any special political wisdom. Busia failed because he relied too heavily on his personal capacity to make effective policy. His party could

[8] See K. A. Busia, *Africa in Search of Democracy* (London: Routledge and Kegan Paul, 1967), p. 168.

neither survive in a field of parties nor depend on Busia's skill in putting together policy packages where the voters were. The alienation of the workers, the students, and the army was sufficiently complete by the end of 1971 that when Busia, his government, and parliamentary government disappeared from the political scene, they went quietly. Today the public mood is one of cynicism and indifference.

With these general comments as a backdrop, we now turn to the major changes that took place under Nkrumah, the National Liberation Council which replaced him, the Busia government, and the National Redemption Council. Each period deserves a much more detailed review than we will be able to provide. In brief, behind the changes in regime were the following factors: Ghana inherited from the British a parliamentary democratic political system which Nkrumah and the C.P.P. had shared in establishing. This framework was never formally dismantled. Rather, it changed in spirit, became a cabinet dictatorship, and then, changing in form, with a revised republican constitutional structure, it became an amalgam of "people's democracy" and a single party state with a legislature which never became a complete rubber stamp. Quite lively debate continued right to the end. The legislature could not, however, exert any control over the executive. By 1966 this system was beginning to change into a dual government. A new set of political institutions had arisen on the basis of a militant pan-African role which, operating out of the office of the President, had no constitutional basis and a great deal of power. This duality also reflected itself in the army, which was divided between the presidential guard regiment and the regular army—a dualism which was to become a specific cause of the first coup in 1966.

The second major phase was rule by the military. But it was not rule by the military alone. The soldiers surrounded themselves with civil servants as well as a corps of intellectuals, particularly those from the universities who had achieved prominence over the years by a more or less uncompromising stand against Nkrumah. They had earned the respect of those officers who, themselves not so long out of secondary school and military training schools, looked up to them and sought guidance and ideas.

The third phase, the return of parliamentary government, was designed to prevent cabinet dictatorship. Fulfilling the requirements of British practice as previously established in Ghana, the pattern was revived, but without a very effective party system. Parliamentarians quickly returned to the habits of party debate. The styles of legislation, trappings, seals, and formulas all represented a symbolism that was reassuring, especially the sense of ceremony and respect for democratic government. Gone from the scene were the capricious politicians, unmannerly slogans and programs, and the sinister practices of the old—that is, the Nkrumah—regime.

The final phase occurred on January 13, 1972, the week after a visit by President Richard Nixon's wife and after Prime Minister Busia had left for London for medical treatment. The first infantry brigade of the Ghanaian army, under the command of Colonel Ignatius K. Acheampong, overthrew the government of the Second Republic of Ghana. The constitution was suspended, political parties banned, and cabinet ministers jailed. General Afrifa, one of the key figures in the coup against Nkrumah, was arrested for allegedly planning a countercoup. We have said that there were few public displays of remorse or regret for the overthrown regime. The reasons were concrete enough. The army budget had been cut by 16 per cent. The cedi, the main Ghana currency unit, had been devalued by 44 per cent, after which prices had risen from between 30 per cent and 40 per cent. There was widespread unemployment. Repressive measures had been employed to stamp out any revival of Nkrumaism. The Trades Union Congress had been dissolved and its assets frozen. Cocoa prices had dropped sharply, and to make matters worse Ghana's share of the world cocoa market, which in 1965 had been approximately 40 per cent, had dropped to 28 per cent. The most important problem of all, and one which remains to confront the National Redemption Council, is the burden of foreign indebtedness, which amounts to approximately $840 million. This debt, which the Busia government had in large measure inherited from Nkrumah, was never completely renegotiated.

Colonel Acheampong, who had been involved in the coup against Nkrumah and served as a regional commissioner in the National Liberation Council, has set up a National Redemption Council composed of civil servants, police, and military officers, and promised the return of civilian rule at the appropriate time. For the civilians, life goes on as usual.

The Mobilization System as a Method of Development

At independence the principles of parliamentary government which were embodied in the constitution were these. There was a democratic local government system, a parliamentary single member constituency electoral system, a reasonable treasury with substantial reserves, and an organized party system dominated by the C.P.P. In this combination of mechanisms the British saw their own norms of government at work, including parliamentary control over the executive, the exclusion of the civil service from politics, and a voice for traditional and regional interests in decision-making.

From the standpoint of the Convention People's Party, all these were primarily a matter of tactical action. They were accepted as part of the independence bargain. They provided a graceful means for the British to withdraw, and, with the electoral strength of the C.P.P. so overwhelming, it remained useful to accomplish policy objectives in a parliamentary manner. Although it rarely inhibited the leadership, the local back-bench opposition often served as a useful device for ventilating local grievances and serving as a barometric indicator of public response to policy beyond the C.P.P. orbit.

This system was in part a transitional one for the C.P.P., and in part more durable. It was never completely dismantled. What did occur, however, was the transformation of the parliamentary mechanism into a personal instrument of Nkrumah's rule. Nkrumah used parliament as a theater. He enjoyed his role as chief actor, although he was not a particularly good debater. He even accepted back-bench revolts within his own parliamentary party as part of the game, which he continued to play as long as he could maintain discipline both in the party as a whole and in the parliamentary party. The issue of discipline was perhaps the key both to Nkrumah's attempt to control various aspects of political life and to his socialism. If socialism had any meaning in Ghana, it was as a demand for collective action. For this reason Nkrumah could with one hand centralize power and with the other decentralize it. He saw himself not as a dictator but as a person privileged by an exceptional and creative personality to employ instrumentalities of party and state in order to bring about a changed social environment for Ghanaians specifically and Africans generally. This notion of the exceptional man, exemplified in the titles he took (which had their traditional counterparts) was perhaps less a matter of enjoying power for its own sake (although there is little doubt that he did that, too) than of a sense of mission. He broke into the relatively conventional society of Ghana like a breath of air. He attacked the intellectuals who remained separated in life style and views from the public. He offered the population, which was bound by relatively limited choices and options, a sense of the future. He used his political strength to open up alternatives. In this sense he had a predisposition to be radical and militant, and knew that any concern about potentiality, the unfolding future, could only be achieved as an organizational matter. He had his preposterous side. He claimed philosophical skill in projecting himself into the role of an activist radical philosopher who, like Lenin, could integrate theory and practice. But he was no Lenin. At the end, increasingly influenced by Mao, he accepted the "analects of contradiction" as a politically effective means of institutionalizing radicalization.[9] He attempted to create a philosophy, "consciencism," which would project him out of the primarily Ghanaian stage of "the struggle" into a more pan-African one, ideologically validating his role as the prime mover of African political integration.

To make this jump required new political and social alternatives. To instill new political ideas and institutionalize new roles he required a new corporate structure. He created new functional bodies, the Young Pioneers, the National Council of Ghana Women, the National Association of Socialist Students Organizations, the Ghana Cooperative Movement, a Ghana Legion of ex-servicemen, and Workers' Brigades. Independent bodies, such as the Trade Union Congress, were turned into party auxiliaries and, having been "nationalized," formed a basis for collaboration with militants elsewhere in Africa. Ghana's T.U.C. formed the nucleus for the All-African Trade Union Federation. The same

---

[9] After he was deposed, Nkrumah produced a little black book (similar to Mao's little red one) composed of various sayings on the subject of imperialism and the tasks of the African revolution.

pattern was followed with respect to farmers. It was to establish control over the increasingly disgruntled farmers that the United Ghana Farmers' Council was formed. Its pan-African equivalent became the All-African Union of Farmers. The Kwame Nkrumah Ideological Institute at Winneba was to provide ideological inspiration. Marxist and C.P.P. study groups were formed, to be disbanded later on. Although largely unsuccessful, Vanguard Activists were used to try and establish C.P.P. units among market women, churches, business enterprises, etc. In short, the object was to penetrate the entire organized network of existing social life with C.P.P. nuclei and create new institutional groupings on a corporate basis for the transformation of social life at home and elsewhere in Africa.[10]

Where they were established, these various bodies changed the core of the party. What declined first were the constituency parties. Then came a change in regional administration and in the functions of parliament. A series of punitive acts followed, all designed to give force to the new corporate structure and aimed at eliminating opposition. Eventually the goal was to transform the governmental structure into a people's democracy and turn Ghana into a base as an African revolutionary center with continental control as its goal. By this time, the systematic dismantling of the parliamentary safeguards left by the British was more or less complete. We have already described how local government authorities were broken up into smaller and less financially viable units under their government-appointed district commissioners. The assemblies of chiefs provided for by the independence constitution were not allowed to function. New legislation effectively abridged free speech and freedom of the press, restricted habeas corpus, "preventative detention," allowed the government to jail opponents without trial. This legislation, accompanied by changes in the constitutional structure, gave special powers to the first President enabling him "whenever he considers it to be in the national interest to do so [to] give directions by legislative instrument." His term of office was open ended. By 1963, the emphasis was to transform society root and branch to a people's democracy at home and a vanguard instrument of pan-Africanism abroad,

[10] See Kwame Nkrumah, *Africa Must Unite* (London: Heinemann, 1963), pp. 118-31.

and a referendum was held in 1964 to validate Marxist-Nkrumaism and pan-Africanism as the goals of the state.[11] This new political emphasis was to serve as a basis for Nkrumah's "second coming."

Hence Ghana's political evolution under Nkrumah was, on one level, a change from populist nationalism in the direction of a more militant socialism as the justification for pan-Africanism even though the latter did not have much chance to develop in substance. This has led observers to conclude that the attempt itself was trivial.[12] I think that this view is too limited. The effort at mobilization failed to achieve its particular objective. The effect was an administrative shambles, providing fresh opportunities for corruption and petty tyranny. The new auxiliaries, far from being models of corporate social development, never functioned properly. Efforts to induce ideological reform, to recruit zealots to positions of local and regional power, and, above all, to discipline the population, all led to opposite results. Discipline led to the exercise of capricious power, sycophancy, manipulation, and eventually to the formation of an underground, capable of throwing bombs. An atmosphere of suspicion, personal fear, and deceit pervaded every aspect of organized life. Each new organization formed a venue for competition and corruption, and each older one it displaced became a potential rallying ground for resistance. A disgruntled population is hardly the basis for effective mobilization. This much was, and is, clear, and always was. The larger question, how much a continued transformation at the top would in time result in a transformation of the aspects of society, remains unanswered. Real changes using real power were clearly under way.

What we do not know is the potential effects of "trickle-down" extremism by the center upon the periphery. Nkrumah was bargaining for a new generation, which he hoped to organize in terms

[11] The referendum which included 95 per cent of the eligible voters was overwhelmingly in favor of the single-party slate with 2,773,920 affirmative and 2,454 negative votes. The election was widely regarded as a joke. See my article, "Ghana," in James S. Coleman and Carl Rosberg, eds., *Political Parties and National Integration in Tropical Africa* (Berkeley: University of California Press, 1964), p. 312.

[12] See, e.g., the view of Henry Bretton, *The Rise and Fall of Kwame Nkrumah* (New York: Praeger, 1966).

of a new crusade, the pan-African one. Socialism at home was now to become effective in the context of pan-Africanism. In effect, what Nkrumah attempted to do, whether deliberately or not, was to repeat the success of the "charismatic" period, 1949-1954, when he had been the essential politician. He wanted to recreate this role at a higher (dialectical) level, e.g., as the essential pan-African leader.

It would not be fair to assume that the reason Nkrumah turned more and more directly to pan-Africanism was because of internal failures in Ghana. However, this external emphasis pushed aside a proper consideration of domestic problems. With a more parochial concern, leakages of money and talent, failures in organization, and the slow decay of social life all could have been arrested and reversed. How much was cause and how much effect is impossible to specify. The difficulty is made worse because the Nkrumah "method" was to create a certain degree of structural randomness that prevented any group or individual from establishing power. Nkrumah never followed a specific plan. He preferred to keep the political situation fluid and his options open. The result was domestic chaos. It is this failure which requires a closer look, for it parallels events in Mali and elsewhere.

Things Fall Apart

It was after 1961 that the party fell apart. It had never been a disciplined body. Its burgeoning superstructure was vastly inflated. Party support, such as it was, became virtually a matter of individual enrichment. The famous dawn broadcast against corruption in April 1961 represented an effort by the "socialist puritans" to force Nkrumah to confront the question of whether or not the party was to be a loose coalition of interests or a militant and organized body. The reaction was that NASSO (the National Association of Socialist Students Organization), the *Evening News*, and the young and militant left were immediately attacked by the right-wing old guard as dangerous dissidents, lacking in loyalty. Eventually NASSO was abolished, and the Marxist study groups which replaced it soon suffered the same fate. By October 1961, after purging a number of his old comrades in arms, Nkrumah had drastically reduced the number of people he could rely on.[13] The following year came the first major attempt to assassinate him at Kulungugu. Those on the "left," including the new general secretary of the party and some of his associates, were immediately put in prison.[14]

From 1961 on most observers agree there was the greatest discrepancy between the sound and the fury of militant socialism and the practice of corrupt payoffs in practical politics. Nkrumah practiced blackmail by holding police dossiers on all his associates. He manipulated them on an increasingly personalistic basis. Relations between the civil service and the party grew extremely tense, and both suffered a progressive demoralization characterized by anxiety in the senior ranks and idleness at more junior levels. To counteract this deterioration, Nkrumah took a number of steps. "A host of high-powered committees, consisting of both state and party representatives, were created to oversee various aspects of policy and party life, and Nkrumah agreed to set aside one day a week to meet representatives of these and other committees. Strong guidelines were given to the committees about procedure, frequency of meetings, and attendance, and expectations were raised about their possible contribution toward the ordering of party life, especially in the area of grass roots coordination and inner party criticism. Almost all respondents agree, however, that very little was achieved by this elaborate reorganization. Nkrumah was too busy or uninterested to keep his commitments, and personal rivalries destroyed the effectiveness of most of the committees."[15]

By 1965, the party consisted of vast networks of committees which did not meet, organizations which failed to function, and personal manipulations which aroused mutual suspicion, mistrust, and recriminations. What grew were the number of posts and positions which had something to do with the party, but actually provided opportunities for political and economic entrepreneur-

[13] In October 1961, he also purged a number of senior leaders, including three of his closest associates, Komla Gbedemah, who went into exile, Kojo Botsio, who later returned to power, as did Krobo Edusei.

[14] They were mainly Ga, one of the few instances where "tribal" factors seemed to be of special significance during the C.P.P. period.

[15] See Selwyn Ryan, "Socialism and the Party System in Ghana, 1947-66," in *Pan-African Journal,* Vol. III, No. 1, Winter 1970, p. 64. For a discussion of how these committees worked see Jan Kraus, "Political Change, Conflict, and Development in Ghana," in Foster and Zolberg, *op. cit.,* pp. 62-65.

ship. At the local level, the district commissioners had real power. They were responsible to the party and government. This, in turn, ensured that they did virtually nothing beyond party instructions, since the district commissioners were themselves caught in a network of conflicting personalities and organizations. So many of them became petty dictators that the need to bypass them opened up new private channels of politics. This reached such proportions that it could be said that the party was riddled with private methods of rule based on the need to cut through the bureaucracy.

In theory, regional party policy was to be laid down by the regional steering committees. But these were large bodies consisting of National Executive members, local council chairmen, district commissioners, members of parliament, party organizers; in short, all those in positions of some party significance. Such bodies were far too unwieldy to take effective action. Similarly, at the district level the district executive was to lay down policy and the district commissioner was obligated to carry it out. But the district commissioner more often than not fell into a role previously occupied by the British and, as in the worst days of colonialism, acted as a local despot.[16]

Because the party degenerated, ideological campaigns, statements of Nkrumaism as a "philosophy" and other efforts to provide an ideological line began to appear more and more absurd. A language of deification, which Nkrumah pretended not to find congenial, pervaded not only the official newspapers and publications of the C.P.P. but also the public statements of senior officials, scholars at the university, and others. Public sycophancy rose almost in direct proportion to private cynicism.

The political effects of all this, i.e., of organizational disintegration, lack of confidence in the leadership, arbitrary imprisonment, a declining economic situation, high corruption, and an ideological environment which had no relationship to facts, combined to create a crisis for Nkrumah which could not be resolved by internal means. An attempt was made to gain more substantial

---

16 See Harriet B. Schiffer, "Political Linkage in Ghana: Bakwai District, a Case Study" (mimeo. n.d.). The discussion of factionalism during the C.P.P. period is particularly useful. See also the detailed discussion of the role of the district commissioner in Kraus, op. cit., pp. 55-56. "Between 1960 and 1962, the number of DC's and districts was increased from 43 to 155."

support from socialist countries for specific targets of pan-African and socialist development. This was essential if Nkrumah was to become the central figure of pan-Africanism. Of his competitors for this role, Nasser he could hold in check because the latter was not part of black Africa (however much continental unity was proclaimed). Modeibo Keita was too vulnerable and Mali too poor to represent a threat. President Sekou Touré of Guinea was another matter, but for the time being he chose to follow Nkrumah's line on pan-African affairs while remaining preoccupied with internal problems in Guinea and other French-speaking West African countries. Relations with Julius Nyerere were more difficult. Nyerere was personally everything that Nkrumah was not, modest, plain-speaking. Clearly not a "man of destiny" in any personalistic way, he had great appeal and inspired trust. But he was not yet well enough known outside of East Africa. Kenyatta had a pan-African appeal, but was too old. Tubman and Haile Selassie had great political influence at a pan-African level, despite their reactionary views. They had to be courted and wooed.

Nkrumah's gamble failed. But he caught up other African states on matters of pan-African principle. He defined the position on South and Portuguese Africa. He argued for the elimination of residual colonialism. Significant for growing numbers of black nationalists in the West Indies and the United States for whom he was a symbol of their own struggles, he became an epic figure in third world terms just as his own political system was disintegrating. His role in foreign and pan-African and socialist affairs loomed larger while the specifically Ghanaian aspects declined.

This last desperate fling in Nkrumah's politics has not been given sufficient attention in the literature dealing with the period 1961-1965. How much of this pan-African role was by original design and how much by default is an open question. In one sense, Nkrumah always intended to use Ghana as a stepping-stone. Indeed, that was the purpose of the first foreign policy move of the Nkrumah government after independence, the convening of the first Conference of Independent African States in April 1958. The ideological slogan—the African Personality—Nkrumah's version of "negritude," like the original character of the C.P.P.'s

Positive Action, had an evocative quality, while remaining vague in meaning, and was designed to appeal to all Africans. The slogan of a pan-African *rassemblement*, it was an attempt to highlight the next level of the struggle. Regional political experiments were tried. Guinea and Ghana "agreed to constitute our two states as the nucleus of a Union of West African states" (joined by Mali in 1961).[17] A different strategy favored in the Sanniquellie conference in Liberia emphasized African unity in very broad terms. The point is that in successive conferences of independent African states Nkrumah sought to identify broad areas of agreement in principle while focusing on specific aspects of racialism and colonialism as the common enemy (the French in Algeria, the remaining areas of colonial rule, particularly the Central African Federation, Portuguese Africa, and finally South Africa). These targets were to serve as the basis for the freedom fighters and justified Ghana's interventions in the activities of other African states.

Nkrumah also used the C.P.P. as a means of engaging in political activities that would have been ruled out by his role as a prime minister and later head of state. As leader of a party, he hoped to deploy the various party wings for political activities elsewhere in Africa. This, indeed, was the distinction he first drew, and would make use of subsequently, between the African conference of heads of state and the first all-African People's Conference of December 1958. In his opening address, Nkrumah made it clear that he was talking to the delegates to the conference as a party leader and that he regarded "this assembly as the opening of a new epoch in our Continent's history. . . . My real role here today is that of the Leader of a Political Party, and it is as the Chairman of that Party that I want to address you."[18]

Thus it could be argued that all along Nkrumah wanted power

[17] See the summary of the proceedings of the conferences of independent African states in *Awakening Africa* (Accra: Bureau of African Affairs). For interesting background materials on the first Conference of Independent African States, see also Alex Quaison-Sackey, *Africa Unbound* (New York: Praeger, 1963), pp. 59-99.

[18] See Kwame Nkrumah, "Africa for Africans," speech given at the inaugural session of the All-African Peoples' Conference at the Accra Community Center, December 8, 1958, in a collection of Nkrumah's speeches published under the title *Hands Off Africa*, by Kwabena Owuwu-Akyem (Accra: Ministry of Local Government, 1960).

in Ghana primarily to use it as a base for funds, training, and, if possible, a showplace for pan-Africanism. Certainly over the years of his rule Nkrumah showed increasing irritation with those Ghanaian political problems which he regarded as essentially provincial. This is one reason why he could put such a trusted party hack as Nathaniel Welbeck in the role of General Secretary of the Party. It was almost a gesture of contempt for the country.

The strategy followed in external affairs was not very different from the one originally employed by Nkrumah internally. Two political "tendencies" were identified, the one militant, based on the idea of a political union of African socialist states (which eventually came to represent the Casablanca powers), and the other conservative (the Brazzaville powers). Conflict between them was to be held in check in a search for unity. This strategy repeated what had been done within the C.P.P. between the more militant left and the more populist right during the early days of C.P.P. organization. Paralleling the pan-African rhetoric was an organizational strategy, the building-up of all-African corporate bodies of a party or extragovernmental nature, the establishment of training centers for freedom fighters and of conference buildings and sites for internal meetings, and the organization of physical facilities for refugees. The foundation for this was the 1964 referendum which turned Ghana into a one-party state. After the referendum, it was possible to develop a dual government in which domestic policy was increasingly a reciprocal of pan-Africanism. This second government, operating out of the President's Office, was run by the National Security Service. A Special Intelligence Unit reported directly to the President's Office and to the Deputy Chief of Staff of the Armed Forces. A Central Bureau directly below the President's Office coordinated military affairs and technical assistance. Under the Central Bureau was the Bureau of African Affairs which in theory also operated the Kwame Nkrumah Ideological Institute, but was in practice semi-autonomous. The National Security Council was responsible for military aspects of pan-Africanism, while the Bureau operated the African Affairs Center where refugees from South Africa and Portuguese Africa and militants from everywhere congregated. The Bureau also ran the Secret Training

Camps for African Freedom Fighters, Ghanaian and others. A Bureau of Technical Assistance was effectively a pan-African revolutionary secretariat, employing information analysts and other specialists in espionage and evaluation. A Special Intelligence Unit maintained its own military force, including the "Guards" regiment whose officers were trained in the U.S.S.R., and was responsible for maintaining the secret training camps whose advisors, first Russian and then Chinese, were experts in guerilla warfare.[19]

If it is true that, in effect, Ghana's political system was transformed into an instrument of pan-Africanism, then explanations of failure that rely on the "shambles" theory of the party (Zolberg, Bretton), or the neoimperialist plot (Fitch and Oppenheimer), or the "paucity" theory of vulnerability to external economic manipulation (Murray), all miss the point.[20]

Nkrumah was very much aware that, as a small country in Africa, Ghana did not have time on her side. He saw that, once the "political moment" of African independence had passed and various countries, among them potentially rich and powerful ones like Nigeria, began to make their impact on the political scene, then the possibilities of forming a militant African union and sustaining a leading role for Ghana in it would inevitably diminish. It was on deepening the "revolutionary" content of the independence movement itself, favoring the most militant elements, identifying the crusade against neoimperialism, that the possibility for influencing African affairs depended. This is why Nkrumah's real project was to foster dissident and militant movements against conservative African governments, using the

---

[19] See my discussion of these matters in "Nkrumah, Charisma, and the Coup," in Dankwart A. Rustow, ed., *Philosophers and Kings: Studies in Leadership* (New York: George Braziller, 1970).

[20] There is a wide variety of explanations for the coup. See Aristide Zolberg's thesis that the party was a myth in *Creating Political Order: The Party-States of West Africa* (Chicago: Rand McNally, 1966), which leads one to conclude that there was no effective party organization. Henry Bretton also argues that the party was never an instrument of mass mobilization nor did Nkrumah want it to perform that function. See Bretton, *op. cit.*, p. 74. In *Ghana: End of an Illusion,* B. Fitch and M. Oppenheimer argue that the political elite bled Ghana at home, while foreign enterprise did the same from abroad under circumstances of pseudo-socialism. See p. 112. Finally, the paucity theory of R. Murray, in the *New Left Review,* which emphasized dependency on overseas capital sources, implies that manipulative economic sanctions from abroad weakened the economic system.

themes of anticolonialism and racism as the basis of unity. To do this, he had always to appear as radical as possible to the radicals and as reasonable as possible to those who might otherwise combine against him.

Indeed, what becomes clear in a review of Nkrumah's views and the specific roles he cast for himself is not so much their consistency as their pattern. He saw himself as the manipulator of opposing factions, but always cast his lot with the left while speaking with the reasonableness of the right. He also saw control as a matter of individuals, people who could be relied on for certain purposes and then gotten rid of. He catered to his colleagues because "the movement" was a continuously changing thing, which with its own internal dynamics required continuous attention if his leadership was not to become imprisoned in its own designs. This, in turn, required a continuous change in both objectives and the concrete political context within which the movement functioned. Such changes were manifested in altering the constitution, abolishing the opposition, voting for a people's republic, etc., all of which in turn required a shifting of the targets and objectives of the society. At each stage, the particular mixture of individuals, the condition of the movement, the political context, and the objective was different. Yet, and this is perhaps the most important point, the political mixture was a personal achievement on Nkrumah's part—a function of his own political skill and ingenuity. As failure became more frequent, coercion was employed to ensure that errors, lack of fit between the different elements, conflict, betrayal, arguments over aims, etc., never got out of control.

One observer who recognized the importance of Nkrumaism in precisely these terms was Professor Ali Mazrui. Describing Nkrumah as a "Leninist Czar," he said that "to make the people's obedience more dependent on persuasion than on naked force, there is always a case for a limited personality cult. That is why Nkrumah's Czarist myths of splendour and sacred leadership helped to reduce the harshness of Leninist notions of 'iron discipline.' "

But the trouble was that Nkrumah carried it too far. He appeared to have become so obsessed with his own myths of grandeur that the whole organization of the Convention People's Party lost its inner efficiency."[21]

Perhaps the emphasis on efficiency is exaggerated. The party was never efficient, nor was it ever intended to be. Nkrumah used the party as the instrument of rule in Ghana, and for this purpose it continued to serve him well for a long time, despite the continuous manipulation, careerism, and petty tyranny that went on within its ranks. What he could not control was the degree to which the party came to be regarded by the public in general as an enemy. Most people tried to minimize its power, softening the impact of the party by accepting it, minimizing it by allowing its adherents to use it as a payoff mechanism. In his study of the C.P.P. in Swedru, Owusu shows how this worked in relations between party stalwarts. The district commissioner had real power. He used it in gifts, patronage, and deals. The basic party units were effective not on the basis of their militancy, but to the extent that they recruited individuals with "strong desires for improving their economic (or class) status."[22] Characteristically, party members were storekeepers, petty merchants, lower officials of the civil service and public works. And because each of these groups was linked to heavily indebted cocoa farming families (whose attitudes toward the party were very mixed), there was a "trickle down" of favors and a reserved commitment upward to the party hierarchs.

This brings us to a particularly sensitive problem in reviewing the Ghanaian nationalist period. Uphoff was undoubtedly right when he suggested that "Ghana and Nkrumah probably started out in 1957 with more influence than their economic and military power warranted."[23] The mounting financial cost which attended this international role reflected itself not only in rural indebtedness, but in the growing importance of local party units as arbiters of economic assistance, success or failure for enterprises, and as a specific means of recruitment, entrepreneurship, and the like. The party always had a Tammany Hall quality. This

[21] See Ali Mazrui, "Nkrumah: the Leninist Czar," in *Transition,* Vol. vi, No. 26, 3-1966, pp. 9-17.

[22] See Maxwell Owusu, *Uses and Abuses of Political Power* (Chicago: University of Chicago Press, 1970), p. 299.

[23] See Norman Thomas Uphoff, "Ghana's Experience in Using External Aid for Development," 1957-66, Ph.D. dissertation, 1970.

intensified and became more important as time went on. Basically, the local party organizations gained their loyalties by payoff and petty manipulation. The rhetoric of revolution was remote from the local practices of local politics.

Certainly, Nkrumah's conception of his role and its relation to the future of Ghana was a grand design that alienated many. What can never be known, of course, is how effective his pan-Africanism was likely to have become. If it had succeeded, he would have become the mover and shaker of African politics. The odds are that he would have failed in this, if only because there were increasingly powerful alternatives in Nigeria, the Congo, and elsewhere. The gamble was both clear and rational. It was taken and lost.

The Nkrumah period can hardly be regarded as superficial. It has left deep scars. It promised too much. It broke the atmosphere of deference to traditional authorities, to the educated, and to foreign culture. African ways and objects came more and more to occupy the center of the stage. The social and political effects of all this will, along with other ingredients of Ghana's history, remain a subject for reinterpretation and analysis.

Ghanaians will, in the last analysis, discover in it in retrospect what they want. For some, it will be heroic time when Ghana made African and world history. For others, it will be racial, when Nkrumah incorporated Garvey, Padmore, and W. E. B. DuBois into the Ghanaian pantheon, either symbolically or in the flesh and blood individuals themselves, and, by doing so, profoundly affected the movement toward racial equality in the United States and elsewhere. Some will see in it an attempt to create a pragmatic form of socialism, while others will see in it the mouthing of radical phrases as a cover for personal rule and dictatorship. It was an epic period, and, therefore, like all such phenomena when observed closely, full of absurdities, overblown rhetoric, and petty authoritarianism vulnerable to those whose postures and gesticulations were exaggerated.

It was a time, too, when, despite the need for modesty and links with the masses, there was generated instead much pomposity and corruption. But it also gave many ordinary people a conscious concern for the future. In short, it had all the advantages and disadvantages of that form of populism in which the few speak in the name of the many. Perhaps a fair standard of evaluation is the one which Nkrumah himself laid down when he was a young man "(1) *Political Freedom*, i.e., complete and absolute independence from the control of any foreign government; (2) *Democratic Freedom*, i.e., freedom from political tyranny and the establishment of a democracy in which sovereignty is vested in the broad masses of the people; (3) *Social Reconstruction*, i.e., freedom from poverty and economic exploitation and the improvement of social and economic conditions of the people so that they will be able to find better means of achieving livelihood [sic] and asserting their right to human life and happiness."[24]

Twenty years later, Nkrumah added "one matter on which my views have been expanded, and that is regarding African unity. Since I have had the opportunity of putting my ideas to work, and personally experiencing the bitter and arduous test of wit, patience, and endurance that was necessary before our own victory over colonialism was won, I lay even greater stress on the vital importance to Africa's survival of a political union of the African continent. Twenty years ago, my ideas on African unity, important as I considered them even at that time, were limited to West African unity. Today, as I sit at my desk in Accra and glance at the several maps of Africa surrounding me, I see the wider horizon of the immense possibilities open to Africans—the only guarantee, in fact, for our survival—in a total continental political union of Africa."[25]

Nkrumah accomplished the first objective. The second he helped to construct and then obliterate. The third was ambiguous, with the economy in a highly precarious condition by the time the coup occurred. But, if we assume that all these were to be ultimately realized in Africa as a whole and not within Ghana, then it is this final objective which is the key to Nkrumah's Ghana. How one feels about that is perhaps the appropriate place for future debate.[26]

[24] See Kwame Nkrumah, *Towards Colonial Freedom* (London: Heinemann, 1962), p. 43.
[25] *Ibid.*, p. xi.
[26] For a thorough analysis of Nkrumah's foreign policy and its effect on Ghana, see W. Scott Thompson, *Ghana's Foreign Policy, 1957-66* (Princeton: Princeton University Press, 1969).

The Coup and Its Aftermath

If Ghana in the Nkrumah days was noisy, cynical, and full of half-believing C.P.P. sympathizers and leaders (whose motives were perhaps one part political purpose and three parts opportunism) during the period in which the National Liberation Council ruled, it was as if the British colonial system had been reimposed.

The coup was a moratorium on bargains struck and a chance for the settling of scores that were economic and familial, as well as political, nursed in quiet, now generating a sudden crescendo. Most celebrated a very real liberation. Only a few seemed to have private regrets and memories.

It came while Nkrumah, acting in his role as a world figure, was on his way to Hanoi "to end the Vietnam War." This provided the opportunity for the military coup organized by Colonel E. K. Kotoka, Commander of the Second Infantry Brigade, Major A. A. Afrifa, and J. W. K. Harlley, Commissioner of Police, while Nkrumah was en route to Peking on February 24, 1966.

The specific reasons for the coup are many. What is clear is that Nkrumah's political method of creating new alternatives without foreclosing others could not go on indefinitely. The restrictions on political opposition and personal freedom, rising prices, higher taxes, and other economic burdens, exaggerated by an inadequate administrative and inefficient managerial infrastructure (under the form of state capitalism which passed for socialism) all contributed. Everyone in the end was affected. The civil service, although it had expanded greatly under the increased state responsibilities, was subject to continuing harassment from the party. The army, which received particular privileges, was concerned about the superior status of the guards regiment. The party bureaucracy was a nest of intrigue. Those with special economic advantages were made vulnerable in political terms. All this was part of the policy of piecemeal control by Nkrumah. There was manipulation and intrigue everywhere, but relatively little loyalty.

What should also be borne in mind is that the economic instability, sectoral incompatibility, and political desires experienced in Ghana were not so very different from what was experienced in other African political systems. Such domestic difficulties would have been endemic no matter what form the political system took. In all modernizing societies, the conditions of dependence grow as development occurs. Each country becomes more locked into international commercial and industrial arrangements, whether socialist or capitalist. Moreover, political instability in Africa is now a commonplace. The reason that the downfall of the Nkrumah regime received so much attention is due to several factors. First, the mixture of intelligence and shrewdness of Nkrumah himself and his apparent rationality as a political leader were sufficiently outstanding for his government to remain attractive even when its adventures were not. Secondly, by attempting so much so fast, Nkrumah had captured a kind of political momentum which had universal consequences, particularly in broadening the attack on racism and neoimperialism. In both these respects, the Nkrumah government had appealed to people in other parts of the world in ways which they could respect and which helped them in their own struggles by giving encouragement and psychological and moral support, and they were dismayed when he fell.

It was Nkrumah's stress on the "big" themes in African politics which made the coup so important. Otherwise, the coup itself would hardly be worth mentioning. Nkrumah himself blamed the coup on the "Sandhurst mentality" of certain officers whose attitudes he regarded as neocolonialist and whose affiliations were bourgeois.[27] This view is shared by scholars such as Robert Dowse and Robert Price, who suggest that the main reason that the army moved was in order to protect its special elite position.[28] There is a good deal of evidence for this view.

Price regards the dismissal of two senior generals by Nkrumah, the decline of military uniforms and stores, and other factors germane to the military as such, as the "motivation" for the

[27] See Kwame Nkrumah, *Dark Days in Ghana* (London: Lawrence and Wishart, 1968), p. 45.
[28] See Robert E. Dowse, "The Military and Political Developments," in Colin Leys, ed., *Politics and Change in Developing Countries* (Cambridge: Cambridge University Press, 1969), p. 234. See also Robert M. Price, "A Theoretical Approach to Military Rule in New States," *World Politics,* Vol. xxxII, No. 3, pp. 399-430. For the best discussion of the Ghanaian army and police under Nkrumah see Jon Kraus, "Arms and Politics in Ghana," in Claude Welch, ed., *Soldier and State in Africa* (Evanston, Ill.: Northwestern University Press, 1970), pp. 154-221.

coup.[29] There was no doubt such grievances led to professional dissatisfaction and induced conspiratorial actions. The military, like the civil service, harbored few preferences for Nkrumah. They were dubious about Nkrumah's pan-Africanism. Nor did the party security network regard the military very highly.[30] There was always conflict between the party and the police, who were responsible for internal security. Although he gave lip service to the principle of civilian supremacy, Nkrumah preferred a loyal "red guard" similar to other people's democracies. If the Presidential Guards, with their Soviet trained officers, were hardly that, their position caused noticeable disgruntlement. For all these reasons, the army had been acutely sensitive to threats to its own autonomy and role.

As personalities, the leaders of the coup were very different. The most powerful (and unassuming), Colonel Kotoka, was a professional soldier who doubted that political democracy was appropriate for Ghana for the foreseeable future. He was a bluff outspoken man, and his assassination removed what might have been a persuasive force to delay the return to civilian rule.[31] Commissioner Harlley, an Ewe like Kotoka, was very much at home in the role of a British style police officer. He was the member of the triumvirate most in favor of the return of former C.P.P. members to politics, "since much of the talent of the country had been absorbed by the C.P.P." He opposed "punitive justice" in favor of an atmosphere in which the law could be respected by all, and counseled leniency for rank and file C.P.P. members. Brigadier Afrifa was the most dramatic presence. Tall, elegant, charming, he had studied classics in secondary school and represented the Sandhurst ideal of the gentleman soldier committed to Westminster style politics. Indeed, on this score he was very explicit:

"What have we fought for? I believe that my country is a beautiful country and has everything that will make us all proud

29 See Robert M. Price, "Military Officers and Political Leadership, the Ghanaian Case," *Comparative Politics*, Vol. III, No. 3, April 1971, p. 366.

30 In the C.P.P. itself, one faction preferred a people's militia.

31 The author had a lengthy interview with Colonel Kotoka in 1967. Kotoka said that he was opposed to the return to civilian rule because the people in the villages would agree with whoever seemed the most likely to win and that illiterates had no business voting.

of her. It was unfortunate that we fell into unscrupulous hands, and it is again unfortunate that we had to adopt the means we adopted. But I believe that we who were architects of the coup owed a duty to our country. We were not unaware of the consequences in the event of failure. We were prepared to accept the risk. We want to build a new Ghana, a country ruled by men of integrity and conscience; for, when one's conscience pronounces judgment, there is no court of appeal against its verdict. It was bitter to realize that those to whom the people gave the leadership of this country had sold their souls, and thought that the use of absolute power and tyranny and the love of money were all that mattered. We will stand against anything undemocratic. I believe that all men are born free. Democracy based on the freedom of the individual is more acceptable than any form of totalitarianism. We are against fascism and communism. I cherish the hope that in our history no one man will ever be allowed to lord it over us again. I am a great admirer of the British way of life, its legal system, the Magna Carta, the Petition of Rights and the Bill of Rights. These are institutions on which the civil liberties of the people are founded. The British Constitution safeguards not only the rule of law but also the freedom of the press, of thought, of action within the law, and of the individual. It is these things that make Britain the home of democracy."[32]

Such ideas were similar to both the lawyers and academicians who, approached by the military, shared in the preparation of new economic and administrative policies. From the start, the impression was created that the military was to provide a caretaker regime, not a permanent government. By committing itself to the return of civilian authority, and defining its role as a caretaker regime, the N.L.C. established a high degree of legitimacy. It received credit for an act of selflessness in having disposed of what was regarded as a corrupt and tyrannical dictatorship. By taking immediate steps to restore a democratic constitution, the officers were shown in their best light. A senior ranking officer (previously removed from his command by Nkrumah) was chosen to serve as the Chairman of the National

[32] See A. A. Afrifa, *The Ghana Coup* (London: Frank Cass & Co., 1967), pp. 107-108.

Liberation Council. (The officer selected, General Ankrah, although a capable administrator, was later forced to resign because of certain corrupt practices.) He had the advantage of belonging to the generation of senior politicians who had opposed Nkrumah from the start. The N.L.C. attempted to discredit Nkrumah by a full disclosure of improper financial and other practices by C.P.P. officials and politicians. It sought to restore financial austerity and legality. Hearings and trials were, by and large, conducted under standard legal procedures, and, in the commissions of inquiry which were established, safeguards for the defendants were, for the most part, readily available. Although "protective custody" replaced preventive detention, on the whole this was used sparingly, and only immediately following the coup.

If for all its emphasis on sobriety and fairness the regime had the character of a colonial system, this was, in part, due to the ban on national party politics. But it was also because of the system of administration. The politically appointed district and regional commissioners of the C.P.P. were replaced by army and police officers. They, in turn, performed very much in the British tradition of fair-minded but tough administrators strongly preoccupied with matters of efficiency. We stress the colonial *role* adopted by the military because, on the whole, that period embodied the norms and styles which seemed to them appropriate.

Of the top military leadership during the N.L.C. period, the most politically articulate were Brigadier A. A. Afrifa and Major-General A. K. Ocran. Both were models of the professional Ghanaian soldier. Afrifa was perhaps more overtly a budding politician. Ocran did not regard the caretaker function of the army as having come to an end and supported a view of the military which in Latin America is called the "pendulum role." According to the "pendulum theory," the army remains "outside" politics, but steps in to restore a certain propriety and institutional autonomy when political conditions distort the structure too much. As it happened, this was a prophetic view indeed. Afrifa's political views have a copybook quality to them which incline him to speculate on whether or not the people could live up to high political precepts. Behind his rather simple version of the Westminster ideal was a shrewd argument for returning power to the military if the regime was inadequate. This proved to be the case, but Afrifa was caught by events and unable to capitalize on his foresight.

More generally, most senior officers of the army shared a conception of a nonpolitical military linked explicitly to parliamentary politics. This tied them to a tradition in Ghana which is best described as liberal in the nineteenth-century sense of the word. Like the intellectuals and civil servants, then, the military was very much a part of the political elite.[33]

And, by accepting these liberal premises, it also accepted the political class which represented them, in effect inviting that class to take power. One consequence was to give office to those long excluded from their rightful place in politics to the detriment of a new and younger generation of potential politicians. Thus the N.L.C. shaped subsequent Ghanaian politics in a particular mold. Essentially, its members regarded the democratic polity as both necessary and sufficient cause for political development. Indeed, one might say it was political development. The N.L.C. never considered another formula and, given its internal factionalism, had no idea what other alternatives might have been more feasible.

The N.L.C. was antisocialist in the same way as it was anti-Nkrumah. Those to whom it looked for guidance, particularly members of the Political and Constitutional Committees, had strongly advised a return to civilian power sooner rather than later. Moreover, near the end of three and one-half years of N.L.C. rule, growing labor unrest and a severe and continuing economic crisis generated strong pressures to relinquish power.

The main achievements of the National Liberation Council were as follows. It established the "legitimacy" of the coup by discrediting the old regime. It was Nkrumah who was "illegit-

---

[33] Elite nationalism began developing prior to the First World War. The movement included such men as the Cape Coast barrister, J. E. Casely Hayford; the Accra physician, Dr. B. W. Quartey-Papafio; and Frans Dove, a Sierra Leonean who founded a professional family dynasty. A political "class" formed which, embodying merchant and professional interests along with some coastal chiefs and others, produced municipal parties and political associations. This group, the precursors of the United Gold Coast Convention, eventually found its way into the Ghana Congress Party and, subsequently, the United Party. Although favoring a liberal interpretation of parliamentary rule, they were not necessarily "pro-British." See David Kimble, *A Political History of Ghana, 1850-1928* (Oxford: Clarendon Press, 1963).

imate," because he had effectively usurped legal power and made it his own personal property. He was charged with being corrupt, capricious, and subversive.[34] The regime was out to destroy the "myth" of the *Osagyefo*.

What changed were the men at the top and the form and spirit of government. However, by and large, the civil servants, including permanent secretaries, remained in their posts. The number of ministries and other offices was reduced, and military and police officers were appointed as commissioners of the nine regions of Ghana. With considerable publicity, an austerity program was launched to improve economic conditions. "An economic council to advise the N.L.C. was formed on the day of the coup, consisting solely of government officials, together with the governors of the Bank of Ghana and the Ghana Commercial Bank."[35] But its efforts were not noticeably successful.

Although political activity was banned, Professor K. A. Busia quickly reemerged as the foremost political leader. He became head of a newly formed political committee, as well as the national chairman of the Centre for Civic Education. The latter body

[34] "To those who have suggested that Nkrumah was concentrating his efforts on legitimate freedom fighters from colonial territories, it will be enlightening to learn the names of some of the houses at this African Affairs Centre. There were two Sawaba Houses (for malcontents from Niger), but there was no South African House; a Cameroon House, but no Rhodesian House; and an Ethiopian House, but no Angolan House. And is it not ironic that Nkrumah saw fit to succour and encourage 'freedom fighters' from Ethiopia—the single country in Africa with a history of independence that stretches back three thousand years.

"But, as in so many other cases, Nkrumah's determination as to which were and which were not independent African nations was based on the purely personal criterion of whether the leaders of their governments did or did not kowtow to the name Nkrumah. Those who did not, no matter how objectively impeccable was the escutcheon of their independence, became in Nkrumah's lexicon 'neo-colonial' and thus targets for his subversion.

"Who can doubt the credentials of Jomo Kenyatta, either as a freedom fighter or as the elected leader of a truly independent African nation? Yet Nkrumah's off-centre view of African affairs permitted him to train dissident members of the Kamba tribe who were to form a guerilla cadre loyal to Oginga Odinga, Kenyatta's chief antagonist in Kenya.

"The end result of Nkrumah's egocentric view of African realities is that his guerilla warfare camps trained more nationalists from independent countries than they did from the imperialist and colonial areas of Angola, Mozambique, Rhodesia, and South Africa combined." See Ministry of Information, *Nkrumah's Subversion in Africa* (Accra: State Publishing Corporation, 1966).

[35] See the very useful account in Robert E. Dowse, "The Military and Political Development," in Colin Leys, ed., *Politics and Change in Developing Countries* (Cambridge: Cambridge University Press, 1969), p. 240.

developed working relationships with various groups in the government and with the Institute of Adult Education, local councils, churches, the Trade Union Congress, and the Department of Social Welfare and Community Development. Busia's political prominence rose while at the same time a series of commissions of inquiry, reviewing the files and records of senior C.P.P. members, publicized the privileged quality of C.P.P. leadership and its misappropriation of funds.

As Dowse suggests, the regime was suspicious of the "masses" (this perhaps ought to be rephrased as the "urban masses"). The rural populations, which all along had had the least affection for Nkrumah, became most favored. Before this it was the urban middle and lower classes that were highly privileged. A qualified but clearly favorable attitude towards chiefs was also manifested, encouraging the political revival of chieftaincy.[36] The emphasis on rural support and chieftaincy renewed a familiar structure which, created during colonial times, had been deliberately dismantled by Nkrumah over the years. The restoration of the alliance formed the backbone of the Progress Party.[37] The party itself was the creation of Professor Busia.

As head of the Political Committee, Busia had been responsible for the establishment of centers for civic education which stressed citizen training and the need for democratic institutions. In effect, while formal party activity was banned under the N.L.C., Busia organized the Progress Party.[38]

Despite their method of coming to power, the military and police officers who ruled Ghana believed deeply in the principles of law and order regulated by the legislative process. They were

[36] The deputy speaker of the Constitutional Assembly was Nene Azu Mate Kole, Konor of Manya Krobo, and Vice Chairman of the Chieftaincy Secretariat. See Chapter 12.

[37] Moreover, after the Busia government came to power, the management committee of the local councils were heavily Progress party. See the discussion of this point in Kwame Afreh, "The Future of the Opposition," in *The Legon Observer*, Vol. v, No. 1, January 1970, p. 16.

[38] Dowse points out that of the twenty-three members of the political committee, "no less than twelve were ex-members of the U.P. and most of the rest were people who had no associations with the C.P.P." See Dowse, *op. cit.*, p. 241. The statement is not quite correct. Kraus notes that fourteen had opposed the C.P.P. Some had been C.P.P. supporters at one time. See Kraus, "Arms and Politics in Ghana," *op. cit.*

anxious to get the country "back on the right track." In an attempt to promote economic recovery, they denationalized some enterprises and closed others which were unprofitable. These actions were taken despite rising unemployment. The *cedi* was devalued and the economic commission sought ways of renegotiating Ghana's debts and attracting foreign capital. Moreover, despite the ban on politics, the constitutional commission established a year after the coup held hearings which enabled representatives of thousands of people to participate under the shrewd chairmanship of the then Chief Justice and later President of Ghana. The draft constitution was debated by a constituent assembly consisting of some nominated and some elected members representing the Trades Union Congress, the Market Women's Association, the Bar Association, Civil Servants, Houses of Chiefs, Farmers, the Judiciary and others, with fifteen members nominated directly by the N.L.C.

An almost exaggerated atmosphere of legalism pervades the period. An electoral commission was established under the chairmanship of an Appeal Court judge which, reviewing previous election proceedings, established a permanent Electoral Commission under the experienced chairmanship of Justice V. C. R. A. C. Crabbe. A new electoral register was prepared (out of 3,222,060 potential voters, 2,356,897, or about 73 per cent, registered), and a week after the new constitution was promulgated general elections were held.

The Restoration of Parliamentary Democracy

However one regards the ideas and political shortcomings of the National Liberation Council, and they were many, the Constitution of the Second Republic of Ghana and the elections which followed its promulgation were in significant part its achievement. It represented a commitment by the army to parliamentary government. The question is whether or not the pattern will be repeated. Not only were parliamentary government and party politics restored, but the army and police, and more practically the key members of the N.L.C., retired from politics. It was an exemplary exercise which placed extraordinary burdens on the Busia government, because it stood on trial not only as the government of the day but as a testimonial to the potential for democratic government in Africa.

The constitution itself reflected both the desire to correct the excessive unitarism of the previous constitution and to prevent the revival of domestic dictatorship while still enabling a government of the day to govern effectively. The difficulties that plagued the Busia government were not constitutional. They derived from the quality of political judgment being exercised in the cabinet, its strategy, and the complex of social and economic problems which remained unsolved.

Indeed, the constitution worked rather better than was to be expected. The outlook for it was not overly sanguine. As one shrewd appraisal summarized it, "the constitution is a *potpourri* of constitutional ideas drawn from many diverse sources." A prominent Ghanaian constitutional lawyer observed that "it appears to be a combination of the French Civil Code, the Swiss criminal code with the original features of the Fifth French Republic tied together with the British concept of common law. The bicephalous executive is, at best, an ambivalent attempt to divide powers between the indirectly elected presidency . . . and the parliament-selected prime minister. With the weakened executive and the enormous emphasis on the division of powers, the framework envisioned by the constitution may lead to political inaction and thus prove to be inadequate to deal with the myriad problems of a developing nation."[39]

Most of the structural weaknesses were a result of efforts to prevent the revival of the kind of constitutional authoritarianism which enabled Nkrumah, by legal steps, to tighten his control over the country. It was an enormous document, full of details and containing 177 articles. For example, a few constitutions specifically mention political parties. The Ghana constitution did, and went on to state that "Parliament shall have no power to pass a law establishing a one-party state."[40]

[39] See Emily Card and Barbara Callaway, "Ghanaian Politics: The Elections and After," in *Africa Report*, Vol. xv, No. 3, March 1970, p. 15. See also D. E. Apter and Martin Doornbos, "Development and the Political Process," in *The African Review*, No. 1, March 1971.

[40] Article 3 (1). Clause 2 further specified that "any person, persons, or group of persons which suppresses or seeks to suppress the lawful political activity of any other person or persons generally or any class of persons shall be an unlawful act."

Such defensive clauses were piled on as if the combination of legal safeguards would, by their predominance and weight, reduce the likelihood of coups and dictatorships. The previous constitution had affirmed certain civil liberties as fundamental principles and obligations not in the form of a legally enforceable bill of rights but as a solemn declaration by the president on taking office.[41] The new constitution provided an elaborate charter of fundamental human rights enforceable in the courts.[42] This was, of course, a fundamental improvement. Other features were more questionable. The power of the president to govern under emergency regulations was delimited, as well as the treatment of persons detained under emergency legislation. Perfectly understandable was a clause of questionable value to express restriction on political parties which recruited members on the basis of primordial loyalties, such as tribal or religious affiliations.[43]

More seriously, as most observers agreed, the potential powers of the president and the prime minister were not always clear vis-à-vis each other. Nor was there a clear enough division of function. The president was to act on the advice of a Council of State with respect to appointments. Membership in the council included the prime minister, the leader of the opposition, the speaker of the Assembly, and other distinguished individuals, some of whom were appointed by the president.[44] There was a National Security Council presided over by the prime minister, which included among its members the ministers of foreign affairs, defense, interior, finance, and the attorney general. Its functions

---

[41] "That subject to such restrictions as may be necessary for preserving public order, morality, or health, no person should be deprived of freedom of religion or speech, or the right to move and assemble without hindrance or of the right of access to courts of law."

[42] Compare Article 13, Clause 1, of the Republican constitution with Chapter 4, "Liberty of the Individual," in the Busia constitution. The latter details in a most elaborate way those rights and freedoms which must be preserved, including fundamental rights, family welfare, protection of the right to life, personal liberty, protection from slavery, forced labor, inhuman treatment, deprivation of property, protection of privacy, freedom of conscience, freedom of expression, assembly, movement, and protection from discrimination.

[43] Article 35.

[44] Article 53. The power of appointment also included public servants, the Electoral Commission, the Ombudsman, the Chief of Defense, the Chief Justice, etc. See Kwame Afreh, "Lt. General Afrifa and the Constitution," in *The Legon Observer,* August 14, 1970.

were "to ensure the collection of information relating to the
national security and the integration of the domestic, foreign
and military policies."[45] It was also responsible for policy relevant
to such issues.

All these needed to be made compatible with responsible cabinet
government. The prime minister was appointed on the basis of
party distribution in the National Assembly, which, organized on
Westminster lines, consisted of 140 members. In addition to a
cabinet, appointed by the prime minister, there was a Supreme
Court with the right of judicial review, an ombudsman to protect
persons from actions taken by any member of a department or
ministry of state, armed forces, statutory corporation, or public
service.[46] Finally, there was also provision for a National House
of Chiefs and regional houses, as well as local district and regional
councils.[47]

The most controversial provision of the constitution was Article 71. This listed the qualifications and disqualifications of
members of the National Assembly and was used as a weapon
against certain former C.P.P. officials.

What was perhaps most curious about the constitution was
not how the various offices and institutions divided power but the
ways in which it remained ambiguous on certain principles. It
was not, as in the American system, an explicit system of checks
and balances in which established tripartite principles determine
the basis on which power is distributed. Rather it was a unitary
and parliamentary instrument with distribution of jurisdictions
within and between extraparliamentary institutional bodies. Some
of these, like the Council of State, appeared to provide substantive power to the president. In contrast, the National Security
Council appeared to provide redundant powers to the prime
minister. All this would have made the role of the Supreme Court
difficult. Clearly able to act to preserve civil liberties, it was less
clear on what basis to decide the appropriate scope of powers
embodied in the various offices and institutions of government. In

[45] Article 55.
[46] Chapter 8, "The Ombudsman."
[47] On each council there was express provision for traditional representation
consisting of two-thirds on local councils and one-third on district councils.

this respect, the decisive clause in the constitution was Article 38. "In the performance of his functions under this Constitution, the President shall act in accordance with the advice of the Cabinet or a Minister acting under the general authority of the Cabinet." Without establishing parliamentary supremacy, the constitution affirmed the preeminence of the prime minister and his cabinet, a curious procedure. In addition, a difficult amending procedure exempted from alteration those clauses dealing with basic rights and liberties. The latter required a two-thirds majority of the members of the National Assembly.

It was forthright only in the preamble: "In the name of Almighty God from Whom all authority is derived and to Whom all actions, both of men and States must be referred, we, the chiefs and people of Ghana, having experienced a regime of tyranny, remembering with gratitude the heroic struggle against oppression, having solemnly resolved never again to allow ourselves to be subjected to a like regime, determined to secure for all of us a Constitution which shall establish the Sovereignty of the People and the Rule of Law as the foundation of our society and which shall guarantee freedom of thought, expression and religion, justice—social, economic, and political—respect for the dignity of the individual, and equality of opportunity, do hereby . . . adopt, enact and give to ourselves this constitution."

It remained in effect for just under two and a half years.

The Election of 1969

With the promulgation of the constitution and prior to the elections which followed, the Chairman of the National Liberation Council appealed to the electorate not to make reckless choices "influenced in any way by considerations other than merit and ability." A rash of political parties broke out. One purported to be a "third force" between the C.P.P. and the U.P. Others had marvelous names and no followers, such as the National Reconstruction Crusade, the Black Power Party, the United Jehovah Party, and the Saviour's Party. One, the People's Popular Party, was banned on the grounds that it had a predisposition in favor of communism and Nkrumah. Another, of some significance, was the People's Action Party, which produced a most unfortunate acronym (P.A.P.).[48]

Excluding minor parties, five contested the elections, with Busia's Progress Party and Gbedemah's National Alliance of Liberals the main contenders.[49] Distinguished more by their ethnic support than basic differences in ideology, both were concerned about similar issues—inflation, unemployment, welfare. The P.P.'s emphasis was on rural development and on decentralized administration, both of which found favor with chiefs and among the older sectors of the population.

Of the two, the National Alliance of Liberals employed campaign tactics that were familiar in the early days of C.P.P. politics. N.A.L. colors, propaganda vans, and motorcycles were visible everywhere, although its slogan was perhaps less than appetizing ("Let the People Eat"). The N.A.L. also emphasized a new agricultural policy, which promised to turn Ghana into an agricultural exporting country to bridge the gap between "rural farmer and the city industrialist, and between the children of the Senior Civil Servant in Accra and those of the small blacksmith in Mamprusi." No wonder that Mr. Gbedemah suggested the need for a crusade for "efficient government" in order to "transform Ghana into a new Israel."

The election results showed some interesting patterns, particularly in the light of previous elections. Dennis Austin commented on one similarity between the first Nkrumah and Busia elections. "As in 1951, so in 1969, popular emotion and private interests have come down overwhelmingly on the side of the party which seemed most likely to make a new beginning. And, in 1969, as in 1951, the main check to the triumphal march of Progress has been the trans-Volta vote, east and north among the non-Akan. There is every reason, also, to suspect that history will repeat itself—of course, with a difference—in the sense that at the next election, Progress, like the old C.P.P., may find itself troubled as much by internal differences as by external enemies."[50]

[48] Perhaps the party with the most magnificent title was the Congress of Continental Africa, founded by A. C. de Profundis.

[49] These were the Progress Party, National Alliance of Liberals, United Nationalist Party, and the People's Action Party, and the All People's Republican Party.

[50] See Dennis Austin, "Caesar's Laurel Crown," in *West Africa,* September 13, 1969.

The seats were distributed as follows:

DISTRIBUTION OF SEATS

Party	Number of Seats
Progress Party	105
National Alliance of Liberals	29
People's Action Party	2
United Nationalist Party	2
All People's Republican Party	1
Independent	1

PARTY DISTRIBUTION*

REGIONAL DISTRIBUTION BETWEEN P.P. AND N.A.L. OF SEATS

Region	P.P.	N.A.L.
Ashanti	22	—
Brong Ahafo	13	—
Central	15	—
Eastern	18	4
Volta	2	14
Western	10	—
Greater Accra	3	3
Northern	9	5
Upper	13	3
	105	29

* From Max Assimeng, "The Electoral Panorama," in *The Legon Observer,* September 5, 1969, p. 3.

Comparing these figures with 1956, we find that then opposition to the C.P.P. was strongest in Ashanti as a whole, which voted in favor of the National Liberation Movement (N.L.M. 119,033 to C.P.P. 96,968)[51] except in the Brong Ahafo area of Ashanti, where the 1956 vote was 38,373 for the C.P.P. and 25,633 for the opposition. In 1969, the total Ashanti and Brong Ahafo vote was 429,978, of which Ashanti alone gave 215,272 votes for the P.P. and 64,522 for the combined opposition and Brong Ahafo 127,707 for the P.P. and 22,477 for the combined opposition. The transformation in that area could not be put down to the fact that Dr. Busia was a Brong from Wenchi (since he

[51] These figures included Brong Ahafo which subsequently became a separate region.

also ran in 1956) but rather said a good deal about the status of the old dispute between Brongs and Ashanti, as it did in 1956 when providing the original basis of the Brong pro-C.P.P. position.[52]

In Transvolta in 1956, the combined opposition was 46,076, while the C.P.P. obtained 55,508 votes. In 1969, this region was, with the exception of two seats, entirely N.A.L. In part, this may have been due to the fact that Gbedemah, the leader of the N.A.L., was himself an Ewe. But this region had always had a strong anti-Akan vote. For example, in 1956 the party receiving the largest number of votes in the Volta region was the Togoland Congress, a predominantly Ewe political party.[53]

Figures for the Greater Accra constituency were also interesting. In the heavily Ga areas, P.P. and N.A.L. divided with three seats each, while the United Nationalist Party under the leadership of a distinguished Ga medical practitioner, Dr. H. S. Bannerman, won two. The U.N.P. included several very well-known politicians who had been in opposition to Nkrumah, including Mr. Joe Appiah, Mr. Modesto K. Apaloo, and Mr. Attoh Quarshie.[54]

The U.N.P., essentially a Ga party, represented a revival of the old Ga Shifmo Kpee, a local separatist movement which had flourished briefly in 1957.

The parliamentary victory of the P.P. thus has a certain consistency to it. Where in 1956 the C.P.P. obtained 72 seats out of 104 with a popular majority of 57 per cent, the P.P. in 1969 won 105 seats out of 140, with a popular majority of 59 per cent.[55] Clearly, given even exceptional elections, Ghanaian voters retained an independence of spirit and a substantial opposition which could only be based on regional and tribal preferences and loyalties. Analyzing the vote makes clear that ethnic factors have played, and continue to play, a very important part in elections. Ethnicity is one way of organizing interests and, precisely be-

[52] See the analysis of the 1956 election in D. E. Apter, "Ghana," in *Political Parties and National Integration in Tropical Africa,* J. S. Coleman and Carl G. Rosberg, eds. (Berkeley: University of California Press, 1964), pp. 288-89.

[53] *Ibid.,* p. 290.

[54] With the exception of Dr. Bannerman and Mr. Alex Hutton-Mills, all the members of the United Nationalist Party outside Accra were defeated in their home constituencies.

[55] A fuller analysis is in Norman Uphoff, "An Element of Repetition in Ghanaian Directions," in *The Legon Observer,* January 2, 1970.

cause there is no sharp urban–rural split, ethnicity helps serve as the basis for demands upon government for a distributive share. As we have already suggested, there is a danger that the casual observer may come to place too many aspects of political life in Ghana under the heading of tribalism. Except for periods of elections and in local party organization (and in these it is not so different from the regional and ethnic loyalties found in most democratic countries), neither under Nkrumah or the Busia government was ethnicity per se a distinguishing feature. "Tribal politicking" does not necessarily lead to "tribal politics." A quick comparison with Nigeria would show the difference. Hence, despite charges of tribal favoritism and the undoubted relevance of ethnicity in elections, the Busia government, while remaining sensitive to the issue, dealt with it in the form of rural development, economic reform, and chieftaincy, an emphasis which proved to be disastrous.[56]

Like the first "nationalist" election in 1951, the symbolism of the campaign went far beyond its immediate objects of obtaining a popular government. The election was a public demonstration of African faith in parliamentary institutions. What was affirmed was the vitality of democratic government. To underscore this point, at the inauguration of the Presidential Commission Brigadier Afrifa released those political prisoners still held under protective custody: "Today we stand at the threshold of a new era in the political evolution of our country, as we are embarking on a great experiment with a constitution forged out of our bitter experience and sufferings of the past. We hope that no Ghanaian will be unjustifiably deprived of his birthright of the fundamental human rights and freedoms of the individual guaranteed by the Constitution. To commemorate this historic occasion, we have decided that all persons still being held in protective custody under the Protective Custody Decree, 1966, and subsequent amendments should be released forthwith. I am happy to say that the Protective Custody Decree now becomes a dead letter. We expect

---

[56] The problem of ethnicity reached its height during the period of National Liberation Council rule where, because of the disproportionate number of Ewes on the Council, the Ewe's had "taken over." For a useful discussion of the ethnicity problem, see "Three Dimensions of Ethnic Politics" by David L. Horowitz, *World Politics,* Vol. xxiii, January 1971.

that the persons so released will be rehabilitated and given the opportunity of taking their place as worthy citizens of their country."[57]

The election by and large followed procedures similar to those of the general elections of 1954 and 1956, with appropriate modifications according to the new constitution. If the campaign was colorful, one surprise was the relative drabness of the N.A.L. party leader, K. A. Gbedemah.[58] In contrast, Busia was a more lively campaigner. He traveled continuously. He made many whistle-stop appearances. According to one observer, "it looked like the Nixon campaign style in America. He even went so far as to arrive at rallies with his wife and his children in one car. This was a novelty in Ghanaian political campaigning. He endeared himself, his family, and the Party to the Ghanaian public. He offered himself for national examination."[59]

The executive of the new government consisted of a Presidential Commission composed of three key military and police officers: Brigadier Afrifa, Chairman; Mr. J. W. K. Harlley, Deputy Chairman; and Lt. General A. K. Ocran, member.[60] Dr. Busia, the new Prime Minister, composed his cabinet carefully. Included were long-term associates such as William Ofori-Atta, one of the last surviving senior members of the old United Gold Coast Convention. Other members were Victor Owusu, R. R. Amponsah, and Simon Dombo (the former leader of the opposition in Nkrumah days), all of whom had been in prison under Nkrumah. Another old-line political leader, Kwesi Lamptey, originally a member of the C.P.P., who had resigned as far back as 1952 and gone into opposition, was made Minister of Defense.[61]

[57] See address by Brigadier A. A. Afrifa, in *Civil Rule Returns to Ghana* (Accra: Ministry of Information, 1969).

[58] Under Article 71 of the constitution, the leader of the N.A.L., Mr. K. A. Gbedemah, who would have taken his seat in parliament and become the Leader of the Opposition, was disqualified.

[59] See Kwame Kesse-Adu, "The Election—Before and After," in Moses Danquah, ed., *The Birth of the Second Republic* (Accra: Editorial and Publishing Services, 1970), p. 82.

[60] The Commission was a transitional executive. A year later, the then Chief Justice, Mr. Edward Akufo-Addo, became the first President.

[61] The members of the first Busia cabinet were Kwesi Lamptey, Defense; William Ofori-Atta, Education; Richard Quarshie, Trade and Industries; Simon Dombo, Interior; R. R. Amponsah, Lands and Mineral Resources; Kwabena Kwakye Anti, Local Administration; Victor Owusu, External Affairs; S. W. A. Darko, Works; Jatoe Kaleo, Labor and Social Welfare; N. Y. B. Adade, Attorney

Excluding Dr. Busia, the occupational composition of the cabinet was seven lawyers, two doctors, four teachers, three senior civil servants, and one businessman. Overwhelmingly professional and technocratic, its ethnic origins were heavily Akan (where the National Liberation Council had been heavily Ewe).[62]

The Busia government was highly educated, consisting of leading citizens, many of whom had suffered deeply for their opposition to Nkrumah. Few except for Kwesi Lamptey, R. R. Amponsah, and to a lesser extent Victor Owusu had been populist politicians. Some, like Busia himself, had intimate connections with chiefly houses. Absent were representatives of the urban workers and trade unionists. No one spoke for youth. No matter what the chronological ages of members of the cabinet, the government represented the "seniors," i.e., the generation which traced its lineage to that generation of lawyers and middle-class professionals which had earned its credentials through consistent and courageous opposition to Nkrumah.

The Democratic Performance

If the Busia government took office with an overwhelming mandate, it also confronted exceptionally grave problems. The worst of these were economic. The overseas debt, high recurrent costs, inflation, unemployment, a steadily deteriorating situation in the world price of cocoa—all demanded instant and dramatic attention. Renegotiation of loans, devaluation of the *cedi*, and elimination of noneconomic enterprises continued to be high priorities. Previous economic failures were analyzed. For example, it was discovered that rural decline under Nkrumah was not caused by low investment but rather by high investment in agriculture, which had been a failure. The state farms employing heavy machinery had proved uneconomic. Indeed, they were so badly managed that the result was an increase rather than a decline in agri-

---

General; J. H. Mensah, Finance; G. D. Ampaw, Health; T. D. Brodia-Mends, Information; Dr. Kwame Safo-Adu, Agriculture; Dr. William G. Bruce-Konuah, Housing; A. A. Munufie, Social and Rural Development; and H. Esseku, Transport and Communications. On January 29, 1971, three ministers were dropped and Dr. Busia assumed responsibility for Economic Planning and Information.

62 By a rough calculation on the basis of place of birth (a hazardous procedure), there were two northerners, five Fanti, four Ashanti, two Brong, four Akim and Akwapim, one Ga, and no Ewe. Since the latter voted almost entirely N.A.L., this was not surprising. The pattern was similar among the ministerial secretaries.

cultural imports. Ghana was one of the few countries which, during the so-called development decade of the 1960's, suffered an average drop in per capita production and a net per capita income decline.

In addition to economic problems, the civil service had been considerably undermined during the Nkrumah period and was in a chronic state of low morale and poor organization. There was underutilization of those with specialized educational and technical skills. Indeed, instead of a shortage, it was discovered that Ghana had been exceptionally well endowed with experts.[63] As one observer put it, "At the moment, it is felt that it is more the strategy for the utilization of the trained personnel which constitutes a problem. What is needed is that, when Government and other industrialists want to start an enterprise, they should use the personnel they have in Ghana and call in the foreign experts only as a last result."[64]

Many of the problems of Busia's Ghana can be laid to the specific policies pursued by Nkrumah, i.e., showpiece projects, hastily organized development schemes, expenditures on enterprises with excessive recurrent costs, expanded educational and social service facilities without provision for sufficient means, lack of maintenance, corruption at home, manipulation by unscrupulous businessman abroad, rising costs of the military and the police because of their growing punitive use and increasing coercion, expensive party and paramilitary operations, overextensive diplomatic facilities, etc. However, with or without Nkrumah, Ghana would still have had what might be called second-stage development problems which, not yet as common in African countries as elsewhere (particularly in Latin America), are the accumulated results of initial policies and the latent and unforeseen difficulties which these produce. These result from (1) inadequacies of the

[63] In a recent paper dealing in part with the utilization of manpower, Dr. R. G. J. Butler comments that the "calculated scientists/residents (Peter Nonkoh) ratio for Ghana in 1967 exceeded by 44 per cent the ratio of 200 scientists/million residents which was recommended by the UNESCO/UNECA Conference at Lagos, Nigeria, 1964, as a minimum target for African countries by 1970." See R. G. J. Butler, "Problems in the Execution of Research Programs in Physical and Technological Sciences in Ghana," conference paper presented to the Joint Council for Scientific and Industrial Research, National Science Foundation Conference, January 1971, Accra.

[64] The problem of under-employed technical personnel is a growing one in many modernizing countries.

market mechanism as a balance wheel of production and consumption; (2) the growth of a large consumption sector with needs that can only be satisfied by imports from industrial countries; (3) the increasing complexity of the planning mechanism, so that projections and predictions become obsolete almost before they are completed; (4) growing dependency on external sources for investment, goods, and services; (5) increasing economic vulnerability as the economy becomes more differentiated and locked into the world market system; (6) administrative "indigestion," specialized agencies, enclave communities of technical experts, commissions, institutes, and operating units which find themselves at odds over priorities and leading to bureaucratic provincialism and confused ends; and (7) the attrition of technical personnel to the expanding administrative system (technical wastage).

The magnitude of the problems must be borne in mind prior to any evaluation of the policy record of the Busia government. In addition, the government had inherited a two-year plan initiated by the National Liberation Council, which, although designed to promote economic recovery, on the whole was not very successful. When the second coup occurred a new five-year plan for comprehensive economic development was being prepared.[65] What the government patently failed to do was to restore the balance of payments by cutting back government expenditure, encouraging private enterprise, and seeking price stabilization in the world marketing of cocoa.[66] Rather, in a politically unsavory gesture to combat unemployment, the Busia government ordered almost all non-Ghanaians without residence permits to leave the country within two weeks.[67]

In a sudden austerity move and to tighten up the civil service, 568 civil servants were dismissed, a high proportion of whom were Ewe and Ga. The educational structure was remodeled at all levels

[65] The Two-Year Development Plan was presented in 1968 and prepared by a Joint Central Planning Agency team assisted by the Harvard Advisory Service.

[66] With respect to the encouragement of private enterprise, Firestone Rubber took over the Czechoslovakian built tire plant and, as well, 45 per cent of the state rubber farms. Lonrho bought the Ashanti Goldfield Company, and the United Africa Company bought 49 per cent of the shares of a Chinese built textile factory, etc.

[67] Approximately 170,000 "strangers" from Togo, Niger, Upper Voltaics, and Nigerians, left the country. For a good analysis of this, see Margaret Piel, "The Expulsion of West African Aliens," in *Journal of Modern African Studies*, Vol. IX, No. 2, August 1971, pp. 205-29.

in order to reduce the number of unemployable middle school leavers who could not find places in secondary schools. This was done before continuation and technical or commercial classes could be expanded. The university bursary system was altered so that the system of providing scholarships for all students was replaced by one of grants for students of exceptional merit only.[68] A twenty-year plan for education, drafted to deal with the entire educational structure, never went into effect. Replacing the old Workers' Brigade was a new National Service Corps based on voluntary service.[69] But it quickly lapsed into somnambulance, and was badly led and poorly financed.

The best efforts were extensions of the general policy directive first laid down by the N.L.C. government, which emphasized developments in the following terms: (a) the general modernization of rural areas; (b) the bridging of the gap between rural and urban areas; (c) the bridging of regional disparities; and (d) agricultural expansion as an aspect of rural development. The emphasis was on agricultural development and improvement in the conditions of village life. It included heavy expenditures on feeder roads and the increasing availability of agricultural credit and other measures to facilitate food and agricultural production. Such a policy, directly economic in its objects, also strengthened the hand of traditional authorities, in particular chiefs, who became more closely identified with local government than ever before.[70]

---

68 This applies to student upkeep. Tuition remains free at the universities in Ghana.

69 "The National Service Corps is conceived as a joint all-embracing effort of the whole nation; it is, in other words, brotherhood action, everyone contributing his or her bit toward solving our problems of hunger, illiteracy, disease and unemployment. The National Service Corps will undertake such projects as farming, building roads, health posts, market sheds, toilets, low cost houses, schools and community centers, wells and boreholds, and generally concern itself with spreading amenities to town and village communities, particularly in the rural areas." See Dr. K. A. Busia, "A Call to Service," radio and television broadcast, reprinted by the Ministry of Information (Accra: Ghana Publishing Corp., December 15, 1969).

70 See the statement by Dr. Busia in his Bolgatanga speech, November 26, 1969. "I would like to assure you, the Chiefs, that under the Constitution of the Second Republic, my Government is committed to the maintenance of the institution of chieftaincy and will encourage our Chiefs to play an increasingly important role in national development as well as in local and regional affairs." Printed in *Progress in Unity* (Ministry of Information: Accra, Ghana Publishing Corp., 1970), p. 27.

In hindsight, perhaps, one can point to the following three critical blunders. First, the smashing of the Trades Union Congress, hitherto the most effective organization in Ghana, aroused deep discontent in urban areas. After a lengthy campaign of harassment by government, not only was the T.U.C. dissolved, but its popular and effective chairman was imprisoned. Secondly, a drastic second devaluation of the *cedi* had an intense impact in the urban areas where the effects of inflation (due in large measure to heavy external indebtedness) were felt more directly in the rising cost of basic necessities of life than in the rural areas. Finally, when members of the cabinet and high officials of the party and government were accused of corruption, the response was to muzzle the press and ignore the charges—actions which particularly angered the military, the students, and the growing political opposition generally.

Not all the blunders were national. In a local crisis which had arisen during the N.L.C. period over the "skin" of Yendi, the government intervened on behalf of one contender to the "skin." This, a deeply traditional matter, was a disaster. In the ensuing riots, a number of people were killed by the police.[71]

The editor of an outspoken opposition newspaper, *The Spokesman*, which attacked the government was threatened with libel.[72] An editor of a progovernment newspaper, *The Daily Graphic*, who had become too critical of government, was invited to take an extended leave from his duties.

In short the record is a mixed one. There was a great deal of public criticism of the kind heard in all developing countries and which arises because of the formidable gaps between promise, plan, and reality. There was also a growing incidence of corruption.[73]

The government was particularly vulnerable because it exuded

---

[71] See S. M. Sibidow, *Background of the Yendi Skin Crisis* (Accra: New Times Press, 1969).

[72] *The Spokesman* charged that the General Secretary of the Progress Party, Mr. B. J. da Rocha, a lawyer, had enriched himself after assuming his post. Major-General A. K. Ocran queried the government on the failure of its Ministers to make public their assets as required by the constitution. Charges were made that government officials had a Mercedes Benz "syndrome."

[73] Neither the Justice Party which (succeeded the N.A.L. as the opposition party) nor the Progress Party paid sufficient attention to the needs of urban workers nor seemed to realize what a potentially effective force the T.U.C. might be.

a rather prim Christianity. Its response to widespread complaints about governmental inactivity was didactic or schoolmasterish. It shocked many Ghanaians by its willingness to "dialogue" with South Africa, while remaining more or less aloof from pan-African affairs. The result of all this was widespread malaise and disappointment.

Some Tentative Conclusions

From one standpoint, the Busia government's emphasis on rural development was a correct basis of policy. Certainly the rural areas represented the main source of votes and income. Moreover, real economic decline in Ghana was suffered in many villages during the years of Nkrumah, except in the north. The Ghanaian farmer knew that he paid for the failures of the Nkrumah regime. From every standpoint, the line on rural policy taken by the Progress Party seemed to make good economic sense. However, there are basic political difficulties with rural reform which plague all governments. One is that it is relatively undramatic, a matter of boreholes, feeder roads, new schools. These are soon taken for granted and are slow to produce results (which occur in small increments), leaving the impression that government is more or less inactive. A second difficulty is that rural reform starves the urban areas. Busia made much of the fact that in Ghana there was no real rural–urban split and that what helps the farmers therefore helps the members of his family in the town. But rural policy can never succeed politically unless accompanied by drastic measures on behalf of urban workers. Today's urban working force is more than a generation old. It was effectively organized in a democratic trade union movement under the leadership of an exceptionally dynamic General Secretary, Mr. B. A. Bentum. Composed of sixteen national unions with effective political and economic committees, it was perhaps the most militant and efficient national organization in Ghana. It was smashed by the Busia government because it was perfectly capable of taking strike action which would turn the precarious economy of Ghana into a shambles overnight and wreck any tentative efforts at recovery.[74] It is now being restored under the N.R.C.

[74] I am grateful to Mr. B. A. Bentum, Chairman of the T.U.C., and Mr. John Gould, Principal of the Labour College, for their extremely stimulating and insightful discussions on these and other points.

A third effect of "ruralism" is its influence on the political parties. The Progress Party, like the constituency parties of the C.P.P., quickly became a lackluster body. The rural branches hardly existed. Having served their purpose during election time, they were left to wither on the vine.

Indeed, instead of using the party, Busia preferred traditional authorities, local elected officials, and the civil service as his chosen instruments. Perhaps, as a former district commissioner, this was appropriate to Dr. Busia's experience, but it helped rob the party of power and made it organizationally vulnerable.

To summarize briefly, the emphasis on rural development policy produced slow and not very visible results. Reliance on local authorities, chiefs, and civil servants worked at the expense of the national party. More and more there was a "civil service" quality about the government. It did little to alter the scale of life between civil servants, university teachers, successful businessmen, and other educated people, which contrasted ever more sharply with the everyday life of the people. The equalization policy was applied in name only and aroused great antagonism not only among urban workers but also among university students and others who more and more represented a disenchanted youth. Meanwhile, the attitude of the government toward youth itself can only be described as musty. It was as if youth had had its day during the Nkrumah period and was now to be reminded of its deferential place in society.[75]

The teachers, university professors, senior civil servants, and chiefs, who were under constant attack during the Nkrumah period, came to power with a heightened sense of virtue and piety that was almost Victorian. Manifested in a style of dignity (or pomposity), it disguised very real inefficiencies in work, created a mutually protective society of "betters," and opened the opportunity for quiet corruption so undermining to standards of hard work. The educated, professional, and bureaucratic elites became a huge excrescence on the society, and the political system became increasingly absurd.

[75] See the interesting discussion on the educated minority and the "verandah boys" in Robert K. A. Gardiner, "The Role of Educated Persons in Ghana Society," in *Proceedings of the Ghana Academy of Arts and Sciences,* Vol. vii, 1970, pp. 8-9.

Dissatisfaction among youth and trade union militancy were never transformed into appropriate political organization. Many of the young remained diffident. They believed that those who for years had suffered in opposition should have an opportunity to rule. But by the time the coup occurred there were many signs that they were profoundly disturbed by what they saw.

More difficult to understand was the position of the T.U.C. Why it did not fight back or try to form a Labor Party (which could also capture the youth) is not exactly clear. Perhaps for the T.U.C. also it was a matter of timing. For one thing, a Labor Party in a developing country cannot function very well when the economic outlook is bleak. It needs a "reallocatable" surplus for welfare and developmental tasks. Even if it could come to power, the problem of what to do would remain. Committed as it was to democratic trade unionism, the ideology of the T.U.C. favored bargaining with power for worker benefits rather than seeking political power.[76] This dominant view was the familiar "fair day's work for a fair day's wage" philosophy of the American trade union movement.[77]

In the unfulfilled needs of youth and the urban trade unionists, there was a possible basis for an effective opposition party. The Justice Party, which emerged out of a coalition between the N.A.L. and several other smaller opposition parties, was beginning to take such a position. Its major difficulty, however, stemmed from the fact that as long as rural votes counted the Progress Party would remain in power. The leader of the Justice Party, Dr. G. K. Agama, a young academic, was very much aware of this predicament. The party he tried to fashion has been described in the following terms. "Social justice, self-reliance, parliamentary democracy, anti-imperialism and anti-

[76] In a speech opening the second biennial congress of the T.U.C., Bentum put this general point of view as follows: "Let us, therefore, make the period ahead of us a period of moral revival—workers to do a good day's job—employers to pay a good day's wage—and government to be sympathetic and concerned about the needs of the people they govern. On our part, let us resolve that the independence that the trade unions in this country have fought and gained shall never be compromised to any institution no matter how paternalistic that institution may be, for our salvation is in our own hands." See "Comprehensive Report," mimeo., Ghana Trades Union Congress, held at Tamale, July 26-28, 1968.

[77] See Obed Y. Asamoah, "Policy Differences Between Government and Opposition," in *The Legon Observer,* Special Edition on Opposition, November 6-19, 1970, pp. 8-9.

racism sum up the outline of Justice Party thinking. In terms of the major ideologies of our time, the Justice Party stands midway between capitalism and socialism—a little left of the center. It is reformative and not revolutionary, and it rejects the implication of the Marxist interpretation of history. It is, however, firmly committed to the eradication of exploitation, and it accepts as inevitable such conscious state planning compatible with political freedom."

The Busia government offended the youth and the workers, and made them the new "marginals" of Ghana. Both groups had had important access to power during the Nkrumah period. For them as time went on the memory of the worst excesses of the Nkrumah regime began to fade from memory and a more charitable view of Nkrumah or a certain nostalgia for past glories could be discerned. Although the Busia government reacted to this very sharply, it dealt with effects rather than causes.

In retrospect, perhaps it was an atmosphere of error rather than any specific mistakes which brought the government into disrepute. As a government it was inept. It experienced many embarrassing political incidents.[78] It alienated students, workers, and trade union officials. And most of all it offended the military by retiring or posting abroad all the senior military and police officials who had made the revolution, and then antagonized the junior officers by cutting the military budget 16 per cent in July 1971. This had a major impact on the training and organizational objectives of the army, and particularly affected the younger officers who had little else to do with their time but talk "coup-politics."[79]

The main lesson which can be learned is that democratic government is a matter of policy "payments" and marginal distributions. These create coalitions which, although they compete, retain a mutual stake in the system. Democratic politicians can perhaps inspire cooperation, or manage competitive groupings, but they cannot afford to define any one group as an enemy. In

[78] Such matters as the "trawler" incident, the Drevici "affair," the Sallah "case," etc., may each have been trivial, but the negative publicity they aroused was bad for the government.

[79] The likely role of such figures as Afrifa Harlley and Deku, crucial Ewe figures in the N.L.C., remains an interesting speculation. So far they have not participated in the National Redemption Council.

short, democratic governments work best when they transform matters of principle into matters of interest. The Busia government did not understand that simple rule of thumb, just as the Nkrumah government did not understand that to transform matters of interest into questions of principle would create cynicism and disbelief. The problem of all politics is how to build a durable framework on the shaky ground between principles and interests.

What this review of Ghana shows is how trying the issues of development really are. Political change in Ghana, as in most other modernizing societies, is a function of powerful and durable incongruities which reflect themselves both in ideology and leadership. The search for a stable political form to contain the contradictions of development and reshape an appropriate social structure will go on. What becomes oppressive to a long-term observer is the sheer effort and energy consumed in the process; the high personal cost of failure. Despite these, what has also emerged out of the trials of Ghanaian politics is a large reservoir of talented and experienced people whose political and technical skills need an appropriate political framework in order to work properly. This, and the impatience of a new generation, wait around the corner for today's regime. The next round in Ghana's transition is for them.

▯⋮▯⋮▯   APPENDIX   ▯⋮▯⋮▯

A NOTE ON METHODOLOGY

THE general theoretical presuppositions which underlie this work relate to three major components. The first is the actor-situation frame of reference which assumes as a dynamic element actors motivated towards the achievement of certain goals; hence the preoccupation, in this study, with the widening of goal opportunities under British rule, and its consequences for action. Second, we assume the significance of the actor's subjective frame of reference. Hence, we use the concept of role to indicate patterns of action as structured by the members of the system. Three, we use a concept of institutionalized norms which we specifiy as the relational substance of political institutional transfer. These three components form the major framework of the analytical system utilized here, excepting that through the use of structural-functional requisite analysis as developed by Parsons[1] and expanded by Levy for use in the analysis of comparative societies the patterns or stable paths of activity found in society have been viewed at a very general level. This supplies a vantage point for discussing social systems, including political sub-systems in comparative societies. For this latter consideration, Levy's work seems admirably suitable, casting the data in a setting which has a wider relevance than the Gold Coast itself and which provides a basis for theory construction (at some future date) in comparative analysis.

It is not our purpose here to go into an elaborate discussion of the theories used in the actual research on political institutional transfer in the Gold Coast. A few words on the methodological background are in order, however, because of the somewhat peculiar treatment entailed in this study.

Research theory attempts the construction of analytical models of a selected unit of social behavior for examination. In the present research, two such models were constructed, derived from the traditional system and the secular system. The usefulness of this sort of exercise depends upon the derivation of meaningful units for comparison between the two models, in which qualifying differences can be articulated out of actual behavior. The level of reliability depends upon the elegance of prior theories regarding human behavior, the careful limiting of the unit for analysis, the construction of research

---

[1] See Parsons, T. and Shils, E., "Values, Motives, and Systems of Action" in *Towards a General Theory of Action*, Harvard, 1952.

models, and the care with which concepts are derived. Research is ultimately faced with the problems of evaluation of data which must be perceived, weighted, and related to other materials.

All social analysis, regardless of whether or not it deals specifically with political structures, has common ground insofar as some aspect of human action is its purview. In this study one cannot find "purely political" elements. In our discussion we have discarded precinctual niceties to get at the substantive aspects of political institutional transfer. We may find them in the family system, in the administrative service, in the history, the pattern of land tenure, the ceremonies of the people of the Gold Coast. At times, perhaps, it appears as if the aspect of human action disappears in a maze of complex terminology and relational categories—a kind of brave new world unpeopled by people. Yet the test of such terms and categories is whether or not, at the end, our understanding of complex sociopolitical phenomena has been improved.

Significance

When we select both a problem and its research boundaries, a number of difficulties are raised. Either explicitly or implicitly the selection of the problem *qua* problem involves prior notions of significance. In this research, significance, it is held, falls into a number of categories.

First, there is the significance which derives from our comprehension of problems of social change. It is held here that in examining social behavior, or some aspects of it, in underdeveloped areas, basic authority-conflict situations are readily observable. These can contribute to our understanding of general social and political behavior over time.

Second, there is the significance which derives from the specific authority struggles between the Western and indigenous systems. Can a political system such as ours in the West be satisfactorily adjusted to the needs of aspiring peoples in underdeveloped areas in Africa? Such a question, it is held here, is one of the overwhelming issues of our time: the suitability of democratic political structures in areas suffering under grave economic and social handicaps.

Methodological Framework

a. Requisite Analysis. Two approaches were used in the research on political institutional transfer. The first involved a methodological framework adapted from a volume devoted to methods of comparative analysis of societies. This material, from *The Structure of So-*

ciety[2] by Marion J. Levy, Jr., follows the general approach of structural-functional requisite analysis. It provides both qualifying concepts for the examination of behavioral materials and a conceptual hierarchy of relational levels making for effective comparative studies. This material has provided the basis for deriving the two models—traditional and secular—in which elements of the first are crucial for an examination of the processes of political institutional transfer at its present stage.

b. Role Analysis. The second approach involves the use of role theory[3] as the specific research lever for the examination of actual political behavior. Role theory provides an initial conceptual tool for the discrimination of data to be qualified in the larger conceptual focus of Levy's methodological framework. In addition, role analysis depends in part upon assumptions made about motivation which are, in this view, inadequately treated in *The Structure of Society* for purposes of studying political institutional transfer.

Theoretical Assumptions

Two types of theories were implicit in the development of a working outline designed to shed light on the specific problem of political institutional transfer in the Gold Coast. One involves a somewhat pragmatic notion of man as an individual actor orienting his action towards the achievement of certain goals.[4] The other involves a notion of society as a complex of culture, social sub-systems (including predominantly political structures), and personality, having effective integration. Particular attention to political sub-structures was paid in the research regarding the models of a society contained in the concepts of traditional and secular in terms of role prescriptions, role pattern, and role modalities. Certain aspects of traditional societies, for example, were found to involve role patterns which were crucial to the maintenance of traditional tribal life and which survived after the tribal pattern had by and large broken down. Such patterns, pursued within secular politics, inhibited the growth and adaptation of secular political structures, as well as acting as malintegrative factors for political institutional transfer.

Concrete Foci of Analysis

Certain concrete social sub-structures were given particular examination in the light of the predominantly political focus of the study. Comparisons were made between the substantive aspects, such as norms and sanctions of the indigenous councils of elders, for

2 Princeton, Princeton University Press, 1952.
3 See Merton, Robert K., *Social Theory and Social Structure*, Glencoe, 1949.
4 Parsons, *Towards a General Theory . . . , op.cit.*

example, as compared with transferred political structures such as
the Legislative Assembly, or the cabinet, modeled on British practice.
The guide to selection of predominantly political structures was
roughly on the range of their decision-making impact over the membership of the society. Membership is determined by examining subjective awareness of belonging, and the observed limits of authority,
for the traditional stage, as compared with non-tribal awareness and
acceptance of authority. In our analysis therefore we are concerned
with the orientational foci of members of both of the systems, at a
most general level, with specific attention paid to the institutionalization of new social norms exhibited in role prescriptions and role
behavior. Substantive conflicts in authority patterns between older
and current political behavioral requirements provide an empirical
guide to problems of institutionalization.

Concept of Perception

Underlying the methodological approach is a concept of perception as a function of socialization. In these terms, for example, the
persistence of the family as a socializing unit according to traditional
criteria promotes behavioral conflict particularly for individuals
brought up in tribal areas, educated, and operating within the secular social and political framework. Again, the evidence of varied
perception is found in behavior categorized as roles and multiple
reference associations. As Parsons indicates:

"Roles are, from the point of view of the functioning of the social
system, the primary mechanisms through which the essential functional prerequisites of the system are met. There is the same order
of relationship between roles and functions in the organism. There is
not, with certain exceptions to be noted, an inherently limited supply
of roles which has to be allocated among claimants. However, if the
role is to serve the requisite functions in the social system, it must be
adapted to such conditions as the possibility of the same individual
combining a given set of roles in his own activity. . . ."[5]

In societies undergoing rapid change, the individual often combines
sets of antithetical roles, moving from one pattern to another as the
situation demands. We can indicate when one set of political roles,
those relating to traditional social systems, is not any longer incorporated in the individual's perceptive and behavioral frame of reference that political institutional transfer has been achieved on the
individual level. When, from the point of view of standard performances within the society, the individual process has been repeated in
regard to the significant groups in the society exhibiting plenary

[5] Parsons, T., *The Social System*, Glencoe, 1952, p. 115.

control through the transferred structures with generalized public support as manifested in both voting behavior, local government, and the nature of the opposition, then political institutional transfer will be deemed achieved. Needless to say, such a point is extremely difficult to determine, and in the material it is abundantly clear that such a level is not yet to be found in the Gold Coast. The range of compatibility and incompatibility of role structures as indicated by value conflicts, contrary and diverse reference orientations, and the multiplicity of patterns of expectancies would indicate a partial institutional transfer, with that at a tentative level.[6]

The two systems, traditional and secular, as integrated role systems, were viewed as the sources of conflicting values, as the framework of concrete socio-political sub-groups and concrete membership groups, as the base of conflicting expectancy patterns, and the source of differing reference groups.

Analysis of Norms

The two systems are descriptively and historically determined models. In their normative aspects they are ideal types.[7] A reconstruction of traditional patterns results in a selective bias based upon a pragmatic survival concept. If patterns of action found extant in the Gold Coast in the process of activating secular political and social structures have predominant reference to behavior suitable under the traditional patterns, they are given an important place in our examination.

More particularly, we are concerned with only those values directly related to the legitimization of authority. They are roughly categorized under Weber's classification of traditional authority, charismatic authority, and legal-rational authority. The development of secular government, in our present meaning, refers in the Gold Coast to public legitimization of a legal-rational set of political norms in relation to parliamentary structures. In examination it has been found that a primary *functional* vehicle of institutionalization has been the personal charisma of the nationalist leader, Kwame Nkrumah. An interesting problem presents itself therefore in a hypothesis about a shift in political norms taking place via charisma. *Are the functions of charisma essential for the successful transfer of*

[6] See Merton et al., "Contributions to the Theory of Reference Group Behavior" in *Studies in the Scope and Method of the "American Soldier,"* by Merton and Lazarsfeld, Glencoe, p. 51: "In general, then, reference group theory aims to systematize the determinants and consequences of those processes of evaluation and self-appraisal in which the individual takes the values or standards of other individuals and groups as a comparative frame of reference."

[7] See Weber, Max, *The Theory of Social and Economic Organization,* edited by Henderson and Parsons, London, 1947.

alien political structures to the larger affiliational ties of an integrated national society?[8]

The Behavioral Fields

The two systems used as working models for the derivation of value orientations and political behavior are fully stated as the traditionally oriented behavioral field, and the secularly oriented behavioral field. Each of these terms refers to a predominating form of legitimization of authority, and whether or not it conforms to a culturally enshrined perceptive focus: e.g., the indigenous past, or the secular future.

The two systems represent particular cultural predispositions which serve as cognitive and communications sources as well as moral commitments for the members of each system. One particular aspect of these cultural predispositions centers on the legitimization of authority around concrete power structures as membership units. These concrete power structures are the means whereby decisions are taken and implemented and therefore provide the empirical units from which data are derived.

The particular patterns by which action takes place derive in some part from the acceptance of certain modes of behavior. The particular type of legitimacy, the political sub-structures where decisions are taken, and political organizations themselves result in value frames (including procedural) in which specific forms of political activity are sanctioned, subject to: (1) threats to the members of the society from outside or external forces; (2) threats to the maintenance of order and procedure; (3) failures within the society to maintain the satisfactions of the members.

Regarding the first, threats to the members of the society from outside or external forces include not only the protection of members from territorial violations, but economic and social pressures as well. This is particularly significant for tribal areas which faced cultural imperialism as well as political domination.

Regarding the second, threats to the maintenance of order and procedure represent the value complex surrounding the structures of problem solving at the political level, as threatened from either internal or external sources. It is at this level that the issue of legitimacy is basic since the development of consensus in institutional transfer is, in itself, a value problem.

Regarding the third, failures within the society to maintain the

---

[8] See Weber, *op.cit.*, p. 301, where charismatic grounds of legitimacy are stated as "resting on devotion to the specific and exceptional sanctity, heroism or exemplary character of an individual person, and of the normative patterns of order revealed or ordained by him (charismatic authority)."

satisfactions of the members refers to what we can roughly classify as an internal political problem. That is, when adequate provisions for the needs of the members as defined on the one hand by their biological needs and on the other hand by their range of tolerance vis-à-vis expectancies are lacking, a political problem arises insofar as constituted authorities must cope with these failures. Long-term failures by the authorities themselves can either lead to changes in the occupants of authority or power roles, or changes in value orientations on the part of the members regarding types of legitimate authority and/or changes in the political sub-structures.

In the Gold Coast itself at the secular-national level, external threats are lacking. Protection from potential enemies is still afforded by Imperial Britain. The development of parliamentary procedure and a larger environment of social order under secular terms is the objective of political institutional transfer. We are therefore concerned with the structural aspects maintained in residual terms by the authority of the governor and in process aspects—as institutional transfer—by the charismatic authority of Kwame Nkrumah, the prime minister. Too weighty burdens, placed upon political institutional transfer, however, would be evidenced in repudiation of secular political structures and norms deriving from failures within the society to maintain the satisfactions of the members.

What we seek to examine, therefore, is a set of two differing systems, deriving from differing cultural traditions, only one of which is a relatively indigenous type to the territorial area. We view sets of political value orientations (or political norms) as they are integrated with individual behavior as a complex of need-dispositions and gratification-expectancies patterns within the structures by which certain aspects of those needs are satisfied (modalities of political behavior), as integrated with institutionalized procedures of choice and political organizations devoted to the effectuation of decisions.

Since we have assumed that political value orientations are part of a cultural heritage which is prior to any given individual actor, the degree to which conflicting value orientations exist within prescribed power structures are examined particularly in role behavior reaching out to larger cultural segments of the population via multiple reference group orientations. These, it is assumed, form certain patterns within each particular cultural nexus. These patterns form the sub-structures of competing social systems and indicate the significance of differing patterns of role behavior relating to authority and legitimacy. Hence the peculiar treatment of indirect rule.

Within this general framework institutional transfer in the Gold Coast has been articulated. Behind the terms "traditional" and "secular" is a notion of social action as a complex of culture, personality, and social systems but categorized in terms of relevances to political behavior. The general description of each predominating type of complex as action has been considered as an integrated behavioral field. Discrepancies between ideal and actual behavior patterns illuminate perceptive and affective shifts by members of the society as measured in roles found in political sub-structures both under indirect rule and under the present parliamentary secular system, particularly for those participants in formal positions of authority and decision-making. The degree of institutionalization thus refers to problems of adaptation and change from one behavioral field to another.

It is important to distinguish the vantage point from which degrees of integration or order as a normative system have been observed. When, from the point of view of the researcher, a genuine perceptive or cognitive shift involving normative acceptance of a secular complex of legitimacy and authority structures has occurred, then a genuine shift in behavioral fields has taken place and political institutional transfer has been realized. There is obviously no specific point at which "genuine" can be ascertained. However, since the observational focus rests on political sub-structures, which operate on the British parliamentary model in the Gold Coast today, then comparisons with the British model are in order. Again, this raises difficulties in questions of relevance and questions of significant comparison. The way out which is taken in this study circumvents the problem in two ways. First of all, one clue is provided in terms of problems which arise on a concrete level in which questions of substantive authority—or legitimacy—are involved (where public apathy is not the rule). If legitimacy issues disappear and questions of the nature of sanctional authority give way to ordinary questions of government, then by one standard political institutional transfer has been achieved. Secondly, the real question of success in institutional transfer cannot be examined in any final terms since complete self-government on the British model has not been fully achieved. Until that time it seems as if successful institutional transfer can be studied only in terms of political issues which have already arisen.

Techniques of Data-Gathering

Within this general theoretical framework, the burden of research has been the following. The enumeration of the two behavioral fields, traditional and secular, has proceeded out of published materials and interviews with key participants. Delineation and analysis of the traditionally oriented behavioral field, which is extremely important since it imposes a kind of base point of analysis, was derived from historical writings, early government documents, sociological and anthropological studies, and interviews with those who occupy important roles in the traditional systems, particularly chiefs and elders.

The second model, or secularly oriented behavioral field, assumes the British parliamentary structural framework, involving elections, parties, and the usual paraphernalia of Western political activity. Again, difficulties arise in the construction of a useful model of the British parliamentary system for comparative purposes. British government operates with a host of subtleties best referred to from an empirical point of view as intangibles which make precise judgments almost impossible. Unfortunately, whether accurately or not, the British governmental pattern is the specific source of transfer legally being constructed. Inasmuch as some form of this pattern is in the minds of constitution-makers and British administrators, it was crucial to devise a secular model theoretically constructed for comparative and analytical purposes. In any case, the secular system forms the main area of empirical research in the field.

Aside from the general interviews of persons occupying important political roles in formal organizations as set up by the relevant orders in council and ordinances, a particular piece of legislation, the Local Government Ordinance of 1951, was followed through from its inception to its administration. The ordinance in question was particularly relevant from the point of view of this study, insofar as it enforced a shift from tribal to conciliar forms of local government, striking at the substantive authority of chieftainship.

Four problem areas where conflicts over legitimized authority were particularly striking were examined in detail, of which two (Wenchi and Manya Krobo) were used in this study for illustrative purposes.

Some attention was devoted to a single personality, the prime minister, partly because of the historical role which he has played in the independence movement of the Gold Coast, and partly because of the particular type of influence which he wields, and the relation of this influence to the legitimization of a predominantly alien political complex.

Written materials included an array of published and unpublished statistics, documents (official and unofficial), letters, books, and legal papers. While some of these materials have been put to unusual use, it is hoped that the results will justify the usage.

From the foregoing discussion it should be clear that the methodological frame of reference departs drastically from the older approaches of such theorists as Hobson, Lenin, Schumpeter, and others who have dealt with problems in the colonial sphere. Here we sought to examine rather than judge. We sought to "research" a problem of great complexity involving as it does the gamut of human emotions and man's ability to adapt to and survive shocks of great magnitude.

INDEX

INDEX

Weber, Max, 82n, 174n, 211, 212n, 228n, 303n

Welbeck, N. A., 210, 216, 232, 300, 381

Wenchi, 87; dispute, 264-270; enstoolment process in, 111-112

West Africa, obstacles to self-government in, 5-8

West African National Congress, 37, 137

Westermann, D., 88

Westernization, implications of land tenure for, 58; regional differentials in, 6

Wight, M., 33n, 42n, 119n, 131n, 136n, 137, 142, 143n, 177n

Wolseley, Sir Garnet, 26, 34

Woode, Anthony, 224, 230, 231, 239-240, 299

Wraith, R. E., 185n

ya na, allegiance to, 14

youngmen, definition of, 14n

youth movements, and formation of nationalism, 127-129; role in formation of Convention People's Party, 170-171; 326, 328, 335, 344-347, 373